THE

AMERICAN ORATOR:

WITH

AN APPENDIX,

CONTAINING

THE DECLARATION OF INDEPENDENCE, WITH THE FAC-SIMILES OF THE AUTOGRAPHS OF THE SIGNERS; THE CONSTITUTION OF THE UNITED STATES; WASHINGTON'S FAREWELL ADDRESS; AND FAC-SIMILES OF THE AUTOGRAPHS OF A LARGE NUMBER OF DISTINGUISHED INDIVIDUALS.

BY LEWIS C. MUNN.

BOSTON:
PUBLISHED BY THE COMPILER,
120 WASHINGTON STREET.
1853.

Stereotyped by
HOBART & ROBBINS,
BOSTON.
PRINTED BY STACY AND RICHARDSON, NO. 11 Milk street.

PREFACE.

It has long been the belief of the compiler of "THE AMERICAN ORATOR" that a work of its character could not fail to be of interest to the public. We are emphatically a nation of talkers. The ambition of nearly all our men of intellectual eminence seems to be to succeed in the field of oratorical display. From those fortunate individuals who have secured for themselves a seat in our national and state legislatures, down to the more humble, but not less ambitious, personage who edifies the public on Fourth of July occasions, or from the village lyceum rostrum, all exhibit the most unconquerable desire to obtain the reputation which Brutus possessed and Antony disclaimed.

It would be singular, indeed, if out of this mass of matter continually given to the public, much that is meritorious should not be produced. With this conviction, it has been the aim of the compiler to endeavor to present, in a necessarily limited compass, what he deemed the fairest specimens of the abilities of those who had attained the highest rank in their vocation. In this somewhat arduous labor, he has in some instances been kindly assisted by the authors themselves, and he would avail himself of this occasion to return to them his grateful acknowledgments.

In selecting the "Specimens," the design has been to represent both the pulpit and the forum. If the extracts from efforts made in the latter field shall seem to preponderate, the compiler offers as his excuse the fact that it is here the American mind seems most naturally to seek its development, and consequently here we find its most characteristic representation.

In the Appendix to the work, it is believed, there is presented an entirely original feature. Allusion is made to the large collection of *fac similes* of the autographs of distinguished men of this and other countries; and, in this connection, the compiler cannot omit to acknowledge his great obligations to that "prince" of autograph collectors, CHARLES H. MORSE, Esq., of Cambridgeport, Mass., who has, with the kindest liberality, placed his invaluable collection entirely at his service, in preparing the work.

BOSTON, *January*, 1853.

TABLE OF CONTENTS.

INDEX TO AUTOGRAPHS.

SPECIMENS

OF

AMERICAN ELOQUENCE.

IN COMMEMORATION OF THE FIRST SETTLEMENT OF NEW ENGLAND. — *D. Webster.*

Let us rejoice that we behold this day! Let us be thankful that we have lived to see the bright and happy breaking of the auspicious morn which commences the third century of the history of New England! Auspicious, indeed, — bringing a happiness beyond the common allotment of Providence to men, full of present joy, and gilding with bright beams the prospect of futurity, — is the dawn that awakens us to the commemoration of the landing of the Pilgrims.

Living at an epoch which naturally marks the progress of the history of our native land, we have come hither to celebrate the great event with which that history commenced. Forever honored be this, the place of our fathers' refuge! Forever remembered the day which saw them, weary and distressed, broken in everything but spirit, poor in all but faith and courage, at last secure from the dangers of wintry seas, and impressing this shore with the first footsteps of civilized man!

We have come to this rock to record here our homage for our Pilgrim Fathers; our sympathy in their sufferings, our gratitude for their labors, our admiration of their virtues, our veneration for their piety, and our attachment to those principles of civil and religious liberty, which they encountered the dangers of the ocean, the storms of heaven, the violence of savages, disease, exile and famine, to enjoy and to establish. And we would leave here, also, for the generations which are rising up rapidly to fill our places, some proof that we have endeavored to transmit the great inheritance unimpaired; that in our estimate of public principles and private virtue, in our veneration of religion and piety, in our devotion to civil and religious liberty, in our regard to whatever advances human knowledge or improves human happiness, we are not altogether unworthy of our origin.

There is a local feeling connected with this occasion, too strong to be resisted, — a sort of *genius of the place*, which inspires and awes us. We feel that we are on the spot where the first scene of our history was laid; where the hearths and altars of New England were first placed; where Christianity, and civilization, and letters, made their first lodgment, in a vast extent of country, covered with a wilderness, and peopled by roving barbarians. We are here at the season of the year at which the event took place. The imagination irresistibly and rapidly draws around us the principal features and the leading characters in the original scene. We cast our eyes abroad on the ocean, and we see where the little bark, with the interesting group upon its deck, made its slow progress to the shore. We look around us, and behold the hills and promontories where the anxious eyes of our fathers first saw the places of habitation and of rest. We feel the cold which benumbed and listen to the winds which pierced them. Beneath us is the rock on which New England received the feet of the Pilgrims. We seem even to behold them, as they struggle with the elements, and, with toilsome efforts, gain the shore. We listen to the chiefs in counsel; we see the unexampled exhibition of female fortitude and resignation; we hear the whisperings of youthful impatience, and we see, what a painter of our own has also represented by his pencil, chilled and shivering childhood, houseless but for a mother's arms, couchless but for a mother's breast, till our own blood almost freezes. The mild dignity of Carver, and of Bradford; the decisive and soldier-like air and manner of Standish; the devout Brewster; the enterprising Allerton; the general firmness and thoughtfulness of the whole band; their conscious joy for dangers escaped, their deep solicitude about dangers to come, their trust in Heaven, their high religious faith, full of confidence and anticipations, all of these seem to belong to this place, and to be present upon this occasion, to fill us with reverence and admiration.

The settlement of New England by the colony which landed here on the 22d of December, 1620, although not the first European establishment in what now constitutes the United States, was yet so peculiar in its causes and character, and has been followed, and must still be followed, by such consequences, as to give it a high claim to lasting commemoration. On these causes and consequences, more than on its immediately attendant circumstances, its importance as an historical event depends. Great actions and striking occurrences, having excited a temporary admiration, often pass away and are forgotten, because they leave no lasting results, affecting the prosperity and happiness of communities. Such is, frequently, the fortune of the most brilliant military achievements. Of the ten thousand battles which have been fought, of all the fields fertilized with carnage, of the banners which have been bathed in blood, of the warriors who had hoped that they had risen from the field of conquest to a glory as bright and as durable as the stars, how few that continue long to interest mankind! The victory of yesterday is reversed by the defeat of to-day; the star of military glory, rising like a meteor, like a meteor has fallen; disgrace and disaster hang on the heels of conquest and renown; victor and vanquished presently pass away to oblivion, and the world goes on in its course, with the loss only of so many lives and so much treasure.

But if this be frequently, or generally, the fortune of military achievements, it is not always so. There are enterprises, military as well as civil, which sometimes check the current of events, give a new turn to human affairs, and transmit their consequences through ages. We see their importance in their results, and call them great because great things follow. There have been battles which have fixed the fate of nations. These come down to us in history with a solid and permanent interest, not created by a display of glittering armor, the rush of adverse battalions, the sinking and rising of pennons, the flight, the pursuit, and the victory; but by their effect in advancing or retarding human knowledge, in overthrowing or establishing despotism, in extending or destroying human happiness. When the traveller pauses on the plain of Marathon, what are the emotions which most strongly agitate his breast? What is that glorious recollection which thrills through his frame, and suffuses his eyes? Not, I imagine, that Grecian skill and Grecian valor were here most signally displayed; but that Greece herself was here saved. It is because to this spot, and to the event which has rendered it immortal, he refers all the succeeding glories of the republic. It is because, if that day had gone otherwise, Greece had perished. It is because he perceives that her philosophers and orators, her poets and painters, her sculptors and architects, her governments and free institutions, point backward to Marathon; and that their future existence seems to have been suspended on the contingency whether the Persian or the Grecian banner should wave victorious in the beams of that day's setting sun. And, as his imagination kindles at the retrospect, he is transported back to the interesting moment, he counts the fearful odds of the contending hosts, his interest for the result overwhelms him; — he trembles, as if it were still uncertain, and seems to doubt whether he may consider Socrates and Plato, Demosthenes, Sophocles and Phidias, as secure, yet, to himself and to the world.

If the blessings of our political and social condition have not been too highly estimated, we cannot well overrate the responsibility and duty which they impose upon us. We hold these institutions of government, religion and learning, to be transmitted as well as enjoyed. We are in the line of conveyance, through which whatever has been obtained by the spirit and efforts of our ancestors is to be communicated to our children.

We are bound to maintain public liberty, and by the example of our own systems to convince the world that order and law, religion and morality, the rights of conscience, the rights of persons, and the rights of property, may all be preserved and secured, in the most perfect manner, by a government entirely and purely elective. If we fail in this, our disaster will be signal, and will furnish an argument, stronger than has yet been found, in support of those opinions that maintain that government can rest safely on nothing but power and coërcion. As far as experience may show errors in our establishments, we are bound to correct them; and if any practices exist contrary to the principles of justice and humanity, within the reach of our laws or our influence, we are inexcusable if we do not exert ourselves to restrain and abolish them.

The hours of this day are rapidly flying, and this occasion will soon be past. Neither we nor our children can expect to behold its return. They are in the distant regions of futurity, they exist only in the all-creating power of God, who shall stand here, a hundred years hence, to trace, through us, their descent from the Pilgrims, and to survey, as we have now surveyed, the progress of their country, during the lapse of a century. We would anticipate their concurrence with us in our sentiments of deep regard for our common ancestors. We would anticipate and partake the pleasure with which they will then recount the steps of New England's advancement. On the morning of that day, although it will not disturb us in our repose, the voice of acclamation and gratitude, commencing on the Rock of Plymouth, shall be transmitted through millions of the sons of the Pilgrims, till it lose itself in the murmurs of the Pacific seas.

We would leave for the consideration of those who shall then occupy our places some proof that we hold the blessings transmitted from our fathers in just estimation; some proof of our attachment to the cause of good government, and of civil and religious liberty; some proof of a sincere and ardent desire to promote everything which may enlarge the understandings and improve the hearts of men. And when, from the long distance of an hundred years, they shall look back upon us, they shall know, at least, that we possessed affections, which, running backward, and warming with gratitude for what our ancestors have done for our happiness, run forward also to our posterity, and meet them with cordial salutation, ere yet they have arrived on the shore of being.

Advance, then, ye future generations! We would hail you, as

you rise in your long succession, to fill the places which we now fill, and to taste the blessings of existence, where we are passing, and soon shall have passed, our own human duration. We bid you welcome to this pleasant land of the fathers. We bid you welcome to the healthful skies and the verdant fields of New England. We greet your accession to the great inheritance which we have enjoyed. We welcome you to the blessings of good government and religious liberty. We welcome you to the treasures of science and the delights of learning. We welcome you to the transcendent sweets of domestic life, to the happiness of kindred, and parents, and children. We welcome you to the immeasurable blessings of rational existence, the immortal hope of Christianity, and the light of everlasting truth!

THE CONSEQUENCES OF DISUNION. — *H. Clay.*

I HAVE been accused of ambition in presenting this measure. Ambition! inordinate ambition! If I had thought of myself only, I should have never brought it forward. I know well the perils to which I expose myself; the risk of alienating faithful and valued friends, with but little prospect of making new ones, if any new ones could compensate for the loss of those whom we have long tried and loved, — and the honest misconceptions both of friends and foes. Ambition! If I had listened to its soft and seducing whispers, if I had yielded myself to the dictates of a cold, calculating and prudential policy, I would have stood still and unmoved. I might even have silently gazed on the raging storm, enjoyed its loudest thunders, and left those who are charged with the care of the vessel of state to conduct it as they could. I have been heretofore often unjustly accused of ambition. Low, grovelling souls, who are utterly incapable of elevating themselves to the higher and nobler duties of pure patriotism, — beings who, forever keeping their own selfish aims in view, decide all public measures by their presumed influence on their aggrandizement, — judge me by the venal rule which they prescribe to themselves. I have given to the winds those false accusations, as I consign that which now impeaches my motives. I have no desire for office, not even the highest. The most exalted is but a prison, in which the incarcerated incumbent daily receives his cold, heartless visitants, marks his weary hours, and is cut off from the practical enjoyment of all the blessings of genuine freedom. I am no candidate for any office in the gift of the people of these states, united or separated; I never wish, never expect to be. Pass this bill, tranquillize the country, restore confidence and affection in the Union, and I am willing to go home to Ashland, and renounce public service forever. I should there find, in its groves, under its shades, on its lawns, amidst my flocks and herds, in the bosom of my family, sincerity and truth, attachment, and fidelity, and gratitude, which I have not always found in the walks of public life. Yes, I have ambition; but it is the ambition of being the humble instrument, in the hands of Providence, to reconcile a divided people, once more to revive concord and harmony in a distracted land, — the pleasing ambition of contemplating the glorious spectacle of a free, united, prosperous, and fraternal people!

South Carolina must perceive the embarrassments of her situation. She must be desirous — it is unnatural to suppose that she is not — to remain in the Union.

What! a state whose heroes in its gallant ancestry fought so many glorious battles along with those of the other states of this Union, — a state with which this confederacy is linked by bonds of such a powerful character!

I have sometimes fancied what would be her condition. if she goes out of this Union, — if her five hundred thousand people should at once be thrown upon their own resources. She is out of the Union. What is the consequence? She is an independent power. What then does she do? She must have armies and fleets, and an expensive government; have foreign missions; she must raise taxes, — enact this very tariff, which had driven her out of the Union, in order to enable her to raise money, and to sustain the attitude of an independent power. If she should have no force, no navy to protect her, she would be exposed to piratical incursions. Her neighbor, St. Domingo, might pour down a horde of pirates on her borders, and desolate her plantations. She must have her embassies, — therefore must she have a revenue.

But I will not dwell on this topic any longer. I say it is utterly impossible that South Carolina ever desired, for a moment, to become a separate and independent state. I would repeat that, under all the circumstances of the case, the condition of South Carolina is only one of the elements of a combination, the whole of which together constitutes a motive of action which renders it expedient to resort, during the present session of Congress, to some measure, in order to quiet and tranquillize the country.

If there be any who want civil war,— who want to see the blood of any portion of our countrymen spilt, — I am not one of them. I wish to see war of no kind; but, above all, do I not desire to see a civil war. When war begins, whether civil or foreign, no human foresight is competent to foresee when, or how, or where, it is to terminate. But, when a civil war shall be lighted up in the bosom of our own happy land, and armies are marching, and commanders are winning their victories, and fleets are in motion on our coast, — tell me, if you can, tell me if any human being can tell, its duration! God alone knows where such a war will end!

FROM A EULOGY ON LAFAYETTE. — *E. Everett.*

But it is more than time, fellow-citizens, that I commit the memory of this great and good man to your unprompted contemplation. On his arrival among you, ten years ago, — when your civil fathers, your military, your children, your whole population, poured itself out, as one throng, to salute him, — when your cannons proclaimed his advent with joyous salvos, and your acclamations were responded from steeple to steeple, by the voice of festal bells, — with what delight did you not listen to his cordial and affectionate words: "I beg of you all, beloved citizens of Boston, to accept the respectful and warm thanks of a heart which has for nearly half a century been devoted to your illustrious city!" That noble heart, — to which, if any object on earth was dear, that object was the country of his early choice, of his adoption, and his more than regal triumph, — that noble heart will beat no more for your welfare. Cold and motionless, it is already mingling with the dust. While he lived, you thronged with delight to his presence; you gazed with admiration on his placid features and venerable form, not wholly unshaken by the rude storms of his career; and now that he is departed, you have assembled in this cradle of the liberties for which, with your fathers, he risked his life, to pay the last honors to his memory. You have thrown open these consecrated portals to admit the lengthened train, which has come to discharge the last public offices of respect to his name. You have hung these venerable arches, for the second time since their erection, with the sable badges of sorrow. You have thus associated the memory of Lafayette in those distinguished honors which but a few years since you paid to your Adams and Jefferson; and, could your wishes and mine have prevailed, my lips would this day have been mute, and the same illustrious voice which gave utterance to your filial emotions over their honored graves would have spoken also for you over him who shared their earthly labors, enjoyed their friendship, and has now gone to share their last repose, and their imperishable remembrance.

There is not, throughout the world, a friend of liberty, who has not dropped his head, when he has heard that Lafayette is no more. Poland, Italy, Greece, Spain, Ireland, the South American republics, — every country where man is struggling to recover his birthright, — has lost a benefactor, a patron, in Lafayette. But you, young men, at whose command I speak, — for you a bright and particular loadstar is henceforward fixed in the front of heaven. What young man that reflects on the history of Lafayette, — that sees him in the morning of his days the associate of sages, the friend of Washington, — but will start with new vigor on the path of duty and renown?

And what was it, fellow-citizens, which gave to our Lafayette his spotless fame? The love of liberty. What has consecrated his memory in the hearts of good men? The love of liberty. What nerved his youthful arm with strength, and inspired him in the morning of his days with sagacity and counsel? The living love of liberty. To what did he sacrifice power, and rank, and country, and freedom itself? To the horror of licentiousness, to the sanctity of plighted faith, to the love of liberty protected by law. Thus the great principle of your Revolutionary fathers, of your Pilgrim sires, — the great principle of the age, — was the rule of his life: *The love of liberty protected by law.*

You have now assembled within these celebrated walls to perform the last duties of respect and love, on the birth-day of your benefactor, beneath that roof which has resounded of old with the master voices of American renown. The spirit of the departed is in high communion with that spirit of the place; the temple, worthy of the new name which we now behold inscribed on its walls. Listen, Americans, to the lessons which seem borne to us on the very air we breathe, while we perform these dutiful rites! Ye winds, that wafted the Pilgrims to the land of promise, fan in their children's hearts the love of freedom! Blood which our fathers shed, cry from the ground! Echoing arches of this renowned hall, whisper back the voices of other days! Glorious Washington, break the long silence of that votive canvas! — speak, speak, marble lips! — teach us THE LOVE OF LIBERTY PROTECTED BY LAW!

NEW ENGLAND AND THE UNION. — *S. S. Prentiss.*

GLORIOUS New England! thou art still true to thy ancient fame, and worthy of thy ancestral honors. On thy pleasant valleys rest, like sweet dews of morning, the gentle recollections of our early life; around thy hills and mountains cling, like gathering mists, the mighty memories of the Revolution; and far away in the horizon of thy past gleam, like thy own bright northern lights, the awful virtues of our Pilgrim sires! But, while we devote this day to the remembrance of our native land, we forget not that in which our happy lot is cast. We exult in the reflection that, though we count by thousands the miles which separate us from our birth-place, still our country is the same. We are no exiles meeting upon the banks of a foreign river, to swell its waters with our homesick tears. Here floats the same banner which rustled above our boyish heads, except that its mighty folds are wider, and its glittering stars increased in number.

The sons of New England are found in every state of the broad republic. In the east, the south, and the unbounded west, their blood mingles freely with every kindred current. We have but changed our chamber in the paternal mansion; in all its rooms we are at home, and all who inhabit it are our brothers. To us the Union has but one domestic hearth; its household gods are all the same. Upon us, then, peculiarly devolves the duty of feeding the fires upon that kindly hearth, of guarding with pious care those sacred household gods.

We cannot do with less than the whole Union; to us it admits of no division. In the veins of our children flows northern and southern blood: how shall it be separated? — who shall put asunder the best affections of the heart, the noblest instincts of our nature? We love the land of our adoption; so do we that of our birth. Let us ever be true to both, and always exert ourselves in maintaining the unity of our country, the integrity of the republic.

Accursed, then, be the hand put forth to loosen the golden cord of union! thrice accursed the traitorous lips which shall propose its severance!

IN MEMORY OF WASHINGTON.—*R. C. Winthrop.*

But, fellow-citizens, while we thus commend the character and example of Washington to others, let us not forget to imitate it ourselves. I have spoken of the precise period which we have reached in our own history, as well as in that of the world at large, as giving something of peculiar interest to the proceedings in which we are engaged. I may not, I will not, disturb the harmony of the scene before me, by the slightest allusion of a party character. The circumstances of the occasion forbid it; the associations of the day forbid it; the character of him in whose honor we are assembled forbids it; my own feelings revolt from it. But I may say, I must say, and every one within the sound of my voice will sustain me in saying, that there has been no moment since Washington himself was among us when it was more important than at this moment that the two great leading principles of his policy should be remembered and cherished.

Those principles were, first, the most complete, cordial, and indissoluble Union of the States; and, second, the most entire separation and disentanglement of our own country from all other countries. Perfect union among ourselves, perfect neutrality towards others, and peace, peace, domestic peace and foreign peace, as the result,—this was the chosen and consummate policy of the Father of his Country.

But, above all, and before all, in the heart of Washington, was the Union of the States; and no opportunity was ever omitted by him to impress upon his fellow-citizens the profound sense which he entertained of its vital importance at once to their prosperity and their liberty.

In that incomparable address in which he bade farewell to his countrymen at the close of his presidential service, he touched upon many other topics with the earnestness of a sincere conviction. He called upon them, in solemn terms, to "cherish public credit;" to "observe good faith and justice towards all nations," avoiding both "inveterate antipathies and passionate attachments" towards any; to mitigate and assuage the unquenchable fire of party spirit, "lest, instead of warming, it should consume;" to abstain from "characterizing parties by geographical distinctions;" "to promote institutions for the general diffusion of knowledge;" to respect and uphold "religion and morality, those great pillars of human happiness, those firmest props of the duties of men and of citizens."

But what can exceed, what can equal, the accumulated intensity of thought and of expression with which he calls upon them to cling to the Union of the States. "It is of infinite moment," says he, in language which we ought never to be weary of hearing or of repeating, "that you should properly estimate the immense value of your national union to your collective and individual happiness; that you should cherish a cordial, habitual, immovable attachment to it; accustoming yourselves to think and speak of it as of the palladium of your political safety and prosperity, watching for its preservation with jealous anxiety, discountenancing whatever may suggest even a suspicion that it can *in any event* be abandoned, and indignantly frowning upon the first dawning of every attempt to alienate any portion of our country from the rest, or to enfeeble the sacred ties which now link together the various parts."

The Union — *the Union in any event* — was thus the sentiment of Washington. The Union — *the Union in any event* — let it be our sentiment this day!

Yes, to-day, fellow-citizens, at the very moment when the extension of our boundaries and the multiplication of our territories are producing, directly and indirectly, among the different members of our political system, so many marked and mourned centrifugal tendencies, let us seize this occasion to renew to each other our vows of allegiance and devotion to the American Union, and let us recognize in our common title to the name and the fame of Washington, and in our common veneration for his example and his advice, the all-sufficient centripetal power which shall hold the thick-clustering stars of our confederacy in one glorious constellation forever! Let the column which we are about to construct be at once a pledge and an emblem of perpetual union! Let the foundations be laid, let the superstructure be built up and cemented, let each stone be raised and riveted, in a spirit of national brotherhood! And may the earliest ray of the rising sun — till that sun shall set to rise no more — draw forth from it daily, as from the fabled statue of antiquity, a strain of national harmony, which shall strike a responsive chord in every heart throughout the republic!

Proceed, then, fellow-citizens, with the work for which you have assembled! Lay the corner-stone of a monument which shall adequately bespeak the gratitude of the whole American people to the illustrious Father of his Country! Build it to the skies; you cannot outreach the loftiness of his principles! Found it upon the massive and eternal rock; you cannot make it more enduring than his fame! Construct it of the peerless Parian marble; you cannot make it purer than his life! Exhaust upon it the rules and principles of ancient and of modern art; you cannot make it more proportionate than his character!

But let not your homage to his memory end here. Think not to transfer to a tablet or a column the tribute which is due from yourselves. Just honor to Washington can only be rendered by observing his precepts and imitating his example. *Similitudine decoremus.* He has built his own monument. We, and those who come after us in successive generations, are its appointed, its privileged guardians. This wide-spread republic is the true monument to Washington. Maintain its independence. Uphold its constitution. Preserve its union. Defend its liberty. Let it stand before the world in all its original strength and beauty, securing peace, order, equality and freedom, to all within its boundaries, and shedding light and hope and joy upon the pathway of human liberty throughout the world, — and Washington needs no other monument. Other structures may fitly testify our veneration for him: this, this alone, can adequately illustrate his services to mankind.

Nor does he need even this. The republic may perish; the wide arch of our ranged Union may fall; star by star its glories may expire; stone after stone its columns and its capitol may moulder and crumble; all other names which adorn its annals may be forgotten; but, as long as human hearts shall anywhere pant, or human tongues shall anywhere plead, for a true, rational, constitutional liberty, those hearts shall enshrine the memory, and those tongues shall prolong the fame, of GEORGE WASHINGTON!

SORROW FOR THE DEAD. — *W. Irving.*

SORROW for the dead is the only sorrow from which we refuse to be divorced. Every other wound we seek to heal, every other affliction to forget; but this wound we consider it a duty to keep open, this affliction we cherish and brood over in solitude. Where is the mother that would willingly forget the infant that perished like a blossom from her arms, though every recollection is a pang?

Where is the child that would willingly forget the most tender of parents, though to remember be but to lament? Who, even in the hour of agony, would forget the friend over whom he mourns? Who, even when the tomb is closing upon the remains of her he most loved, and he feels his heart, as it were, crushed in the closing of its portal, would accept consolation that was to be bought by forgetfulness? No! the love which survives the tomb is one of the noblest attributes of the soul. If it has its woes, it has likewise its delights; and, when the overwhelming burst of grief is calmed into the gentle tear of recollection, when the sudden anguish and the convulsive agony over the present ruins of all that we most loved is softened away into pensive meditation on all that it was in the days of its loveliness, who would root out such a sorrow from the heart? Though it may sometimes throw a passing cloud even over the bright hour of gayety, or spread a deeper sadness over the hour of gloom, yet who would exchange it even for the song of pleasure or the burst of revelry? No! there is a voice from the tomb sweeter than song; there is a recollection of the dead to which we turn even from the charms of the living. O, the grave! the grave! It buries every error, covers every defect, extinguishes every resentment. From its peaceful bosom spring none but fond regrets and tender recollections. Who can look down upon the grave even of an enemy, and not feel a compunctious throb, that ever he should have warred with the poor handful of earth that lies mouldering before him?

The grave of those we loved — what a place for meditation! There it is that we call up in long review the whole history of virtue and gentleness, and the thousand endearments lavished upon us almost unheeded in the daily intercourse of intimacy; there it is that we dwell upon the tenderness, the solemn, awful tenderness, of the parting scene: the bed of death, with all its stifled griefs; its noiseless attendance; its mute, watchful assiduities; the last testimonies of expiring love; the feeble, fluttering, thrilling (O, how thrilling!) pressure of the hand; the last fond look of the glazing eye, turning upon us even from the threshold of existence;

the faint, faltering accents, struggling in death to give one more assurance of affection!

Ay, go to the grave of buried love, and meditate! There settle the account with thy conscience for every past benefit unrequited, every past endearment unregarded, of that being who can never, never, never return, to be soothed by thy contrition!

If thou art a child, and hast ever added a sorrow to the soul or a furrow to the silvered brow of an affectionate parent; if thou art a husband, and hast ever caused the fond bosom, that ventured its whole happiness in thy arms, to doubt one moment of thy kindness or thy truth; if thou art a friend, and hast ever wronged in thought, word or deed, the spirit that generously confided in thee; if thou art a lover, and hast ever given one unmerited pang to that true heart that now lies cold and still beneath thy feet; — then be sure that every unkind look, every ungracious word, every ungentle action, will come thronging back upon thy memory, and knocking dolefully at thy soul; then be sure that thou wilt lie down sorrowing and repentant on the grave, and utter the unheard groan, and pour the unavailing tear, — more deep, more bitter, because unheard and unavailing.

Then weave thy chaplet of flowers, and strew the beauties of nature about the grave; console thy broken spirit, if thou canst, with these tender, yet futile tributes of regret; but take warning by the bitterness of this thy contrite affliction over the dead, and be more faithful and affectionate in the discharge of thy duties to the living!

REPUBLICS. — *H. S. Legaré.*

The name of REPUBLIC is inscribed upon the most imperishable monuments of the species; and it is probable that it will continue to be associated, as it has been in all past ages, with whatever is heroic in character, and sublime in genius, and elegant and brilliant in the cultivation of arts and letters. It would not be difficult to prove that the base hirelings who have so industriously inculcated a contrary doctrine have been compelled to falsify history and abuse reason.

It might be asked, triumphantly, what land has ever been visited with the influences of liberty, that has not flourished like the spring? What people has ever worshipped at her altars, without kindling with a loftier spirit, and putting forth more noble energies? Where has she ever acted, that her deeds have not been heroic? Where has she ever spoken, that her eloquence has not been triumphant and sublime?

With respect to ourselves, would it not be enough to say that we live under a form of government and in a state of society to which the world has never yet exhibited a parallel? Is it, then, nothing to be free? How many nations, in the whole annals of human kind, have proved themselves worthy of being so? Is it nothing that we are republicans? Were all men as enlightened, as brave, as proud, as they ought to be, would they suffer themselves to be insulted with any other title? Is it nothing, that so many independent sovereignties should be held together in such a confederacy as ours? What does history teach us of the difficulty of instituting and maintaining such a polity, and of the glory that, of consequence, ought to be given to those who enjoy its advantages in so much perfection and on so grand a scale? For, can anything be more striking and sublime than the idea of an imperial republic, spreading over an extent of territory more immense than the empire of the Cæsars in the accumulated conquests of a thousand years — without prefects or proconsuls or publicans — founded in the maxims of common sense — employing within itself no arms but those of reason — and known to its subjects only by the blessings it bestows or perpetuates, yet capable of directing, against a foreign foe, all the energies of a military despotism, — a republic, in which men are completely insignificant, and principles and laws exercise, throughout its vast dominion, a peaceful and irresistible sway, blending in one divine harmony such various habits and conflicting opinions, and mingling in our institutions the light of philosophy with all that is dazzling in the associations of heroic achievement, and extended domination, and deep-seated and formidable power!

THE DEATH OF WASHINGTON. — *R. T. Paine.*

Having accomplished the embassy of a benevolent Providence, Washington, the founder of one nation, the sublime instructor of all, took his flight to heaven; — not like Mahomet, for his memory is immortal without the fiction of a miracle; not like Elijah, for recording time has not registered the man on whom his mantle should descend; but in humble imitation of that Omnipotent Architect, who returned from a created universe to contemplate from his throne the stupendous fabric he had erected!

The august form whose undaunted majesty could arrest the lightning, ere it fell on the bosom of his country, now sleeps in silent ruin, untenanted of its celestial essence. But the incorruptible example of his virtues shall survive, unimpaired by the corrosion of time, and acquire new vigor and influence from the crimes of ambition and the decay of empires. The invaluable valediction bequeathed to the people who inherited his affections is the effort of a mind whose powers, like those of prophecy, could overleap the tardy progress of human reason, and unfold truth without the labor of investigation. Impressed in indelible characters, this legacy of his intelligence will descend, unsullied as its purity, to the wonder and instruction of succeeding generations; and, should the mild philosophy of its maxims be ingrafted into the policy of nations, at no distant period will the departed hero, who now lives only in the spotless splendor of his own great actions, exist in the happiness and dignity of mankind.

The sighs of contemporary gratitude have attended the sublime spirit to its paternal abode, and the prayers of meliorated posterity will ascend in glowing remembrance of their illustrious benefactor! The laurels that now droop as they shadow his tomb with monumental glory will be watered by the tears of ages; and, embalmed in the heart of an admiring world, the temple erected to his memory will be more glorious than the pyramids, and as eternal as his own imperishable virtues!

ANCIENT AND MODERN PRODUCTIONS. — *C. Sumner.*

The classics possess a peculiar charm, from the circumstance that they have been the models, I might almost say the masters, of composition and thought, in all ages. In the contemplation of these august teachers of mankind, we are filled with conflicting emotions. They are the early voice of the world, better remembered and more cherished still than all the intermediate words that have been uttered, as the lessons of childhood still haunt us when the impressions of later years have been effaced from the mind. But they show with most unwelcome frequency the tokens of the world's childhood, before passion had yielded to the sway of reason and the affections. They want the highest charm of purity, of righteousness, of elevated sentiments, of love to God and man. It is not in the frigid philosophy of the porch and the academy that we are to seek these; not in the marvellous teachings of Socrates, as they come mended by the mellifluous words of Plato; not in the resounding line of Homer, on whose inspiring tale of blood Alexander pillowed his head; not in the animated strain of Pindar, where virtue is pictured in the successful strife of an athlete at the Isthmian games; not in the torrent of Demosthenes, dark with self-love and the spirit of vengeance; not in the fitful philosophy and intemperate eloquence of Tully; not in the genial libertinism of Horace, or the stately atheism of Lucretius. No! these must not be our masters; in none of these are we to seek the way of life. For eighteen hundred years the spirit of these writers has been engaged in weaponless contest with the Sermon on the Mount, and those two sublime commandments on which hang all the law and the prophets. The strife is still pending. Heathenism, which has possessed itself of such siren forms, is not yet exorcised. It still tempts the young, controls the affairs of active life, and haunts the meditations of age.

Our own productions, though they may yield to those of the ancients in the arrangement of ideas, in method, in beauty of form, and in freshness of illustration, are immeasurably superior in the truth, delicacy and elevation of their sentiments, — above all, in the benign recognition of that great Christian revelation, the brotherhood of man. How vain are eloquence and poetry, compared with this heaven-descended truth! Put in one scale that simple utterance, and in the other the lore of antiquity, with its accumulating glosses and commentaries, and the last will be light and trivial in the balance. Greek poetry has been likened to the song of the nightingale as she sits in the rich, symmetrical crown of the palm-tree, trilling her thick-warbled notes; but even this is less sweet and tender than the music of the human heart.

DEATH OF JOHN Q. ADAMS. — *I. E. Holmes.*

The mingled tones of sorrow, like the voice of many waters, have come unto us from a sister state — Massachusetts, weeping for her honored son. The state I have the honor in part to represent once endured, with her, a common suffering, battled for a common cause, and rejoiced in a common triumph. Surely, then, it is meet that in this the day of her affliction we should mingle our griefs.

When a great man falls, the nation mourns; when a patriarch is removed, the people weep. Ours, my associates, is no common bereavement. The chain which linked our hearts with the gifted spirits of former times has been suddenly snapped. The lips from which flowed those living and glorious truths that our fathers uttered are closed in death. Yes, my friends, Death has been among us! He has not entered the humble cottage of some unknown, ignoble peasant; he has knocked audibly at the palace of a nation! His footstep has been heard in the halls of state! He has cloven down his victim in the midst of the councils of a people. He has borne in triumph from among you the gravest, wisest, most reverend head. Ah! he has taken him as a trophy who was once chief over many statesmen, adorned with virtue, and learning, and truth; he has borne at his chariot-wheels a renowned one of the earth.

How often we have crowded into that aisle, and clustered around that now vacant desk, to listen to the counsels of wisdom as they fell from the lips of the venerable sage, we can all remember, for it was but of yesterday. But what a change! How wondrous! how sudden! 'T is like a vision of the night. That form which we beheld but a few days since is now cold in death!

But the last Sabbath, and in this hall he worshipped with others. Now his spirit mingles with the noble army of martyrs and the just made perfect, in the eternal adoration of the living God. With him, "this is the end of earth." He sleeps the sleep that knows no waking. He is gone — and forever! The sun that ushers in the morn of that next holy day, while it gilds the lofty dome of the capitol, shall rest with soft and mellow light upon the consecrated spot beneath whose turf forever lies the PATRIOT FATHER and the PATRIOT SAGE.

THE SEVENTY-FIFTH ANNIVERSARY OF THE FIRST BATTLE OF THE REVOLUTION. — *R. Rantoul, Jr.*

THE prospect before Hancock and Adams, on the ever-glorious nineteenth of April, was, to be soon proclaimed traitors; and, if the giant despotism they had provoked crushed the incipient rebellion, as the world looking on expected, that then their ghastly heads would frown from Temple Bar, and their blasted names be bequeathed to eternal infamy, both in the Old World and the New, — triumphant tyranny having silenced the voice of truth, justice, and patriotism. The "condign punishment" denounced against these champions of the constitutional rights of Englishmen involved atrocities too horrible to be alluded to here; it was an exhibition from which a heathen spectator might naturally infer that not the dove, but the vulture, was the emblem of Christianity. It had been first inflicted on an unfortunate patriot guilty of the precise crime of Hancock and Adams, — David, Prince of Wales, — who, in the eleventh year of Edward I., expiated by a cruel death his fidelity to the cause of his country's independence. At a grand consultation of the peers of the realm, it was agreed that London should be graced with his head, while York and Winchester disputed for the honor of his right shoulder. In a few years other

Welsh chiefs suffered the fate of their prince. This unseemly precedent, adopted in the flush and insolence of victory, then assumed the venerable form of law, and fell next upon the undaunted William Wallace, who nobly died in defence of the liberties and independence of his country, exhibiting to the delighted city of London a terrible example of Edward's vengeance. Such was the beginning of that law of treason, which, originating in the year 1283, continued in force for more than five centuries, as if to warn mankind how easily the most execrable example may be introduced, and with what difficulty a country is purified from its debasing influence. Why should I single out illustrious victims of these rites of Moloch? The ever-hallowed names in the perennial pages of British glory, you may read them in the attainted catalogue of arrant traitors. Long after the ashes of Welsh independence were quenched in the blood of a native prince, — ages after the spirit of Scottish liberty was roused, not crushed, by the ignominious butchery of Wallace, — More and Fisher, learning and piety, Russell and Sidney, integrity and honor, were sacrificed upon the scaffold of treason, beneath the axe of arbitrary power. These lessons of history might have taught our Hancock and Adams that the holy cause to which they were devoted, purity of motive, and a character untouched by any shaft of calumny, were not pleas in bar to a British indictment for treason.

Why, then, was the prospect of coming perils glorious to the eye of far-seeing patriotism? For the high prize that could be won by none but souls tempered to pass through the intervening agony, who, for the joy that was set before them, could endure the cross and despise the shame, — Liberty, the life of life, that gladdens the barren hill-tops of Scotland, and Switzerland, and loved New England, — that makes the sun shine brightly in our cold northern sky, that makes the valleys verdant in blithesome spring, and sober autumn laugh in her golden exuberance, — that nerves the arm of labor and blesses the couch of repose, that clothes with strength our sons and our daughters with beauty, — Liberty, in whose devotion they were nursed, — which their fathers had bequeathed to them, a legacy to be handed down unimpaired, through ourselves, to their and our latest posterity; to which they clung through life, and which inspired the patriotism that could freely testify to die for one's country is a joy and a glory.

Young freedom had ever been consecrated by the baptism of blood. Sparta and Athens, Holland and the mountain-girt Swiss, proud Albion and regenerated France, bought at a cheap purchase, with the lavish expense of their best lives, the rights which they enjoyed. Adams and his compatriots, on the day we have met to celebrate, knew that liberty must be, as it ever had been, a life-bought boon; that only by a mortal struggle could it be wrested from the grasp of power; and that nothing but perpetual vigilance, resolved to do and dare and suffer all things, rather than surrender it, could guarantee the long possession of the blessing afterwards. They had counted the cost, and chose the purchase.

Glorious, thrice glorious, was the morning, then, when the first shot fired at Lexington gave the signal of separation of a free and independent empire from its parent state! The nineteenth of April, and the seventeenth of June, both on the classic ground of the world's freedom, this county of Middlesex, cut out the work for the fourth of July, — world-emancipating work, which the achievements of the heroes of the uprising of America, and the Titanic labors of the transatlantic sons of revolution, yet agitate and roll on towards its grand completion! Middlesex possesses this imperishable glory, before which the lustre of the brightest victories, won in battles between contending tyrants, turns pale. Her children claim a common property in the trophies of these two memorable days; they walk together in the light of these two glowing beacon-fires, kindled on that stormy coast where Liberty has taken up her eternal abode, to illuminate, with the cheering radiance of hope, her benighted pilgrims, who can look nowhere else for hope but to this western world.

It is to the county of Middlesex that the tribes of our American Israel come up to keep holy time. The Mecca and Medina of the advent of freedom are within her borders. Lexington, whose echoes answered to the signal-gun that broke the centennial slumbers of the genius of revolution, to sleep no more till he has trampled on the fetters of the last slave, and wrapped in consuming flames the last throne; to overturn, and overturn, and overturn, until he shall make an end; — Concord, that saw the insulting foe driven back in dire confusion before the children of liberty, as the cloud squadrons of some threatening thunder-storm melt and disperse when the full-orbed sun bursts through and overpowers them; — Acton, whose Spartan band of minute-men withstood the onset and returned the fire of the minions of the tyrant; whose gallant Davis poured out his soul freely in his country's cause, at the moment when the tide of foreign aggression ebbed, at the moment when the beginning of the onward movement of his country's liberty, independence, greatness and glory, by his judgment, promptness and valor, was secured; — Charlestown, the smoke of whose sacrifice mingled with the roar of the murderous artillery, while a holocaust of victims and the apotheosis of Warren consecrated her mount as the thrice holy spot of all New England's hallowed soil; — Cambridge, the head-quarters of the hero, after whom the age of transition from monarchies to republics will be called the age of Washington; — in these, her towns, are the several peculiar shrines of the worship of constitutional liberty that have made the American continent not barren of historical monumental scenes. Where else, in the circuit of the revolving globe, does the sun look on such a clustered group of glories?

Over how broad a portion of the world have we extended the advantages we ourselves enjoy! Our domain unites the noblest valley on the surface of the globe, competent to grow food for human beings many more than now dwell on the face of the earth, with an eastern wing fitted for the site of the principal manufacturing and commercial power of existing Christendom, and a western flank well situated to hold the same position on the Pacific, when Asia shall renew her youth, and Australia shall have risen to the level of Europe. Bewildering, almost, is the suddenness of our expansion to fill these limits, and astounding are the phenomena that accompany this development. This day there stands before the councils of the nation, deputed to participate in their deliberations, a young man born within sight of old Concord Bridge, and educated under the institutions which Concord fight secured, who, when he revisits the old homestead, claims to represent a territory larger than France and the United British kingdom, — capable of containing, if settled to the present density of Great Britain, more than a hundred millions of souls, — a territory lately the joint inheritance of the Indian and the grisly bear, now outstripping, in its instant greatness, all recorded colonies, — the Ophir of our age, richer than Solomon's, richer than the wildest vision that ever dazzled Arabian fancy.

Occupying such a continent, receiving it consecrated by the toils and sufferings and outpouring of ancestral blood, which on the day we now commemorate began, how delightful is the duty which devolves on us, to guard the beacon-fire of liberty, whose flames our fathers kindled! Suffer it not, my friends! suffer it not, posterity that shall come after us! to be clouded by domestic dissension, or obscured by the dank, mephitic vapors of faction! Until now, its pure irradiance dispels doubt and fear, and revivifies the fainting hopes of downcast patriotism. Forever may it shine brightly as now; for as yet its pristine lustre fades not, but still flashes out the ancient, clear, and steady illumination, joy-giving as the blaze that, leaping from promontory to promontory, told the triumph of Agamemnon over fated Troy! It towers and glows, refulgent and beautiful, far-seen by the tempest-tost on the sea of revolution, darting into the dungeons of gaunt despair beams whose benignant glory no lapse of time shall dim; the wanderers in the chill darkness of slavery it guides, and cheers, and warms; it fills the universe with its splendor.

THE UNION. — *H. Clay.*

I DO not desire to see the lustre of one single star dimmed of that glorious confederacy which constitutes our political sun; still less do I wish to see it blotted out, and its light obliterated forever. Has not the State of South Carolina been one of the members of this Union in "days that tried men's souls"? Have not her ancestors fought alongside our ancestors? Have we not, conjointly, won together many a glorious battle? If we had to go into a civil war with such a state, how would it terminate? Whenever it should have terminated, what would be her condition? If she should ever return to the Union, what would be the condition of her feelings and affections? what the state of the heart of her people? She has been with us before, when our ancestors mingled in the throng of battle; and, as I hope our posterity will mingle with hers, for ages and centuries to come, in the united defence of liberty, and for the honor and glory of the Union, I do not wish to see her degraded or defaced as a member of this confederacy.

In conclusion, allow me to entreat and implore each individual member of this body to bring into the consideration of this measure, which I have had the honor of proposing, the same love of country which, if I know myself, has actuated me, and the same desire of restoring harmony to the Union which has prompted this effort. If we can forget for a moment, — but that would be asking too much of human nature, — if we could suppress, for one moment, party feelings and party causes, — and, as I stand here before my God, I declare I have looked beyond these considerations, and regarded only the vast interests of this united people, — I should hope that, under such feelings, and with such dispositions, we may advantageously proceed to the consideration of this bill, and heal, before they are yet bleeding, the wounds of our distracted country.

FREE DISCUSSION. — *T. Burgess.*

Sir, admit — for we must admit — that free discussion has ever been odious to the tyrant, and to all the minions of licentious power, — but can we ever forget how eloquent, how enchanting, the voice of that same freedom of speech has in all ages been, wherever its tones have fallen on the ear of freemen?

Free discussion, and liberty itself, eloquence and freedom of speech, are contemporaneous fires, and brighten and blaze, or languish and go out, together. Athenian liberty was, for years, protracted by that free discussion which was sustained and continued in Athens. Freedom was prolonged by eloquence. Liberty paused and lingered, that she might listen to the divine intonations of her voice. Free discussion, the eloquence of one man, rolled back the tide of Macedonian power, and long preserved his country from the overwhelming deluge.

When the light of free discussion had, throughout all the Grecian cities, been extinguished in the blood of those statesmen by whose eloquence it had been sustained, young Tully, breathing the spirit of Roman liberty on the expiring embers, relumed and transmitted, from the banks of the Ilissus to those of the Tiber, this glorious light of freedom. This mighty master of the forum, by his free discussions, both from the rostrum and in the senate-house, gave new vigor, and a longer duration of existence, to the liberty of his country. Who, more than Marcus Tullius Cicero, was loved and cherished by the friends of that country? Who more feared and hated by traitors and tyrants?

Freedom of speech, Roman eloquence, and Roman liberty, expired together, when, under the proscription of the second triumvirate, the hired bravo of Mark Antony placed in the lap of one of his profligate minions the head and the hands of Tully, the statesman, the orator, the illustrious father of his country. After amusing herself some hours by plunging her bodkin through that tongue which had so long delighted the senate and the rostrum, and made Antony himself tremble in the midst of his legions, she ordered that head and those hands, then the trophies of a savage despotism, to be set up in the forum.

> "Her last good man dejected Rome adored;
> Wept for her patriot slain, and cursed the tyrant's sword."

English statesmen and orators, in the free discussions of the English Parliament, have been formed on those illustrious models of Greek and Roman policy and eloquence. Multiplied by the teeming labors of the press, the works of the master and the disciple have come to our hands; and the eloquence of Chatham, of Burke, of Fox, and of the younger Pitt, reaches us, not in the feeble and

4

evanescent voice of tradition, but preserved and placed before the eye on the more imperishable page. Neither these great originals nor their improved transcripts have been lost to our country. The American political school of free discussion has enriched the nation with some distinguished scholars; and Dexter, and Morris, and Pinkney, will not soon be forgotten by our country, or by the literary world.

Some men who now live may hereafter be found deserving of that life, in the memory of posterity, which very great men have thought no unworthy object of a glorious ambition. Who can censure this anxious wish to live in human memory? When we feel ourselves borne along the current of time, — when we see ourselves hourly approach that cloud, impenetrable to the human eye, which terminates the last visible portion of this moving estuary, — who of us, although he may hope, when he reaches it, to shoot through that dark barren into a more bright and peaceful region, yet who, I say, can feel himself receding swiftly from the eye of all human sympathy, leaving the vision of all human monuments, and not wish, as he passes by, to place on those monuments some little memorial of himself, — some volume of a book, — or, perhaps, but a single page, that it may be remembered,

"When we *are not*, that we *have been*"?

Sir, these models of ancient and modern policy and eloquence, formed in the great schools of free discussion, both in earlier and later time, are in the hands of thousands of those youths who are now, in all the parts of our country, forming themselves for the public service. This hall is the bright goal of their generous, patriotic, and glorious ambition. Sir, they look hither with a feeling not unlike that devotion felt by the pilgrim as he looks towards some venerated shrine. Do not — I implore you, sir, do not — by your decision this day abolish the rites of liberty, consecrated in this place! Extinguish not those fires on her altar, which should here be eternal! Suffer not, suffer not the rude hand of this more than Vandal violence to demolish, "from turret to foundation-stone," this last sanctuary of freedom!

THE RIGHT TO DISCUSS PRESIDENTIAL ACTS. — *W. C. Preston.*

THE gentleman has referred to the contest to be fought between liberty and power; and I say, that if the contest did not originate here, it is made when we are not permitted to speak of the administration in terms that we believe to be true, without being denounced for it. The President of the United States certainly demands a degree of forbearance from his political opponents; but am I to be told that one can only allude to him in the humble language of a degraded Roman senate, speaking of the emperor with his Prætorian guards surrounding the capitol? Am I to be told, when he came into power on principles of reform, after "keeping the word of promise to our ear, and breaking it to our hope," — am I to be told that I must close my lips, or be denounced for want of decorum? Am I to be told, when he promised to prevent official influence from interfering with the freedom of elections, that I must not speak of the broken promise, under pain of the displeasure of his friends? Am I to be told, when he came into power as a judicious tariff man, after advocating his principles and aiding in his election, — believing at the time in his integrity, though I did not believe him possessed of intellectual qualifications, — am I to be told, after pledges that have been violated, promises that have been broken, and principles that have been set at naught, that I must not speak of these things as they are, for fear of being denounced for want of courtesy to the constituted authorities? Why, to what pass are we come! Are we to be gagged — reduced to silence? If nothing else is left to us, the liberty of speech is left; and it is our duty to cry aloud and spare not, when the undenied, admitted, and declared fact before us is, that these pledges have been made, and have been violated. This administration is about to end; and if gentlemen can succeed in preventing us from complaining of being deceived, if they can reduce us to abject slavery, they will also have to expunge the history of the country, the president's written and recorded communications to Congress, and the most ardent professions of his friends, when fighting his battles, before they can conceal the recorded fact, that he has made pledges which he has violated, and promises which he has repeatedly broken. If they succeed in reducing us to slavery, and closing our lips against speaking of the abuses of this administration, thank God! the voice of history, trumpet-tongued, will proclaim these pledges, and the manner in which they have been violated, to future generations!

Neither here nor elsewhere will I use language, with regard to any gentleman, that may be considered indecorous; and the question not easily solved is, how far shall we restrain ourselves in expressing a just and necessary indignation; and whether the expression of such indignation may be considered a departure from courtesy. That indignation, that reprobation, I shall express on all occasions. But those who have taken upon themselves the guardianship of the Grand Lama, who is surrounded by a light which no one can approach, — about whom no one is permitted to speak without censure, — have extended that guardianship to the presiding officer of this house. Gentlemen are not permitted to speak of the qualifications of that officer for the highest office in the government. Shall we, sir, because he is here as presiding officer of this body, keep silent when he is urged upon the people, who are goaded and driven to his support, lest we be guilty of an indecorum against those who are the constituted authorities of the country? Thank God, it is not my practice to "crook the pliant hinges of the knee, that thrift may follow fawning!"

This aggression of power upon our liberties, sir, and this tame submission to aggression, forebode evil to this nation. "Coming events cast their shadows before them," deepening and darkening; and, as the sun sets, the shadows lengthen. It may be the going down of the great luminary of the republic, and that we all shall be enveloped in one universal political darkness!

BURNING OF THE LEXINGTON. — *E. H. Chapin.*

GREAT calamities, though they may startle and appal at first, live but a brief time in the memory of the multitude. There is a vivid flash, a momentary shock, when the noisy world shrinks back and is silent; — and then the vast and busy machinery goes on again, the sentiment of horror is absorbed in the rush of jarring interests and active life, and the event is apparently forgotten; while the hearts that are peculiarly torn and smitten are left to bleed alone, and to heal up slowly in the obscurity of private grief and retirement. But in this instance the cold thrill that ran through every soul upon hearing the "evil tidings" has not yet ceased to vibrate even in the great mass of community at large. The exclamations of surprise and horror which follow the dreadful announcement are yet pealing upon our ears from remote portions of the land. The waters that yawned to receive the wasted treasures, the charred and broken timbers, and the bodies of the drowned, have not yet become quiet and sealed above their awful sepulchres. Still, day after day, disconsolate Love and sorrowing Friendship are called to the sea-shore or the house of the dead, to recognize some lithe and perhaps mangled form, that has been given up and rescued from the deep. Still, ever and anon, some portion of sunken treasure, some relic that was lost with the departed, is plucked all dripping from the bosom of the element, to touch the chord of painful association, and tear the wounds of affection afresh. Still, the anxious wife, or child, or parent, at the hearth of home, and the distant traveller upon the heaving billows, shudder with apprehension and are cold at the heart, as their thought goes back to that scene of death and terror which surrounded the doomed and burning Lexington.

A vessel plying upon the route between two of the most important cities of our country, filled with a multitude of human beings, in sight of a populous shore, in an early hour of the evening, is suddenly enwrapped in flames, — surrounded by the darkness of the night, the inclement winter air, and a waste of cold and icy waters; leaving to its wretched inmates, in almost every instance, nothing but the dreadful alternative of death by the consuming flame or by the freezing flood. The alarm-cry bursts from lip to lip of that startled throng, smiting awfully and solemnly upon each heart, like the tone of its own deep death-knell. Imagination cannot picture, or conceive, the dread reality. In what various moods of thought, in what different occupations, were they engaged! They had left, but a little while ago, the thronged and busy city, through whose streets, filled with light and life, and presenting all the diversities of a mimic world, they had so lately passed; and they were now, calmly as if under the roof of their own dwellings, borne on with all the speed of mighty engines towards other thoroughfares of life and action and joy, where they might mingle among men. Some had grasped warm hands and pressed warm hearts at parting, and bidden a gay or sad, but, as they thought, a brief farewell. Some had left the couch of the sick friend, hurried forth by the urgency of business, with the promise and the thought speedily to return. Some had parted with the traveller's haste, who had already passed over a long and wearisome route, and were looking forward with eager expectation to the welcome of their near and waiting homes. Some had come forth with the gladness and buoyancy of hope, with the strong purpose of gain, with the joyful anticipation of meeting dear and familiar faces. Some had decided to come upon a halting resolution, — O! why *did* they thus decide? Some were far from their homes, and were numbering the days that should bear them back. Some — but we will not pause to enumerate the various circumstances under which the members of that group had set out, and that preceded their solemn end. Suffice it to say, that life and hope, and memories of loved ones, and innumerable thoughts and sympathies and feelings, were stirring in the hearts of the mass of beings that were so soon to go down, amid the chilliness of winter and the flaming shroud of the conflagration, to the cold and unknown chambers of the deep!

What a hurried rush for safety and for life was there! What piercing shrieks, bursting from ashy and quivering lips, rose above the hoarse gurgling of the waters, the roar and crackling of the flames, and rent the flushed and heated brow of night! What frantic cries of the husband for the wife, the wife for the husband, — the mother clutching wildly for her child, the child sobbing for its mother! What strivings of agony with the hot breath of the flame and the suffocating smoke; what moanings of the helpless, the trampled, and the crushed! What invocations for aid, shrieked into the ears of mortals as impotent! What fervent prayers, rising through the tumult and storm of the elements to the eternal throne! But still the fierce flame swept relentlessly on, and the waters chafed and shouted for their prey!

The strong, brave man, perchance, was there, who had toiled in sun and storm, and faced the billows and the wind, and travelled by land and by sea. And with a desperate struggle did he meet his death, grappling and striving with the overwhelming and terrific powers around him, as though they were living and conquerable things. As he saw behind him, in the fiery jaws of one element, certain destruction, with giant energy did he put by the dense and muffling smoke, and plunged with nerved limbs and dauntless heart into the cold arms of the other. And long did he battle with the waves, and shout and gurgle and shriek and madly toss the icy waters to and fro; and then, benumbed and dead, he went down, down, and all was still, — save a hoarse moaning of the deep, above his burial-place!

Beauty, perhaps, was there, in the bloom of youth and health. But when the alarm-cry came, white was that cheek with a paleness that was the seal of death, and horror glared wildly in those beaming eyes, and around her frail and delicate form swept the blast of the wreathing flame. That white hand was lifted for a moment above the ridgy billows, one stifled cry was heard — and she was gone! And now the gentle sunlight lingers and the sorrowful winds lament above her bed; but no flowers shall bloom and no tear be shed upon that spot beneath which, with calm brow, she sleeps, in some rocky and garnished chamber,

"Deep in the silent waters,
A thousand fathoms low."

The esteemed and talented one was there. He who had studied, with the love of the scholar, the sober reason of philosophy, and the earnest faith of religion, — whose lips had poured forth the words of instruction and of genius, and whose voice had been heard in the blessed ministrations of the gospel, — was called upon thus to die, —

to die suddenly and amid a scene of horror, — to die while on his way to fulfil a duty of his sacred station, — to die far away from the graves of his fathers and from his native land, and even from the tombs of those dear to him in the home of his adoption, — and, O! to die away from the arms of that devoted wife, who sorrowed for his absence, and waited with yearning fondness for his return. But he died leaving fresh, green memories in the hearts of those who knew him, and a good name in the world; and, better than all, he died with his armor on, as a soldier of the cross. He passed away amid the strife of the physical elements and the sufferings of keenest bodily anguish; but we may believe that soul that had imbibed the principles of Jesus was calm and triumphant amid it all, and supported and brightened with the undying hope of the Christian.

Maternal affection was there, deep, firm and true, to the last. Doubtless she struggled long for the boon of life; not only for herself, — O! not only for herself! — but for that dear babe. But when death came to relieve the little suffering child, and she gazed upon its pale brow and saw that it was dead, — when she felt the coldness gathering closer about her own yearning heart, and her eyes growing dim, — still, still was she true to the unconquerable impulse of a mother's love; and she tore her veil from off her, and cast it about the face of that sleeping one, that the winds and the waves and the ice might not treat it roughly, and that, when they should find its little corse, it might be all as unmarred and natural as if it had been borne in its mother's arms, and laid in the calmness and beauty of its stony slumber at their feet! And then life fluttered and went out in that true heart, and she sunk to her unknown grave!

And so, in various modes, and under circumstances marked by various degrees of horror, the young, the old, the rich, the poor, the talented, the weak, the strong, — tender woman and haughty manhood, the budding youth and the helpless child, — so they were swept away, upon that night, and devoured by the elements; with wild struggle and terrible agonies of death, with the flames hissing behind them and the waters yawning before, they passed from existence, a fearful mass of human life,

"Unknelled, uncoffined, and unknown!"

O! what, think you, were the thoughts of that dark and terrific death-hour? The reflections and memories of a life breaking at once upon the throbbing brain, more painful, more torturing, than the flame or flood that was devouring their shrinking bodies! The cold and freezing truth rushing over the heart, that they must die — and die thus! The remembrance of loved ones, of eyes that would flow with weeping for them, of homes that would be desolate, of those that would be left destitute, of forms and faces to be seen in this world no more! And then, the many and varied thoughts that surround the idea of death, — the things of religion, the concerns of the soul, — all these breaking in, in one flood, thrilling every artery of the body, and every faculty of the mind! O! who shall attempt to describe that crisis? They were human. They felt as human beings must ever feel, borne at one sweep from this mortal existence, hurried from the relations of this life, suddenly, violently, and forever!

O! the homes and the hearts that were left desolate that night! O! the peculiar nature of that grief, that flowed in upon the mourner's spirit as coldly as the waters flowed over their lost, their ocean-buried dead!

There were children gathered around their mother's knees in a distant home that night, and, perchance, they looked up into her gentle face, and caught from it the beaming smile of joy that accompanied the announcement that their father was on his way to greet them! Alas! the dark sea lay between him and them; and little did they think, when they opened their eyes to hail with gladness another day, that, they thought, brought him nearer to them, — little did they think that the husband, the father, rested cold and still beneath that sea, and that the hours flew on to bring them the tidings that he was lost!

Love lit its watch-fire upon that sad night. It looked out, peering through the darkness, almost in sight of the burning wreck, for the well-known form, so endeared to it by the strongest of earthly bonds. But that form came not. It had passed away from life forever. The bridal altar would never be lighted for him. The true glance of affection should beam upon him no more. His voice of love would never greet the ear, — it went out in a lone, wild shriek upon the night air! The heart that beat for him in anxious expectation would never press *his* heart; — the dashing waves had gone over it, and it was cold and still!

A splendid mansion waited for its owner. Its hall, perchance, was lighted, and its doors left ajar; and there were those who listened to catch the echoes of his well-known step. But that mansion received him, living, no more. That midnight lamp might burn on until the dawn, but he would not return. Those doors should open to his touch never again. Those anxious watchers listened in vain for his tread. O! sad, sad were the tidings that broke upon their ears, instead of the sound of that well-known step! Dark, dark was that hearth, from which his familiar face was absent — absent to greet them there no more!

FORMATION OF CHARACTER. — *W. Wirt.*

The man who is so conscious of the rectitude of his intentions as to be willing to open his bosom to the inspection of the world is in possession of one of the strongest pillars of a decided character. The course of such a man will be firm and steady, because he has nothing to fear from the world, and is sure of the approbation and support of Heaven. While he who is conscious of secret and dark designs, which, if known, would blast him, is perpetually shrinking and dodging from public observation, and is afraid of all around, and much more of all above him.

Such a man may, indeed, pursue his iniquitous plans, steadily, — he may waste himself to a skeleton in the guilty pursuit, — but it is impossible that he can pursue them with the same health-inspiring confidence, and exulting alacrity, with him who feels, at every step, that he is in pursuit of honest ends, by honest means.

The clear, unclouded brow, the open countenance, the brilliant eye, which can look an honest man steadfastly, yet courteously, in the face, the healthfully-beating heart, and the firm, elastic step, belong to him whose bosom is free from guile, and who knows that all his motives and purposes are pure and right. Why should such a man falter in his course? He may be slandered; he may be deserted by the world; but he has that within which will keep him erect, and enable him to move onward in his course with his eyes fixed on Heaven, which he knows will not desert him.

Let your first step, then, in that discipline which is to give you decision of character, be the heroic determination to be honest men, and to preserve this character through every vicissitude of fortune, and in every relation which connects you with society. I do not use this phrase, "honest men," in the narrow sense, merely, of meeting your pecuniary engagements, and paying your debts; for this the common pride of gentlemen will constrain you to do.

I use it in its larger sense of discharging all your duties, both public and private, both open and secret, with the most scrupulous, Heaven-attesting integrity; in that sense, further, which drives from the bosom all little, dark, crooked, sordid, debasing considerations of self, and substitutes in their place a bolder, loftier, and nobler spirit, — one that will dispose you to consider yourselves as born, not so much for yourselves as for your country and your fellow-creatures, and which will lead you to act on every occasion sincerely, justly, generously, magnanimously.

There is a morality on a larger scale, perfectly consistent with a just attention to your own affairs, which it would be the height of folly to neglect, — a generous expansion, a proud elevation and conscious greatness of character, which is the best preparation for a decided course, in every situation into which you can be thrown; and it is to this high and noble tone of character that I would have you to aspire.

I would not have you to resemble those weak and meagre streamlets, which lose their direction at every petty impediment that presents itself, and stop, and turn back, and creep around, and search out every little channel through which they may wind their feeble and sickly course. Nor yet would I have you to resemble the headlong torrent, that carries havoc in its mad career. But I would have you like the ocean, that noblest emblem of majestic decision, which, in the calmest hour, still heaves its resistless might of waters to the shore, filling the heavens, day and night, with the echoes of its sublime declaration of independence, and tossing and sporting on its bed, with an imperial consciousness of strength that laughs at opposition. It is this depth, and weight, and power, and purity of character, that I would have you to resemble; and I would have you, like the waters of the ocean, to become the purer by your own action.

THE DECLARATION OF INDEPENDENCE. — *J. Q. Adams.*

The interest which, in that paper, has survived the occasion upon which it was issued, — the interest which is of every age and every clime, — the interest which quickens with the lapse of years, spreads as it grows old, and brightens as it recedes, — is in the principles which it proclaims. It was the first solemn declaration by a nation of the only legitimate foundation of civil government. It was the corner-stone of a new fabric, destined to cover the surface of the globe. It demolished, at a stroke, the lawfulness of all governments founded upon conquest. It swept away all the rubbish of accumulated centuries of servitude. It announced, in practical form, to the world, the transcendent truth of the inalienable sovereignty of the people. It proved that the social compact was no figment of the imagination, but a real, solid and sacred bond of the social union. From the day of this declaration, the people of North America were no longer the fragment of a distant empire, imploring justice and mercy from an inexorable master, in another hemisphere. They were no longer children, appealing in vain to the sympathies of a heartless mother; no longer subjects, leaning upon the shattered columns of royal promises, and invoking the faith of parchment to secure their rights. They were a nation, asserting as of right, and maintaining by war, its own existence. A nation was born in a day.

"How many ages hence
Shall this, their lofty scene, be acted o'er,
In states unborn, and accents yet unknown?"

It will be acted o'er, fellow-citizens, but it can never be repeated. It stands, and must forever stand, alone; a beacon on the summit of the mountain, to which all the inhabitants of the earth may turn their eyes, for a genial and saving light, till time shall be lost in eternity, and this globe itself dissolve, nor leave a wreck behind. It stands forever, a light of admonition to the rulers of men, a light of salvation and redemption to the oppressed. So long as this planet shall be inhabited by human beings, so long as man shall be of a social nature, so long as government shall be necessary to the great moral purposes of society, so long as it shall be abused to the purposes of oppression, — so long shall this declaration hold out, to the sovereign and to the subject, the extent and the boundaries of their respective rights and duties, founded in the laws of nature and of nature's God.

KOSSUTH'S WELCOME TO BUNKER HILL. — *R. Frothingham, Jr.*

We stand on America's classic ground. The waters that flow beneath us, and every hill-top and valley that spread out in a beautiful amphitheatre around us, have their story of the men who perilled and suffered for the cause of freedom. Here was fought the first great battle of the war of the Revolution; there, near the shades of our venerable Harvard, Washington stood when he first drew his sword in that great struggle; on yonder summit, when our old thirteen colonies had united to form our early country, the Union flag of the thirteen stripes was first unfurled to the battle and the breeze; and it was over our proud metropolis that this flag, for the first time, waved in triumph behind a retreating foe.

Welcome, great patriot, to these enkindling associations! Your noble nature, your fidelity to principle, your labors, triumphs, perils and sufferings, in your country, and your continued and untiring devotion, in exile, to the cause of your father-land, proclaim you to be of kindred spirit with the immortal men whose heroism, in a day of baptism of fire and blood, hallowed this soil forever to the lovers of liberty! Welcome, illustrious exile, to the sacred inspiration, to the awakening power, of this consecrated spot!

And as, to bid you welcome, we come forth from our happy homes, from our schools of learning and our altars of religion, from the shops of a thriving industry and the marts of a prosperous commerce, it is in the full enjoyment of the fruits of political freedom, the quickening power of the principle of liberty animating all into its varied life. Would it were thus with brave and unfortunate Hungary! How can be expressed what here was felt at those occurrences that deprived your people of their rights, and made you an exile from home and country! We know the story of your eventful struggle. We see exhibited in it the traits of love of freedom, of chivalrous heroism, of undying attachment to ancient rights and liberties, of noble self-sacrifice, that marked our own great contest. We saw you, animated by the glorious antecedent of a thousand years' enjoyment of municipal institutions, gallantly carve your way, with your own good swords, to national independence, and thereby acquire the right of ordaining your own institutions. But then came the foreign interference with your internal affairs, when your territory was invaded and your independence was destroyed by the armies of the Czar. An indignant American public opinion must ever pronounce that interference to have been an enormous violation of national law; and also pronounce that each nation has a right to make or to unmake its government, free from interference by any foreign power.

Honored sir, I feel how inadequate are my poor words to serve such an occasion as to welcome the representative man of the cause of liberty in the Old World, on the soil where that cause in the New World first met the shock of regular conflict. Fortunately, the want is supplied. "The powerful speaker stands motionless before us." This majestic column was solemnly dedicated "to the spirit of national independence." Its speech to-day is of welcome and encouragement to the illustrious exile whose life is devoted to this noble cause!

LAYING OF THE CORNER-STONE OF BUNKER HILL MONUMENT.
—*D. Webster.*

We live in a most extraordinary age. Events so various and so important that they might crowd and distinguish centuries are, in our times, compressed within the compass of a single life. When has it happened that history has had so much to record, in the same term of years, as since the 17th of June, 1775? Our own Revolution, which, under other circumstances, might itself have been expected to occasion a war of half a century, has been achieved; twenty-four sovereign and independent states erected, and a general government established over them, so safe, so wise, so free, so practical, that we might well wonder its establishment should have been accomplished so soon, were it not far the greater wonder that it should have been established at all. Two or three millions of people have been augmented to twelve; and the great forests of the west prostrated beneath the arm of successful industry; and the dwellers on the banks of the Ohio and the Mississippi become the fellow-citizens and neighbors of those who cultivate the hills of New England. We have a commerce that leaves no sea unexplored; navies which take no law from superior force; revenues adequate to all the exigencies of the government, almost without taxation; and peace with all nations, founded on equal rights and mutual respect.

Europe, within the same period, has been agitated by a mighty revolution, which, while it has been felt in the individual condition and happiness of almost every man, has shaken to the centre her political fabric, and dashed against one another thrones which had stood tranquil for ages. On this, our continent, our own example has been followed; and colonies have sprung up to be nations. Unaccustomed sounds of liberty and free government have reached us from beyond the track of the sun; and at this moment the dominion of European power in this continent, from the place where we stand to the south pole, is annihilated forever.

In the mean time, both in Europe and America, such has been the general progress of knowledge, such the improvements in legislation, in commerce, in the arts, in letters, and, above all, in liberal ideas, and the general spirit of the age, that the whole world seems changed.

Yet, notwithstanding that this is but a faint abstract of the things which have happened since the day of the battle of Bunker Hill, we are but fifty years removed from it; and we now stand here, to enjoy all the blessings of our own condition, and to look abroad on the brightened prospects of the world, while we hold still among us some of those who were active agents in the scenes of 1775, and who are now here, from every quarter of New England, to visit once more, and under circumstances so affecting, I had almost said so overwhelming, this renowned theatre of their courage and patriotism.

Venerable men! you have come down to us from a former generation. Heaven has bounteously lengthened out your lives, that you might behold this joyous day. You are now where you stood fifty years ago, this very hour, with your brothers and your neighbors, shoulder to shoulder, in the strife of your country. Behold how altered! The same heavens are indeed over your heads, the same ocean rolls at your feet, — but all else how changed! You hear now no roar of hostile cannon; you see no mixed volumes of smoke and flame rising from burning Charlestown. The ground strewed with the dead and the dying, — the impetuous charge, — the steady and successful repulse, — the loud call to repeated assault, — the summoning of all that is manly to repeated resistance, — a thousand bosoms freely and fearlessly bared in an instant to whatever of terror there may be in war and death; — all these you have witnessed, but you witness them no more. All is peace. The heights of yonder metropolis, its towers and roofs, which you then saw filled with wives and children and countrymen in distress and terror, and looking with unutterable emotions for the issue of the combat, have presented you to-day with the sight of its whole happy population come out to welcome and greet you with a universal jubilee. Yonder proud ships, by a felicity of position appropriately lying at the foot of this mount, and seeming fondly to cling around it, are not means of annoyance to you, but your country's own means of distinction and defence. All is peace; and God has granted you this sight of your country's happiness ere you slumber in the grave forever. He has allowed you to behold and to partake the reward of your patriotic toils; and he has allowed us, your sons and countrymen, to meet you here, and in the name of the present generation, in the name of your country, in the name of liberty, to thank you!

But, alas! you are not all here! Time and the sword have thinned your ranks! Prescott, Putnam, Stark, Brooks, Read, Pomeroy, Bridge! — our eyes seek for you in vain amidst this broken band! You are gathered to your fathers, and live only to your country in her grateful remembrance, and your own bright example! But let us not too much grieve that you have met the common fate of men. You lived, at least, long enough to know that your work had been nobly and successfully accomplished. You lived to see your country's independence established, and to sheathe your swords from war. On the light of liberty you saw arise the light of peace, like

"another morn
Risen on mid-noon; —"

and the sky on which you closed your eyes was cloudless.

But — ah! — him! the first great martyr in this great cause! Him! the premature victim of his own self-devoting heart! Him! the head of our civil councils, and the destined leader of our military bands; whom nothing brought hither, but the unquenchable fire of his own spirit! Him! cut off by Providence in the hour of overwhelming anxiety and thick gloom; falling ere he saw the star of his country rise; pouring out his generous blood, like water, before he knew whether it would fertilize a land of freedom or of bondage! — how shall I struggle with the emotions that stifle the utterance of thy name! Our poor work may perish; but thine shall endure! This monument may moulder away, — the solid ground it rests upon may sink down to a level with the sea; but thy memory shall not fail! Wheresoever among men a heart shall be found that beats to the transports of patriotism and liberty, its aspirations shall be to claim kindred with thy spirit!

But the scene amidst which we stand does not permit us to confine our thoughts or our sympathies to those fearless spirits who hazarded or lost their lives on this consecrated spot. We have the happiness to rejoice here in the presence of a most worthy representation of the survivors of the whole Revolutionary army.

Veterans! you are the remnant of many a well-fought field. You bring with you marks of honor from Trenton and Monmouth, from Yorktown, Camden, Bennington, and Saratoga. Veterans of half a century! when, in your youthful days, you put everything at hazard in your country's cause, good as that cause was, and sanguine as youth is, still your fondest hopes did not stretch onward to an hour like this! At a period to which you could not reasonably have expected to arrive, at a moment of national prosperity such as you could never have foreseen, you are now met here to enjoy the fellowship of old soldiers, and to receive the overflowings of a universal gratitude.

But your agitated countenances and your heaving breasts inform me that even this is not an unmixed joy. I perceive that a tumult of contending feelings rushes upon you. The images of the dead, as well as the persons of the living, throng to your embraces. The scene overwhelms you, and I turn from it. May the Father of all mercies smile upon your declining years, and bless them! And, when you shall here have exchanged your embraces, — when you shall once more have pressed the hands which have been so often extended to give succor in adversity, or grasped in the exultation of victory, — then look abroad into this lovely land, which your young valor defended, and mark the happiness with which it is filled; yea, look abroad into the whole earth, and see what a name you have contributed to give to your country, and what a praise you have added to freedom, and then rejoice in the sympathy and gratitude which beam upon your last days from the improved condition of mankind!

It is, indeed, a touching reflection, that while, in the fulness of our country's happiness, we rear this monument to her honor, we look for instruction, in our undertaking, to a country which is now in fearful contest, not for works of art or memorials of glory, but for her own existence. Let her be assured that she is not forgotten in the world; that her efforts are applauded, and that constant prayers ascend for her success. And let us cherish a confident hope for her final triumph. If the true spark of religious and civil liberty be kindled, it will burn. Human agency cannot extinguish it. Like the earth's central fire, it may be smothered for a time, the ocean may overwhelm it, mountains may press it down, — but its inherent and unconquerable force will heave both the ocean and the land, and at some time or another, in some place or another, the volcano will break out, and flame up to heaven!

THE DISINTERESTEDNESS OF WASHINGTON. — *R. T. Paine.*

To the pen of the historian must be resigned the more arduous and elaborate tribute of justice to those efforts of heroic and political virtue which conducted the American people to peace and liberty. The vanquished foe retired from our shores, and left to the controlling genius who repelled them the gratitude of his own country, and the admiration of the world. The time had now arrived which was to apply the touchstone to his integrity — which was to assay the affinity of his principles to the standard of immutable right. On the one hand, a realm to which he was endeared by his services almost invited him to empire; on the other, the liberty to whose protection his life had been devoted was the ornament and boon of human nature. Washington could not depart from his own great self. His country was free — he was no longer a general. Sublime spectacle! more elevating to the pride of virtue than the sovereignty of the globe united to the sceptre of ages! Enthroned in the hearts of his countrymen, the gorgeous pageantry of prerogative was unworthy the majesty of his dominion. That effulgence of military character which in ancient states has blasted the rights of the people whose renown it had brightened, was not here permitted, by the hero from whom it emanated, to shine with so destructive a lustre. Its beams, though intensely resplendent, did not wither the young blossoms of our independence and liberty, like the burning bush, flourished unconsumed by the glory which surrounded it.

To the illustrious founder of our republic was it reserved to exhibit the example of a magnanimity that commanded victory, of a moderation that retired from triumph. Unlike the erratic meteors of ambition, whose flaming path sheds a disastrous light on the pages of history, his bright orb, eclipsing the luminaries among which it rolled, never portended "fearful change" to religion, nor from its "golden tresses" shook pestilence on empire. What to other heroes has been glory, would to him have been disgrace. To his intrepidity it would have added no honorary trophy, to have waded, like the conqueror of Peru, through the blood of credulous millions, to plant the standard of triumph at the burning mouth of a volcano. To his fame it would have erected no auxiliary monument, to have invaded, like the ravager of Egypt, an innocent though barbarous nation, to inscribe his name on the pillar of Pompey.

AMERICAN SCHOLARS NOT DEPENDENT UPON PRIVILEGED ORDERS. — *G. C. Verplanck.*

In other lands, pecuniary dependence is too often connected with reverence for rank, so that they produce together the most complete vassalage. The market for intellectual labor is overstocked. Nature's rich banquet is crowded with titled and hereditary guests; "the table is full." To emerge from the crowd of menials, and obtain some share of the feast, the unbidden scholar must attach himself to the train of a patron, and feed on the alms his niggard bounty may bestow. Such has been the degrading history of literary men, poets, authors, and, I blush to add, philosophers, throughout the world, for many centuries. The facility with which a sure and comfortable subsistence may be obtained in this country, and the certainty with which educated talent, directed by ordinary discretion and industry, may obtain to a decent competency, are such as to exclude all temptation, much more all necessity, to follow in this respect the humiliating example of European learning.

To such evils "the lack of means need never drive us." If dazzled by the false glitter of office, if bribed by the doles of political patronage, or by such paltry boons as private interest can bestow, the American scholar is ever weak enough to sell his conscience, or bow down his independence before a master, he falls a voluntary victim. His sin is his own: his own be the shame. Let him not seek to divide it with his country. Is it not, then, a glorious privilege, to be wholly free from the necessity of such dependence, — never to be forced by the tyrannous compulsion of need to man-worship, the meanest of all idolatries? Far nobler, far happier than kings can make him, is the lot of him who dedicates his life and his intellect to instruct and delight the people; who looks to them, not for alms or bounty, but for a just compensation in honor and in profit, for the pleasure or the instruction he affords them; who seeks to serve them as a friend, not to fawn on them as a flatterer, — to please them or to teach them, yet as having a higher master, and knowing the solemn responsibility of one who acts upon the happiness or the morals of many. Happy he who, in the discharge of such duties, leads none into dangerous error, lulls none into careless or contemptuous negligence of right, nor ever sullies the whiteness of an innocent mind. Happier, still happier, he who has scattered abroad into many hearts those moral seeds whence benevolent and heroic actions spring up, who has "given ardor to virtue and confidence to truth," or, in more sacred language, "has turned many unto righteousness." Such genius, fired from heaven's own light, will continue to the end of time to burn and spread, kindling congenial flames far and wide, until they lift up their broad, united blaze on high, enlightening, cheering and gladdening, the nations of the earth.

THE SUSPENSION OF DIPLOMATIC RELATIONS WITH AUSTRIA.

— *L. Cass.*

I DO not mistake the true position of my country, nor do I seek to exaggerate her importance. I am perfectly aware that, whatever we may do or say, the immediate march of Austria will be onward in the course of despotism, with a step feebler or firmer as resistance may appear near or remote, till she is stayed by one of those upheavings of the people, which is as sure to come as that man longs for freedom, and longs to strike the blow which shall make it his.

Pride is blind, and power tenacious; and Austrian pride and power, though they may quail before the signs of the times, before barricades and fraternization, by which streets are made fortresses and armies revolutionists, new and mighty engines in popular warfare, will hold out in their citadel till the last extremity. But many old things are passing away; and Austrian despotism will pass away, in its turn. Its bulwarks will be shaken by the rushing of mighty winds, by the voice of the world, wherever its indignant expression is not restrained by the kindred sympathies of arbitrary power.

I desire, sir, not to be misunderstood. I do not mean that in all the revolutionary struggles which political contests bring on it would be expedient for other governments to express their feelings of interest or sympathy. I think they should not; for there are obvious considerations which forbid such action, and the value of this kind of moral interposition would be diminished by its too frequent recurrence. It should be reserved for great events, — events marked by great crimes and oppressions on the one side, and great exertions and misfortunes on the other, and under circumstances which carry with them the sympathies of the world, like the partition of Poland and the subjugation of Hungary. We can offer public congratulations, as we have done, to people crowned by success in their struggle for freedom. We can offer our recognition of their independence to others, as we have done, while yet the effort was pending. Have we sympathy only for the fortunate? Or is a cause less sacred or less dear because it is prostrated in the dust by the foot of power? Let the noble sentiments of Washington, in his spirit-stirring reply to the French minister, answer these questions: "Born, sir, in a land of liberty, — having early learned to estimate its value, — having, in a word, devoted the best years of my life to its maintenance, — I rejoice whensoever in any country I see a nation unfold the banner of freedom. To call your nation brave, were but common praise. Wonderful people! Ages to come will read with astonishment the history of your exploits."

I freely confess that I shall hail the day with pleasure when this government, reflecting the true sentiments of the people, shall express its sympathy for struggling millions seeking, in circumstances of peril and oppression, that liberty which was given to them by God, but has been wrested from them by man. I do not see any danger to the true independence of nations by such a course; and, indeed, I am by no means certain that the free interchange of public views in this solemn manner would not go far towards checking the progress of oppression, and the tendency to war.

THE UNION. — *D. S. Dickinson.*

But a few days since, I visited the hall where the immortal Washington, after carving out the liberty which we, in common with twenty-five millions of our fellow-beings, this day enjoy, with a victorious yet unpaid army, who adored him, under his command, surrendered his commission and his sword voluntarily to the representatives of a few exhausted colonies. That sublime occasion yet imparts its sacred influences to the place, and there is eloquence in its silent walls. But where, said I, are the brave and patriotic spirits who here fostered the germ of this mighty empire? Alas! they have gone to their rewards, and the clods of the valley lie heavily on their hearts; while we, their ungrateful children, with every element of good before us, forgetting the mighty sacrifices they made for their descendants, trifle with the rich blessings we inherited, and are ready, with sacrilegious hands, to despoil the temple of liberty which they reared by years of toil and trial, and cemented in blood and tears. O! could we not have deferred this inhuman struggle until the departure from amongst us of the Revolutionary soldier, with his bowed and tottering frame, and his once bright eye dimmed? Ask him the cost of liberty, and he will "shoulder his crutch and tell how fields were won," and tell you of its priceless value. And yet we are shamelessly struggling in his sight, like mercenary children, for the patrimony, around the death-bed of a common parent, by whose industry and exertion it was accumulated, before the heart of him who gave them existence had ceased to pulsate. Amid all these conflicts, it has been my policy to give peace and stability to the Union, to silence agitation, to restore fraternal relations to an estranged brotherhood, and to lend my feeble aid in enabling our common country to march onward to the glorious fruition which awaits her. I have opposed, and will hereafter oppose, the monster disunion, in any and every form, and howsoever disguised, or in whatsoever condition, — whether in the germ, or the stately upas, with its wide-spread branches; whether it comes from the North or the South, or the East or the West; and whether it consists in denying the South her just rights, or in her demanding that to which she is not entitled. The Union of these States, in the true spirit of the constitution, is a sentiment of my life. It was the dream of my early years; it has been the pride and joy of manhood; and, if it shall please Heaven to spare me to age, I pray that its abiding beauty may beguile my vacant and solitary hours. I do not expect a sudden disruption of the political bonds which unite the states of this confederacy; but I greatly fear a growing spirit of jealousy and discontent and sectional hate, which must, if permitted to extend itself, finally destroy the beauty and harmony of the fabric, if it does not raze it to its foundation. It cannot be maintained by force, and majorities in a confederacy should be admonished to use their power justly. Let no one suppose that those who have been joined together will remain so, despite the commission of mutual wrongs, because they have once enjoyed each other's confidence and affection, and propriety requires them to remain united. A chafed spirit, whether of a community or an individual, may be goaded beyond endurance; and the history of the world has proved that the season of desperation which succeeds is awfully reckless of consequences. But woe be to him by whom the offence of disunion comes! He will be held accursed when the bloody mandates of Herod and Nero shall be forgiven; and be regarded as a greater monster in this world than he who, to signalize his brutal ferocity, reared a monument of thousands of human skulls; and, in the next,

> "The common damned will shun his society,
> And look upon themselves as fiends less foul."

THE INFLUENCE OF CHRISTIANITY. — *J. A. Dix.*

The influence of Christianity upon the political condition of mankind, though silent and almost imperceptible, has doubtless been one of the most powerful instruments of its amelioration. The principles and the practical rules of conduct which it prescribes; the doctrine of the natural equality of men, of a common origin, a common responsibility, and a common fate; the lessons of humility, gentleness and forbearance, which it teaches, are as much at war with political as they are with all moral injustice, oppression, and wrong. During century after century, excepting for brief intervals, the world too often saw the beauty of the system marred by the fiercest intolerance and the grossest depravation. It has been made the confederate of monarchs in carrying out schemes of oppression and fraud. Under its banner armed multitudes have been banded together, and led on by martial prelates to wars of desolation and revenge. Perpetrators of the blackest crimes have purchased from its chief ministers a mercenary immunity from punishment.

But nearly two thousand years have passed away, and no trace is left of the millions who, under the influence of bad passions, have dishonored its holy precepts; or of the far smaller number who, in seasons of general depravation, have drunk its current of living water on the solitary mountain or in the hollow rock. Its simple maxims, outliving them all, are silently working out a greater revolution than any which the world has seen; and long as the period may seem since its doctrines were first announced, it is almost imperceptible when regarded as one of the divisions of that time which is of endless duration. To use the language of an eloquent and philosophical writer, "The movements of Providence are not restricted to narrow bounds; it is not anxious to deduce to-day the consequences of the premises it laid down yesterday. It may defer this for ages, till the fulness of time shall come. Its logic will not be less conclusive for reasoning slowly. Providence moves through time as the gods of Homer through space; it makes a step, and years have rolled away. How long a time, how many circumstances, intervened before the regeneration of the moral powers of man by Christianity exercised its great, its legitimate function upon his social condition! Yet who can doubt or mistake its power?"

THE EXAMPLE OF OUR FOREFATHERS. — *J. Sparks.*

THE instructive lesson of history, teaching by example, can nowhere be studied with more profit, or with a better promise, than in the Revolutionary period of America; and especially by us, who sit under the tree our fathers have planted, enjoy its shade, and are nourished by its fruits. But little is our merit or gain, that we applaud their deeds, unless we emulate their virtues. Love of country was in them an absorbing principle, an undivided feeling; not of a fragment, a section, but of the whole country. Union was the arch on which they raised the strong tower of a nation's independence. Let the arm be palsied that would loosen one stone in the basis of this fair structure, or mar its beauty; the tongue mute, that would dishonor their names, by calculating the value of that which they deemed without price!

They have left us an example already inscribed in the world's memory; an example portentous to the aims of tyranny in every land; an example that will console in all ages the drooping aspirations of oppressed humanity. They have left us a written charter as a legacy, and as a guide to our course. But every day convinces us that a written charter may become powerless. Ignorance may misinterpret it; ambition may assail and faction destroy its vital parts; and aspiring knavery may at last sing its requiem on the tomb of departed liberty. It is the spirit which lives: in this are our safety and our hope, — the spirit of our fathers; and while this dwells deeply in our remembrance, and its flame is cherished, ever burning, ever pure, on the altar of our hearts, — while it incites us to think as they have thought, and do as they have done, — the honor and the praise will be ours, to have preserved unimpaired the rich inheritance which they so nobly achieved.

PUBLIC FAITH. — *F. Ames.*

To expatiate on the value of public faith may pass with some men for declamation; — to such men I have nothing to say. To others I will urge, Can any circumstance mark upon a people more turpitude and debasement? Can anything tend more to make men think themselves mean, or degrade to a lower point their estimation of virtue, and their standard of action?

It would not merely demoralize mankind; it tends to break all the ligaments of society, to dissolve that mysterious charm which attracts individuals to the nation, and to inspire in its stead a repulsive sense of shame and disgust.

What is patriotism? Is it a narrow affection for the spot where a man was born? Are the very clods where we tread entitled to this ardent preference because they are greener? No, sir; this is not the character of the virtue, and it soars higher for its object. It is an extended self-love, mingling with all the enjoyments of life, and twisting itself with the minutest filaments of the heart. It is thus we obey the laws of society, because they are the laws of virtue. In their authority we see, not the array of force and terror, but the venerable image of our country's honor. Every good citizen makes that honor his own, and cherishes it not only as precious, but as sacred. He is willing to risk his life in its defence, and is conscious that he gains protection while he gives it. For what rights of a citizen will be deemed inviolable when a state renounces the principles that constitute their security? Or, if his life should not be invaded, what would its enjoyments be in a country odious in the eyes of strangers, and dishonored in his own?

Could he look with affection and veneration to such a country as his parent? The sense of having one would die within him; he would blush for his patriotism, if he retained any; and justly, for it would be a vice. He would be a banished man in his native land.

I see no exception to the respect that is paid among nations to the law of good faith. If there are cases in this enlightened period when it is violated, there are none when it is decried. It is the philosophy of politics, the religion of governments. It is observed by barbarians, — a whiff of tobacco-smoke, or a string of beads, gives not merely binding force, but sanctity, to treaties. Even in Algiers, a truce may be bought for money, but, when ratified, even Algiers is too wise, or too just, to disown and annul its obligation. Thus, we see, neither the ignorance of savages, nor the principles of an association for piracy and rapine, permit a nation to despise its engagements. If, sir, there could be a resurrection from the foot of the gallows, — if the victims of justice could live again, collect together and form a society, — they would, however loath, soon find themselves obliged to make justice — that justice under which they fell — the fundamental law of their state. They would perceive it was their interest to make others respect, and they would therefore soon pay some respect themselves to the obligations of good faith.

It is painful, — I hope it is superfluous, — to make even the supposition that America should furnish the occasion of this opprobrium. No! let me not even imagine that a republican government, sprung, as our own is, from a people enlightened and uncorrupted, — a government whose origin is right, and whose daily discipline is duty, — can, upon solemn debate, make its option to be faithless, can dare to act what despots dare not avow, what our own example evinces, the states of Barbary are unsuspected of. No! rather let me make the supposition that Great Britain refuses to execute the treaty after we have done everything to carry it into effect. Is there any language of reproach pungent enough to express your commentary on the fact? What would you say, or, rather, what would you not say? Would you not tell them, wherever an Englishman might travel, shame would stick to him — he would disown his country? You would exclaim: England! proud of your wealth, and arrogant in the possession of power, blush for these distinctions, which become the vehicles of your dishonor! Such a nation might truly say to corruption, thou art my father, and to the worm, thou art my mother and my sister. We should say of such a race of men, their name is a heavier burden than their debt.

THE STABILITY OF OUR GOVERNMENT. — *C. Sprague.*

If there be on the earth one nation more than another whose institutions must draw their life-blood from the individual purity of its citizens, that nation is our own. Rulers by divine right, and nobles by hereditary succession, may, perhaps, tolerate with impunity those depraving indulgences which keep the great mass abject. Where the many enjoy little or no power, it were a trick of policy to wink at those enervating vices which would rob them of both the ability and the inclination to enjoy it. But, in our country, where almost every man, however humble, bears to the omnipotent ballot-box his full portion of the sovereignty, — where, at regular periods, the ministers of authority, who went forth to rule, return to be ruled, and lay down their dignities at the feet of the monarch multitude, — where, in short, public sentiment is the absolute lever that moves the political world, the purity of the people is the rock of political safety.

We may boast, if we please, of our exalted privileges, and fondly imagine that they will be eternal; but, whenever those vices shall abound which undeniably tend to debasement, steeping the poor and ignorant still lower in poverty and ignorance, and thereby destroying that wholesome mental equality which can alone sustain a self-ruled people, it will be found, by woful experience, that our happy system of government, the best ever devised for the intelligent and good, is the very worst to be intrusted to the degraded and vicious. The great majority will then truly become a many-headed monster, to be tamed and led at will. The tremendous

6*

power of suffrage, like the strength of the eyeless Nazarite, so far from being their protection, will but serve to pull down upon their heads the temple their ancestors reared for them. Caballers and demagogues will find it an easy task to delude those who have deluded themselves; and the freedom of the people will finally be buried in the grave of their virtues. National greatness may survive; splendid talents and brilliant victories may fling their delusive lustre abroad; — these can illumine the darkness that hangs round the throne of a despot, but their light will be like the baleful flame that hovers over decaying mortality, and tells of the corruption that festers beneath. The immortal spirit will have gone; and along our shores, and among our hills, — those shores made sacred by the sepulchre of the pilgrim, those hills hallowed by the uncoffined bones of the patriot, — even there, in the ears of their degenerate descendants, shall ring the last knell of departed Liberty!

THE AMERICAN UNION. — *E. Everett.*

It would be an unprofitable consumption of time to attempt to point out the innumerable ways in which the Union has auspiciously influenced the destinies of the country. Could any doubt arise on this point, it ought to be removed by a glance at the disastrous effects of discord among the republics of ancient Greece; among the Italian cities in the middle ages, or even at the present day, when we behold that lovely region, once the garden of Europe and the mistress of the world, by the sole want of a comprehensive nationality, lying at the mercy of foreign foes, and, what is worse, of foreign friends; or at more than one of the groups of states which have been carved out of the colonial dominions of Spain, in the southern portions of this continent. These are all so many warning examples of the disastrous effects of a want of union among kindred states; like discordant brothers, in danger of being led into fiercer warfare by those very circumstances of common language and origin, which, under a well-adjusted central power, would form the natural cement of the union.

It was the great happiness of the American people, that they followed the counsels of their patriotic and thoughtful leaders. In the midst of a wholesome jealousy in favor of local rights (which they carefully secured), and in opposition to some strong centrifugal tendencies, they had the discernment to perceive the advantages of a common bond, and followed with steadiness that line of policy which gave us our constitution. Nor have the conditions of our well-being, as it seems to me, been at all changed in the course of seventy-five years. What was matter of prospective prudence on the morning of the Revolution, is matter of experienced wisdom now. The same patriotic instinct (if I may adhere to that language) which brought the men of Massachusetts and Connecticut, of New Hampshire and Rhode Island, side by side, to the summit of Bunker Hill, and mingled their blood on that day, has, at every subsequent period of our national existence, cried out not less loudly for the preservation of the Union.

There is one view of this subject of so much importance, that I cannot forbear to present it more particularly to your consideration. Among the great ideas of the age, we are authorized in reckoning a growing sentiment in favor of peace. An impression is unquestionably gaining strength in the world, that public war is no less reproachful to our Christian civilization than the private wars of the feudal chiefs in the middle ages. The hope of adjusting national controversies by some system of friendly arbitration — a hope which philanthropic minds have distrustfully cherished in other periods — has of late been openly avowed by men of a more practical class, by men conversant with the policy of the world, and fresh from its struggles. The last year witnessed the assembling of a peace convention, of a very imposing character, at Paris; a similar one is about to be held at Frankfort-on-the-Main. Delegates from this country are on the way to join it. A congress of nations begins to be regarded as a practicable measure. Statesmen, and orators, and philanthropists, are flattering themselves that the countries of Europe, which have existed as independent sovereignties for a thousand years, and have never united in one movement since the crusades, may be brought into some community of action for this end. They are calling conventions and digesting projects, by which governments the most diverse, — empires, kingdoms, and republics, — inhabited by different races of men, — tribes of Sclavonian, Teutonic, Latin and mixed descent; speaking different languages, believing different creeds, — Greeks, Catholics and Protestants, — men who are scarcely willing to live on the same earth with each other, or go to the same heaven, can yet be made to agree in some great plan of common umpirage. If, while these sanguine projects are pursued, — while we are thinking it worth while to compass sea and land in the expectation of bringing these jarring nationalities into some kind of union, in order to put a stop to war; if, I say, at this juncture, the people of these thirty United States, most of which are of the average size of a European kingdom, — destined, if they remain a century longer at peace with each other, to equal in numbers the entire population of Europe, — states which, drawn together by a general identity of descent, language and faith, have not so much formed as grown up into a national confederation, — possessing, in its central legislature, executive and judiciary, an efficient tribunal for the arbitration and decision of public controversies; an actual peace congress, clothed with all the powers of a common constitution and law, and with a jurisdiction extending to the individual citizen (which this projected congress of nations does not even hope to exercise), — if, while they grasp at this shadow of a congress of nations, the people of these states let go of — nay, break up and scatter to the winds — this substantial Union, this real peace congress, which for sixty years has kept the country, with all its conflicting elements, in a state of prosperity never before equalled in the world, — the admiration and the envy of mankind, — they will commit a folly for which the language we speak has no name; against which, if we rational beings should fail to protest, the dumb stones of yonder monument would immediately cry out in condemnation!

Friends and fellow-citizens! we live at an eventful period. Mighty changes in human affairs are of daily occurrence, at home and abroad. In Europe, the strongest governments are shaken;

the pillars of tradition, rooted in the depths of antiquity, are heaved from their basis; and that fearful war of opinion, so long foretold, is raging, with various fortune, from Lisbon to Archangel. Have you not noticed that in the midst of the perplexity and dismay, — of the visions and the hopes, — of the crisis, the thoughts of men have been turned more and more to what has passed and what is passing in America? They are looking anxiously to us for lessons of practical freedom, — for the solution of that great mystery of state, that the strongest government is that which, with the least array of force, is deepest seated in the welfare and affections of the people. The friends of republican government in France, taunted with the impossibility of making such a government efficient and respectable, point to our example as the sufficient answer. Austria, breaking down beneath the burden of her warring races, offers them too late a federal constitution modelled on our own; and even in England, from which the original elements of our free institutions were derived, scarce a debate arises in Parliament, on an important question, without reference to the experience of the United States. The constitutional worship of mankind is reversed; they turn their faces to the west. Happy for them, happy for us, should they behold naught in this country to disappoint the hopes of progress, to discourage the friends of freedom, to strengthen the arm of the oppressor; and may God grant that those who look to us for guidance and encouragement may be able to transplant the germs of constitutional liberty to the ancient gardens of the earth, that the clouds which now darken the horizon of Europe may clear away, and the long-deferred hopes of the friends of freedom be fulfilled!

But chiefly let us trust that the principles of our fathers may more and more prevail throughout our beloved country. We have erected a noble monument to their memory; but we shall not have performed all our duty, unless we catch ourselves some portion of their spirit. O! that the contemplation of their bright example and pure fame might elevate our minds above the selfish passions, the fierce contentions, and the dark forebodings, of the day! We need the spirit of '75 to guide us safely amidst the dizzy activities of the times. While our own numbers are increasing in an unexampled ratio, Europe is pouring in upon us her hundreds of thousands annually, and new regions are added to our domain, which we are obliged to count by degrees of latitude and longitude. In the mean time, the most wonderful discoveries of art, and the most mysterious powers of nature, combine to give an almost fearful increase to the intensity of our existence. Machines of unexampled complication and ingenuity have been applied to the whole range of human industry. We rush across the land and the sea by steam; we correspond by magnetism; we paint by the solar ray; we count the beats of the electric clock at the distance of a thousand miles; — we do all but annihilate time and distance; — and, amidst all the new agencies of communication and action, the omnipotent press, the great engine of modern progress, not superseded or impaired, but gathering new power from all the arts, is daily clothing itself with louder thunders.

While we contemplate with admiration, — almost with awe, — the mighty influences which surround us, and which demand our coöperation and our guidance, let our hearts overflow with gratitude to the patriots who have handed down to us this great inheritance. Let us strive to furnish ourselves, from the storehouse of their example, with the principles and virtues which will strengthen us for the performance of an honored part on this illustrious stage. Let pure patriotism add its bond to the bars of iron which are binding the continent together; and, as intelligence shoots with the electric spark from ocean to ocean, let public spirit and love of country catch from heart to heart!

ATTENTION THE SOUL OF GENIUS. — *O. Dewey.*

The favorite idea of a genius among us is of one who never studies, or who studies nobody can tell when, — at midnight, or at odd times and intervals; and now and then strikes out, "at a heat," as the phrase is, some wonderful production. "The young man," it is often said, "has genius enough, if he would only study." Now, the truth is, that the genius will study; it is that in the mind which does study: that is the very nature of it. I care not to say that it will always use books. All study is not reading, any more than all reading is study.

Attention is the very soul of genius; not the fixed eye, not the poring over a book, but the fixed thought. It is, in fact, an action of the mind which is steadily concentrated upon one idea, or one series of ideas, which collects in one point the rays of the soul, till they search, penetrate, and fire the whole train of its thoughts. And while the fire burns within, the outside may be, indeed, cold, indifferent, negligent, absent in appearance; he may be an idler, or a wanderer, apparently without aim or intent; but still the fire burns within. And what though "it bursts forth," at length, as has been said, "like volcanic fires, with spontaneous, original, native force"? It only shows the intense action of the elements beneath. What though it breaks forth, like lightning from the cloud? The electric fire had been collecting in the firmament through many a silent, clear, and calm day. What though the might of genius appears in one decisive blow, struck in some moment of high debate, or at the crisis of a nation's peril? That mighty energy, though it may have heaved in the breast of Demosthenes, was once a feeble, infant thought. A mother's eye watched over its dawnings. A father's care guarded its early youth. It soon trod, with youthful steps, the halls of learning, and found other fathers to wake and to watch for it, even as it finds them here. It went on; but silence was upon its path, and the deep strugglings of the inward soul silently ministered to it. The elements around breathed upon it, and "touched it to finer issues." The golden ray of heaven fell upon it, and ripened its expanding faculties. The slow revolutions of years slowly added to its collected energies and treasures, till, in its hour of glory, it stood forth embodied in the form of living, commanding, irresistible eloquence. The world wonders at the manifestation, and says, "Strange, strange that it should come thus unsought, unpremeditated, unprepared!" But the truth is, there is no more a miracle in it than there is in the towering of the preëminent forest-tree, or in the flowing of the mighty and irresistible river, or in the wealth and waving of the boundless harvest.

THE SOUTH AND THE UNION. — *A. P. Butler.*

There has been much said about the feeling of a portion of this Union, as being ready to dissolve it. I am not to be terrified or controlled by any imputations of that kind. This Union has its uses, just according to the use that is made of it. It may be used as a great trust to effect the greatest ends that time ever committed to human institutions; and it is in the power of patriots and statesmen to make it subserve these ends. But when it shall be made a mere instrument of partial legislation, and to pander to the views and ends of hypocritical demagogues, it will cease to be an object of veneration, unless its worshippers shall be like those of Juggernaut, who regard it as a pious service to prostrate themselves and be crushed by the wheels of his car. I believe I am one of its real friends, and the charge of criminal design upon its duration comes with an ill grace from those who have adhered to selfish and unjust purposes.

Those who have introduced here the doctrines which we are called upon to question have no right to measure the extent of my opposition. What that measure will be I do not know. I am willing to accede to any peaceful constitutional measure which will tend to preserve the Union itself; these means may be too long disregarded; there is a limit. I am astonished when I hear the language sometimes used by the representatives from the "old thirteen," — from Massachusetts, Connecticut, Rhode Island, New York, and New Jersey, — making war upon their brethren of the southern sections of the Union, which seems to me but the policy that results in their own suicide. They give way to these wild, fanatical suggestions of policy, in disregard of those admonitions which should address themselves to them from their past history, as well as in view of their future destiny. They are waging a war against their interest, under the influence of feelings which were inculcated by their ancestors, and sowing the seeds of disunion.

I have said what I designed to say at this time; but with it I would, if I dared, make a suggestion to the administration, which has now, in a measure, the control of the destinies of this country;

and it would be that they should not experiment upon the disaffection which exists in one portion of this Union. I know, sir, it is deeper, far deeper, than has ever been exhibited on this floor. I fear it has been too much disguised. And it is not confined to South Carolina, as some seem to consider. Some would be glad to see her isolated from others, and thereby made an easier victim. The people of other Southern States are speaking out; and, if events are not arrested, there will be but one voice, and that voice will come from the mass of the people. The press and politicians cannot much longer delude them. What state may be the first to be involved in measures of resistance, I know not. South Carolina has sometimes cried out as a sentinel. But there are others having greater interests at stake, and which will be put ultimately in great danger. They will look to their security and interests, and all will move as one man. It is for those who have the destinies of this nation in their hands to say how far they will respect the feelings of the South.

IGNORANCE A CRIME IN A REPUBLIC. — *H. Mann.*

In all the dungeons of the Old World, where the strong champions of freedom are now pining in captivity beneath the remorseless power of the tyrant, the morning sun does not send a glimmering ray into their cells, nor does night draw a thicker veil of darkness between them and the world, but the lone prisoner lifts his iron-laden arms to heaven in prayer, that we, the depositaries of freedom, and of human hopes, may be faithful to our sacred trust; — while, on the other hand, the pensioned advocates of despotism stand, with listening ear, to catch the first sound of lawless violence that is wafted from our shores, to note the first breach of faith or act of perfidy amongst us, and to convert them into arguments against liberty and the rights of man.

The experience of the ages that are past, the hopes of the ages that are yet to come, unite their voices in an appeal to us; — they implore us to think more of the character of our people than of its numbers; to look upon our vast natural resources, not as tempters to ostentation and pride, but as a means to be converted, by the refining alchemy of education, into mental and spiritual treasures; they supplicate us to seek for whatever complacency or self-satisfaction we are disposed to indulge, not in the extent of our territory, or in the products of our soil, but in the expansion and perpetuation of the means of human happiness; they beseech us to exchange the luxuries of sense for the joys of charity, and thus give to the world the example of a nation whose wisdom increases with its prosperity, and whose virtues are equal to its power. For these ends they enjoin upon us a more earnest, a more universal, a more religious devotion to our exertions and resources, to the culture of the youthful mind and heart of the nation. Their gathered voices assert the eternal truth, that, in a republic, ignorance is a crime; and that private immorality is not less an opprobrium to the state than it is guilt in the perpetrator.

OBEDIENCE TO THE CONSTITUTION. — *S. A. Douglass.*

Our forefathers held that the people had an inherent right to establish such constitution and laws, for the government of themselves and their posterity, as they should deem best calculated to insure the protection of life, liberty, and the pursuit of happiness; and that the same might be altered and changed, as experience should satisfy them to be necessary and proper. Upon this principle the constitution of the United States was formed, and our glorious Union established. All acts of Congress passed in pursuance of the constitution are declared to be the supreme laws of the land, and the Supreme Court of the United States is charged with expounding the same. All officers and magistrates, under the federal and state governments, — executive, legislative, judicial, and ministerial, — are required to take an oath to support the constitution, before they can enter upon the performance of their respective duties. Every person born under the constitution owes allegiance to it; and every naturalized citizen takes an oath to support it. Fidelity to the constitution is the only passport to the enjoyment of rights under it. When a senator elect presents his credentials, he is not allowed to take his seat until he places his hand upon the holy evangelist, and appeals to his God for the sincerity of his vow to support the constitution. He who does this with a mental reservation, or secret intention to disregard any provision of the constitution, commits a double crime — is morally guilty of perfidy to his God, and treason to his country!

If the constitution of the United States is to be repudiated upon the ground that it is repugnant to the divine law, where are the friends of freedom and Christianity to look for another and a better? Who is to be the prophet to reveal the will of God, and establish a theocracy for us?

I will not venture to inquire what are to be the form and principles of the new government, or to whom is to be intrusted the execution of its sacred functions; for, when we decide that the wisdom of our Revolutionary fathers was foolishness, and their piety wickedness, and destroy the only system of self-government that has ever realized the hopes of the friends of freedom and commanded the respect of mankind, it becomes us to wait patiently until the purposes of the Latter Day Saints shall be revealed unto us.

For my part, I am prepared to maintain and preserve inviolate the constitution as it is, with all its compromises; to stand or fall by the American Union, clinging with the tenacity of life to all its glorious memories of the past, and precious hopes of the future.

THE HEROISM OF THE PILGRIMS. — *R. Choate.*

If one were called on to select the most glittering of the instances of military heroism to which the admiration of the world has been most constantly attracted, he would make choice, I imagine, of the instance of that desperate valor, in which, in obedience to the laws, Leonidas and his three hundred Spartans cast themselves headlong, at the passes of Greece, on the myriads of their Persian invaders. From the simple page of Herodotus, longer than from the Amphyctionic monument, or the games of the commemoration, that act speaks still to the tears and praise of all the world.

Judge if, that night, as they watched the dawn of the last morning their eyes could ever see; as they heard with every passing hour the stilly hum of the invading host, his dusky lines stretched out without end, and now almost encircling them around; as they remembered their unprofaned home, city of heroes and of the mother of heroes, — judge if, watching there, in the gateway of Greece, this sentiment did not grow to the nature of madness, if it did not run in torrents of literal fire to and from the laboring heart; and when morning came and passed, and they had dressed their long locks for battle, and when, at a little after noon, the countless invading throng was seen at last to move, was it not with a rapture, as if all the joy, all the sensation of life, was in that one moment, that they cast themselves, with the fierce gladness of mountain torrents, headlong on that brief revelry of glory?

I acknowledge the splendor of that transaction in all its aspects. I admit its morality, too, and its useful influence on every Grecian heart, in that greatest crisis of Greece.

And yet, do you not think that whoso could, by adequate description, bring before you that winter of the Pilgrims, — its brief sunshine; the nights of storm, slow waning; the damp and icy breath, felt to the pillow of the dying; its destitutions, its contrasts with all their former experience in life, its utter insulation and loneliness, its death-beds and burials, its memories, its apprehensions, its hopes; the consultations of the prudent; the prayers of the pious; the occasional cheerful hymn, in which the strong heart threw off its burden, and, asserting its unvanquished nature, went up, like a bird of dawn, to the skies; — do ye not think that whoso could describe them calmly waiting in that defile, lonelier and darker than Thermopylæ, for a morning that might never dawn, or might show them, when it did, a mightier arm than the Persian raised as in act to strike, would he not sketch a scene of more difficult and rarer heroism? A scene, as Wordsworth has said, "melancholy, yea, dismal, yet consolatory and full of joy;"

a scene even better fitted to succor, to exalt, to lead the forlorn hopes of all great causes, till time shall be no more!

I have said that I deemed it a great thing for a nation, in all the periods of its fortunes, to be able to look back to a race of founders, and a principle of institution, in which it might rationally admire the realized idea of true heroism. That felicity, that pride, that help, is ours. Our past, with its great eras, that of settlement, and that of independence, should announce, should compel, should spontaneously evolve as from a germ, a wise, moral, and glowing future. Those heroic men and women should not look down on a dwindled posterity. That broad foundation, sunk below frost or earthquake, should bear up something more permanent than an encampment of tents, pitched at random, and struck when the trumpet of march sounds at next daybreak. It should bear up, as by a natural growth, a structure in which generations may come, one after another, to the great gift of the social life.

THE DEATH OF O'CONNELL. — *W. H. Seward.*

THERE is sad news from Genoa. An aged and weary pilgrim, who can travel no further, passes beneath the gate of one of her ancient palaces, saying, with pious resignation, as he enters its silent chambers, "Well, it is God's will that I shall never see Rome. I am disappointed. But I am ready to die. It is all right." The superb though fading queen of the Mediterranean holds anxious watch, through ten long days, over that majestic stranger's wasting frame. And now death is there — the Liberator of Ireland has sunk to rest in the cradle of Columbus.

Coincidence beautiful and most sublime! It was the very day set apart by the elder daughter of the Church for prayer and sacrifice throughout the world, for the children of the sacred island, perishing by famine and pestilence in their homes and in their native fields, and on their crowded paths of exile, on the sea and in the havens, and on the lakes, and along the rivers of this far distant land. The chimes rung out by pity for his countrymen were O'Connell's fitting knell; his soul went forth on clouds of incense that rose from altars of Christian charity; and the mournful anthems which recited the faith, and the virtue, and the endurance of Ireland, were his becoming requiem.

It is a holy sight to see the obsequies of a soldier, not only of civil liberty, but of the liberty of conscience; of a soldier, not only of freedom, but of the cross of Christ; of a benefactor, not merely of a race of people, but of mankind. The vault lighted by suspended worlds is the temple within which the great solemnities are celebrated; the nations of the earth are mourners; and the spirits of the just made perfect, descending from their golden thrones on high, break forth into songs.

Behold, now, a nation that needeth not to speak its melancholy precedence. The lament of Ireland comes forth from palaces deserted, and from shrines restored; from Boyne's dark water, witness of her desolation, and from Tara's lofty hill, ever echoing her renown. But louder and deeper yet that wailing comes from the lonely huts on mountain and on moor, where the people of the greenest island of all the seas are expiring in the midst of insufficient though world-wide charities. Well, indeed, may they deplore O'Connell; for they were his children, and he bore them

"A love so vehement, so strong, so pure,
That neither age could change nor art could cure."

DESTINY OF AMERICA. — *J. Story.*

What is to be the destiny of this republic? In proposing this question, I drop all thought of New England. She has bound herself to the fate of the Union. May she be true to it, now and forever; true to it, because true to herself, true to her own principles, true to the cause of religion and liberty throughout the world. I speak, then, of our common country; of that blessed mother that has nursed us in her lap, and led us up to manhood. What is her destiny? Whither does the finger of fate point? Is the career on which we have entered to be bright with ages of onward and upward glory? Or is our doom already recorded in the past history of the earth, in the past lessons of the decline and fall of other republics?

I would not willingly cloud the pleasures of such a day, even with a transient shade. I would not that a single care should flit across the polished brow of Hope, if considerations of the highest moment did not demand our thoughts, and give us counsel of our duties. Who, indeed, can look around him upon the attractions of this scene, upon the faces of the happy and the free, the smiles of youthful beauty, the graces of matron virtue, the strong intellect of manhood, and the dignity of age, and hail these as the accompaniments of peace and independence; — who can look around him and not at the same time feel that change is written on all the works of man, — that the breath of a tyrant, or the fury of a corrupt populace, may destroy in one hour what centuries have slowly consolidated?

The Old World has already revealed to us, in its unsealed books, the beginning and end of all its own marvellous struggles in the cause of liberty. Greece, lovely Greece, "the land of scholars and the nurse of arms," where sister republics in fair possessions chanted the praises of liberty and the gods, — where, and what is she? For two thousand years the oppressor has bound her to the earth. Her arts are no more. The last sad relics of her temples are but the barracks of a ruthless soldiery; the fragments of her columns and her palaces are in the dust, yet beautiful in ruin. She fell not when the mighty were upon her. Her sons were united at Thermopylæ and Marathon, and the tide of her triumph rolled back upon the Hellespont. She was conquered by her own factions. She fell by the hands of her own people. The man of Macedonia did not the work of destruction. It was already done, by her own corruptions, banishments, and dissensions. Rome, republican Rome, whose eagles glanced in the rising and setting sun, — where and what is she? The eternal city yet remains, proud even in her desolation, noble in her decline, venerable in the majesty of religion, and calm as in the composure of death!

And where are the republics of modern times, which clustered round immortal Italy? Venice and Genoa exist but in name. The Alps, indeed, look down upon the brave and peaceful Swiss in their native fastnesses; but the guarantee of their freedom is in their weakness, and not in their strength. The mountains are not easily crossed, and the valleys are not easily retained. When the invader comes, he moves like an avalanche, carrying destruction in his path.

We stand the latest, and, if we fail, probably the last experiment of self-government by the people. We have begun it under circumstances of the most auspicious nature. We are in the vigor of youth. Our growth has never been checked by the oppressions of tyranny. Our constitutions have never been enfeebled by the vices or luxuries of the Old World. Such as we are, we have been from the beginning, — simple, hardy, intelligent, accustomed to self-government and self-respect. The Atlantic rolls between us and any formidable foe. Within our own territory, stretching through many degrees of latitude and longitude, we have the choice of many products, and many means of independence. The government is mild. The press is free. Religion is free. Knowledge reaches, or may reach, every home. What fairer prospect of success could be presented? What means more adequate to accomplish the sublime end? What more is necessary than for the people to preserve what they themselves have created?

Already has the age caught the spirit of our institutions. It has already ascended the Andes, and snuffed the breezes of both oceans. It has infused itself into the life-blood of Europe, and warmed the sunny plains of France, and the low lands of Holland. It has touched the philosophy of Germany and the north; and, moving onward to the south, has opened to Greece the lessons of her better days.

Can it be that America, under such circumstances, can betray herself? That she is to be added to the catalogue of republics, the inscription upon whose ruins is, "They were, but they are not"? Forbid it, my countrymen! forbid it, Heaven!

I call upon you, fathers, by the shades of your ancestors, by the dear ashes which repose in this precious soil, by all you are and all you hope to be, — resist every object of disunion; resist every encroachment upon your liberties; resist every attempt to fetter your consciences, or smother your public schools, or extinguish your system of public instruction.

I call upon you, mothers, by that which never fails in woman — the love of your offspring; teach them, as they climb your knees, or lean on your bosoms, the blessings of liberty. Swear them at the altar, as with their baptismal vows, to be true to their country, and never to forget or forsake her.

I call upon you, young men, to remember whose sons you are — whose inheritance you possess. Life can never be too short, which brings nothing but disgrace and oppression. Death never comes too soon, if necessary in defence of the liberties of your country.

I call upon you, old men, for your counsels, and your prayers, and your benedictions. May not your gray hairs go down in sorrow to the grave with the recollection that you have lived in vain! May not your last sun sink in the west upon a nation of slaves!

No! I read in the destiny of my country far better hopes, far brighter visions. We who are now assembled here must soon be gathered to the congregation of other days. The time of our departure is at hand, to make way for our children upon the theatre of life. May God speed them and theirs! May he who, at the distance of another century, shall stand here to celebrate this day, still look round upon a free, happy and virtuous people! May he have reason to exult as we do! May he, with all the enthusiasm of truth as well as of poetry, exclaim that here is still his country!

DUTIES OF AMERICANS. — *G. S. Hillard.*

We may betray the trust reposed in us — we may most miserably defeat the fond hopes entertained of us. We may become the scorn of tyrants and the jest of slaves. From our fate, oppression may assume a bolder front of insolence, and its victims sink into a darker despair.

In that event, how unspeakable will be our disgrace! with what weight of mountains will the infamy lie upon our souls! The gulf of our ruin will be as deep, as the elevation we might have attained is high. How wilt thou fall from heaven, O Lucifer, son of the morning! Our beloved country with ashes for beauty; the golden cord of our union broken; its scattered fragments presenting every form of misrule, from the wildest anarchy to the most ruthless despotism; our "soil drenched with fraternal blood;" the life of man stripped of its grace and dignity; the prizes of honor gone, and virtue divorced from half its encouragements and supports; — these are gloomy pictures, which I would not invite your imaginations to dwell upon, but only to glance at, for the sake of the warning lessons we may draw from them.

Remember that we can have none of those consolations which sustain the patriot who mourns over the undeserved misfortunes of his country. Our Rome cannot fall, and we be innocent. No conqueror will chain us to the car of his triumph; no countless swarm of Huns and Goths will bury the memorials and trophies of civilized life beneath a living tide of barbarism. Our own selfishness, our own neglect, our own passions, and our own vices, will furnish the elements of our destruction. With our own hands we shall tear down the stately edifice of our glory. We shall die by self-inflicted wounds.

But we will not talk of themes like these. We will not think of failure, dishonor and despair. We will elevate our minds to the contemplation of our high duties, and the great trust committed to us. We will resolve to lay the foundations of our prosperity on that rock of private virtue which cannot be shaken until the laws of the moral world are reversed. From our own breasts shall flow the salient springs of national increase. Then our success, our happiness, our glory, is inevitable. We may calmly smile at all the croakings of all the ravens, whether of native or foreign breed.

The whole will not grow weak by the increase of its parts. Our growth will be like that of the mountain oak, which strikes its roots more deeply into the soil, and clings to it with a closer grasp, as its lofty head is exalted and its broad arms stretched out. The loud burst of joy and gratitude which this, the anniversary of our independence, is breaking from the full hearts of a mighty people, will never cease to be heard. No chasms of sullen silence will interrupt its course; no discordant notes of sectional madness mar the general harmony. Year after year will increase it, by tributes from now unpeopled solitudes. The furthest West shall hear it and rejoice; the Oregon shall swell it with the voice of its waters; the Rocky Mountains shall fling back the glad sound from their snowy crests.

OUR COUNTRY'S ORIGIN — *D. Webster.*

Our fathers came hither to a land from which they were never to return. Hither they had brought, and here they were to fix, their hopes, their attachments, and their objects. Some natural tears they shed, as they left the pleasant abodes of their fathers; and some emotions they suppressed, when the white cliffs of their native country, now seen for the last time, grew dim to their sight.

A new existence awaited them here; and when they saw these shores, rough, cold, barbarous and barren, as then they were, they beheld their country. Before they reached the shore they had established the elements of a social system, and at a much earlier period had settled their forms of religious worship. At the moment of their landing, therefore, they possessed institutions of government and institutions of religion. The morning that beamed on the first night of their repose saw the Pilgrims already established in their country. There were political institutions, and civil liberty, and religious worship. Poetry has fancied nothing in the wanderings of heroes so distinct and characteristic. Here was man indeed unprotected, and unprovided for, on the shore of a rude and fearful wilderness; but it was politic, intelligent and educated man. Everything was civilized but the physical world. Institutions containing in substance all that ages had done for human government were established in a forest. Cultivated mind was to act on uncultivated nature; and, more than all, a government and a country were to commence with the very first foundations laid under the divine light of the Christian religion. Happy auspices of a happy futurity! Who would wish that his country's existence had otherwise begun? Who would desire the power of going back to the ages of fable? Who would wish for an origin obscured in the darkness of antiquity? Who would wish for other emblazoning of his country's heraldry, or other ornaments of her genealogy, than to be able to say that her first existence was with intelligence, her first breath the inspirations of liberty, her first principle the truth of divine religion?

AGRICULTURE. — *D. S. Dickinson.*

We have the high authority of history, sacred and profane, for declaring that agriculture is a dignified and time-honored calling — ordained and favored of Heaven, and sanctioned by experience; and we are invited to its pursuit by the rewards of the past and the present, and the rich promises of the future. While the fierce spirit of war, with its embattled legions, has, in its proud triumphs, "whelmed nations in blood and wrapped cities in fire," and filled the land with lamentation and mourning, it has not brought peace or happiness to a single hearth, dried the tears of the widows or hushed the cries of the orphans it has made, bound up or soothed one crushed or broken spirit, nor heightened the joys of domestic or social life in a single bosom. But how many dark recesses of the earth has agriculture illumined with its blessings! How many firesides has it lighted up with radiant gladness! How many hearts has it made buoyant with domestic hope! How often, like the good Samaritan, has it alleviated want and misery, while the priest and Levite of power have passed by on the other side! How many family altars, and gathering places of affection, has it erected! How many desolate homes has it cheered by its consolations! How have its peaceful and gentle influences filled the land with plenteousness and riches, and made it vocal with praise and thanksgiving!

It has pleased the benevolent Author of our existence to set in boundless profusion before us the necessary elements for a high state of cultivation and enjoyment. Blessings cluster around us like fruits of the land of promise, and science unfolds her treasures and invites us to partake, literally without money and without price. The propensities of our nature, as well as the philosophy of our being, serve to remind us that man was formed for care and labor, for the acquisition and enjoyment of property, for society and government, to wrestle with the elements around him; and that, by an active exercise of his powers and faculties alone, can he answer the ends of his creation, or exhibit his exalted attributes. His daily wants, in all conditions of life, prompt him to exertion; and the spirit of acquisition, so deeply implanted in the human breast, — that "ruling passion strong in death," so universally diffused through the whole family of man, — is the parent of that laudable enterprise which has caused the wilderness to bud and blossom like the rose, planted domestic enjoyments in the lair of the beast of prey, and transformed the earth from an uncultivated wild into one vast storehouse of subsistence and enjoyment. What can be more acceptable to the patriot or the philanthropist, than to behold the great mass of mankind raised above the degrading influences of tyranny and indolence, to the rational enjoyment of the bounties of their Creator? To see, in the productions of man's magic powers, the cultivated country, the fragrant meadow, the waving harvest, the smiling garden, and the tasteful dwelling, and himself, chastened by the precepts of religion and elevated by the refinements of science, partaking of the fruits of his own industry, with the proud consciousness that he eats not the bread of idleness or fraud; that his gains are not met with the tears of misfortune, nor wrung from his fellow by the devices of avarice or extortion; his joys heightened, his sorrows alleviated, and his heart rectified, by the cheering voice and heaven-born influences of woman. Well may he sit down under his own vine and fig-tree without fear of molestation, and his nightly repose be more quiet than that of the stately monarch of the east upon his down of cygnets, or the voluptuous Sybarite upon his bed of roses.

SECTIONAL SERVICES IN THE LAST WAR. — *C. Cushing.*

The gentleman from South Carolina taunts us with counting the cost of that war in which the liberties and honor of the country, and the interests of the North, as he asserts, were forced to go elsewhere for their defence. Will he sit down with me and count the cost now? Will he reckon up how much of treasure the State of South Carolina expended in that war, and how much the State of Massachusetts? — how much of the blood of either state was poured out on sea or land? I challenge the gentleman to the test of patriotism, which the army roll, the navy lists, and the treasury books, afford. Sir, they who revile us for our opposition to the last war have looked only to the surface of things. They little know the extremities of suffering which the people of Massachusetts bore at that period, out of attachment to the Union, — their families beggared, their fathers and sons bleeding in camps, or pining in foreign prisons. They forget that not a field was marshalled, on this side of the mountains, in which the men of Massachusetts did not play their part as became their sires, and their "blood fetched from mettle of war proof." They battled and bled, wherever battle was fought or blood drawn.

Nor only by land. I ask the gentleman, who fought your naval battles in the last war? Who led you on to victory after victory, on the ocean and the lakes? Whose was the triumphant prowess before which the red cross of England paled with unwonted shames? Were they not men of New England? Were these not foremost in those maritime encounters which humbled the pride and power of Great Britain? I appeal to my colleague before me from our common county of brave old Essex, — I appeal to my respected colleagues from the shores of the Old Colony. Was there a village or a hamlet on Massachusetts Bay which did not gather its hardy seamen to man the gun-decks of your ships of war? Did they not rally to the battle, as men flock to a feast?

I beseech the House to pardon me, if I may have kindled, on this subject, into something of unseemly ardor. I cannot sit tamely by, in humble acquiescent silence, when reflections, which I know to be unjust, are cast on the faith and honor of Massachusetts. Had I suffered them to pass without admonition, I should have deemed that the disembodied spirits of her departed children, from their ashes mingled with the dust of every stricken field of the Revolution, — from their bones mouldering to the consecrated earth of Bunker's Hill, of Saratoga, of Monmouth, — would start up in visible shape before me, to cry shame on me, their recreant countryman! Sir, I have roamed through the world, to find hearts nowhere warmer than hers, soldiers nowhere braver, patriots nowhere purer, wives and mothers nowhere truer, maidens nowhere lovelier, green valleys and bright rivers nowhere greener or brighter; and I will not be silent, when I hear her patriotism or her truth questioned with so much as a whisper of detraction. Living, I will defend her; dying, I would pause, in my last expiring breath, to utter a prayer of fond remembrance for my native New England!

AN APPEAL FOR UNION. — *J. M. Berrien.*

I do not limit my appeal to Southern senators: I address myself to senators from whatever quarter of the Union; I appeal to them as American senators, and I adjure them, by their recollections of the past, by their hopes of the future, as they value the free institutions which the mercy of Providence permits us to enjoy, — by all these considerations, I entreat them to unite with us in excluding from the national councils this demon of discord. The acquisition of territory which it is proposed to accomplish by this bill must bring upon us, with accumulated force, a question which even now menaces the permanence of our Union. I know the firmness of your determination to exert your constitutional powers to prevent the extension of our domestic institutions. I know the various considerations which unite to constitute that determination, and to give to it its unyielding, irrevocable character. I do not mean to discuss this question with you, still less to speak in the language of menace. That is alike forbidden by my respect for myself, for you, and for the dignity and the interests of my constituents; but I entreat you to listen to truth, dispassionately, calmly announced to you.

Your determination to deny this right to the South is not more fixed and unwavering than theirs to assert it. You do not believe that Southern men will silently acquiesce in, will tamely submit to, the denial to them of that which in their deliberate judgment is the common right of all the people of the United States. If we have a right to acquire territory, — if that acquisition be made by the common effort of all the states, by the blood and treasure of all, — if all have a common right to share what all have united to acquire, then the exclusion of the South must result in one of two things. They must give an unexampled manifestation of their devotion to the bond of our Federal Union, by submitting to this exclusion, or sadly though resolutely determine, at whatever hazard, and even against you their brothers in that sacred bond, to assert and maintain their rights. You know them well enough to know which of these alternatives they will adopt. I do most earnestly hope that we may never be brought to so fearful a crisis. The danger menaces us even now; but the patriotism and intelligence of the American people will, I trust, avert it, — will teach us, and will teach you, that our safety, that your safety, that the common safety of all alike, forbid the acquisition of territory, if we would continue to enjoy the precious legacy which has been transmitted to us, — a rich, almost boundless domain, capable of ministering to all our wants, of gratifying all our desires, and a glorious constitution, which a world in arms would vainly assail while we rally round it in our united strength.

UNION LINKED WITH LIBERTY. — *A. Jackson.*

Without union, our independence and liberty would never have been achieved; without union, they can never be maintained. Divided into twenty-four, or even a smaller number of separate communities, we shall see our internal trade burdened with numberless restraints and exactions; communication between distant points and sections obstructed, or cut off; our sons made soldiers, to deluge with blood the fields they now till in peace; the mass of our people borne down and impoverished by taxes to support armies and navies; and military leaders, at the head of their victorious legions, becoming our lawgivers and judges. The loss of liberty, of all good government, of peace, plenty and happiness, must inevitably follow a dissolution of the Union. In supporting it, therefore, we support all that is dear to the freeman and the philanthropist.

The time at which I stand before you is full of interest. The eyes of all nations are fixed on our republic. The event of the existing crisis will be decisive, in the opinion of mankind, of the practicability of our federal system of government. Great is the stake placed in our hands; great is the responsibility which must rest upon the people of the United States. Let us realize the importance of the attitude in which we stand before the world. Let us exercise forbearance and firmness. Let us extricate our country from the dangers which surround it, and learn wisdom from the lessons they inculcate. Deeply impressed with the truth of these observations, and under the obligation of that solemn oath which I am about to take, I shall continue to exert all my faculties to maintain the just powers of the constitution, and to transmit unimpaired to posterity the blessings of our Federal Union.

At the same time, it will be my aim to inculcate, by my official acts, the necessity of exercising, by the general government, those powers only that are clearly delegated; to encourage simplicity and economy in the expenditures of the government; to raise no more money from the people than may be requisite for these objects, and in a manner that will best promote the interests of all classes of the community, and of all portions of the Union. Constantly bearing in mind that, in entering into society, "individuals must give up a share of liberty to preserve the rest," it will be my desire so to discharge my duties as to foster with our brethren, in all parts of the country, a spirit of liberal concession and compromise; and, by reconciling our fellow-citizens to those partial sacrifices which they must unavoidably make, for the preservation of a greater good, to recommend our invaluable government and Union to the confidence and affections of the American people. Finally, it is my most fervent prayer to that Almighty Being before whom I now stand, and who has kept us in his hands from the infancy of our republic to the present day, that he will so overrule all my intentions and actions, and inspire the hearts of my fellow-citizens, that we may be preserved from dangers of all kinds, and continue forever a UNITED AND HAPPY PEOPLE.

SUPPOSED SPEECH OF JOHN ADAMS. — *D. Webster.*

SINK or swim, live or die, survive or perish, I give my hand and my heart to this vote! It is true, indeed, that in the beginning we aimed not at independence. But there is a divinity which shapes our ends. The injustice of England has driven us to arms; and, blinded to her own interest for our good, she has obstinately persisted, till independence is now within our grasp. We have but to reach forth to it, and it is ours. Why, then, should we defer the declaration? Is any man so weak as now to hope for a reconciliation with England, which shall leave either safety to the country and its liberties, or safety to his own life, and his own honor? Are not you, sir, who sit in that chair, — is not he, our venerable colleague near you, — are not both already the proscribed and predestined objects of punishment and of vengeance? Cut off from all hope of royal clemency, what are you, what can you be, while the power of England remains, but outlaws?

If we postpone independence, do we mean to carry on, or give up, the war? Do we mean to submit to the measures of Parliament, Boston port-bill and all? Do we mean to submit, and consent that we ourselves shall be ground to powder, and our country and its rights trodden down in the dust? I know we do not mean to submit. We never shall submit. Do we intend to violate that most solemn obligation ever entered into by men, — that plighting, before God, of our sacred honor to Washington, when, putting him forth to incur the dangers of war, as well as the political hazards of the times, we promised to adhere to him, in every extremity, with our fortunes and our lives?

I know there is not a man here who would not rather see a general conflagration sweep over the land, or an earthquake sink it, than one jot or tittle of that plighted faith fall to the ground. For myself, having, twelve months ago, in this place, moved you that George Washington be appointed commander of the forces raised, or to be raised, for defence of American liberty, may my right hand forget its cunning, and my tongue cleave to the roof of my mouth, if I hesitate or waver in the support I give him! The war, then, must go on. We must fight it through.

And, if the war must go on, why put off longer the declaration of independence? That measure will strengthen us. It will give us character abroad. The nations will then treat with us, which they never can do while we acknowledge ourselves subjects, in arms against our sovereign. Nay, I maintain that England herself will sooner treat for peace with us on the footing of independence, than consent, by repealing her acts, to acknowledge that her whole conduct towards us has been a course of injustice and oppression. Her pride will be less wounded by submitting to that course of things which now predestinates our independence, than by yielding the points in controversy to her rebellious subjects. The former she would regard as the result of fortune; the latter, she would feel as her own deep disgrace. Why, then, sir, do we not, as soon as possible, change this from a civil to a national war? And, since we must fight it through, why not put ourselves in a state to enjoy all the benefits of victory, if we gain the victory? If we fail, it can be no worse for us. But we shall not fail!

The cause will raise up armies; — the cause will create navies. The people, — the people, — if we are true to them, will carry us, and will carry themselves, gloriously through this struggle. I care not how fickle other people have been found. I know the people of these colonies; and I know that resistance to British aggression is deep and settled in their hearts, and cannot be eradicated. Every colony, indeed, has expressed its willingness to follow, if we but take the lead. Sir, the declaration will inspire the people with increased courage. Instead of a long and bloody war for restoration of privileges, for redress of grievances, for chartered immunities, held under a British king, set before them the glorious object of entire independence, and it will breathe into them anew the breath of life. Read this declaration at the head of the army; — every sword will be drawn from its scabbard, and the solemn vow uttered, to maintain it, or to perish on the bed of honor. Publish it from the pulpit; — religion will approve it, and the love of religious liberty will cling round it, resolved to stand with it, or fall with it. Send it to the public halls; proclaim it there; let them hear it who heard the first roar of the enemy's cannon, — let them see it who saw their brothers and their sons fall on the field of Bunker Hill, and in the streets of Lexington and Concord, — and the very walls will cry out in its support!

Sir, I know the uncertainty of human affairs; but I see clearly through this day's business. You and I, indeed, may rue it. We may not live to see the time when this declaration shall be made good. We may die, — die colonists; die slaves; die, it may be, ignominiously, and on the scaffold! Be it so! be it so! If it be the pleasure of Heaven that my country shall require the poor offering of my life, the victim shall be ready, at the appointed hour of sacrifice, come when that hour may. But, while I do live, let me have a country, — or, at least, the hope of a country, and that a free country.

But, whatever may be our fate, be assured that this declaration will stand. It may cost treasure, and it may cost blood; but it will stand, and it will richly compensate for both. Through the thick gloom of the present, I see the brightness of the future, as the sun in heaven. We shall make this a glorious, an immortal day. When we are in our graves, our children will honor it. They will celebrate it with thanksgiving, with festivity, with bonfires, and illuminations. On its annual return, they will shed tears, — copious, gushing tears, — not of subjection and slavery, not of agony and distress, — but of exultation, of gratitude, and of joy. Sir, before God, I believe the hour is come! My judgment approves this measure, and my whole heart is in it. All that I have, and all that I am, and all that I hope, in this life, I am now ready here to stake upon it; and I leave off as I began, that, live or die, survive or perish, I am for the declaration! It is my living sentiment, and, by the blessing of God, it shall be my dying sentiment, — INDEPENDENCE *now*, and INDEPENDENCE FOREVER!

THE DEVELOPMENT OF OUR COUNTRY. — *C. S. Henry.*

It is but a few years since we entered upon the conquest of a country wilder than Germany in the days of Cæsar, and ten times more extensive; and yet in that short space we have reached a point of physical development which twenty centuries have not accomplished there. The forests have fallen down, the earth has been quarried, cities and towns have sprung up all over the immense extent of our land, thronged with life, and resounding with the multitudinous hum of traffic; and from hundreds of ports the canvas of ten thousand sails whitens all the ocean and every sea, bearing the products of our soil and manufactures, and bringing back the wealth and luxuries of every quarter of the globe. Then, too, the tremendous agencies of nature — the awful forces evolved by chemical and dynamic science — have been subdued to man's dominion, and have become submissive ministers to his will, more prompt and more powerful than the old fabled genii of the Arabian tales. Little did our fathers, little did we ourselves, even the youngest of us, dream, in the days of our childhood, when we fed our wondering imaginations with the prodigies wrought by those elemental spirits evoked by the talismanic seal of Solomon, that these were but faint foreshadowings of what our eyes should see in the familiar goings on of the every-day life around us. Yet so it truly is. Ha! gentlemen, the steam-engine is your true elemental spirit; it more than realizes the gorgeous ideas of the old oriental imagination. That had its different orders of elemental spirits, — genii of fire, of water, of earth, and of air, whose everlasting hostility could never be subdued to unity of purpose: this combines the powers of all in one, and a child may control them! Across the ocean, along our coast, through the length of a hundred rivers, with the speed of wind, we plough our way against currents, wind and tide; while, on iron roads, through the length and breadth of the land, innumerable trains, thronged with human life and freighted with the wealth of the nation, are urging their way in every direction, — flying through the valleys, thundering across the rivers, panting up the sides or piercing through the hearts of the mountains, with the resistless force of lightning, and scarcely less swift!

All this is wonderful! The old limitations to human endeavor seem to be broken through; the everlasting conditions of time and space seem to be annulled! Meanwhile the magnificent achievements of to-day lead but to grander projects for to-morrow. Success in the past serves but to enlarge the purposes of the future; and the people are rushing onward in a career of physical development to which no bounds can be assigned.

THE SOUTH. — *Jef. Davis.*

I CAN but consider it as a tribute of respect to the character for candor and sincerity which the South maintains, that every movement which occurs in the Southern States is closely scrutinized; but what shall we think of the love for the Union of those in whom this brings no corresponding change of conduct, who continue the wanton aggressions which have produced and justify the action they deprecate? Is it well, is it wise, is it safe, to disregard these manifestations of public displeasure, though it be the displeasure of a minority? Is it proper, or prudent, or respectful, when a representative, in accordance with the known will of his constituents, addresses you the language of solemn warning, in conformity to his duty to the constitution, the Union, and to his own conscience, that his course should be arraigned as the declaration of ultra and dangerous opinions? If these warnings were received in the spirit they are given, it would augur better for the country. It would give hopes which are denied us, if the press of the country — that great lever of public opinion — would enforce these warnings, and bear them to every cottage, instead of heaping abuse upon those whose ease would prompt them to silence — whose speech, therefore, is evidence of sincerity. Lightly and loosely representatives of Southern people have been denounced as disunionists by that portion of the Northern press which most disturbs the harmony and endangers the perpetuity of the Union. Such, even, has been my own case; though the man does not breathe at whose door the charge of disunion might not as well be laid as at mine. The son of a Revolutionary soldier, attachment to this Union was among the first lessons of my childhood; bred to the service of my country from boyhood, to mature age I wore its uniform. Through the brightest portion of my life I was accustomed to see our flag, historic emblem of the Union, rise with the rising and fall with the setting sun. I look upon it now with the affection of early love, and seek to maintain it by a strict adherence to the constitution, from which it had its birth, and by the nurture of which its stars have come so much to outnumber its original stripes. Shall that flag, which has gathered fresh glory in every war, and become more radiant still by the conquest of peace, — shall that flag now be torn by domestic faction, and trodden in the dust by petty sectional rivalry? Shall we of the South, who have shared equally with you all your toils, all your dangers, all your adversities, and who equally rejoice in your prosperity and your fame, — shall we be denied those benefits guaranteed by our compact, or gathered as the common fruits of a common country? If so, self-respect requires that we should assert them, and, as best we may, maintain that which we could not surrender without losing your respect, as well as our own.

If, sir, this spirit of sectional aggrandizement shall cause the disunion of these states, the last chapter of our history will be a sad commentary upon the justice and the wisdom of our people. That this Union, replete with blessings to its own citizens, and diffusive of hope to the rest of mankind, should fall a victim to a selfish aggrandizement and a pseudo philanthropy, prompting one portion of the Union to war upon the domestic rights and peace of another, would be a deep reflection on the good sense and patriotism of our day and generation.

Sir, I ask Northern senators to make the case their own: to carry to their own fireside the idea of such intrusion and offensive discrimination as is offered to us, — realize these irritations, so galling to the humble, so intolerable to the haughty, and wake, before it is too late, from the dream that the South will tamely submit. Measure the consequences to us of your assumption, and ask yourselves whether, as a free, honorable and brave people, you would submit to it.

It is essentially the characteristic of the chivalrous that they never speculate upon the fears of any man; and I trust that no such speculations will be made upon either the condition or the supposed weakness of the South. They will bring sad disappointments to those who indulge them. Rely upon her devotion to the Union; rely upon the feeling of fraternity she inherited, and has never failed to manifest; rely upon the nationality and freedom from sedition which has in all ages characterized an agricultural people; give her justice, sheer justice, and the reliance will never fail you!

THE FEDERAL COMPACT. — *G. Morris.*

Our situation is peculiar. At present, our national compact can prevent a state from acting hostilely towards the general interest. But, let this compact be destroyed, and each state becomes vested instantaneously with absolute sovereignty. Is there no instance of a similar situation to be found in history? Look at the states of Greece. By their divisions they became at first victims of the ambition of Philip, and were at length swallowed up in the Roman empire. Are we to form an exception to the general principles of human nature, and to all the examples of history? and are the maxims of experience to become false, when applied to our fate?

Some, indeed, flatter themselves that our destiny will be like that of Rome. But we have not that strong, aristocratic arm, which can seize a wretched citizen, scourged almost to death by a remorseless creditor, turn him into the ranks, and bid him, as a soldier, bear our eagle in triumph round the globe. I hope to God we shall never have such an abominable institution. But what, I ask, will be the situation of these states, organized as they now are, if, by the dissolution of our national compact, they be left to themselves? What is the probable result? We shall either be victims of foreign intrigue, and, split into factions, fall under the domination of a foreign power, or else, after the misery and torment of civil war, become the subjects of a usurping military despot. What but this compact, — what but this specific part of it, — can save us from ruin! The judicial power — that fortress of the constitution — is now to be overturned. Yes, with honest Ajax, I would not only throw a shield before it — I would build around it a wall of brass!

THE FATE OF THE INDIANS. — *J. Story.*

There is, indeed, in the fate of the unfortunate Indians, much to awaken our sympathy, and much to disturb the sobriety of our judgment; much which may be urged to excuse their own atrocities; much in their characters which betrays us into an involuntary admiration. What can be more melancholy than their history? By a law of their nature, they seem destined to a slow but sure extinction. Everywhere, at the approach of the white man, they fade away. We hear the rustling of their footsteps, like that of the withered leaves of autumn, and they are gone forever. They pass mournfully by us, and they return no more.

Two centuries ago, the smoke of their wigwams and the fires of their councils rose in every valley, from Hudson's Bay to the furthest Florida, from the ocean to the Mississippi and the lakes. The shouts of victory and the war-dance rang through the mountains and the glades. The thick arrows and the deadly tomahawk whistled through the forests, and the hunter's trace and the dark encampment startled the wild beasts in their lairs.

But where are they? Where are the villages, and warriors, and youth, the sachems and the tribes, the hunters and their families? They have perished. They are consumed. The wasting pestilence has not alone done the mighty work. No: nor famine, nor war. There has been a mightier power, a moral canker, which hath eaten into their heart-cores, — a plague, which the touch of the white man communicated, — a poison which betrayed them into a lingering ruin. The winds of the Atlantic fan not a single region which they may now call their own. Already the last feeble remnants of the race are preparing for their journey beyond the Mississippi. I see them leave their miserable homes, the aged, the helpless, the women, and the warriors, "few and faint, yet fearless still."

The ashes are cold on their native hearths. The smoke no longer curls round their lowly cabins. They move on with a slow, unsteady step. The white man is upon their heels, for terror or despatch; but they heed him not. They turn to take a last look of their deserted villages. They cast a last glance upon the graves of their fathers. They shed no tears; they utter no cries; they heave no groans. There is something in their hearts which passes speech. There is something in their looks, not of vengeance or submission, but of hard necessity, which stifles both, which chokes all utterance, which has no aim or method. It is courage absorbed in despair. They linger but for a moment. Their look is onward. They have passed the fatal stream. It shall never be repassed by them; no, never! Yet there lies not between us and them an impassable gulf. They know and feel that there is for them still one remove further, — not distant, nor unseen. It is to the general burial-ground of the race!

THE LIGHT OF KNOWLEDGE. — *D. D. Barnard.*

We know the enemy we have to contend with — which is ignorance; and we know where to find him, though he hath his habitation in darkness. We are acquainted with his haunts and his associations; and the weapon of his certain destruction is in our hands. That weapon is LIGHT, — the light of genuine learning added to the light of a genuine faith, — a light which heretofore has not been permitted to burn with brightness and purity, chiefly because it was not originally kindled at the right fountain; a light which has often gone out in the keeping of unfaithful vestals; which has often been hid, when it should have been made manifest; which has always been, more or less, fed from sources which could not supply or support it; which, at best, has been kept as a lamp to the feet of the few, when it should have been made to illumine the pathway of the many; which, for the most part, having only glimmered faintly from a few sequestered and solitary places, has served but to deepen the shadows of the general gloom around them. This is that light which is now beginning to be fed from better and purer sources; which has its fountain in nature; which is to be supplied from her fulness, by the aid of the educated; which ought to be made, and may be made, to increase, spreading wide and mounting high, and passing rapidly from heart to heart, and from dwelling to dwelling, till all the valleys shall answer to all the mountain-tops in one universal and healthful glow of brightness and illumination!

AN APPEAL TO SOUTH CAROLINA. — *A. Jackson.*

FELLOW-CITIZENS of my native state! Let me not only admonish you, as the first magistrate of our common country, not to incur the penalty of its laws, but to use the influence that a father would over his children whom he saw rushing to certain ruin. In that paternal language, with that paternal feeling, let me tell you, my countrymen, that you are deluded by men who are either deceived themselves, or wish to deceive you. Mark under what pretences you have been led on to the brink of insurrection and treason, on which you stand! First, a diminution of the value of your staple commodity, lowered by over production in other quarters, and the consequent diminution in the value of your lands, were the sole effect of the tariff laws. The effects of those laws are confessedly injurious, but the evil was greatly exaggerated by the unfounded theory you were taught to believe, that its burthens were in proportion to your exports, not to your consumption of imported articles. Your pride was roused by the assertion that a submission to those laws was a state of vassalage, and that resistance to them was equal, in patriotic merit, to the opposition our fathers offered to the oppressive laws of Great Britain. You were told that this opposition might be peaceably, might be constitutionally made, — that you might enjoy all the advantages of the Union, and bear none of its burthens.

Eloquent appeals to your passions, to your state pride, to your native courage, to your sense of real injury, were used to prepare you for the period when the mask which concealed the hideous features of DISUNION should be taken off. It fell, and you were made to look with complacency on objects which, not long since, you would have regarded with horror.

Contemplate the condition of that country of which you still form an important part. Consider its government, uniting in one bond of common interest and general protection so many different states, giving to all their inhabitants the proud title of AMERICAN CITIZENS, protecting their commerce, securing their literature and their arts, facilitating their intercommunication, defending their frontiers, and making their name respected in the remotest parts of the earth! Consider the extent of its territory, its increasing and happy population, its advance in arts which render life agreeable, and the sciences which elevate the mind! See education spreading the lights of religion, humanity and general information, into every cottage in this wide extent of our territories and states! Behold it as the asylum where the wretched and the oppressed find a refuge and support! Look on this picture of happiness and honor, and say, WE, TOO, ARE CITIZENS OF AMERICA; Carolina is one of these proud states; her arms have defended, her best blood has cemented, this happy Union! And then add, if you can without horror and remorse, This happy Union we will dissolve; this picture of peace and prosperity we will deface; this free intercourse we will interrupt; these fertile fields we will deluge with blood; the protection of that glorious flag we renounce; the very names of Americans we discard. And for what, mistaken men,— for what do you throw away these inestimable blessings,—for what would you exchange your share in the advantages and honor of the Union? For the dream of a separate independence, a dream interrupted by bloody conflicts with your neighbors, and a vile dependence on a foreign power. If your leaders could succeed in establishing a separation, what would be your situation? Are you united at home,—are you free from the apprehension of civil discord, with all its fearful consequences? Do our neighboring republics, every day suffering some new revolution, or contending with some new insurrection,—do they excite your envy? But the dictates of a high duty oblige me solemnly to announce that you cannot succeed.

The laws of the United States must be executed. I have no discretionary power on the subject; my duty is emphatically pronounced in the constitution. Those who told you that you might peaceably prevent their execution deceived you; they could not have been deceived themselves. They know that a forcible opposition could alone prevent the execution of the laws, and they know that such opposition must be repelled. Their object is disunion;—but be not deceived by names,—disunion by armed force is TREASON. Are you really ready to incur its guilt? If you are, on the heads of the instigators of the act be the dreadful consequences; on their heads be the dishonor, but on yours may fall the punishment; on your unhappy state will inevitably fall all the evils of the conflict you force upon the government of your country. It cannot accede to the mad project of disunion, of which you would be the first victims; its first magistrate cannot, if he would, avoid the performance of his duty; the consequences must be fearful for you, distressing to your fellow-citizens here, and to the friends of good government throughout the world. Its enemies have beheld our prosperity with a vexation they could not conceal; it was a standing refutation of their slavish doctrines, and they will point to our discord with the triumph of malignant joy. It is yet in your power to disappoint them. There is yet time to show that the descendants of the Pinckneys, the Sumpters, the Rutledges, and of the thousand other names which adorn the pages of your Revolutionary history, will not abandon that Union, to support which so many of them fought, and bled, and died. I adjure you, as you honor their memory, as you love the cause of freedom to which they dedicated their lives, as you prize the peace of your country, the lives of its best citizens, and your own fair fame, to retrace your steps. Snatch from the archives of your state the disorganizing edict of its convention; bid its members to reässemble and promulgate the decided expressions of your will to remain in the path which alone can conduct you to safety, prosperity and honor; — tell them that, compared to disunion, all other evils are light, because that brings with it an accumulation of all; — declare that you will never take the field unless the star-spangled banner of your country shall float over you, — that you will not be stigmatized when dead, and dishonored and scorned while you live, as the authors of the first attack on the constitution of your country! Its destroyers you cannot be. You may disturb its peace, you may interrupt the course of its prosperity, you may cloud its reputation for stability, — but its tranquillity will be restored, its prosperity will return, and the stain upon its national character will be transferred, and remain an eternal blot on the memory of those who caused the disorder.

Fellow-citizens of the United States! The threat of unhallowed disunion, — the names of those, once respected, by whom it is uttered, — the array of military force to support it, — denote the approach of a crisis in our affairs on which the continuance of our unexampled prosperity, our political existence, and, perhaps, that of all free governments, may depend. The conjunction demanded a free, a full and explicit enunciation, not only of my intentions, but of my principles of action; and as the claim was asserted of a right by a state to annul the laws of the Union, and even to secede from it at pleasure, a frank exposition of my opinions in relation to the origin and form of our government, and the construction I give to the instrument by which it was created, seemed to be proper. Having the fullest confidence in the justness of the legal and constitutional opinion of my duties which has been expressed, I rely with equal confidence on your undivided support in my determination to execute the laws, — to preserve the Union by all constitutional means, — to arrest, if possible, by moderate but firm measures, the necessity of a recourse to force; and, if it be the will of Heaven that the recurrence of its primeval curse on man for the shedding of a brother's blood should fall upon our land, that it be not called down by any offensive act on the part of the United States.

Fellow-citizens! the momentous case is before you. On your undivided support of your government depends the decision of the great question it involves, whether your sacred Union will be preserved, and the blessings it secures to us as one people shall be perpetuated. No one can doubt that the unanimity with which that decision will be expressed will be such as to inspire new confidence in republican institutions, and that the prudence, the wisdom and the courage which it will bring to their defence, will transmit them unimpaired and invigorated to our children.

SELF-SACRIFICING AMBITION. — *H. Greeley.*

We need a loftier ideal to nerve us for heroic lives. To know and feel our nothingness without regretting it, — to deem fame, riches, personal happiness, but shadows of which human good is the substance, — to welcome pain, privation, ignominy, so that the sphere of human knowledge, the empire of virtue, be thereby extended, — such is the soul's temper in which the heroes of the coming age shall be cast. When the stately monuments of mightiest conquerors shall have become shapeless and forgotten ruins, the humble graves of earth's Howards and Frys shall still be freshened by the tears of fondly admiring millions, and the proudest epitaph shall be the simple entreaty,

"Write me as one who *loved* his fellow-men."

Say not that I thus condemn and would annihilate ambition.

The love of approbation, of esteem, of true glory, is a noble incentive, and should be cherished to the end. But the ambition which points the way to fame over torn limbs and bleeding hearts, which joys in the Tartarean smoke of the battle-field and the desolating tramp of the war-horse, — *that* ambition is worthy only of "archangel ruined." To make one conqueror's reputation, at least one hundred thousand bounding, joyous, sentient beings must be transformed into writhing and hideous fragments, must perish untimely by deaths of agony and horror, leaving half a million widows and orphans to bewail their loss in anguish and destitution. This is too mighty, too awful a price to be paid for the fame of any hero, from Nimrod to Wellington. True fame demands no such sacrifices of others; it requires us to be reckless of the outward well-being of but one. It exacts no hecatomb of victims for each triumphal pile; for the more who covet and seek it, the easier and more abundant is the success of each and all. With souls of the celestial temper, each human life might be a triumph, which angels would lean from the skies delighted to witness and admire.

PARTY SPIRIT — *W. Gaston.*

Parties and party men may deserve reprobation for their selfishness, their violence, their errors, or their wickedness. They may do our country much harm. They may retard its growth, destroy its harmony, impair its character, render its institutions unstable, pervert the public mind, and deprave the public morals. These are, indeed, evils, and sore evils; but the principle of life remains, and will yet struggle, with assured success, over these temporary maladies.

Still we are great, glorious, united, and free; still we have a name that is revered abroad and loved at home, — a name which is a tower of strength to us against foreign wrong, and a bond of internal union and harmony, — a name which no enemy pronounces but with respect, and which no citizen hears but with a throb of exultation. Still we have that blessed constitution, which, with all its pretended defects, and all its alleged violations, has conferred more benefit on man than ever yet flowed from any other human institution, — which has established justice, insured domestic tranquillity, provided for the common defence, promoted the general welfare, and which, under God, if we be true to ourselves, will insure the blessings of liberty to us and our posterity.

Surely, such a country, and such a constitution, have claims upon you, my friends, which cannot be disregarded. I entreat and adjure you, then, by all that is near and dear to you on earth, by all the obligations of patriotism, by the memory of your fathers who fell in the great and glorious struggle, for the sake of your sons, whom you would not have to blush for your degeneracy, — by all your proud recollections of the past, and all the fond anticipations of the future renown of our nation, — preserve that country, uphold that constitution! Resolve that they shall not be lost while in your keeping; and may God Almighty strengthen you to perform that vow!

THE DEATH OF HAMILTON. — *A. Nott.*

Guilty, absurd and rash as duelling is, it has its advocates. And had it not had its advocates, had not a strange preponderance of opinion been in favor of it, never, O lamentable Hamilton! hadst thou thus fallen, in the midst of thy days, and before thou hadst reached the zenith of thy glory!

O that I possessed the talent of eulogy, and that I might be permitted to indulge the tenderness of friendship, in paying the last tribute to his memory! O that I were capable of placing this great man before you! Could I do this, I should furnish you with an argument, the most practical, the most plain, the most convincing, except that drawn from the mandate of God, that was ever furnished against duelling — that horrid practice, which has in an awful moment robbed the world of such exalted worth. But I cannot do this; I can only hint at the variety and exuberance of his excellence: —

The Man, on whom nature seems originally to have impressed

the stamp of greatness, whose genius beamed from the retirement of collegiate life with a radiance which dazzled and a loveliness which charmed the eye of sages.

The Hero, called from his sequestered retreat, whose first appearance in the field, though a stripling, conciliated the esteem of Washington, our good old father. Moving by whose side, during all the perils of the Revolution, our young chieftain was a contributor to the veteran's glory, the guardian of his person, and the copartner of his toils.

The Conqueror, who, sparing of human blood, when victory favored, stayed the uplifted arm, and nobly said to the vanquished enemy, "Live!"

The Statesman, the correctness of whose principles, and the strength of whose mind, are inscribed on the records of Congress, and on the annals of the council chamber; whose genius impressed itself upon the constitution of his country, and whose memory the government — illustrious fabric, resting on this basis — will perpetuate while it lasts; and, shaken by the violence of party, should it fall, which may Heaven avert, his prophetic declarations will be found inscribed on its ruins.

The Counsellor, who was at once the pride of the bar and the admiration of the court; whose apprehensions were quick as lightning, and whose development of truth was luminous as its path; whose argument no change of circumstances could embarrass; whose knowledge appeared intuitive; and who by a single glance, and with as much facility as the eye of the eagle passes over the landscape, surveyed the whole field of controversy, saw in what way truth might be most successfully defended, and how error must be approached; and who, without ever stopping, ever hesitating, by a rapid and manly march led the listening judge and the fascinated juror, step by step, through a delightsome region, brightening as he advanced, till his argument rose to demonstration, and eloquence was rendered useless by conviction; whose talents were employed on the side of righteousness; whose voice, whether in the council chamber or at the bar of justice, was virtue's consolation; at whose approach oppressed humanity felt a secret rapture, and the heart of injured innocence leaped for joy.

Where Hamilton was, in whatever sphere he moved, the friendless had a friend, the fatherless a father, and the poor man, though unable to reward his kindness, found an advocate. It was when the rich oppressed the poor, when the powerful menaced the defenceless, when truth was disregarded, or the eternal principles of justice violated, — it was on these occasions that he exerted all his strength, — it was on these occasions that he sometimes soared so high and shone with a radiance so transcendent, I had almost said, so "heavenly, as filled those around him with awe, and gave to him the force and authority of a prophet."

The Patriot, whose integrity baffled the scrutiny of inquisition; whose manly virtue never shaped itself to circumstances; who, always great, always himself, stood amidst the varying tides of party, firm like the rock which, far from land, lifts its majestic top above the waves, and remains unshaken by the storms which agitate the ocean.

The Friend who knew no guile, whose bosom was transparent and deep; in the bottom of whose heart was rooted every tender and sympathetic virtue; whose various worth opposing parties acknowledged while alive, and on whose tomb they unite, with equal sympathy and grief, to heap their honors.

I know he had his failings. I see, on the picture of his life, — a picture rendered awful by greatness, and luminous by virtue, — some dark shades. On these let the tear that pities human weakness fall; on these let the veil which covers human frailty rest. As a hero, as a statesman, as a patriot, he lived nobly; — and would to God I could add, he nobly fell. Unwilling to admit his error in this respect, I go back to the period of discussion. I see him resisting the threatened interview. I imagine myself present in his chamber. Various reasons, for a time, seem to hold his determination in arrest. Various and moving objects pass before him, and speak a dissuasive language. His country, which may need his counsels to guide, and his arm to defend, utters her veto. The partner of his youth, already covered with weeds, and whose tears flow down into her bosom, intercedes! His babes, stretching out their little hands and pointing to a weeping mother, with lisping eloquence, but eloquence which reaches a parent's heart, cry out, "Stay, stay, dear papa, and live for us!" In the mean time, the spectre of a fallen son, pale and ghastly, approaches, opens his bleeding bosom, and, as the harbinger of death, points to the yawning tomb, and warns a-hesitating father of the issue! He pauses, reviews these sad objects, and reasons on the subject. I admire his magnanimity, I approve his reasoning, and I wait to hear him reject, with indignation, the murderous proposition, and to see him spurn from his presence the presumptuous bearer of it. But I wait in vain. It was a moment in which his great wisdom forsook him; a moment in which Hamilton was not himself. He yielded to the force of an imperious custom; and, yielding, he sacrificed a life in which all had an interest, and he is lost, — lost to his country, lost to his family, lost to us!

Would to God I might be permitted to approach for once the late scene of death! Would to God I could there assemble, on the one side, the disconsolate mother, with her seven fatherless children, and on the other those who administer the justice of my country. Could I do this, I would point them to these sad objects. I would entreat them, by the agonies of bereaved fondness, to listen to the widow's heartfelt groans, to mark the orphan's sighs and tears. And, having done this, I would uncover the breathless corpse of Hamilton, — I would lift from his gaping wound his bloody mantle, — I would hold it up to heaven before them, and I would ask, in the name of God I would ask, whether, at the sight of it, they felt no compunction!

Ah! ye tragic shores of Hoboken, crimsoned with the richest blood, I tremble at the crimes ye record against us — the annual register of murders which you keep and send up to God! Place of inhuman cruelty! beyond the limits of reason, of duty and of religion, where man assumes a more barbarous nature, and ceases to be man. What poignant, lingering sorrows do thy lawless combats occasion to surviving relatives! Ye who have hearts of pity, — ye who have experienced the anguish of dissolving friendship, — who have wept, and still weep, over the mouldering ruins of departed kindred, ye can enter into this reflection.

O thou disconsolate widow! robbed, so cruelly robbed, and in so short a time, both of a husband and a son, what must be the plenitude of thy sufferings! Could we approach thee, gladly would we drop the tear of sympathy, and pour into thy bleeding bosom the balm of consolation. But how can we comfort her whom God hath not comforted? To His throne let us lift up our voice and weep!

A short time since, and he who is the occasion of our sorrows was the ornament of his country. He stood on an eminence, and glory covered him. From that eminence he has fallen, — suddenly, forever fallen. His intercourse with the living world has now ended; and those who would hereafter find him must seek him in the grave. There, cold and lifeless, is the heart which just now was the seat of friendship. There, dim and sightless, is the eye whose radiant and enlivening orb beamed with intelligence; and there, closed forever, are those lips, on whose persuasive accents we have so often and so lately hung with transport! From the darkness which rests upon his tomb there proceeds, methinks, a light in which it is clearly seen that those gaudy objects which men pursue are only phantoms. In this light how dimly shines the splendor of victory, — how humble appears the majesty of grandeur! The bubble, which seemed to have so much solidity, has burst, and we again see that all below the sun is vanity!

True, the funeral eulogy has been pronounced, — the sad and solemn procession has moved, — the badge of mourning has already been decreed, and presently the sculptured marble will lift up its front, proud to perpetuate the name of Hamilton, and rehearse to the passing traveller his virtues. Just tributes of respect! And to the living useful. But to him, mouldering in his narrow and humble habitation, what are they? How vain! — how unavailing!

Approach, and behold, while I lift from his sepulchre its covering! Ye admirers of his greatness, ye emulous of his talents and his fame, approach, and behold him now. How pale! how silent No martial bands admire the adroitness of his movements; no fascinated throng weep, and melt, and tremble, at his eloquence! Amazing change! A shroud! a coffin! a narrow, subterraneous cabin! This is all that now remains of Hamilton!

INTELLIGENCE A NATIONAL SAFEGUARD. — *L. Woodbury.*

Our history constantly points her finger to a most efficient resource, and indeed to the only elixir to secure a long life to any popular government, in increased attention to useful education and sound morals, with the wise description of equal measures and just practices they inculcate on every leaf of recorded time. Before their alliance, the spirit of misrule will always, in time, stand rebuked, and those who worship at the shrine of unhallowed ambition must quail.

Storms in the political atmosphere may occasionally happen by the encroachments of usurpers, the corruption or intrigues of demagogues, or in the expiring agonies of faction, or by the sudden fury of popular phrensy; but, with the restraints and salutary influences of the allies before described, these storms will purify as healthfully as they often do in the physical world, and cause the tree of liberty, instead of falling, to strike its roots deeper.

In this struggle, the enlightened and moral possess also a power, auxiliary and strong, in the spirit of the age, which is not only with them, but onward, in everything to ameliorate or improve.

When the struggle assumes the form of a contest with power, in all its subtlety, or with undermining and corrupting wealth, as it sometimes may, rather than with turbulence, sedition, or open aggression by the needy and desperate, it will be indispensable to employ still greater diligence; to cherish earnestness of purpose, resoluteness in conduct; to apply hard and constant blows to real abuses, and encourage not only bold, free and original thinking, but determined action.

In such a cause, our fathers were men whose hearts were not

accustomed to fail them, through fear, however formidable the obstacles. We are not, it is trusted, such degenerate descendants as to prove recreant, and fail to defend with gallantry and firmness as unflinching all which we have either derived from them or since added to the rich inheritance.

At such a crisis, therefore, and in such a cause, yielding to neither consternation nor despair, may we not all profit by the vehement exhortations of Cicero to Atticus: "If you are asleep, awake; if you are standing, move; if you are moving, run; if you are running, fly!"

All these considerations warn us, — the gravestones of almost every former republic warn us, — that a high standard of moral rectitude, as well as of intelligence, is quite as indispensable to communities, in their public doings, as to individuals, if they would escape from either degeneracy or disgrace.

PEACE AND NATIONAL HONOR. — *G. Morris.*

My object is peace. I will not pretend, like my honorable colleague, to describe to you the waste, the ravages, and the horrors of war. I have not the same harmonious periods, nor the same musical tones; neither shall I boast of Christian charity, nor attempt to display that ingenuous glow of benevolence so decorous to the cheek of youth, which gave a vivid tint to every sentence he uttered, and was, if possible, as impressive even as his eloquence. But though we possess not the same pomp of words, our hearts are not insensible to the woes of humanity. We can feel for the misery of plundered towns, the conflagration of defenceless villages, and the devastation of cultured fields. Turning from these features of general distress, we can enter the abodes of private affliction, and behold the widow weeping as she traces, in the pledges of connubial affection, the resemblance of him whom she has lost forever. We see the aged matron bending over the ashes of her son. He was her darling, for he was generous and brave, and, therefore, his spirit led him to the field in defence of his country.

Hard, hard indeed must be that heart which can be insensible to scenes like these, and bold the man who dares present to the Almighty Father a conscience crimsoned with the blood of his children.

Yes, sir, we wish for peace; but how is that blessing to be preserved? In my opinion, there is nothing worth fighting for but national honor; for in the national honor is involved the national independence. I know that prudence may force a wise government to conceal the sense of indignity; but the insult should be engraven on tablets of brass with a pencil of steel. And when that time and change, which happen to all, shall bring forward the favorable moment, then let the avenging arm strike home. It is by avowing and maintaining this stern principle of honor that peace can be preserved.

THE TRUE REFORMERS. — *H Greeley.*

To the rightly constituted mind, to the truly developed man, there always is, there always must be, opportunity — opportunity to be and to learn, nobly to do and to endure; and what matter whether with pomp and eclat, with sound of trumpets and shout of applauding thousands, or in silence and seclusion, beneath the calm, discerning gaze of Heaven? No station can be humble on which that gaze is approvingly bent; no work can be ignoble which is performed uprightly, and not impelled by sordid and selfish aims.

Not from among the children of monarchs, ushered into being with boom of cannon and shouts of revelling millions, but from amid the sons of obscurity and toil, cradled in peril and ignominy, from the bulrushes and the manger, come forth the benefactors and saviors of mankind. So when all the babble and glare of our age shall have passed into a fitting oblivion, when those who have enjoyed rare opportunities and swayed vast empires, and been borne through life on the shoulders of shouting multitudes, shall have been laid at last to rest in golden coffins, to moulder forgotten, the stately marble their only monuments, it will be found that some humble youth, who neither inherited nor found, but hewed out his opportunities, has uttered the thought which shall render the age memorable, by extending the means of enlightenment and blessing to our race. The great struggle for human progress and elevation proceeds noiselessly, — often unnoted, often checked and apparently baffled, amid the clamorous and debasing strifes impelled by greedy selfishness and low ambition. In that struggle, maintained by the wise and good of all parties, all creeds, all climes, bear ye the part of men. Heed the lofty summons, and, with souls serene and constant, prepare to tread boldly in the path of highest duty. So shall life be to you truly exalted and heroic; so shall death be a transition neither sought nor dreaded; so shall your memory, though cherished at first but by a few humble, loving hearts, linger long and gratefully in human remembrance, a watchword to the truthful and an incitement to generous endeavor, freshened by the proud tears of admiring affection, and fragrant with the odors of heaven!

ON THE DEATH OF HON. WILLIAM PINCKNEY. — *J. Sparks.*

No object is so insignificant, no event so trivial, as not to carry with it a moral and religious influence. The trees that spring out of the earth are moralists. They are emblems of the life of man. They grow up; they put on the garments of freshness and beauty. Yet these continue but for a time; decay seizes upon the root and the trunk, and they gradually go back to their original elements. The blossoms that open to the rising sun, but are closed at night, never to open again, are moralists. The seasons are moralists, teaching the lessons of wisdom, manifesting the wonders of the Creator, and calling on man to reflect on his condition and destiny. History is a perpetual moralist, disclosing the annals of past ages, showing the impotency of pride and greatness, the weakness of human power, the folly of human wisdom. The daily occurrences in society are moralists. The success or failure of enterprise, the prosperity of the bad, the adversity of the good, the disappointed hopes of the sanguine and active, the sufferings of the virtuous, the caprices of fortune in every condition of life, — all these are fraught with moral instructions, and, if properly applied, will fix the power of religion in the heart.

But there is a greater moralist still, and that is DEATH. Here is a teacher who speaks in a voice which none can mistake; who comes with a power which none can resist. Since we last assembled in this place as the humble and united worshippers of God, this stern messenger, this mysterious agent of Omnipotence, has come among our numbers, and laid his withering hand on one whom we have been taught to honor and respect, whose fame was a nation's boast, whose genius was a brilliant spark from the ethereal fire, whose attainments were equalled only by the grasp of his intellect, the profoundness of his judgment, the exuberance of his fancy, the magic of his eloquence.

It is not my present purpose to ask your attention to any picture drawn in the studied phrase of eulogy. I aim not to describe the commanding powers and the eminent qualities which conducted the deceased to the superiority he held, and which were at once the admiration and the pride of his countrymen. I shall not attempt to analyze his capacious mind, nor to set forth the richness and variety of its treasures. The trophies of his genius are a sufficient testimony of these, and constitute a monument to his memory, which will stand firm and conspicuous amidst the faded recollections of future ages. The present is not the time to recount the sources or the memorials of his greatness. He is gone. The noblest of Heaven's gifts could not shield even him from the arrows of the destroyer. And this behest of the Most High is a warning summons to us all. When death comes into our doors, we ought to feel that he is near. When his irreversible sentence falls on the great and the renowned, when he severs the strongest bonds which can bind mortals to earth, we ought to feel that our hold on life is slight, that the thread of existence is slender, that we walk amidst perils, where the next wave of the agitated sea of life may baffle all our struggles, and carry us back into the dark bosom of the deep.

When we look at the monuments of human greatness, and the

powers of human intellect, all that genius has invented, or skill executed, or wisdom matured, or industry achieved, or labor accomplished, — when we trace these through the successive gradations of human advancement, what are they? On these are founded the pride, glory, dignity of man. And what are they? Compared with the most insignificant work of God, they are nothing, less than nothing. The mightiest works of man are daily and hourly becoming extinct. The boasted theories of religion, morals, government, which took the wisdom, the ingenuity of ages, to invent, have been proved to be shadowy theories only. Genius has wasted itself in vain; the visions it has raised have vanished at the touch of truth. Nothing is left but the melancholy certainty that all things human are imperfect, and must fail and decay. And man himself, whose works are so fragile, where is he? The history of his works is the history of himself. He existed; — he is gone!

The nature of human life cannot be more forcibly described than in the beautiful language of eastern poetry, which immediately precedes the text: "Man, that is born of woman, is of few days, and full of trouble. He cometh forth like a flower, and is cut down; he fleeth as a shadow, and continueth not. There is hope of a tree, if it be cut down, that it will sprout again, and that the tender branch thereof will not cease. Though the root thereof wax old in the earth, and the stock thereof die in the ground; yet, through the scent of water, it will bud and bring forth boughs like a plant. But man wasteth away; yea, man giveth up the ghost, and where is he?" Such are the striking emblems of human life; such is the end of all that is mortal in man. And what a question is here for us to reflect upon! "Man giveth up the ghost, *and where is he?*"

Yes, when we see the flower of life fade on its stalk, and all its comeliness depart, and all its freshness wither; when we see the bright eye grow dim, and the rose on the cheek lose its hue; when we hear the voice faltering its last accents, and see the energies of nature paralyzed; when we perceive the beams of intelligence grow fainter and fainter on the countenance, and the last gleam of life extinguished; when we deposit all that is mortal of a fellow-being in the dark, cold chamber of the grave, and drop a pitying tear at a spectacle so humiliating, so mournful, — then let us put the solemn question to our souls, Where is he? His body is concealed in the earth; but where is the spirit? Where is the intellect that could look through the works of God, and catch inspiration from the divinity which animates and pervades the whole? Where are the powers that could command, the attractions that could charm? where the boast of humanity, wisdom, learning, wit, eloquence, the pride of skill, the mystery of art, the creations of fancy, the brilliancy of thought? where the virtues that could win, and the gentleness that could soothe? where the mildness of temper, the generous affections, the benevolent feelings, all that is great and good, all that is noble, and lovely, and pure, in the human character, — where are they? They are gone. We can see nothing; the eye of faith only can dimly penetrate the region to which they have fled. Lift the eye of faith; follow the light of the gospel, and let your delighted vision be lost in the glories of the immortal world. Behold, there, the spirits of the righteous dead rising up into newness of life, gathering brightness and strength, unencumbered by the weight of mortal clay and mortal sorrows, enjoying a happy existence, and performing the holy service of their Maker.

Let our reflections on death have a weighty and immediate influence on our minds and characters. We cannot be too soon or too entirely prepared to render the account which we must all render to our Maker and Judge. All things earthly must fail us; the riches, power, possessions and gifts of the world will vanish from our sight; friends and relatives will be left behind; our present support will be taken away; our strength will become weakness, and the earth itself, and all its pomps, and honors, and attractions, will disappear. Why have we been spared even till this time? We know not why, nor yet can we say that a moment is our own. The summons for our departure may now be recorded in the book of Heaven. The angel may now be on his way to execute his solemn commission. Death may already have marked us for his victims. But, whether sooner or later, the event will be equally awful, and demand the same preparation.

One, only, will then be our rock and our safety. The kind Parent, who has upheld us all our days, will remain our unfailing support. With him is no change; he is unmoved from age to age; his mercy, as well as his being, endures forever; and, if we rely on him, and live in obedience to his laws, all tears shall be wiped from our eyes, and all sorrow banished from our hearts. If we are rebels to his cause, slaves to vice, and followers of evil, we must expect the displeasure of a holy God — the just punishment of our folly and wickedness; for a righteous retribution will be awarded to the evil as well as to the good.

Let it be the highest, the holiest, the unceasing concern of each one of us, to live the life, that we may be prepared to die the death, of the righteous; that, when they who come after us shall ask, Where is he? unnumbered voices shall be raised to testify, that, although his mortal remains are mouldering in the cold earth, his memory is embalmed in the cherished recollections of many a friend who knew and loved him; and all shall say, with tokens of joy and confident belief, If God be just, and piety be rewarded, his pure spirit is now at rest in the regions of the blessed.

THE DISSOLUTION OF THE UNION. — *A. Stewart.*

THE gentleman from South Carolina has painted, in the most glowing colors and fascinating forms, the glorious advantages to the South of a dissolution of this Union. But is there not another side to this picture? — and to this I beg the gentlemen to turn their calm and dispassionate attention. Before they take this fearful plunge, let them look over the precipice on which they stand into the yawning gulf beneath. On the other side of this picture is written, in flaming capitals, Treason, Rebellion, Civil War, with all its fearful consequences. Let it be remembered that no state can go out of this Union until it has conquered all the rest. When one state is gone, no two remain united. We have heard of the benefits of destroying this Union; but what will be its cost to those who may attempt it? From imaginary ills they fly to "others that they know not of."

They now complain of taxation! But what will be the taxation necessary to raise and sustain armies and navies to contend against this government? — a government which now, with fond and parental affection, guards and protects the South. But taxation would be the smallest item in the frightful catalogue of their calamities. There is still another leaf in this book, to which gentlemen should look. And can they behold it with indifference? It is the page on which posterity will write the epitaph of the authors of the destruction of this happy and glorious Union; of those who should involve us in all the horrors of civil war; who should arm father against son, and brother against brother; who should destroy this bright and glorious example — the only free government on earth.

How deep and how loud would be their denunciations, how bitter and how blasting would be the curses, with which posterity would brand the memories of those men! And will not their sentence be just? Where will they look for extenuation or excuse? Taxation! — it is imaginary, not real. All contributions here are voluntary, not compulsory. No people under heaven are half so lightly taxed, or half so highly blessed. In other countries, the people are taxed twenty times the amount, to support despots; imposed, not by themselves, but by arbitrary power. Compared with this country, in England taxation is as eighteen to one; yet they submit, and we rebel. Will not the people of the South look at these facts, and pause before they do the fatal deed that must seal forever their own destruction? In this Union the gentleman from South Carolina has everything to hope; — his name may go down to posterity among the most distinguished men of the age; his talents may adorn its highest offices, to which he has a just right to aspire; and, much as I may differ with that gentleman, both as to men and measures, yet such is my opinion of his talents and his worth, that I would rejoice to see him at this moment filling the highest of the executive departments of this government, or the highest of its diplomatic stations. That gentleman may be carried away by momentary excitement; still I cannot doubt his attachment to this Union, which I trust he will never sacrifice to imaginary evils. The blessings of this government, and the value of this Union, I have never heard so forcibly urged, or so eloquently portrayed, as by the gentleman from South Carolina himself; and I cannot, in conclusion, better express my own feelings than by repeating the very words uttered by that gentleman in concluding an able and eloquent speech on another occasion, when he said, "The liberty of this country is a sacred depository — a vestal fire, which Providence has committed to our hands for the general benefit of mankind. It is the world's last hope: extinguish it, and the earth will be covered with eternal darkness; but once 'put out that light, I know not where is that Promethean heat that shall that light relume.'"

I appeal to the gentleman; I ask him, is he prepared to destroy that "sacred depository," the Union and liberties of his country? Is he prepared to extinguish, in fraternal blood, that "vestal fire committed to his hands by Providence, for the benefit of mankind?" Is he prepared to destroy "the world's last hope;" to put out and extinguish forever that great and glorious light of liberty and union now blazing up to the heavens, illumining the path and cheering the onward march of the friends of freedom throughout the world, and thus to cover the earth with eternal darkness? Is he prepared for this? I pause for a reply.

MADISON AND THE CONSTITUTION. — *J. Q. Adams.*

Mr. Madison was associated with his friend Jefferson in the institution of the University of Virginia, and after his decease was placed at its head, under the modest and unassuming title of rector. He was also the president of an agricultural society in the county of his residence, and in that capacity delivered an address which the practical farmer and the classical scholar may read with equal profit and delight.

In the midst of these occupations the declining days of the philosopher, the statesman, and the patriot, were past, until the 21st day of June last, the anniversary of the day on which the ratification of the convention of Virginia in 1788 had affixed the seal of JAMES MADISON as the father of the constitution of the United States, when his earthly part sunk without a struggle into the grave, and a spirit bright as the seraphim that surround the throne of Omnipotence ascended to the bosom of his God.

This constitution is the great result of the North American Revolution. This is the giant stride in the improvement of the condition of the human race, consummated in a period of less than one hundred years. Of the signers of the address to George the Third in the Congress of 1774, of the signers of the Declaration of Independence in 1776, of the signers of the articles of confederation in 1781, and of the signers of the federal and national constitution of government under which we live, with enjoyments never before allotted to man, — not one remains in the land of the living. The last survivor of them all was he to honor whose memory we are here assembled at once with mourning and with joy. We reverse the order of sentiment and reflection of the ancient Persian king, — we look *back* on the century gone by — we look around with anxious and eager eye for *one* of that illustrious host of patriots and heroes under whose guidance the Revolution of American Independence was begun and continued and completed. We look around in vain. To them this crowded theatre, full of human life, in all its stages of existence, full of the glowing exultation of youth, of the steady maturity of manhood, the sparkling eyes of beauty, and the gray hairs of reverend age, — all this to them is as the solitude of the sepulchre. We think of this, and say, How short is human life! But then, *then*, we turn back our thoughts again, to the scene over which the falling curtain has but now closed upon the drama of the day. From the saddening thought that they are no more, we call for comfort upon the memory of what they *were*, and our hearts leap for joy that they were our fathers. We see them, true and faithful subjects of their sovereign, first meeting with firm but respectful remonstrance the approach of usurpation upon their rights. We see them, fearless in their fortitude, and confident in the righteousness of their cause, bid defiance to the arm of power, and declare themselves independent states. We see them, waging for seven years a war of desolation and of glory, in most unequal contest with their own unnatural step-mother, the mistress of the seas, till under the sign manual of their king their independence was acknowledged; and, last and best of all, we see them toiling in war and in peace to form and perpetuate a union, under forms of government intricately but skilfully adjusted so as to secure to themselves and their posterity the priceless blessings of inseparable liberty and law.

Their days on earth are ended, and yet their century has not passed away. *Their* portion of the blessings which they thus labored to secure, they have enjoyed, and transmitted to *us* their posterity. We enjoy them as an inheritance, — won, not by our toils; watered, not with our tears; saddened, not by the shedding of any blood of ours. The gift of Heaven through their sufferings and their achievements, — but not without a charge of correspondent duty incumbent upon ourselves.

And what, my friends and fellow-citizens, what is that duty of our own? Is it to remonstrate to the adder's ear of a king beyond the Atlantic wave, and claim from him the restoration of violated rights? No. Is it to sever the ties of kindred and of blood with the people from whom we sprang? to cast away the precious name of Britons, and be no more the countrymen of Shakspeare and Milton, of Newton and Locke, of Chatham and Burke? Or more and worse, is it to meet *their* countrymen in the deadly conflict of a seven years' war? No. Is it the last and greatest of the duties fulfilled by them? Is it to lay the foundations of the fairest government and the mightiest nation that ever floated on the tide of time? No! These awful and solemn duties were allotted to them, and by them they were faithfully performed. What, then, is our duty?

Is it not to preserve, to cherish, to *improve* the inheritance which they have left us, — won by their toils, watered by their tears, saddened but fertilized by their blood? Are we the sons of worthy sires, and in the onward march of time have they achieved in the career of human improvement so much, only that our posterity and theirs may blush for the contrast between their unexampled energies and our nerveless impotence? between their more than herculean labors and our indolent repose? No, my fellow-citizens, far be from us, far be from you, — for he who now addresses you has but a few short days before he shall be called to join the multitudes of ages past, — far be from you the reproach or the suspicion of such a degrading contrast! You, too, have the solemn duty to perform of improving the condition of your species, by improving your own. Not in the great and strong wind of a revolution, which rent the mountains and brake in pieces the rocks before the Lord, — for the Lord is not in the wind; not in the earthquake of a revolutionary war, marching to the onset between the battle-field and the scaffold, — for the Lord is not in the earthquake; not in the fire of civil dissension, in war between the members and the head, in nullification of the laws of the Union by the forcible resistance of one refractory state, — for the Lord is not in the fire, and *that* fire was never kindled by your fathers! No! it is in the still small voice that succeeded the whirlwind, the earthquake, and the fire. The voice that stills the raging of the waves and the tumults of the people, — that spoke the words of peace, of harmony, of union. And for that voice, may you and your children's children, "to the last syllable of recorded time," fix your eyes upon the memory, and listen with your ears to the life, of JAMES MADISON.

HOPE. — *G. Spring.*

OF all the prospective emotions, Hope is the most prolific source of happiness, especially to the youthful mind. In the bloom of man's brightening existence, when everything about him is gay and alluring, and at that anxious and perilous moment when he steps forward to the duties of life, the impulse which encourages and charms him is found in his eager and vivid expectations. This is, indeed, the principal source of every man's happiness. We do not live for the present, but are perpetually carried forward by a sort of natural instinct to halcyon days to come. There are few present joys so absorbing, and few present trials so fraught with depression, that in the midst of the former we are not looking for others yet to come, and in the midst of the latter we are not anticipating relief. Men differ in this respect from the inferior animals. We are not, like them, environed as with a dense wall, beyond which we can catch but a glimmering light. We have a prospect brighter and wider than theirs. In poverty and sickness, in disappointment and sorrow, we are rich, and well, and happy in expectation; and in the midst of happiness we are still happier in expectation. In our dreams we hope. Even sleep, when it covers us with its heavy pall, does not so overpower the mind but pleasant visions creep gently beneath its folds, — visions of present happiness and happiness to come. Enjoyment is nothing without hope. I have sometimes thought that those winged messengers of celestial mercy, who are "ministering spirits" to many an agitated and trembling mind, never fulfil their errands of love more opportunely than when, in times of deep depression and unmingled darkness, they light up the glowing anticipations of the soul. It is but to touch some secret spring within, to inspire this glowing bosom with the expectation of some great though distant good, — and the same circumstances which were just now dreary and dark, are changed as though by magic, and become radiant with light and beauty. But who does not know that his hopes depend on nothing so much as those habits of enterprise which give character to the thoughts and feelings, and are always presenting some delightful as well as reasonable object of expectation? A regard to the present only would leave the common business of life well nigh undone. The agriculturist ploughs, and sows, and reaps, in hope. The mariner, reckless of his present comfort, exposes his life amid the breathings of the tempest under the influence of hope. The merchant shrinks from no hardship, omits no opportunity of exertion, avoids no hazard, and all under the powerful influence of hope. Hope moves the tongue of the orator, fills the imagination of the poet, and lights the lamp of the scholar. Hope gives courage to the heart and strength to the arm of the mighty on the field of battle; while, through a thousand valves, hope, with its airy enchantments, conveys the impulse to the complicated machinery of the deep and sage politician. A man never lays out himself in diligent and useful exertion, but he secures or increases his own good, or that of his fellow-men. And this is a prospect which supports and cheers him; and thus, while his hopes call forth his exertions, they, in their turn, are themselves fostered by the exertions which they call forth. Hope makes him active, and action gives him hope. The actual scenes of human life never present themselves in their true coloring to an indolent mind, but tinged with many a dark and melancholy hue. That complaining spirit, which is habitually looking to sources of darkness, and turning away from those of light and encouragement, is the natural growth of an unelastic, effeminate, slothful mind. That absorbing sentimentalism, that morbid sensibility, so often affected by the young, and which, when not affected, is the bane of every manly and energetic quality, finds no welcome in the bosom of a man whose highest ambition is gratified in the prospect of responsible exertion. No matter what may be the aspect of his condition, no matter what he is called to do or to suffer, no matter how vividly or how mournfully imagination may paint his prospects, so long as he has energy of purpose, patiently and cheerfully to address himself to his duty, and to augment his courage and increase his exertions by all the difficulties that beset his path.

VALUE OF THE UNION.— *C. T. Russell.*

The union of these states has been accomplished by the contributions of nations and centuries, for no transient or insignificant purpose. In its sublime and ultimate end it has a mission to humanity. In the language of Washington, "The preservation of the sacred fire of liberty, and the destiny of the republican model of government, are justly considered as deeply, perhaps as finally, staked on the experiment intrusted to the hands of the American people." Thus, as Madison has truly said, are we "responsible for the greatest trust ever confided to a political society." Ours is not the duty of forming, but preserving. The fathers were faithful to every exigency, by which God created it; we are responsible for a like faithfulness to every exigency, by which He would preserve and perpetuate it. To such fidelity the past urges, the future calls, and the highest law commands us. Evils and defects within our Union we may well and earnestly seek to remove, by the development and operation of the principles upon which it rests. But whosoever lays his hand upon the fabric itself, or seeks, by whatever means, or under whatever pretence, or from whatever source, to undermine its foundations, is treacherous to humanity, false to liberty, and, more than all, culpable to God.

This is the inference of duty. To its performance hope, by its smile, encourages us. All efforts for the dissolution of our Union will be as disastrously unsuccessful as they are singularly criminal. Never in its existence has it been more earnestly and truly performing its appropriate work than now. A people, in the aggregate happy and blessed as the sun shines upon, repose in its protection. Every rolling tide brings to its shores multitudes seeking its shelter. Each receding wave carries back to the people they have left its liberalizing influence. Rising midway of the continent, and reaching to either ocean, it throws over both its radiant and cheering light. Intently the struggling nations contemplate its no longer doubtful experiment. Moral and religious truth are penetrating every part of its vast domain, and planting, in the very footsteps of the first settlers, the church, the school, and the college. Its Christian missionaries have girdled the globe with their stations, and in all of them heroic men and women, under its protection, with the religion of Jesus, are silently diffusing the principles of American liberty. Already a nation in the far-off islands of the Pacific has been redeemed by them from barbarism, assumed its place among the powers of the earth, and the very last mails tell us is at this moment seeking admission to our republic.

Thus meeting its grand purposes, it will not fall. Man alone has not reared it, the tabernacle of freedom, and man alone cannot prostrate it, or gently, beam by beam, take it down. Heaven-directed in its formation and growth, while true to its origin it will be Heaven-protected in its progress and maturity. The stars of God will shine down kindly upon it, and angels on the beats of their silvery wings will linger and hover above it. To-day it is as firmly seated as ever in the affections of its citizens. Guarded by its hardly-seen power, reposing in its prosperity, not stopping to contemplate the character of its origin, or to realize its transcendent purpose, men, for a moment, may cast its value, speculate on its duration, and even threaten its dissolution. In the administration of its affairs, conflicts of opinion will exist, sectional interests will become excited, and sometimes hostile. The views of ardent men will be maintained with the ardor in which they are held. A clear and fair field of combat will be left to error and truth. The largest freedom of discussion will be scrupulously preserved. In the consequent excitement there may sometimes seem to be danger to the Union itself. But in the hour of peril experience shows, and ever will show, that a whole people will rally to its support, and sink its foes beneath a weight of odium a lifetime cannot alleviate. The rain may descend, the floods come, and the winds blow and beat upon it, — it will not fall, for it is founded upon a rock. It rests upon guarantees stronger even than laws and compromises. For it our interests combine in overwhelming potency; around it cluster the most glorious associations of our history; in it the hopes of humanity are involved; to it our hearts cling with undying love; for it religion, liberty and conscience plead; and, beyond all, upon it, in its riper years, as in its infancy, the protection of God rests, a sheltering cloud for its fiercer day, a pillar of fire in its darker night.

THE NOBILITY OF LABOR. — *O. Dewey.*

Why, in the great scale of things, is labor ordained for us? Easily, had it so pleased the great Ordainer, might it have been dispensed with. The world itself might have been a mighty machinery for producing all that man wants. Houses might have risen like an exhalation, —

> "With the sound
> Of dulcet symphonies, and voices sweet,
> Built like a temple."

Gorgeous furniture might have been placed in them, and soft couches and luxurious banquets spread by hands unseen; and man, clothed with fabrics of nature's weaving, rather than with imperial purple, might have been sent to disport himself in those Elysian palaces.

But where, then, had been human energy, perseverance, patience, virtue, heroism? Cut off labor with one blow from the world, and mankind had sunk to a crowd of Asiatic voluptuaries.

Better that the earth be given to man as a dark mass, whereupon to labor. Better that rude and unsightly materials be provided in the ore-bed, and in the forest, for him to fashion in splendor and beauty. Better, not because of that splendor and beauty, but because the act of creating them is better than the things themselves; because exertion is nobler than enjoyment; because the laborer is greater and more worthy of honor than the idler.

Labor is Heaven's great ordinance for human improvement. Let not the great ordinance be broken down. What do I say? It is broken down; and it has been broken down for ages. Let it, then, be built again; here, if anywhere, on the shores of a new world, of a new civilization.

But how, it may be asked, is it broken down? Do not men toil? it may be said. They do, indeed, toil; but they too generally do because they must. Many submit to it, as in some sort a degrading necessity; and they desire nothing so much on earth as an escape from it. This way of thinking is the heritage of the absurd and unjust feudal system, under which serfs labored, and gentlemen spent their lives in fighting and feasting. It is time that this opprobrium of toil were done away.

Ashamed to toil! Ashamed of thy dingy work-shop and dusty labor-field; of thy hard hand, scarred with service more honorable than that of war; of thy soiled and weather-stained garments, on which mother Nature has embroidered mist, sun and rain, fire and steam, — her own heraldic honors! Ashamed of those tokens and titles, and envious of the flaunting robes of imbecile idleness and vanity! It is treason to nature, — it is impiety to Heaven, — it is breaking Heaven's great ordinance! Toil, toil, either of the brain, of the heart, or of the hand, is the only true manhood, the only true nobility!

AMERICAN INSTITUTIONS. — *D. Webster.*

Who is there among us, that, should he find himself on any spot of the earth where human beings exist, and where the existence of other nations is known, would not be proud to say, I am an American! I am a countryman of Washington! I am a citizen of that republic which, although it has suddenly sprung up, yet there are none on the globe who have ears to hear and have not heard of it, who have eyes to see and have not read of it, who know anything and yet do not know of its existence and its glory? And, gentlemen, let me now reverse the picture. Let me ask, Who there is among us, if he were to be found to-morrow in one of the civilized countries of Europe, and were there to learn that this goodly form of government had been overthrown, — that the United States were no longer united, — who is there whose heart would not sink within him? Who is there who would not cover his face for very shame?

At this very moment, gentlemen, our country is a general refuge for the distressed and the persecuted of other nations. Whoever is in affliction from political occurrences in his own country, looks here for shelter. Whether he be republican, flying from the oppression of thrones, or whether he be monarch or monarchist, flying from thrones that crumble and fall under or around him, — he feels equal assurance that, if he get foothold on our soil, his person is safe, and his rights will be respected.

We have tried these popular institutions in times of great excitement and commotion, and they have stood substantially firm and steady, while the fountains of the great political deep have been elsewhere broken up; while thrones, resting on ages of prescription, have tottered and fallen; and while, in other countries, the earthquake of unrestrained popular commotion has swallowed up all law, and all liberty, and all right together. Our government has been tried in peace, and it has been tried in war, and has proved itself fit for both. It has been assailed from without, and it has successfully resisted the shock; it has been disturbed within, and it has effectually quieted the disturbance. It can stand trial, it can stand assault, it can stand adversity, — it can stand everything but the marring of its own beauty, and the weakening of its own strength. It can stand everything but the effects of our own rashness and our own folly. It can stand everything but disorganization, disunion, and nullification.

HUMAN LIFE. — *H. Greeley.*

HUMAN life! how inspiring, how boundless the theme! Sadly, wildly has the poet sung of it; calmly, lucidly has the historian traced its meanderings; earnestly, gravely have the priest and the sage exposed and reproved its errors, from the birth of the race. The muse's story depicts it, the scholar's research illustrates, the statesman's harangue illumines and exalts. From the cradle over which the young mother bends with a novel sensation of wondering delight, to the bier around which all are melted in the brotherhood of a common sorrow, this life of ours is a marvel and a poem. The very vitality within us, the warm current flowing so impetuously, yet steadily, from centre to extremities, and returning to renew its ceaseless errand; the beating heart, the seething, working brain, the apt, instinctive eye and ear, — can chemist or geologist, juggler or magician, show us wonders greater than these? The probing physiologist, the deep searcher into the hidden reason of things, begins by assuming the great mystery of all — life; for this he dare not hope to unravel. Not his the capacity or the hope to explain how or why it is; here he must content him with the simple fact — IT IS.

Human life! How is our every sympathy entwined with each emotion awakened by its contemplation! On every side it is putting forth manifestations to the observing eye of its energy and its beauty. Are we dwellers in the country? From that low-roofed cottage a youth is going forth with lofty heart to do and dare on the great battle-field of manly adventure. He has given ear to a father's counsel; he has knelt to receive a mother's blessing; he has smiled at the fears and regrets expressed by younger or tenderer hearts around him, — for a sanguine spirit urges him on, and he sees, already, fortune and honors awaiting him in the distant city to which his eager footsteps tend. Not till the hour of parting has come and passed does he feel how heavy the chain *he* drags who goes forth for years from all he loves on earth; not till the stately-branching elms which overhang the dear spot have waved their last mute adieus to his backward glances; not till the stream which was the companion of his boyish pastimes has bent away from his rigid course and buried itself among wooded hills, does he feel that he has shaken off the companionships and supports of his youth, and is utterly alone. Now nerve your quivering heart, young adventurer! Summon every thought of hope, and pride, and shame, and press sternly onward, — for a feather's weight might almost suffice to dash all your high resolutions, to chase away the dreams of hope and ambition, and send you back, an early penitent, to that lowly home which never seemed half so dear before.

Are we dwellers by the sea-side? Here the sailor is bending the white canvass for a voyage, it may be, around the world, Before he shall again drop anchor in the haven which he deems his home, he may from his vessel's deck gaze on the peaks of the Andes, the sulphurous flames of Kirauea, or may thread with his bark the perilous windings of the forest-mantled Oregon, may survey the porcelain towers of Canton, or the naked site of Troy, whose very ruins have vanished, leaving no monument of their existence, save in Homer's undying song.

Here, too, the emigrant is bidding adieu to the ungenial land of his birth and his love, and, with his household gods around him, is seeking, on a distant shore, a soil on which his hopes may expand and flourish. Then is sadness, then is anguish in the parting hour; the tree most carefully transplanted must leave too many fibres in its native soil; and the life-long dweller in some secluded valley who first finds himself confronted with a thousand leagues of raging brine, across which lies the way to his unknown future home, may well recoil and shudder at the prospect. But the hoarse order to embark is given and obeyed; the last adieus are looked from streaming eyes; the vessel swings slowly from her moorings; the young look out in wonder on the bleak waste of stormy waters, and turn inquiringly to those who are, perchance, as young in this hour's sensations as they. And so wears on the passage; and, at length, amid new scenes, new toils, anxieties and troubles, the pilgrim finds that care rests its eternal burden on man wherever he is found, — that earth has no more an Eden. What recks it? The same blue heaven bends lovingly over all the children of men. New scenes, new hopes, new prospects speedily dim the memory of keenest disappointments, of deepest regrets; and the heart transplanted sends out its tendrils in every direction, and learns to bloom and grow again. And thus do all of us, each in his appointed sphere and season, open new chapters in the great volume of human life.

But let us not contemplate only individual aspects. This life of ours has grander proportions, if we can but widen the sweep of our vision so as to reach its far horizon. Those daily acts, those common impulses, which, viewed individually, and with microscopic or with soulless gaze, seem insignificant or trifling, take a different aspect if regarded in a more catholic spirit. Those myriad hammers which, impelled by brawny arms, are ringing out their rude melody day by day, contributing to the comfort and sustenance of man, — those fleets of hardy fishers now chasing the whale on the other side of the globe to give light to the city mansion, and celerity to the wheels of the village factory, — those armies of trappers, scattered through the glens of the Rocky Mountains, each in stealthy solitude pursuing his deadly trade, whence dames of London and belles of Pekin alike shall borrow warmth and comeliness,

— let us contemplate these in their several classes, unmindful of the leagues of wood, or plain, or water, which chance to divide them. Readily enough do we perceive and acknowledge the grandeur of the great army which some chief or despot assembles and draws out to feed his vanity by display, or his ambition by carnage; but the larger and nobler armies, whose weapons are the mattock and the spade, who overspread the hills and line the valleys, until, beneath their rugged skill and persevering effort, a highway of commerce is opened where late the panther leaped, the deer disported, — is not theirs the nobler spectacle, more worthy of the orator's apostrophe, the poet's song? Let us look boldly, broadly out on nature's wide domain. Let us note the irregular yet persistent advance of the pioneers of civilization, the forest conquerors, before whose lusty strokes and sharp blades the century-crowned wood-monarchs, rank after rank, come crushing to the earth. From age to age have they kept apart the soil and the sunshine, as they shall do no longer. Onward, still onward pours the army of axe-men, and still before them bow their stubborn foes. But yesterday, their advance was checked by the Ohio; to-day, it has crossed the Missouri, the Kansas, and is fast on the heels of the flying buffalo. In the eye of a true discernment, what host of Xerxes or Cæsar, of Frederick or Napoleon, ever equalled this in majesty, in greatness of conquest, or in true glory?

The mastery of man over nature, — this is an inspiring truth, which we must not suffer, from its familiarity, to lose its force. By the might of his intellect, man has not merely made the elephant his drudge, the lion his diversion, the whale his magazine, but even the subtlest and most terrible of the elements are the submissive instruments of his will. He turns aside or garners up the lightning; the rivers toil in his workshop; the tides of ocean bear his burdens; the hurricane rages for his use and profit. Fire and water struggle for mastery that he may be whisked over hill and valley with the celerity of the sunbeam. The stillness of the forest midnight is broken by the snort of the iron horse, as he drags the long train from lakes to ocean with a slave's docility, a giant's strength. Up the long hill he labors, over the deep glen he skims the tops of the tall trees swaying around and below his narrow path. His sharp, quick breathing speaks his impetuous progress; a stream of fire reflects its course. On dashes the resistless, tireless steed, and the morrow's sun shall find him at rest in some far mart of commerce, and the partakers of his wizard journey scattered to their vocations of trade or pleasure, unthinking of their night's adventure. What has old romance wherewith to match the every-day realities of the nineteenth century?

WAR WITH FRANCE. — *J. Buchanan.*

France has been placed before the world by her rulers in the most false position ever occupied by a brave and gallant nation. She believes herself to be insulted; and what is the consequence? She refuses to pay a debt now admitted to be just by all the branches of her government. Her wounded feelings are estimated by dollars and cents; and she withholds twenty-five millions of francs, due to a foreign nation, to soothe her injured pride. How are the mighty fallen! Truly it may be said the days of her chivalry are gone. Have the pride and the genius of Napoleon left no traces of themselves under the constitutional monarchy? In private life, if you are insulted by an individual to whom you are indebted, what is the first impulse of a man of honor? To owe no pecuniary obligation to the man who has wounded your feelings; to pay him the debt instantly, and to demand reparation for the insult; or, at the least, to hold no friendly communication with him afterwards.

The only question with you now, is not one of substance, but merely whether these explanations are in proper form. But in regard to the United States, the question is far different. What is with you mere etiquette, is a question of life and death to them. Let the president of the United States make the apology which you have dictated, let him once admit the right of a foreign government to question his messages to Congress, and to demand explanations of any language at which they may choose to take offence, and their independent existence as a government, to that extent, is virtually destroyed.

We must remember that France may yield with honor; *we* never can without disgrace. Will she yield? That is the question. She must still believe that the people of this country are divided in opinion in regard to the firm maintenance of their rights. In this she will find herself entirely mistaken. But should Congress, at the present session, refuse to sustain the president, by adopting measures of defence, — should the precedent of the last session be followed for the present year, then I shall entertain the most gloomy forebodings. The father of his country has informed us that the best mode of preserving peace is to be prepared for war. I firmly believe, therefore, that a unanimous vote of the senate in favor of the resolutions now before them, to follow to Europe the acceptance of the mediation, would, almost to a certainty, render it successful. It would be an act of the soundest policy, as well as of the highest patriotism. It would prove, not that we intend to menace France, because such an attempt would be ridiculous, but that the American people are unanimous in the assertion of their rights, and have resolved to prepare for the worst. A French fleet is now hovering upon our coasts; and shall we sit still, with an overflowing treasury, and leave our country defenceless? This will never be said with truth of the American Congress.

If war should come, — which God forbid, — if France should still persist in her efforts to degrade the American people in the person of their chief magistrate, we may appeal to Heaven for the justice of our cause, and look forward with confidence to victory from that Being in whose hands is the destiny of nations.

POPULAR EXCITEMENT IN ELECTIONS. — *G. McDuffie.*

I NOT only maintain that the people are exempt from the charge of violence, but that there is a tendency to carry the feeling of indifference to public affairs to a dangerous extreme. From the peculiar structure and commercial spirit of modern society, and the facilities presented in our country for the acquisition of wealth, the eager pursuit of gain predominates over our concern for the affairs of the republic. This is, perhaps, our national foible. Wealth is the object of our idolatry; and even liberty is worshipped in the form of property. Although this spirit, by stimulating industry, is unquestionably excellent in itself, yet it is to be apprehended that, in a period of peace and tranquillity, it will become too strong for patriotism, and produce the greatest of national evils — popular apathy.

We have been frequently told that the farmer should attend to his plough, and the mechanic to his handicraft, during the canvass for the presidency. A more dangerous doctrine could not be inculcated. If there is any spectacle from the contemplation of which I would shrink with peculiar horror, it would be that of the great mass of the American people sunk into a profound apathy on the subject of their highest political interests. Such a spectacle would be more portentous to the eye of intelligent patriotism, than all the monsters of the earth, and fiery signs of the heavens, to the eye of trembling superstition. If the people could be indifferent to the fate of a contest for the presidency, they would be unworthy of freedom. If I were to perceive them sinking into this apathy, I would even apply the power of political galvanism, if such a power could be found, to rouse them from their fatal lethargy. Keep the people quiet! Peace! peace! Such are the whispers by which the people are to be lulled to sleep, in the very crisis of their highest concerns. "You make a solitude, and call it peace!" Peace? 'T is death! Take away all interest from the people in the election of their chief ruler, and liberty is no more. What is to be the consequence? If the people do not elect the president, somebody must. There is no special providence to decide the question. Who, then, is to make the election, and how will it operate? You throw a general paralysis over the body politic, and excite a morbid action in particular members. The general patriotic excitement of the people, in relation to the election of the president, is as essential to the health and energy of the political system, as circulation of the blood is to the health and energy of the natural body. Check that circulation, and you inevitably produce local inflammation, gangrene, and, ultimately, death. Make the people indifferent, destroy their legitimate influence, and you communicate a morbid violence to the efforts of those who are ever ready to assume the control of such affairs, — the mercenary intriguers and interested office-hunters of the country. Tell me not of popular violence! Show me a hundred political factionists, —men who look to the election of a president as the means of gratifying their high or their low ambition, — and I will show you the very materials for a mob, ready for any desperate adventure connected with their common fortunes. The reason of this extraordinary excitement is obvious. It is a matter of self-interest, of personal ambition. The people can have no such motives. They look only to the interest and glory of the country.

THE SPIRIT OF HUMAN LIBERTY. — *D. Webster.*

The spirit of human liberty and of free government, nurtured and grown into strength and beauty in America, has stretched its course into the midst of the nations. Like an emanation from heaven, it has gone forth, and it will not return void. It must change, it is fast changing, the face of the earth. Our great, our high duty is to show, in our own examples, that this spirit is a spirit of health as well as a spirit of power; that its benignity is as great as its strength; that its efficiency to secure individual rights, social relations, and moral order, is equal to the irresistible force with which it prostrates principalities and powers. The world, at this moment, is regarding us with a willing, but something of a fearful, admiration. Its deep and awful anxiety is to learn, whether free states may be stable as well as free; whether popular power may be trusted as well as feared; — in short, whether wise, regular and virtuous self-government is a vision for the contemplation of theorists, or a truth, established, illustrated, and brought into practice, in the country of Washington.

For the earth which we inhabit, and the whole circle of the sun, for all the unborn races of mankind, we seem to hold in our hands, for their weal or woe, the fate of this experiment. If we fail, who shall venture the repetition? If our example shall prove to be one, not of encouragement, but of terror, — not fit to be imitated, but fit only to be shunned, — where else shall the world look for free models? If this great western sun be struck out of the firmament, at what other fountain shall the lamp of liberty hereafter be lighted? What other orb shall emit a ray to glimmer, even, on the darkness of the world?

THE DESTINY OF THE UNITED STATES. — *H. W. Hilliard.*

WHEN Oregon shall be in our possession, when we shall have established a profitable trade with China through her ports, when our ships traverse the Pacific as they now cross the Atlantic, and all the countless consequences of such a state of things begin to flow in upon us, then will be fulfilled that vision which rapt and filled the mind of Nunez as he gazed over the placid waves of the Pacific.

I will now address myself for a moment to the moral aspect of this great question. Gentlemen have talked much and eloquently about the horrors of war. I should regret the necessity of a war; I should deplore its dreadful scenes; — but if the possession of Oregon gives us a territory opening upon the nation prospects such as I describe, and if, for the simple exercise of our rights in regard to it, Great Britain should wage war upon us, — an unjust war, — the regret which every one must feel will, at least, have much to counterbalance it. One of England's own writers has said: "The possible destiny of the United States of America, as a nation of one hundred millions of freemen, stretching from the Atlantic to the Pacific, living under the laws of Alfred, and speaking the language of Shakspeare and Milton, is an august conception."

It is an august conception, finely embodied; and I trust in God that it will, at no distant time, become a reality. I trust that the world will see, through all time, our people living, not only under the laws of Alfred, but that they will be heard to speak, throughout our wide-spread borders, the language of Shakspeare and Milton. Above all, is it my prayer that, as long as our posterity shall contine to inhabit these mountains and plains, and hills and valleys, they may be found living under the sacred institutions of Christianity. Put these things together, and what a picture do they present to the mental eye! Civilization and intelligence started in the East; they have travelled, and are still travelling, westward; but when they shall have completed the circuit of the earth, and reached the extremest verge of the Pacific shores, then, unlike the fabled god of the ancients, who dipped his glowing axle in the western wave, they will take up their permanent abode; then shall we enjoy the sublime destiny of returning these blessings to their ancient seat; then will it be ours to give the priceless benefits of our free institutions, and the pure and healthful light of the gospel, back to the dark family which has so long lost both truth and freedom; then may Christianity plant herself there, and while with one hand she points to the Polynesian isles, rejoicing in the late-recovered treasure of revealed truth, with the other present the Bible to the Chinese. It is our duty to aid in this great work. I trust we shall esteem it as much our honor as our duty. Let us not, like some of the British missionaries, give them the Bible in one hand and opium in the other, but bless them only with the pure word of truth. I hope the day is not distant, — soon, soon may its dawn arise! — to shed upon the farthest and the most benighted of nations the splendor of more than a tropical sun.

THE NATIONAL DEFENCES. — *F. Pierce.*

In this age of progress, in this land of invention and almost boundless resources, we are not the people to stand still. We have not stood still. But while individual enterprise has kept pace, in all the various pursuits of life, with the best improvements of the day, it must be admitted, considering our position upon the globe, — the immense extent of our maritime frontier, — the mode in which we must be assailed, if ever successfully, by a foreign foe, — the easy access to our most commanding harbors, — the vast importance and exposed condition of our great commercial cities, especially since the successful application of steam-power to ocean navigation, — that we have been singularly regardless of the improvements which in other countries, especially in France and England, have been and are rapidly changing the character of military operations, offensive and defensive, both on the land and on the sea.

There are some things about the military defences of this country which may be considered as settled. I regard it as certain that no large standing army is ever to be maintained here, in time of peace, while our free institutions remain unshaken. In this we differ entirely from those nations with whom, from our position and political relations, we are in the greatest danger of a collision. It is equally certain, in my judgment, that stationary fortifications, in the best condition, with abundance of *materiêl*, and well manned, will prove entirely inadequate to the defence of even our large commercial cities. It must be regarded as not less clear, that no foreign power can ever embark in the Quixotic enterprise of *conquering* this country, unless its constitution shall first be trampled in the dust by its children. Such a project can never be soberly contemplated while we are a united people. During our Revolution, — in the weakness of our infancy, — the invaders could scarcely command more ground than they were able immediately to occupy.

The leading purposes of an enemy will be, by the celerity and boldness of his movements on our coast, to keep up a constant alarm; to harass and cut off our commerce; to destroy our naval depots and public works; and, if possible, to lay our great commercial cities under contribution or in ashes. It is against prompt movements and vigorous exertions for objects like these, that we should prepare and provide. France and England have, and always must maintain, large and well-appointed standing armies;

they are the indispensable appendages of royal power and dominion, without which no monarch in Europe can retain his crown a single year. They have not only armies, but they have now the means of planting them upon our shores, — nay, of quartering them in the heart of our cities, — before we can set in order our insufficient and now deserted fortresses, or call into the field any effective force, organized as our militia at present is. Indeed, in some of the states there is no organization whatever; it is wholly disbanded, and men, whose thoughts were never elevated above the contemplation of loss and gain, are out in the newspapers with their calculations to show *exactly* how many dollars and cents may be saved annually by the "disbandment" of this safe and sure auxiliary in our national defence.

I cannot help feeling strongly upon this subject, because I have witnessed the deep lethargy in which the spirit of the nation, easily roused to everything else, has seemed to slumber here. Within the last few years war-clouds have lowered most portentously upon our horizon, and on one or two occasions seemed ready to burst, and scatter far and wide the calamities of that dreadful scourge. What was the effect upon the government and the country, when, upon the question of *money*, we were upon the eve of a war with one of the most powerful and gallant nations of the earth? Did we manifest a willingness to apply our money in preparation for the contest? No! There was, as usual, no want of patriotic demonstration in the way of speeches, but they were followed by nothing like decisive action. Through the country there appeared to be a profound repose, and blind trusting to luck, in the face of admitted imminent danger. In the beneficent ordination of Providence, and through the energy and wisdom of that extraordinary man, who always proved equal to great occasions, the impending danger was happily averted.

How was it more recently, when, for a long time, there had been a quasi war along our whole border, from St. John's to the lakes? In what condition did the evening of the 2d of March, 1839, find the country? In what state did it find us in our places here? Like the nation generally — calm and undisturbed. Senators then present will not soon forget the scene that followed the arrival of the eastern mail that night. The stirring report soon passed around the chamber, "There has been a battle upon our eastern frontier; the blood of our citizens has been shed upon our own soil!" A change came over the spirit of our dream. Every countenance was lighted up with high excitement. We were at last, when the strange spell of fancied security could no longer bind us, roused as from the delusion of a charm; we awoke as from the trance of years; as from a dream we opened our eyes upon a full view of the nearness and magnitude of our danger. I shall never forget the bearing, on that occasion, nor the burning words of an honorable senator on the other side of the chamber, not now in his place. He seemed to feel that, by our culpable neglect to provide the means of defence, we had invited aggression, and that we ought ourselves to take our places in the fiercest of the eddying storm which, it was then supposed, had already burst upon our border brethren. What was done? All that could be done under the circumstances. The constitutional term of one branch of Congress had but a few more hours to run. There was little time for deliberation; but we showed that there was one contingency in which we could merge everything like party, and present an unbroken front. We passed a bill, placing at the disposal of the president the whole militia of the United States, to be compelled to serve for a term not exceeding six months; to raise fifty thousand volunteers; to equip, man, and employ in active service all the naval force of the United States; and to build, purchase or charter, arm, equip and man such vessels and steamboats on the northern lakes and rivers, whose waters communicated with the United States and Great Britain, as he should deem necessary. This fearful responsibility was cast upon one individual. This vast command, with ten millions of dollars to make it effectual, was committed to the sole discretion and patriotism of the president. No man who loves his country can but deprecate the necessity of placing such tremendous and fearful powers in the hands of one man, however wise and disinterested.

I warn the people against another such crisis. Sooner or later it will come, and perhaps unattended by that good fortune which has thus far borne us on in peace. At all events, it is the most fatal temerity to depend upon it, and neglect the necessary preparations. We should provide our harbors, in addition to the stationary fortifications, with the best floating defences known to the world. We should make our navy equal at least to one sixth of that of Great Britain. We should provide for an organization of the militia to be efficient and uniform throughout the Union. Thus prepared, with our large cities in a suitable state of defence, and with six hundred thousand disciplined citizen soldiers, so enrolled and organized as to admit of being promptly mustered and called into the field, we shall be ready for the conflict which, under such circumstances, will hardly be pressed upon us.

ANNIVERSARY OF THE BOSTON MASSACRE.—*J. Warren.*

You have, my friends and countrymen, frustrated the designs of your enemies, by your unanimity and fortitude; it was your union and determined spirit which expelled those troops who polluted your streets with innocent blood. You have appointed this anniversary as a standard memorial of the bloody consequences of placing an armed force in a populous city, and of your deliverance from the dangers which then seemed to hang over your heads; and I am confident that you will never betray the least want of spirit when called upon to guard your freedom. None but they who set a just value upon the blessings of liberty are worthy to enjoy her; your illustrious fathers were her zealous votaries;—when the blasting frowns of tyranny drove her from public view, they clasped her in their arms; they cherished her in their generous bosoms; they brought her safe over the rough ocean, and fixed her seat in this then dreary wilderness; they nursed her infant age with the most tender care; for her sake, they patiently bore the severest hardships; for her support, they underwent the most rugged toils; in her defence, they boldly encountered the most alarming dangers; neither the ravenous beasts that ranged the woods for prey, nor the more furious savages of the wilderness, could damp their ardor! Whilst with one hand they broke the stubborn glebe, with the other they grasped their weapons, ever ready to protect her from danger. No sacrifice, not even their own blood, was esteemed too rich a libation for her altar. God prospered their valor; they preserved her brilliancy unsullied; they enjoyed her whilst they lived, and, dying, bequeathed the dear inheritance to your care. And, as they left you this glorious legacy, they have undoubtedly transmitted to you some portion of their noble spirit, to inspire you with virtue to merit her, and courage to preserve her. You surely cannot, with such examples before your eyes as every page of the history of this country affords, suffer your liberties to be ravished from you by a lawless force, or cajoled away by flattery and fraud.

The voice of your fathers' blood cries to you from the ground, My sons, scorn to be slaves! In vain we met the frowns of tyrants; in vain we crossed the boisterous ocean, found a new world, and prepared it for the happy residence of liberty; in vain we toiled, in vain we fought, we bled in vain, if you, our offspring, want valor to repel the assaults of her invaders! Stain not the glory of your worthy ancestors; but, like them, resolve never to part with your birthright. Be wise in your deliberations, and determined in your exertions for the preservation of your liberties. Follow not the dictates of passion, but enlist yourselves under the sacred banner of reason. Use every method in your power to secure your rights. At least, prevent the curses of posterity from being heaped upon your memories.

If you, with united zeal and fortitude, oppose the torrent of oppression; if you feel the true fire of patriotism burning in your breasts; if you from your souls despise the most gaudy dress that slavery can wear; if you really prefer the lonely cottage (whilst blessed with liberty) to gilded palaces, surrounded with the ensigns of slavery, — you may have the fullest assurance that tyranny, with her whole accursed train, will hide their hideous heads in confusion, shame and despair. If you perform your part, you must have the strongest confidence that the same Almighty

Being, who protected your pious and venerable forefathers, who enabled them to turn a barren wilderness into a fruitful field, who so often made bare his arm for their salvation, will still be mindful of you, their offspring.

May this Almighty Being graciously preside in all our councils. May he direct us to such measures as he himself shall approve, and be pleased to bless. May we ever be a people favored of God. May our land be a land of liberty, the seat of virtue, the asylum of the oppressed, a name and a praise in the whole earth, until the last shock of time shall bury the empires of the world in one common, undistinguished ruin!

THE PERMANENCE OF AMERICAN LIBERTY. — *G. McDuffie.*

The election of a chief magistrate by the mass of the people of an extensive community, was, to the most enlightened nations of antiquity, a political impossibility. Destitute of the art of printing, they could not have introduced the representative principle into their political systems, even if they had understood it. In the very nature of things, that principle can only be coëxtensive with popular intelligence. In this respect, the art of printing, more than any invention since the creation of man, is destined to change and elevate the political condition of society. It has given a new impulse to the energies of the human mind, and opens new and brilliant destinies to modern republics, which were utterly unattainable by the ancients. The existence of a country population, scattered over a vast extent of territory, as intelligent as the population of the cities, is a phenomenon which was utterly and necessarily unknown to the free states of antiquity. All the intelligence which controlled the destiny and upheld the dominion of republican Rome was confined to the walls of the great city. Even when her dominion extended beyond Italy to the utmost known limits of the inhabited world, the city was the exclusive seat both of intelligence and empire. Without the art of printing, and the consequent advantages of a free press, that habitual and incessant action of mind upon mind, which is essential to all human improvement, could no more exist among a numerous and scattered population, than the commerce of disconnected continents could traverse the ocean without the art of navigation. Here, then, is the source of our superiority, and our just pride as a nation. The statesmen of the remotest extremes of the Union can converse together, like the philosophers of Athens in the same portico, or the politicians of Rome in the same forum. Distance is overcome, and the citizens of Georgia and of Maine can be brought to coöperate in the same great object, with as perfect a community of views and feelings as actuated the tribes of Rome in the assemblies of the people. It is obvious that liberty has a more extensive and durable foundation in the United States than it ever has had in any other age or country. By the representative principle, — a principle unknown and impracticable among the ancients, — the whole mass of society is brought to operate in constraining the action of power and in the conservation of public liberty.

THE EXPERIMENT OF SELF-GOVERNMENT. — *E. Everett.*

We are summoned to new energy and zeal by the high nature of the experiment we are appointed in Providence to make, and the grandeur of the theatre on which it is to be performed. When the Old World afforded no longer any hope, it pleased Heaven to open this last refuge of humanity. The attempt has begun, and is going on, far from foreign corruption, on the broadest scale, and under the most benignant auspices; and it certainly rests with us to solve the great problem in human society, to settle, and that forever, the momentous question, whether mankind can be trusted with a purely popular system. One might almost think, without extravagance, that the departed wise and good of all places and times are looking down from their happy seats to witness what shall now be done by us; that they, who lavished their treasures and their blood of old, who labored and suffered, who spake and wrote, who fought and perished, in the one great cause of freedom and truth, are now hanging from their orbs on high, over the last solemn experiment of humanity. As I have wandered over the spots once the scene of their labors, and mused among the prostrate columns of their senate-houses and forums, I have seemed almost to hear a voice from the tombs of departed ages, from the sepulchres of the nations which died before the sight. They exhort us, they adjure us to be faithful to our trust. They implore us, by the long trials of struggling humanity; by the blessed memory of the departed; by the dear faith which has been plighted by pure hands to the holy cause of truth and man; by the awful secrets of the prison-houses where the sons of freedom have been immured; by the noble heads which have been brought to the block; by the wrecks of time; by the eloquent ruins of nations, — they conjure us not to quench the light which is rising on the world. Greece cries to us, by the convulsed lips of her poisoned, dying Demosthenes; and Rome pleads with us in the mute persuasion of her mangled Tully.

In that high romance, if romance it be, in which the great minds of antiquity sketched the fortunes of the ages to come, they pictured to themselves a favored region beyond the ocean, a land of equal laws and happy men. The primitive poets beheld it in the islands of the blest; the Doric bards surveyed it in the hyperborean regions; the sage of the academy placed it in the lost Atlantis; and even the sterner spirit of Seneca could discern a fairer abode of humanity in distant regions then unknown. We look back upon these uninspired predictions, and almost recoil from the obligations they imply. By us must these fair visions be realized; by us must be fulfilled these high promises, which burst in trying hours from the longing hearts of the champions of truth. There are no more continents or worlds to be revealed; Atlantis hath arisen from the ocean; the farthest Thule is reached; there are no more retreats beyond the sea, no more discoveries, no more hopes. Here, then, a mighty work is to be fulfilled, or never, by the race of mortals. The man, who looks with tenderness on the sufferings of good men in other times; the descendant of the Pilgrims, who cherishes the memory of his fathers; the patriot, who feels an honest glow at the majesty of the system of which he is a member; the scholar, who beholds with rapture the long-sealed book of unprejudiced truth expanded to all to read; — these are they by whom these auspices are to be accomplished. Yes, brethren, it is by the intellect of the country that the mighty mass is to be inspired, that its parts are to communicate and sympathize, its bright progress to be adorned with becoming refinements, its strong sense uttered, its character reflected, its feelings interpreted to its own children, to other regions, and to after ages.

Meantime, the years are rapidly passing away and gathering importance in their course. With the present year will be completed the half century from that most important era in human history, the commencement of our Revolutionary War. The jubilee of our national existence is at hand.

The space of time that has elapsed from that momentous date, has laid down in the dust, which the blood of many of them had already hallowed, most of the great men to whom, under Providence, we owe our national existence and privileges. A few still survive among us to reap the rich fruits of their labors and sufferings; and one has yielded himself to the united voice of a people, and returned in his age to receive the gratitude of the nation to whom he devoted his youth.

Welcome, friend of our fathers, to our shores! Happy are our eyes that behold those venerable features. Enjoy a triumph, such as never conqueror or monarch enjoyed, — the assurance that throughout America there is not a bosom which does not beat with joy and gratitude at the sound of your name. You have already met and saluted, or will soon meet, the few that remain of the ardent patriots, prudent counsellors, and brave warriors, with whom you were associated in achieving our liberty. But you have looked round in vain for the faces of many who would have lived years of pleasure on a day like this with their old companion in arms and brother in peril. Lincoln, and Greene, and Knox, and Hamilton, are gone; the heroes of Saratoga and Yorktown have fallen before the only foe they could not meet. Above all, the first of heroes and of men, the friend of your youth, the more than friend of his country, rests in the bosom of the soil he redeemed. On the banks of his Potomac he lies in glory and peace. You will revisit the hospitable shades of Mount Vernon, but him whom you venerated as we did, you will not meet at its door. His voice of consolation, which reached you in the Austrian dungeons, cannot now break its silence, to bid you welcome to his own roof. But the grateful children of America will bid you welcome, in his name. Welcome, thrice welcome to our shores! and whithersoever throughout the limits of the continent your course shall take you, the ear that hears you shall bless you, the eye that sees you shall bear witness to you, and every tongue exclaim, with heartfelt joy, Welcome, welcome, Lafayette!

NORTHERN LABORERS. — *C. C. Naylor.*

The gentleman has misconceived the spirit and tendency of northern institutions. He is ignorant of northern character. He has forgotten the history of his country. Preach insurrection to the northern laborers! Who are the northern laborers? The history of your country is their history. The renown of your country is their renown. The brightness of their doings is emblazoned on its every page. Blot from your annals the deeds and the doings of northern laborers, and the history of your country presents but a universal blank.

Who was he that disarmed the thunderer; wrested from his grasp the bolts of Jove; calmed the troubled ocean; became the central sun of the philosophical system of his age, shedding his brightness and effulgence on the whole civilized world; whom the great and mighty of the earth delighted to honor; who participated in the achievement of your independence; prominently assisted in moulding your free institutions, and the beneficial effects of whose wisdom will be felt to the last moment of "recorded time"? Who, I ask, was he? A northern laborer, a Yankee tallow-chandler's son, a printer's runaway boy!

And who, let me ask the honorable gentleman, who was he that, in the days of our Revolution, led forth a northern army, — yes, an army of northern laborers, — and aided the chivalry of South Carolina in their defence against British aggression, drove the spoilers from their firesides, and redeemed her fair fields from foreign invaders? Who was he? A northern laborer, a Rhode Island blacksmith, — the gallant General Greene, —who left his hammer and his forge, and went forth conquering and to conquer in the battle for our independence! And will you preach insurrection to men like these?

Our country is full of the achievements of northern laborers! Where are Concord, and Lexington, and Princeton, and Trenton, and Saratoga, and Bunker Hill, but in the north? And what has shed an imperishable renown on the never-dying names of those hallowed spots, but the blood and the struggles, the high daring and patriotism, and sublime courage, of northern laborers? The whole north is an everlasting monument of the freedom, virtue, intelligence, and indomitable independence of northern laborers! Go, preach insurrection to men like these!

The fortitude of the men of the north, under intense suffering for liberty's sake, has been almost godlike! History has so recorded it. Who comprised that gallant army, that, without food, without pay, shelterless, shoeless, penniless, and almost naked, in that dreadful winter, — the midnight of our Revolution, — whose wanderings could be traced by their blood-tracks in the snow, whom no arts could seduce, no appeal lead astray, no sufferings disaffect, but who, true to their country and its holy cause, continued to fight the good fight of liberty, until it finally triumphed? Who were these men? Why, northern laborers!

THE MILITIA OF THE REVOLUTION. — *H. Hubbard.*

No body of troops were more patriotic, no men were more ardent in the prosecution of the war of the Revolution, no men in the public service endured more or suffered more, no men were clothed less, fed less, or paid less than they were. In every point of view they have as strong claims upon the justice and gratitude of the country as any of the surviving soldiers of the Revolution.

The peculiar services and sacrifices of the militia during the war of the Revolution give to that class a powerful claim upon the justice of the common country. For these services, for these sacrifices, they could not have been paid. The debt is yet due; it still remains unsatisfied; and, on every consideration, the militia are equally well entitled to the benefit of the pension system as any other class of revolutionary soldiers.

It was the pure patriotism, it was the unwavering devotion to the best interests of the republic, it was the virtue and the valor of the militia, that gave to our cause an impulse which was irresistible, an impulse which the whole physical force of England, aided by her subsidized Hessians, proved wholly incompetent to control and to vanquish.

The battles of Lexington, Concord, Bunker Hill, taught the enemy that the soil of freemen could not be invaded with impunity, that the spirit of freemen could never be subdued by skill however consummate, by force however powerful. The enemy then saw and felt too much not to believe that the sacred soil of freedom might be run over, but could not be conquered. Were it necessary to advert to events to show forth the value of the militia, I would direct your attention to every great battle that was fought in the war of the Revolution.

At the north, it was the militia that gave a turn to our hostile operations which inspired confidence in the cause of America. The battle of Bennington, under the brave Stark, of my own state, with his regiments of militia, after a series of disaster and defeat had attended the army in Canada and upon the lakes, served to animate the drooping spirit of despondency, to fill the soul of patriotism with hope, with confidence, with courage.

In the south as well as in the north the militia of the country was equally distinguished for the purity of its patriotism and the ardor of its zeal. If any invidious foe to our country has cast imputations upon the bravery and the conduct of our militia at any particular period of that war, it should be replied, that want of discipline, not want of heroism, subjected our militia, in certain memorable battles, to great disadvantages.

There was no cowardice, no treachery in the composition of the militia. In every battle fought, in every victory won, they were breast to breast, side by side, with state and continental troops. When the enemy of the country cried "havoc, and let slip the dogs of war," the militia came forth in their might. All the battles of 1775, before a regular army could have been organized, — of Lexington, of Bunker Hill, of Ticonderoga, of St. John's and of Norfolk, — evince the most unwavering courage and conduct. If a doubt could be supposed to exist as to the value of the militia service in the war of the Revolution, I would refer to the battles of Fort Moultrie, of Bennington, of Saratoga, of Long Island, of Trenton, of Germantown, and of Yorktown. These engagements speak a language which cannot be mistaken, and which will not be forgotten.

We are now happy at home, enjoying every blessing which can pertain to freemen. We are respected abroad, participating in every right guaranteed to the most honored nation. We cannot fail to realize that every interest of our beloved country is most prosperous. Every citizen in this great republic is made secure in the enjoyment of all his rights, by the moral influence of our free institutions. How wonderful have been the practical effects of the American Revolution! How great has been the advance of our general population, the march of improvement, the progress of the arts! Our extended and extending West comes forth in all her majesty, in all her physical and moral power, to bear evidence to the wondering world of the great and glorious fruits of the Revolution. The cause of learning, the pure spirit of Christianity, trace their astonishing advancement to the impulse received in that eventful period. The science of self-government, the free institutions of our land, rest upon a deep and enduring foundation, laid in the war of the Revolution. In every latitude, in every region, in every part of Christendom, are to be found the effects of American genius, American enterprise, and of American industry.

And while we contemplate the universal prosperity and happiness which pervade our land, can we fail to take a retrospect, and bring to mind by whose efforts and energies, by whose services and sacrifices, these invaluable blessings have been secured? In the dark days of the Revolution our beloved country was poor, of limited resources, little able to fulfil to the letter her engagements; her soldiers were neither fed nor clothed nor paid according to the stipulations of the government; the general currency of the country was greatly depreciated. These unfailing friends could not at such a time have received their honest, their just demands.

Nevertheless, their devotion to her cause suffered no change. Through good report and through evil report, in her prosperity and in her adversity, they went for their country, and for nothing but their country.

Let us then unite with one mind and with one heart to effect a satisfactory payment of this debt, — a debt which we should most willingly admit, a debt which our country is now well able satisfactorily to discharge. And shall we stop, the descendants of our revolutionary fathers, the children of the patriots of that day; shall we, *freemen*, the native sons of the soil, stop to calculate the dollars and cents, the pounds and the pence, which the passage of this bill may annually draw from our treasury? God forbid! I would have never entered upon any such inglorious work, had it not been time and again reiterated, that the passage of such a bill as this would impoverish our country, bring ruin upon our republic. I would pass this bill, were I certain that the consequent exaction upon me would require the surrender of the better half of my estate. I would then have left the consolation that the claims of our revolutionary patriots had been satisfied, without whose triumphant efforts everything here would have been valueless; political rights and political privileges would have been anything but political blessings.

The surviving soldiers of the Revolution have already passed that boundary which has been assigned by high authority as the duration of human existence. If by reason of their strength they should continue until fourscore years, yet will their strength be labor and sorrow. They must be soon cut off; their places will soon know them no more forever. The day of their departure must be at hand; their years must be nearly numbered. I would then most solemnly urge this committee not to delay the passage of this bill; and my fervent prayer to the Father of the faithful would be, that many may long live to enjoy its benefits; that they may be induced to call around them their children and their children's children, and by one more patriotic effort rivet their affections still stronger to the republic, by pointing out to them this act of the justice and the gratitude of their beloved country.

THE FAMINE IN IRELAND. — *S. S. Prentiss.*

There lies upon the other side of the wide Atlantic a beautiful island, famous in story and in song. It has given to the world more than its share of genius and of greatness. It has been prolific in statesmen, warriors, and poets. Its brave and generous sons have fought successfully in all battles but its own. In wit and humor it has no equal; while its harp, like its history, moves to tears by its sweet but melancholy pathos. In this fair region God has seen fit to send the most terrible of all those fearful ministers who fulfil his inscrutable decrees. The earth has failed to give her increase; the common mother has forgotten her offspring, and her breast no longer affords them their accustomed nourishment. Famine, gaunt and ghastly famine, has seized a nation with its strangling grasp; and unhappy Ireland, in the sad woes of the present, forgets, for a moment, the gloomy history of the past.

In battle, in the fulness of his pride and strength, little recks the soldier whether the hissing bullet sing his sudden requiem, or the cords of life are severed by the sharp steel. But he who dies of hunger, wrestles alone, day after day, with his grim and unrelenting enemy. He has no friends to cheer him in the terrible conflict; for if he had friends how could he die of hunger? He has not the hot blood of the soldier to maintain him; for his foe, vampire-like, has exhausted his veins.

Who will hesitate to give his mite, to avert such awful results? Give, then, generously and freely. Recollect that in so doing you are exercising one of the most godlike qualities of your nature, and at the same time enjoying one of the greatest luxuries of life. We ought to thank our Maker that he has permitted us to exercise equally with himself that noblest of even the Divine attributes — benevolence. Go home and look at your family, smiling in rosy health, and then think of the pale, famine-pinched cheeks of the poor children of Ireland; and you will give, according to your store, even as a bountiful Providence has given to you, — not grudgingly, but with an open hand; for the quality of benevolence, like that of mercy,

> "Is not strained;
> It droppeth like the gentle rain from heaven
> Upon the place beneath. It is twice blessed;
> It blesses him that gives, and him that takes."

CLASSICAL STUDIES — *J Story.*

There is not a single nation, from the north to the south of Europe, from the bleak shores of the Baltic to the bright plains of immortal Italy, whose literature is not imbedded in the very elements of classical learning. The literature of England is, in an emphatic sense, the production of her scholars; of men who have cultivated letters in her universities, and colleges, and grammar-schools; of men who thought any life too short, chiefly because it left some relic of antiquity unmastered, and any other fame humble, because it faded in the presence of Roman and Grecian genius. He who studies English literature without the lights of classical learning, loses half the charms of its sentiments and style, of its force and feelings, of its delicate touches, of its delightful allusions, of its illustrative associations. Who, that reads the poetry of Gray, does not feel that it is the refinement of classical taste which gives such inexpressible vividness and transparency to his diction? Who, that reads the concentrated sense and melodious versification of Dryden and Pope, does not perceive in them the disciples of the old school, whose genius was inflamed by the heroic verse, the terse satire, and the playful wit of antiquity? Who, that meditates over the strains of Milton, does not feel that he drank deep at

"Siloa's brook, that flowed
Fast by the oracle of God" —

that the fires of his magnificent mind were lighted by coals from ancient altars?

It is no exaggeration to declare, that he who proposes to abolish classical studies proposes to render, in a great measure, inert and unedifying the mass of English literature for three centuries; to rob us of the glory of the past, and much of the instruction of future ages; to blind us to excellences which few may hope to equal, and none to surpass; to annihilate associations which are interwoven with our best sentiments, and give to distant times and countries a presence and reality as if they were in fact his own.

THE FREEDOM OF SCIENCE IN AMERICA. — *G. C. Verplanck.*

The quick and keen sense of self-interest, that gives such sagacity and energy to the business operations of this country, is equally propitious to the success of every art, every discovery, invention, undertaking, and science, that involves in it any amount of practical improvement or power. Hence, whatever of theoretical science, inventive skill, ingenious speculation, or reasoning eloquence, can be made to tell upon any of the multitudinous affairs making up the business of life, or to minister in any way to the increased power or enjoyment of man, will soon find ready attention for their claims. Here no prejudices in favor of time-honored usages are strong enough long to resist the advance of scientific improvement or wise innovation. Society is not divided into castes, each one of them watching with jealous vigilance against any encroachment of their several exclusive walks by any rude intruder from another class, themselves clinging to the settled usages and old forms of their own clan, with the steady pertinacity of men whose unexamined prejudices are interwoven with their earliest habits and their most valuable personal interests. If Science, descending from her starry throne in the heavens, light the student to any discovery or invention in any manner applicable to the wants of his fellow-creatures, — if Genius prompt the lofty thought, — if love of God or of man inspire the generous design, no matter how the novelty may astonish for the moment, no matter what prejudices may be shocked, no matter what interests may be alarmed and band themselves against the innovator, let him go on undismayed, — he advances to certain victory.

WAR WITH FRANCE. — *J. C. Calhoun.*

The first thing that strikes me, sir, in casting my eyes to the future, is the utter impossibility that war, should there unfortunately be one, can have an honorable termination. The capacity of France to inflict injury upon us is ten times greater than ours to inflict injuries on her; while the cost of the war, in proportion to her means, would be in nearly the same proportion less than ours to our means. She has relatively a small commerce to be destroyed, while we have the largest in the world, in proportion to our capital and population. She may threaten and harass our coast, while her own is safe from assault. I do not hesitate to pronounce that a war with France will be among the greatest calamities, — greater than a war with England herself. The power of the latter to annoy us may be greater than that of the former; but so is ours, in turn, greater to annoy England than France. Nothing can be more destructive to our commerce and navigation than for England to be neutral while we are belligerent in a contest with such a country as France. The whole of our commercial marine, with our entire shipping, would pass almost instantly into the hands of England. With the exception of our public armed vessels, there would be scarcely a flag of ours afloat on the ocean. We grew rich by being neutral while England was belligerent. It was that which so suddenly built up the mighty fabric of our prosperity and greatness. Reverse the position: let England be neutral while we are belligerent, and the sources of our wealth and prosperity would be speedily exhausted.

In a just and necessary war, all these consequences ought to be fearlessly met. Though a friend to peace, when a proper occasion occurs I would be among the last to dread the consequences of war. I think the wealth and blood of a country are well poured out in maintaining a just, honorable, and necessary war; but, in such a war as that with which the country is now threatened, — a mere war of etiquette, — a war turning on a question so trivial as whether an explanation shall or shall not be given, — no, whether it has or has not been given (for that is the real point on which the controversy turns), — to put in jeopardy the lives and property of our citizens, and the liberty and institutions of our country, is worse than folly, — is madness. I say the liberty and institutions of the country. I hold them to be in imminent danger. Such has been the grasp of executive power, that we have not been able to resist its usurpations, even in a period of peace; and how much less shall we be able, with the vast increase of power and patronage which a war must confer on that department? In a sound condition of the country, with our institutions in their full vigor, and every department confined to its proper sphere, we would have nothing to fear from a war with France, or any other power; but our system is deeply diseased, and we may fear the worst in being involved in a war at such a juncture.

THE SURVIVORS OF THE REVOLUTION. — *E. Everett.*

LET us not forget the men who, when the conflict of counsel was over, stood forward in that of arms; yet let me not, by faintly endeavoring to sketch, do deep injustice to the story of their exploits. The efforts of a life would scarce suffice to paint out this picture in all its astonishing incidents, in all its mingled colors of sublimity and woe, of agony and triumph.

But the age of commemoration is at hand. The voice of our

fathers' blood begins to cry to us from beneath the soil which it moistened. Time is bringing forward, in their proper relief, the men and the deeds of that high-souled day. The generation of contemporary worthies is gone; the crowd of the unsignalized great and good disappears; and the leaders in war as well as council are seen, in Fancy's eye, to take their stations on the mount of remembrance.

They come from the embattled cliffs of Abraham; they start from the heaving sods of Bunker's Hill; they gather from the blazing lines of Saratoga and Yorktown, from the blood-dyed waters of the Brandywine, from the dreary snows of Valley Forge, and all the hard-fought fields of the war. With all their wounds and all their honors, they rise and plead with us for their brethren who survive, and bid us, if indeed we cherish the memory of those who bled in our cause, to show our gratitude, not by sounding words, but by stretching out the strong arm of the country's prosperity to help the veteran survivors gently down to their graves.

AGRICULTURE AND COMMERCE. — *J. S. Buckminster.*

No situation in life is so favorable to established habits of virtue, and to powerful sentiments of devotion, as a residence in the country, and rural occupations. I am not speaking of a condition of peasantry, of which in this country we know little, who are mere vassals of an absent lord, or the hired laborers of an intendant, and who are, therefore, interested in nothing but the regular receipt of their daily wages; but I refer to the honorable character of an owner of the soil, whose comforts, whose weight in the community, and whose very existence depend upon his personal labors, and the regular returns of abundance from the soil which he cultivates. No man, one would think, would feel so sensibly his immediate dependence upon God, as the husbandman. For all his peculiar blessings, he is invited to look immediately to the bounty of Heaven. No secondary cause stands between him and his Maker. To him are essential the regular succession of the seasons, and the timely fall of the rain, the genial warmth of the sun, the sure productiveness of the soil, and the certain operations of those laws of nature which must appear to him nothing less than the varied exertions of omnipresent energy. In the country, we seem to stand in the midst of the great theatre of God's power, and we feel an unusual proximity to our Creator. His blue and tranquil sky spreads itself over our heads, and we acknowledge the intrusion of no secondary agent in unfolding this vast expanse. Nothing but Omnipotence can work up the dark horrors of the tempest, dart the flashes of the lightning, and roll the long-resounding rumor of the thunder. The breeze wafts to his senses the odors of God's beneficence; the voice of God's power is heard in the rustling of the forest; and the varied forms of life, activity and pleasure, which he observes at every step in the fields, lead him irresistibly, one would think, to the source of being and beauty and joy. How auspicious such a life to the noble sentiments of devotion! Besides, the situation of the husbandman is peculiarly favorable, it should seem, to purity and simplicity of moral sentiment. He is brought acquainted, chiefly, with the real and native wants of mankind. Employed solely in bringing food out of the earth, he is not liable to be fascinated with the fictitious pleasures, the unnatural wants, the fashionable follies and tyrannical vices of more busy and splendid life.

Still more favorable to the religious character of the husbandman is the circumstance, that, from the nature of agricultural pursuits, they do not so completely engross the attention as other occupations. They leave much time for contemplation, for reading, and intellectual pleasures; and these are peculiarly grateful to the resident in the country. Especially does the institution of the Sabbath discover all its value to the tiller of the earth, whose fatigue it solaces, whose hard labors it interrupts, and who feels on that day the worth of his moral nature, which cannot be understood by the busy man, who considers the repose of this day as interfering with his hopes of gain, or professional employments. If, then, this institution is of any moral and religious value, it is to the country we must look for the continuance of that respect and observance which it merits. My friends, — those of you especially who retire annually into the country, — let these periodical retreats from business or dissipation bring you nearer to your God; let them restore the clearness of your judgment on the objects of human pursuits, invigorate your moral perceptions, exalt your sentiments, and regulate your habits of devotion; and if there be any virtue or simplicity remaining in rural life, let them never be impaired by the influence of your presence and example.

After what we have now said upon the virtuous and devotional tendency of a country life, it may, perhaps, be considered as inconsistent, or even paradoxical, to place our commercial character among our moral, much less our religious advantages. But let it be considered, whatever be the influence of traffic upon the personal worth of some of those who are engaged in it, its intrinsic value to the community, and its kind influence upon certain parts of the moral character, are not to be disputed. Hence I do not scruple to state it as one of our great national distinctions, which call for our grateful acknowledgments. Tell me not of Tyre, and Sidon, and Corinth, and Carthage. I know they were commercial and corrupt. But let it be remembered that they flourished long before the true principles of honorable trade were understood; before the introduction of Christianity had given any stability to those virtues of conscientious integrity, and strict fidelity in trusts, which are now indispensable to commercial prosperity. They have passed away, it is true; and so has Sparta, where no commerce was allowed; and Judea, though mostly agricultural, is known no more, except for its national ingratitude and corruption. Besides, when the choice of a nation lies, as, from the present state of the world, it appears long destined to lie, between a commercial and a military character, surely there can be little hesitation about the comparative influence of the peaceful activity of trade, though it may tend to enervate some of the energies of the human character, and that deplorable activity of a mere warlike nation, where plunder is the ruling passion of the great, and destruction the trade of the small; where every new conquest tends only to concentrate, in still fewer hands, the wealth of kingdoms, and to inspire the common people with an undistinguishing ferocity. Surely, we cannot hesitate whether to prefer that warlike state of a nation which poisons at once the sources and security of domestic happiness, — a state in which the lives as well as the virtues of mankind sink into objects of insignificant importance, — or that commercial situation of a people, which rouses and develops all the powers of all classes of the population, which gives a perpetual spring to industry, and which, by showing every man how completely he is dependent upon every other man, makes it his interest to promote the prosperity, to consult the happiness, and to maintain the peace, the health, and the security of the millions with whom he is connected. Surely, that state of a people cannot be unfavorable to virtue, which provides such facilities of intellectual communication between the remotest regions, so that not a bright idea can spring up in the brain of a foreign philosopher, but it darts, like lightning, across the Atlantic; not an improvement obtains in the condition of one society, but it is instantly propagated to every other. By this perpetual interchange of thought, and this active diffusion of understanding, the most favorable opportunities are afforded for the dissemination of useful knowledge, especially for the extension of that most precious of gifts, the gospel of Jesus. I need not add, that the wide intercourse we are keeping up with foreign nations ought to enlarge the sphere of our intelligence, liberalize our sentiments of mankind, polish the manners of the community, and introduce courteousness and urbanity of deportment. Merchants! if I may be permitted to suggest to you any considerations on the value of your order to the community, I would say, that upon your personal character depends much of these favorable influences of commerce. I would beg you to beware of an engrossing love of profit, which invariably narrows the capacity, and debases the noblest tendencies of the human character. I would persuade you to cultivate habits of mental activity, to indulge enlarged views of your connection with mankind, to consider yourselves as forming part of the vast chain of mutual supports and dependencies, by which the activity, the improvement and the pleasure of the inhabitants of every part of the world are secured and promoted. Above all, forget not that you are instruments in the hands of Providence, by which he diffuses his blessings, and promotes his grand purposes in the cultivation, the civilization, and thus the moral and religious advancement, of this wide creation. God grant that you may never feel the remorse of having deliberately contributed to the introduction of a new vice into the community, or to the corruption of an old or established principle; of having aided the tyranny of a worthless fashion, or assisted the gradual encroachments of selfishness, vanity, pomp, and slavish imitation, on the freedom and dignity of social life!

THE PRESERVATION OF THE UNION.—*L. Cass.*

I MAY well appeal to those who find in the constitution or out of the constitution this power to control the territories, whether it is a power that ought to be exercised under existing circumstances. Here is one half of a great country which believes, with a unanimity perhaps without a parallel in grave national questions, that the constitution has delegated to Congress no such power whatever. And there is a large portion of the other half which entertains similar views; while of those who see in the constitution sufficient grounds for legislative action, there are many who admit,—indeed, probably, there are few who deny,—that the question is not free from serious doubts.

Besides the want of constitutional power, there are at least fourteen states of this Union which see in this measure a direct attack upon their rights, and a disregard of their feelings and interests, as injurious in itself as it is offensive to their pride of character, and incompatible with the existence of those bonds of amity which are stronger than constitutional ties to hold us together. No man can shut his eyes to the excitement which prevails there, and which is borne to us by the press in countless articles coming from legislative proceedings, from popular assemblies, and from all the sources whence public opinion is derived, and be insensible to the evil day that is upon us. I believe this Union will survive all the dangers with which it may be menaced, however trying the circumstances in which it may be placed. I believe it is not destined to perish till long after it shall have fulfilled the great mission confided to it, of example and encouragement to the nations of the earth who are struggling with the despotism of centuries, and groping their way in a darkness once impenetrable, but where the light of knowledge and freedom is beginning to disperse the gloom. But to maintain this proud position, this integrity of political existence, on which so much for us and for the world depends, we must carefully avoid those sectional questions so much and so forcibly deprecated by the father of his country, and, cultivating a spirit of mutual regard, adding to the considerations of interest which hold us together the higher motives of affection and of affinity of views and of sympathies. Sad will be the day when the first drop of blood is shed in the preservation of this Union. That day need never come, and never will come, if the same spirit of compromise and concession by each to the feelings of all, which animated our fathers, continues to animate us and our children. But if powers offensive to one portion of the country, and of doubtful obligation, to say the least of it, are to be exercised by another, and under circumstances of peculiar excitement, this confederation may be rent in twain, leaving another example of that judicial blindness with which God, in his providence, sometimes visits the sins of nations.

A REPUBLIC THE STRONGEST GOVERNMENT. — *T. Jefferson.*

During the throes and convulsions of the ancient world, — during the agonizing spasms of infuriated man, seeking, through blood and slaughter, his long-lost liberty, — it was not wonderful that the agitation of the billows should reach even this distant and peaceful shore; that this should be more felt and feared by some, and less by others, and should divide opinions as to measures of safety. But every difference of opinion is not a difference of principle. We have called by different names brethren of the same principle. We are all Republicans; we are all Federalists.

If there be any among us who would wish to dissolve this Union, or to change its republican form, let them stand, undisturbed, as monuments of the safety with which error of opinion may be tolerated where reason is left free to combat it. I know, indeed, that some honest men fear a republican government cannot be strong, — that this government is not strong enough. But would the honest patriot, in the full tide of successful experiment, abandon a government which has so far kept us free and firm, on the theoretic and visionary fear that this government, the world's best hope, may, by possibility, want energy to preserve itself? I trust not. I believe this, on the contrary, the strongest government on earth. I believe it the only one where every man, at the call of the law, would fly to the standard of the law, and would meet invasions of the public order, as his own personal concern. Sometimes it is said that man cannot be trusted with the government of himself. Can he, then, be trusted with the government of others? Or have we found angels, in the form of kings, to govern him? Let history answer this question.

Let us, then, with courage and confidence, pursue our own federal and republican principles, — our attachment to union and representative government. Kindly separated, by nature and a wide ocean, from the exterminating havoc of one quarter of the globe, — too high-minded to endure the degradations of the others, — possessing a chosen country, with room enough for our descendants to the thousandth and thousandth generation, — entertaining a due sense of our equal right to the use of our own faculties, to the acquisitions of our own industry, to honor and confidence from our fellow-citizens, resulting not from birth, but from our actions, and their sense of them, — enlightened by a benign religion, professed, indeed, and practised in various forms, yet all of them inculcating honesty, truth, temperance, gratitude, and the love of man, — acknowledging and adoring an overruling Providence, which, by all its dispensations, proves that it delights in the happiness of man here, and his greater happiness hereafter; with all these blessings, what more is necessary, to make us a happy and prosperous people?

Still one thing more, fellow-citizens: a wise and frugal government, which shall restrain men from injuring one another, shall leave them otherwise free to regulate their own pursuits of industry and improvement, and shall not take from the mouth of labor the bread it has earned. This is the sum of good government; and this is necessary to close the circle of our felicities.

THE INFLUENCE OF FREE INSTITUTIONS ENNOBLING. — *G. C. Verplanck.*

It has been said by shrewd though unfriendly observers, that in America the practical and the profitable swallow up every other thought. There, say they, fancy withers, art languishes, taste expires; there the mind looks only to the material and the mechanical, and loses its capacity for the ideal and the abstract. But while the intelligent American citizen is surrounded by the strongest temptations to devote himself solely to selfish pursuits, he is at the same time everywhere invited to conform his own spirit to that of our liberal institutions, and instructed to uplift his mind to the consideration of large principles, and to regard himself as being but a small part of the vast whole which claims his best affections.

With such a choice before him, pitiable indeed is the lot of him who turns from the nobler and manlier side, to think, to live, and to drudge, for himself alone. He cuts himself off from the best delights of the heart, its endearing charities and its elevating sympathies. He paralyzes his own intellect by suffering it to become half dead through inaction, and that in its nobler parts. The mighty ladder of thought and reason, reaching from the visible to the invisible, — from the crude knowledge gained through the senses to the sublimest inferences of the pure reason, — from the earth to the very footstool of God's own throne, — is before him, and invites his ascent. But he bends his eyes obstinately downwards upon the glittering ores at his feet, until he loses the wish or the hope for anything better.

That such grovelling materiality, such mean selfishness, is not the necessary, nor the constant, no, nor the frequent result of our ardent industry in the affairs of life, let the discoveries of Franklin, and the magnificent far-drawn speculations of Edwards, — let the grand philosophy and the poetic thought, flashing quick and thick through the cloudy atmosphere of political discussion in our senate-house, — let the open-handed charity, the more than princely munificence, the untiring personal labors of benevolence, exhibited by our most devoted and successful men of business, bear splendid testimony.

LIBERTY. — *E. P. Whipple.*

To the Anglo-Saxon mind, liberty is not apt to be the enthusiast's mountain nymph, with cheeks wet with morning dew, and clear eyes that mirror the heavens; but rather is she an old dowager lady, fatly invested in commerce and manufactures, and peevishly fearful that enthusiasm will reduce her establishment, and panics cut off her dividends. Now, the moment property becomes timid, agrarianism becomes bold; and the industry which liberty has created liberty must animate, or it will be plundered by the impudent and rapacious idleness its slavish fears incite.

Our political institutions, again, are but the body of which liberty is the soul; their preservation depends on their being continually inspired by the light and heat of the sentiment and idea whence they sprung; and when we timorously suspend, according to the latest political fashion, the truest and dearest maxims of our freedom at the call of expediency or threat of passion, — when we convert politics into a mere game of interests, unhallowed by a single great and unselfish principle, — we may be sure that our worst passions are busy "forging our fetters;" that we are proposing all those intricate problems which red republicanism so swiftly solves, and giving manifest destiny pertinent hints to shout new anthems of atheism over victorious rapine.

The liberty which our fathers planted, and for which they sturdily contended, and under which they grandly conquered, is a rational and temperate but brave and unyielding freedom, the august mother of institutions, the hardy nurse of enterprise, the sworn ally of justice and order; a liberty that lifts her awful and rebuking face equally upon the cowards who would sell, and the braggarts who would pervert, her precious gifts of rights and obligations. And this liberty we are solemnly bound at all hazards to protect, at any sacrifice to preserve, and by all just means to extend, against the unbridled excesses of that ugly and brazen hag, originally scorned and detested by those who unwisely gave her infancy a home, but which now, in her enormous growth and favored deformity, reels, with blood-shot eyes, and dishevelled tresses, and words of unshamed slavishness, into halls where Liberty should sit enthroned!

PUBLIC VIRTUE. — *H. Clay.*

I HOPE, that in all that relates to personal firmness, all that concerns a just appreciation of the insignificance of human life, — whatever may be attempted to threaten or alarm a soul not easily swayed by opposition, or awed or intimidated by menace, — a stout heart and a steady eye, that can survey, unmoved and undaunted, any mere personal perils that assail this poor, transient, perishing frame, I may, without disparagement, compare with other men. But there is a sort of courage, which, I frankly confess it, I do not possess, — a boldness to which I dare not aspire, a valor which I cannot covet. I cannot lay myself down in the way of the welfare and happiness of my country. That I cannot, I have not the courage to do. I cannot interpose the power with which I may be invested — a power conferred, not for my personal benefit, nor for my aggrandizement, but for my country's good — to check her onward march to greatness and glory. I have not courage enough, I am too cowardly, for that. I would not, I dare not, in the exercise of such a trust, lie down, and place my body across the path that leads my country to prosperity and happiness. This is a sort of courage widely different from that which a man may display in his private conduct and personal relations. Personal or private courage is totally distinct from that higher and nobler courage which prompts the patriot to offer himself a voluntary sacrifice to his country's good. Apprehensions of the imputation of the want of firmness sometimes impel us to perform rash and inconsiderate acts. It is the greatest courage to be able to bear the imputation of the want of courage. But pride, vanity, egotism, so unamiable and offensive in private life, are vices which partake of the character of crimes, in the conduct of public affairs. The unfortunate victim of these passions cannot see beyond the little, petty, contemptible circle of his own personal interests. All his thoughts are withdrawn from his country, and concentrated on his consistency, his firmness, himself. The high, the exalted, the sublime emotions of a patriotism which, soaring toward heaven, rises far above all mean, low, or selfish things, and is absorbed by one soul-transporting thought of the good and the glory of one's country, are never felt in his impenetrable bosom. That patriotism which, catching its inspirations from the immortal God, and leaving at an immeasurable distance below all lesser, grovelling, personal interests and feelings, animates and prompts to deeds of self-sacrifice, of valor, of devotion, and of death itself, — that is public virtue; that is the noblest, the sublimest, of all public virtues!

HOWARD, THE PHILANTHROPIST. — *F. Wayland.*

It is not in the field of patriotism alone that deeds have been achieved to which history has awarded the palm of moral sublimity. There have lived men in whom the name of patriot has been merged in that of philanthropist; who, looking with an eye of compassion over the face of the earth, have felt for the miseries of our race, and have put forth their calm might to wipe off one blot from the marred and stained escutcheon of human nature, to strike off one form of suffering from the catalogue of human woe. Such a man was Howard. Surveying our world like a spirit of the blessed, he beheld the misery of the captive, he heard the groaning of the prisoner. His determination was fixed. He resolved, single-handed, to gauge and to measure one form of unpitied, unheeded wretchedness, and, bringing it out to the sunshine of public observation, to work its utter extermination. And he well knew what this undertaking would cost him. He knew what he had to hazard from the infection of dungeons, to endure from the fatigues of inhospitable travel, and to brook from the insolence of legalized oppression. He knew that he was devoting himself to the altar of philanthropy; and he willingly devoted himself. He had marked out his destiny, and he hastened forward to its accomplishment, with an intensity "which the nature of the human mind forbade to be more, and the character of the individual forbade to be less." Thus he commenced a new era in the history of benevolence. And hence the name of Howard will be associated with all that is sublime in mercy, until the final consummation of all things.

THE LAND OF OUR FATHERS. — *E. Everett.*

WHAT American does not feel proud that he is descended from the countrymen of Bacon, of Newton, and of Locke? Who does not know, that while every pulse of civil liberty in the heart of the British empire beat warm and full in the bosom of our fathers, the sobriety, the firmness and the dignity, with which the cause of free principles struggled into existence here, constantly found encouragement and countenance from the sons of liberty there? Who does not remember that when the Pilgrims went over the sea, the prayers of the faithful British confessors, in all the quarters of their dispersion, went over with them, while their aching eyes were strained, till the star of hope should go up in the western skies? And who will ever forget that in that eventful struggle which severed this mighty empire from the British crown, there was not heard, throughout our continent in arms, a voice which spoke louder for the rights of America than that of Burke, or of Chatham, within the walls of the British Parliament, and at the foot of the British throne? No! for myself I can truly say, that after my native land, I feel a tenderness and a reverence for that of my fathers. The pride I take in my own country makes me respect that from which we are sprung.

In touching the soil of England, I seem to return like a descendant to the old family seat, — to come back to the abode of an aged, the tomb of a departed parent. I acknowledge this great consanguinity of nations. The sound of my native language, beyond the sea, is a music to my ear beyond the richest strains of Tuscan softness, or Castilian majesty. I am not yet in a land of strangers, while surrounded by the manners, the habits, the forms in which I have been brought up. I wander delighted through a thousand scenes which the historians, the poets, have made familiar to us, — of which the names are interwoven with our earliest associations. I tread with reverence the spot where I can retrace the footsteps of our suffering fathers; the pleasant land of their birth has a claim on my heart. It seems to me a classic, yea, a holy land, rich in the memories of the great and good; the martyrs of liberty, the exiled heralds of truth; and richer, as the parent of this land of promise in the west.

I am not, I need not say I am not, the panegyrist of England. I am not dazzled by her riches, nor awed by her power. The sceptre, the mitre and the coronet, stars, garters and blue ribbons, seem to me poor things for great men to contend for. Nor is my admiration awakened by her armies, mustered for the battles of Europe; her navies, overshadowing the ocean; nor her empire, grasping the furthest East. It is these, and the price of guilt and blood by which they are maintained, which are the cause why no friend of liberty can salute her with undivided affections. But it is the refuge of free principles, though often persecuted; the school of religious liberty, the more precious for the struggles to which it has been called; the tomb of those who have reflected honor on all who speak the English tongue; it is the birthplace of our fathers, the home of the Pilgrims; — it is these which I love and venerate in England. I should feel ashamed of an enthusiasm for Italy and Greece, did I not also feel it for a land like this. In an American it would seem to me degenerate and ungrateful to hang with passion upon the traces of Homer and Virgil, and follow without emotion the nearer and plainer footsteps of Shakspeare and Milton; and I should think him cold in his love for his native land, who felt no melting in his heart for that other native land, which holds the ashes of his forefathers.

THE DIGNITY OF HUMAN NATURE. — *O. Dewey.*

You are a man; you are a rational and religious being; you are an immortal creature. Yes, a glad and glorious existence is yours: your eye is opened to the lovely and majestic vision of nature; the paths of knowledge are around you, and they stretch onward to eternity; and, most of all, the glory of the infinite God, the all-perfect, all-wise, and all-beautiful, is unfolded to you. What, now, compared with this, is a little worldly renown? The treasures of infinity and of eternity are heaped upon thy laboring thought; — can that thought be deeply occupied with questions of mortal prudence? It is as if a man were enriched by some generous benefactor almost beyond measure, and should find nothing else to do but vex himself and complain, because another man was made a few thousands richer.

Where, unreasonable complainer, dost thou stand, and what is around thee? The world spreads before thee its sublime mysteries, where the thoughts of sages lose themselves in wonder; the ocean lifts up its eternal anthems to thine ear; the golden sun lights thy path; the wide heavens stretch themselves above thee, and worlds rise upon worlds, and systems beyond systems, to infinity; and dost thou stand in the centre of all this, to complain of thy lot and place? Pupil of that infinite teaching, — minister at nature's great altar, — child of heaven's favor, — ennobled being, — redeemed creature, — must thou pine in sullen and envious melancholy, amidst the plenitude of the whole creation?

In that thou art a man, thou art infinitely exalted above what any man can be, in that he is praised. I would rather be the humblest man in the world, than barely be thought greater than the greatest. The beggar is greater, as a man, than is the man, merely as a king. Not one of the crowds that listened to the eloquence of Demosthenes and Cicero, not one who has bent with admiration over the pages of Homer and Shakspeare, not one who followed in the train of Cæsar or of Napoleon, would part with the humblest power of thought, for all the fame that is echoing over the world and through the ages.

THE FIRST BATTLE-GROUND OF THE REVOLUTION. — *R. Choate.*

THAT was a glorious morning, the 19th of April, 1775; and wherein, I would ask, consisted the specific, transcendent glories of that day? Wherein lies that strange charm that belongs to everything connected with this place, its incidents and details? Why is it that our hearts grow liquid, and that we can pour them out like water, when we listen again to that old story, older than the words of our mothers' love, needing none of that brilliant genius which had that day touched their ears, to invest them with power which should never die?

Why is it so pleasant to come up here from the miserable strifes and bickerings of every-day life, to dwell and worship for a short space of time in such charmed presence as this? What is it that makes the specific, transcendent glory of the day? It is because it was an event so rare, so strange, so ominous of good or evil to future generations of man. It was from these instruments, and from these flags, borne by these trembling hands, — it was that essence, so subtile, so rare, so extensive, so mysterious, — that free and that stirring spirit, the sentiment of American nationality, which was first breathed into the life of this people, and made to pour itself through and about the body of the people, and which shall last until the heavens be no more.

Let, then, the events of which we are reminded by these scenes and these men mark the strong birth-love of the American people. On that day, within the space of twelve hours, the old colonial party passed away, like a scroll. The veil of the first temple was that day rent from top to bottom. That day, American liberty was then and there born. Our aged and revered friends of Concord, and Lexington, and Acton, of Carlisle, Sudbury and the surrounding towns, went into that battle British colonists; the baptism of fire was laid upon their charmed brows, and they rose from their knees American citizens! The flag of Massachusetts, the pine-tree flag, that old flag, was carried into battle in the morning; and if the survivor who rolled it up that night had noticed it, he would have seen, gleaming through a blaze of light, on one side, the pine-tree banner, and, on the other, the glorious stars and stripes!

DEDICATION OF THE CEMETERY AT MOUNT AUBURN. — *J. Story.*

Our cemeteries, rightly selected and properly arranged, may be made subservient to some of the highest purposes of religion and human duty. They may preach lessons to which none may refuse to listen, and which all that live must hear. Truths may be there felt and taught, in the silence of our own meditations, more persuasive and more enduring than ever flowed from human lips. The grave hath a voice of eloquence, — nay, of superhuman eloquence, — which speaks at once to the thoughtlessness of the rash, and the devotion of the good; which addresses all times, and all ages, and all sexes; which tells of wisdom to the wise, and of comfort to the afflicted; which warns us of our follies and our dangers; which whispers to us in accents of peace, and alarms us in tones of terror; which steals with a healing balm into the stricken heart, and lifts up and supports the broken spirit; which awakens a new enthusiasm for virtue, and disciplines us for its severer trials and duties; which calls up the images of the illustrious dead, with an animating presence for our example and glory; and which demands of us, as men, as patriots, as Christians, as immortals, that the powers given by God should be devoted to his service, and the minds created by his love should return to him with larger capacities for virtuous enjoyment, and with more spiritual and intellectual brightness.

A rural cemetery seems to combine in itself all the advantages which can be proposed to gratify human feelings, or tranquillize human fears; to secure the best religious influences, and to cherish all those associations which cast a cheerful light over the darkness of the grave.

And what spot can be more appropriate than this, for such a purpose? Nature seems to point it out with significant energy, as the favorite retirement for the dead. There are around us all the varied features of her beauty and grandeur, — the forest-crowned height, the abrupt acclivity, the sheltered valley, the deep glen, the grassy glade, and the silent grove. Here are the lofty oak, the beech, that "wreathes its old fantastic roots so high," the rustling pine, and the drooping willow; the tree that sheds its pale leaves with every autumn, a fit emblem of our own transitory bloom, and the evergreen, with its perennial shoots, instructing us that "the wintry blast of death kills not the buds of virtue." Here is the thick shrubbery to protect and conceal the new-made grave; and there is the wild-flower creeping along the narrow path, and planting its seeds in the upturned earth. All around us there breathes a solemn calm, as if we were in the bosom of a wilderness, broken only by the breeze as it murmurs through the tops of the forest, or by the notes of the warbler pouring forth his matin or his evening song.

Ascend but a few steps, and what a change of scenery to surprise and delight us! We seem, as it were in an instant, to pass from the confines of death to the bright and balmy regions of life! Below us flows the winding Charles, with its rippling current, like the stream of time hastening to the ocean of eternity! In the distance, the city — at once the object of our admiration and our love — rears its proud eminences, its glittering spires, its lofty towers, its graceful mansions, its curling smoke, its crowded haunts of business and pleasure, which speak to the eye, and yet leave a noiseless loneliness on the ear. Again we turn, and the walls of our venerable university rise before us, with many a recollection of happy days passed there in the interchange of study and friendship, and many a grateful thought of the affluence of its learning, which has adorned and nourished the literature of our country. Again we turn, and the cultivated farm, the neat cottage, the village church, the sparkling lake, the rich valley, and the distant hills, are before us through opening vistas; and we breathe amidst the fresh and varied labors of man.

There is, therefore, within our reach, every variety of natural and artificial scenery, which is fitted to awaken emotions of the highest and most affecting character. We stand, as it were, upon the borders of two worlds; and, as the mood of our minds may be, we may gather lessons of profound wisdom by contrasting the one with the other, or indulge in the dreams of hope and ambition, or solace our hearts by melancholy meditations.

Within the flight of one half-century, how many of the great, the good, and the wise, will be gathered here! How many in the loveliness of infancy, the beauty of youth, the vigor of manhood, and the maturity of age, will lie down here, and dwell in the bosom of their mother earth! The rich and the poor, the gay and the wretched, the favorites of thousands and the forsaken of the world, the stranger in his solitary grave and the patriarch surrounded by the kindred of a long lineage! How many will here bury their brightest hopes, or blasted expectations! How many bitter tears will here be shed! How many agonizing sighs will here be heaved! How many trembling feet will cross the pathways, and, returning, leave behind them the dearest objects of their reverence or their love!

And if this were all, sad, indeed, and funereal, would be our thoughts; gloomy, indeed, would be these shades, and desolate these prospects. But, thanks be to God, the evils which he permits have their attendant mercies, and are blessings in disguise. The bruised reed will not be laid utterly prostrate. The wounded heart will not always bleed. The voice of consolation will spring up in the midst of the silence of these regions of death. The mourner will revisit these shades with a secret, though melancholy pleasure. The hand of friendship will delight to cherish the flowers and the shrubs that fringe the lowly grave or the sculptured monument. The earliest beams of the morning will play upon these summits with a refreshing cheerfulness, and the lingering tints of evening hover on them with a tranquillizing glow. Spring will invite thither the footsteps of the young by its opening foliage, and autumn detain the contemplative by its latest bloom. The votary of learning and science will here learn to elevate his genius by the holiest studies. The devout will here offer up the silent tribute of pity, or the prayer of gratitude. The rivalries of the world will here drop from the heart; the spirit of forgiveness will gather new impulses; the selfishness of avarice will be checked; the restlessness of ambition will be rebuked; vanity will let fall its plumes; and pride, as it sees "what shadows we are, and what shadows we pursue," will acknowledge the value of virtue as far, immeasurably far, beyond that of fame.

But that which will be ever present, pervading these shades like the noon-day sun, and shedding cheerfulness around, is the consciousness, the irrepressible consciousness, amidst all these lessons of human mortality, of the higher truth, that we are beings, not of time, but of eternity; "that this corruptible must put on incorruption, and this mortal must put on immortality;" that this is but the threshold and starting point of an existence, compared with whose duration the ocean is but as a drop, nay, the whole creation an evanescent quality.

Let us banish, then, the thought that this is to be the abode of a gloom which will haunt the imagination by its terrors, or chill the heart by its solitude. Let us cultivate feelings and sentiments more worthy of ourselves, and more worthy of Christianity. Here let us erect the memorials of our love, and our gratitude, and our glory. Here let the brave repose, who have died in the cause of their country. Here let the statesman rest, who has achieved the victories of peace, not less renowned than war. Here let genius find a home, that has sung immortal strains, or has instructed with still diviner eloquence. Here let learning and science, the votaries of inventive art, and the teacher of the philosophy of nature, come. Here let youth and beauty, blighted by premature decay, drop, like tender blossoms, into the virgin earth; and here let age retire, ripened for the harvest. Above all, here let the benefactors of mankind, the good, the merciful, the meek, the pure in heart, be congregated, — for to them belongs an undying praise!

THE CONSTITUTION NOT AN EXPERIMENT. — *H. S. Legaré.*

We are told that our constitution — the constitution of the United States — is a mere experiment. Sir, I deny it utterly; and he that says so shows me that he has either not studied at all, or studied to very little purpose, the history and genius of our institutions. The great cause of their prosperous results — a cause which every one of the many attempts since vainly made to imitate them, on this continent or in Europe, only demonstrates the more clearly — is precisely the contrary. It is because our fathers made no experiments, and had no experiments to make, that their work has stood. They were forced, by a violation of their historical, hereditary rights under the old common law of their race, to dissolve the connection with the mother country. But the whole constitution of society in the states, the great body and bulk of their public law, with all its maxims and principles, — in short, all that is republican in our institutions, — remained, after the Revolution, and remains *now*, with some very subordinate modifications, what it was from the beginning.

Our written constitutions do nothing but consecrate and fortify the "plain rules of ancient liberty," handed down with Magna Charta, from the earliest history of our race. It is not a piece of paper, sir, it is not a few abstractions engrossed on parchment, that make free governments. No, sir; the law of liberty must be inscribed on the heart of the citizen; THE WORD, if I may use the expression without irreverence, MUST BECOME FLESH. You must have a whole people trained, disciplined, bred, — yea, and born, — as our fathers were, to institutions like ours. Before the colonies existed, the petition of rights, that Magna Charta of a more enlightened age, had been presented, in 1628, by Lord Coke and his immortal compeers. Our founders brought it with them, and we have not gone one step beyond them. They brought these maxims of civil liberty, not in their libraries, but in their souls; not as philosophical prattle, not as barren generalities, but as rules of conduct; as a symbol of public duty and private right, to be adhered to with religious fidelity; and the very first pilgrim that set his foot upon the rock of Plymouth stepped forth a LIVING CONSTITUTION, armed at all points to defend and to perpetuate the liberty to which he had devoted his whole being.

MILITARY QUALIFICATIONS DISTINCT FROM CIVIL.—*J. Sergeant.*

It has been maintained that the genius which constitutes a great military man is a very high quality, and may be equally useful in the cabinet and in the field; that it has a sort of universality equally applicable to all affairs. We have seen, undoubtedly, instances of a rare and wonderful combination of civil and military qualifications, both of the highest order. That the greatest civil qualifications may be found united with the highest military talents, is what no one will deny who thinks of Washington. But that such a combination is rare and extraordinary, the fame of Washington sufficiently attests. If it were common, why was *he* so illustrious?

I would ask, what did Cromwell, with all his military genius, do for England? He overthrew the monarchy, and he established dictatorial power in his own person. And what happened next? Another soldier overthrew the dictatorship, and restored the monarchy. The sword effected both. Cromwell made one revolution; and Monk another. And what did the people of England gain by it? Nothing. Absolutely nothing! The rights and liberties of Englishmen, as they now exist, were settled and established at the revolution in 1688. Now, mark the difference! By whom was that revolution begun and conducted? Was it by soldiers? by military genius? by the sword? No! It was the work of statesmen and of eminent lawyers,—men never distinguished for military exploits. The faculty — the dormant faculty — may have existed. That is what no one can affirm or deny. But it would have been thought an absurd and extravagant thing to propose, in reliance upon this possible dormant faculty, that one of those eminent statesmen and lawyers should be sent, instead of the Duke of Marlborough, to command the English forces on the continent!

Who achieved the freedom and the independence of this our own country? Washington effected much in the field; but where were the Franklins, the Adamses, the Hancocks, the Jeffersons, and the Lees, — the band of sages and patriots, whose memory we revere? They were assembled in council. The *heart* of the Revolution beat in the hall of Congress. *There* was the power which, beginning with appeals to the king and to the British nation, at length made an irresistible appeal to the world, and consummated the Revolution by the declaration of independence, which Washington established with their authority, and, bearing their commission, supported by arms. And what has this band of patriots, of sages, and of statesmen, given to us? Not what Cæsar gave to Rome; not what Cromwell gave to England, or Napoleon to France: they established for us the great principles of civil, political and religious liberty, upon the strong foundations on which they have hitherto stood. There may have been military capacity in Congress; but can any one deny that it is to the wisdom of the sages, Washington being one, we are indebted for the signal blessings we enjoy?

REMEMBRANCE OF THE GOOD. — *H. Humphrey.*

Why is it that the names of Howard, and Thornton, and Clarkson, and Wilberforce, will be held in everlasting remembrance? Is it not chiefly on account of their goodness, their Christian philanthropy, the overflowing and inexhaustible benevolence of their great minds? Such men feel that they were not born for themselves, nor for the narrow circle of their kindred and acquaintances, but for the world and for posterity. They delight in doing good on a great scale. Their talents, their property, their time, their knowledge and experience and influence, they hold in constant requisition for the benefit of the poor, the oppressed, and the perishing. You may trace them along the whole pathway of life, by the blessings which they scatter far and wide. They may be likened to yon noble river, which carries gladness and fertility, from state to state, through all the length of that rejoicing valley, which it was made to bless ; — or to those summer showers which pour gladness and plenty over all the regions that they visit, till they melt away into the glorious effulgence of the setting sun.

Such a man was Howard, the prisoner's friend. Christian philanthropy was the element in which he lived and moved, and out of which life would have been intolerable. It was to him that kings listened with astonishment, as if doubtful from what world of pure disinterestedness he had come. To him despair opened her dungeons, and plague and pestilence could summon no terrors to arrest his investigations. In his presence, crime, though girt with the iron panoply of desperation, stood amazed and rebuked. With him, home was nothing, country was nothing, health was nothing, life was nothing. His first and last question was, " What is the utmost that I can do for degraded, depraved, bleeding humanity, in all her prison-houses ? " And what wonders did he accomplish ! What astonishing changes in the whole system of prison discipline may be traced back to his disclosures and suggestions, and how many millions yet to be born will rise up and call him blessed ! Away, all ye Cæsars and Napoleons, to your own dark and frightful domains of slaughter and misery ! Ye can no more endure the light of such a godlike presence than the eye, already inflamed to torture by dissipation, can look the sun in the face at noonday !

INFLUENCE OF AMERICA UPON MANKIND. — *G. C. Verplanck.*

The study of the history of most other nations fills the mind with sentiments not unlike those which the American traveller feels on entering the venerable and lofty cathedral of some proud old city of Europe. Its solemn grandeur, its vastness, its obscurity, strike awe to his heart. From the richly-painted windows, filled with sacred emblems, and strange antique forms, a dim religious light falls around. A thousand recollections of romance, and poetry, and legendary story, come thronging in upon him. He is surrounded by the tombs of the mighty dead, rich with the labors of ancient art, and emblazoned with the pomp of heraldry.

What names does he read upon them? Those of princes and nobles who are now remembered only for their vices; and of sovereigns at whose death no tears were shed, and whose memories lived not an hour in the affections of their people. There, too, he sees other names, long familiar to him for their guilty or ambiguous fame. There rest the blood-stained soldier of fortune; the orator, who was ever the ready apologist of tyranny; great scholars, who were the pensioned flatterers of power; and poets, who profaned the high gift of genius to pamper the vices of a corrupted court.

Our own history, on the contrary, like that poetical temple of fame reared by the imagination of Chaucer, and decorated by the taste of Pope, is almost exclusively dedicated to the memory of the truly great. Or, rather, like the Pantheon of Rome, it stands in calm and severe beauty amid the ruins of ancient magnificence and "the toys of modern state." Within, no idle ornament encumbers its bold simplicity. The pure light of heaven enters from above, and sheds an equal and serene radiance around. As the eye wanders about its extent, it beholds the unadorned monuments of brave and good men who have greatly bled or toiled for their country, or it rests on votive tablets inscribed with the names of the best benefactors of mankind.

Doubtless this is a subject upon which we may be justly proud. But there is another consideration, which, if it did not naturally arise of itself, would be pressed upon us by the taunts of European criticism.

What has this nation done to repay the world for the benefits we have received from others? We have been repeatedly told, and sometimes, too, in a tone of affected impartiality, that the highest praise which can fairly be given to the American mind is that of possessing an enlightened selfishness; that if the philosophy and talents of this country, with all their effects, were forever swept into oblivion, the loss would be felt only by ourselves; and that if to the accuracy of this general charge the labors of Franklin present an illustrious, it is still but a solitary, exception.

The answer may be given confidently and triumphantly. Without abandoning the fame of our eminent men, whom Europe has been slow and reluctant to honor, we would reply, that the intellectual power of this people has exerted itself in conformity to the general system of our institutions and manners, and, therefore, that for the proof of its existence, and the measure of its force, we must look not so much to the works of prominent individuals, as to the great aggregate results; and if Europe has hitherto been wilfully blind to the value of our example and the exploits of our sagacity, courage, invention and freedom, the blame must rest with her, and not with America.

Is it nothing for the universal good of mankind to have carried into successful operation a system of self-government uniting personal liberty, freedom of opinion, and equality of rights, with national power and dignity such as had before existed only in the Utopian dreams of philosophers? Is it nothing, in moral science, to have anticipated, in sober reality, numerous plans of reform in civil and criminal jurisprudence, which are but now received as plausible theories by the politicians and economists of Europe? Is it nothing to have been able to call forth on every emergency, either in war or peace, a body of talents always equal to the difficulty? Is it nothing to have, in less than half a century, exceedingly improved the sciences of political economy, of law, and of medicine, with all their auxiliary branches; to have enriched human knowledge by the accumulation of a great mass of useful fact and observations, and to have augmented the power and the comforts of civilized man by miracles of mechanical invention? Is it nothing to have given the world examples of disinterested patriotism, of political wisdom, of public virtue; of learning, eloquence and valor, never exerted save for some praiseworthy end?

It is sufficient to have briefly suggested these considerations; every mind would anticipate me in filling up the details.

No, land of liberty! thy children have no cause to blush for thee. What though the arts have reared few monuments among us, and scarce a trace of the Muse's footstep is found in the paths of our forests, or along the banks of our rivers, — yet our soil has been consecrated by the blood of heroes, and by great and holy deeds of peace! Its wide extent has become one vast temple and hallowed asylum, sanctified by the prayers and blessings of the persecuted of every sect, and the wretched of all nations.

CENTENNIAL BIRTHDAY OF WASHINGTON. — *D. Webster.*

We are met to testify our regard for him whose name is intimately blended with whatever belongs most essentially to the prosperity, the liberty, the free institutions and the renown, of our country. That name was of power to rally a nation in the hour of thick-thronging public disasters and calamities; that name shone, amid the storm of war, a beacon-light to cheer and guide the country's friends; it flamed, too, like a meteor, to repel her foes. That name, in the days of peace, was a loadstone, attracting to itself a whole people's confidence, a whole people's love, and the whole world's respect; that name, descending with all time, spreading over the whole earth, and uttered in all the languages belonging to the tribes and races of men, will forever be pronounced with affectionate gratitude by every one in whose breast there shall arise an aspiration for human rights and human liberty.

A true friend of his country loves her friends and benefactors, and thinks it no degradation to commend and commemorate them. The voluntary outpouring of the public feeling, made to-day, from the north to the south, and from the east to the west, proves this sentiment to be both just and natural. In the cities and in the villages, in the public temples and in the family circles, among all ages and sexes, gladdened voices, to-day, bespeak grateful hearts, and a freshened recollection of the virtues of the Father of his

Country. And it will be so, in all time to come, so long as public virtue is itself an object of regard. The ingenuous youth of America will hold up to themselves the bright model of Washington's example, and study to be what they behold; they will contemplate his character till all its virtues spread out and display themselves to their delighted vision; as the earliest astronomers, the shepherds on the plains of Babylon, gazed at the stars till they saw them form into clusters and constellations, overpowering at length the eyes of the beholders with the united blaze of a thousand lights.

We are at the point of a century from the birth of Washington; and what a century it has been! During its course, the human mind has seemed to proceed with a sort of geometric velocity, accomplishing, for human intelligence and human freedom, more than had been done in fives or tens of centuries preceding. Washington stands at the commencement of a new era, as well as at the head of the new world. A century from the birth of Washington has changed the world. The country of Washington has been the theatre on which a great part of that change has been wrought, and Washington himself a principal agent by which it has been accomplished. His age and his country are equally full of wonders; and of both he is the chief.

If the prediction of the poet, uttered a few years before his birth, be true; if, indeed, it be designed by Providence that the grandest exhibition of human character and human affairs shall be made on this theatre of the western world; if it be true that,

"The four first acts already past,
A fifth shall close the drama with the day, —
Time's noblest offspring is the last;"

how could this imposing, swelling, final scene, be appropriately opened, how could its intense interest be adequately sustained, but by the introduction of just such a character as our Washington?

Washington had attained his manhood when that spark of liberty was struck out in his own country, which has since kindled into a flame, and shot its beams over the earth. In the flow of a century from his birth the world has changed in science, in arts, in the extent of commerce, in the improvement of navigation, and in all that relates to the civilization of man. But it is the spirit of human freedom, the new elevation of individual man, in his moral, social and political character, leading the whole long train of other improvements, which has most remarkably distinguished the era.

The political prosperity which this country has attained, and which it now enjoys, it has acquired mainly through the instrumentality of the present government. While this agent continues, the capacity of attaining to still higher degrees of prosperity exists also. We have, while this lasts, a political life, capable of beneficial exertion, with power to resist or overcome misfortunes, to sustain us against the ordinary accidents of human affairs, and to promote, by active efforts, every public interest. But dismemberment strikes at the very being which preserves these faculties. It would lay its rude and ruthless hand on this great agent itself. It would sweep away, not only what we possess, but all power of regaining lost or acquiring new possessions. It would leave the country, not only bereft of its prosperity and happiness, but without limbs, or organs, or faculties, by which to exert itself, hereafter, in the pursuit of that prosperity and happiness.

Other misfortunes may be borne, or their effects overcome. If disastrous war should sweep our commerce from the ocean, another generation may renew it; if it exhaust our treasury, future industry may replenish it; if it desolate and lay waste our fields, still, under a new cultivation, they will grow green again, and ripen to future harvests. It were but a trifle, even if the walls of yonder capitol were to crumble, if its lofty pillars should fall, and its gorgeous decorations be all covered by the dust of the valley. All these might be rebuilt. But who shall re-construct the fabric of demolished government? Who shall rear again the well-proportioned columns of constitutional liberty? Who shall frame together the skilful architecture which unites national sovereignty with state rights, individual security, and public prosperity? No! if these columns fall, they will be raised not again. Like the Coliseum and the Parthenon, they will be destined to a mournful, a melancholy immortality. Bitterer tears, however, will flow over them, than were ever shed over the monuments of Roman or Grecian art; for they will be the remnants of a more glorious edifice than Greece or Rome ever saw, — the edifice of constitutional American liberty.

But let us hope for better things. Let us trust in that gracious Being who has hitherto held our country as in the hollow of his hand. Let us trust to the virtue and the intelligence of the people, and to the efficacy of religious obligation. Let us trust to the influence of Washington's example. Let us hope that that fear of Heaven which expels all other fear, and that regard to duty which transcends all other regard, may influence public men and private citizens, and lead our country still onward in her happy career. Full of these gratifying anticipations and hopes, let us look forward to the end of that century which is now commenced. A hundred years hence, other disciples of Washington will celebrate his birth with no less of sincere admiration than we now commemorate it. When they shall meet, as we now meet, to do themselves and him that honor, so surely as they shall see the blue summits of his native mountains rise in the horizon, so surely as they shall behold the river on whose banks he lived, and on whose banks he rests, still flowing on toward the sea, — so surely may they see, as we now see, the flag of the Union floating on the top of the capitol; and then, as now, may the sun, in his course, visit no land more free, more happy, more lovely, than this our own country!

AMERICA. — *C. M. Clay.*

I MAY be an enthusiast; but I cannot but give utterance to the conceptions of my own mind. When I look upon the special developments of European civilization; when I contemplate the growing freedom of the cities, and the middle class which had sprung up between the pretenders to divine rule on the one hand, and the abject serf on the other; when I consider the Reformation, and the invention of the press, and see, on the southern shore of the continent, an humble individual, amidst untold difficulties and repeated defeats, pursuing the mysterious suggestions which the mighty deep poured unceasingly upon his troubled spirit, till at last, with great and irrepressible energy of soul, he discovered that there lay in the far western ocean a continent open for the infusion of those elementary principles of liberty which were dwarfed in European soil, — I have conceived that the hand of destiny was there!

When I saw the immigration of the Pilgrims from the chalky shores of England, — in the night fleeing from their native home — so dramatically and ably pictured by Mr. Webster in his celebrated oration, — when father, mother, brother, wife, sister, lover, were all lost, by those melancholy wanderers "stifling," in the language of one who is immortal in the conception, "the mighty hunger of the heart," and landing amidst cold, and poverty, and death, upon the rude rocks of Plymouth, — I have ventured to think the will of Deity was there!

When I have remembered the Revolution of '76, — the seven years' war — three millions of men in arms against the most powerful nation in history, and vindicating their independence, — I have thought that their sufferings and death were not in vain! When I have gone and seen the forsaken hearth-stone, — looked in upon the battle-field, upon the dying and the dead, — heard the agonizing cry, "Water, for the sake of God! water!" seeing the dissolution of this being, — pale lips pressing in death the yet loved images of wife, sister, lover, — I will not deem all these in vain! I cannot regard this great continent, reaching from the Atlantic to the far Pacific, and from the St. John's to the Rio del Norté, a barbarian people of third-rate civilization.

Like the Roman who looked back upon the glory of his ancestors, in woe exclaiming,

> "Great Scipio's ghost complains that we are slow,
> And Pompey's shade walks unavenged among us,"

the great dead hover around me; — Lawrence, "Don't give up the ship!" — Henry, "Give me liberty or give me death!" —

Adams, "Survive or perish, I am for the declaration!"—Allen, "In the name of the living God, I come!"

Come, then, thou Eternal! who dwellest not in temples made with hands, but who, in the city's crowd or by the far forest stream, revealest thyself to the earnest seeker after the true and right, inspire my heart; give me undying courage to pursue the promptings of my spirit; and, whether I shall be called in the shades of life to look upon as sweet and kind and lovely faces as now, or, shut in by sorrow and night, horrid visions shall gloom upon me in my dying hour — O! MY COUNTRY, MAYEST THOU YET BE FREE!

THE MISSOURI QUESTION. — *W. Pinkney.*

I HAVE long since persuaded myself that the Missouri question, as it is called, might be laid to rest, with innocence and safety, by some conciliatory compromise at least, by which, as is our duty, we might reconcile the extremes of conflicting views and feelings, without any sacrifice of constitutional principle; and, in any event, that the Union would easily and triumphantly emerge from those portentous clouds with which this controversy is supposed to have environed it.

Some of the principles announced by the honorable gentleman, with an explicitness that reflected the highest credit on his candor, did, when they were first presented, startle me not a little. They were not, perhaps, entirely new. Perhaps I had seen them before in some shadowy and doubtful shape,

"If shape it might be called, that shape had none,
Distinguishable in member, joint, or limb."

But in the honorable gentleman's speech they were shadowy and doubtful no longer. He exhibited them in forms so boldly and accurately defined, with contours so distinctly traced, with features so pronounced and striking, that I was unconscious for a moment that they might be old acquaintances. I received them as *novi hospites* within these walls, and gazed upon them with astonishment and alarm. I have recovered, however, thank God, from this paroxysm of terror, although not from that of astonishment. I have sought and found tranquillity and courage in my former consolatory faith. My reliance is that these principles will obtain no general currency; for, if they should, it requires no gloomy imagination to sadden the perspective of the future. My reliance is upon the unsophisticated good sense and noble spirit of the American people. I have what I may be allowed to call a proud and patriotic trust, that they will give countenance to no principles which, if followed out to their obvious consequences, will not only shake the goodly fabric of the Union to its foundations, but reduce it to a melancholy ruin. The people of this country, if I do not wholly mistake their character, are wise as well as virtuous. They know the value of that federal association which is to them the single pledge and guarantee of power and peace. Their warm and pious affections will cling to it as to their only hope of prosperity and happiness, in defiance of pernicious abstractions, by whomsoever inculcated, or howsoever seductive and alluring in their aspect.

It is not an occasion like this, although connected, as, contrary to all reasonable expectation, it has been, with fearful and disorganizing theories, which would make our estimates, whether fanciful or sound, of natural law, the measure of civil rights and political sovereignty in the social state, that can harm the Union. It must, indeed, be a mighty storm that can push from its moorings this sacred ark of the common safety. It is not every trifling breeze, however it may be made to sob and howl in imitation of the tempest, by the auxiliary breath of the ambitious, the timid, or the discontented, that can drive this gallant vessel, freighted with everything that is dear to an American bosom, upon the rocks, or lay it a sheer hulk upon the ocean. I will continue to cherish the belief that the Union of these states is formed to bear up against far greater shocks than, through all vicissitudes, it is ever likely to encounter. I will continue to cherish the belief that, although, like all other human institutions, it may for a season be disturbed, or suffer momentary eclipse by the transit across its disk of some malignant planet, it possesses a recuperative force, a redeeming energy in the hearts of the people, that will soon restore it to its wonted calm, and give it back its accustomed splendor. On such a subject I will discard all hysterical apprehensions, I will deal in no sinister auguries, I will indulge in no hypochondriacal forebodings. I will look forward to the future with gay and cheerful hope, and will make the prospect smile, in fancy at least, until overwhelming reality shall render it no longer possible.

It is now avowed that, while Maine is to be ushered into the Union with every possible demonstration of studious reverence on our part, and on hers with colors flying, and all the other graceful accompaniments of honorable triumph, this ill-conditioned upstart of the west, this obscure foundling of a wilderness, that was but yesterday the hunting-ground of the savage, is to find her way into the American family as she can, with a humiliating badge of remediless inferiority patched upon her garments, with the mark of recent, qualified manumission upon her, or rather with a brand upon her forehead to tell the story of her territorial vassalage, and to perpetuate the memories of her evil propensities. It is now avowed that, while the robust district of Maine is to be seated by the side of her truly respectable parent, coördinate in authority and honor, and is to be dandled into that power and dignity of which she does not stand in need, but which undoubtedly she deserves, the more infantine and feeble Missouri is to be repelled with harshness, and forbidden to come at all, unless with the iron collar of servitude about her neck, instead of the civic crown of republican freedom upon her brows, and is to be doomed forever to leading-strings, unless she will exchange those leading-strings for shackles.

There is such a thing as enthusiasm, moral, religious or political, or a compound of all three; — and it is wonderful what it will attempt, and from what imperceptible beginnings it sometimes rises into a mighty agent. Rising from some obscure or unknown source, it first shows itself a petty rivulet, which scarcely murmurs over the pebbles that obstruct its way; then it swells into a fierce torrent, bearing all before it; and then again, like some mountain stream which occasional rains have precipitated upon the valley, it sinks once more into a rivulet, and finally leaves its channel dry. Such a thing has happened. I do not say that it is now happening. It would not become me to say so. But, if it should occur, woe to the unlucky territory that should be struggling to make its way into the Union at the moment when the opposing inundation was at its height, and at the same instant this wide Mediterranean of discretionary powers, which it seems is ours, should open up all its sluices, and, with a consentaneous rush, mingle with the turbid waters of the others!

EDUCATION OF THE YOUNG. — *H. Mann.*

From her earliest colonial history, the policy of Massachusetts has been to develop the minds of all her people, and to imbue them with the principles of duty. To do this work most effectually, she has begun it with the young. If she would continue to mount higher and higher towards the summit of prosperity, she must continue the means by which her present elevation has been gained. In doing this, she will not only exercise the noblest prerogative of government, but will coöperate with the Almighty in one of his sublimest works.

The Greek rhetorician Longinus quotes from the Mosaic account of the creation what he calls the sublimest passage ever uttered: "God said, 'Let there be light,' and there was light." From the centre of black immensity effulgence burst forth. Above, beneath, on every side, its radiance streamed out, silent, yet making each spot in the vast concave brighter than the line which the lightning pencils upon the midnight cloud. Darkness fled as the swift beams spread onward and outward, in an unending circumfusion of splendor. Onward and outward still they move to this day, glorifying, through wider and wider regions of space, the infinite Author from whose power and beneficence they sprang. But not only in the beginning when God created the heavens and the earth did he say "Let there be light." Whenever a human soul is born into the world, its Creator stands over it, and again pronounces the same sublime words, "Let there be light."

Magnificent, indeed, was the material creation, when, suddenly blazing forth in mid space, the new-born sun dispelled the darkness of the ancient night. But infinitely more magnificent is it when the human soul rays forth its subtler and swifter beams; when the light of the senses irradiates all outward things, revealing the beauty of their colors and the exquisite symmetry of their proportions and forms; when the light of reason penetrates to their invisible properties and laws, and displays all those hidden relations that make up all the sciences; when the light of conscience illuminates the moral world, separating truth from error, and virtue from vice. The light of the newly-kindled sun, indeed, was glorious. It struck upon all the planets, and waked into existence their myriad capacities of life and joy. As it rebounded from them, and showed their vast orbs all wheeling, circle beyond circle, in their stupendous courses, the sons of God shouted for joy. That light sped onward, beyond Sirius, beyond the pole-star, beyond Orion and the Pleiades, and is still spreading onward into the abysses of space. But the light of the human soul flies swifter than the light of the sun, and outshines its meridian blaze. It can embrace not only the sun of our system, but all suns and galaxies of suns; ay! the soul is capable of knowing and of enjoying Him who created the suns themselves: and when these starry lustres that now glorify the firmament shall wax dim, and fade away like a wasted taper, the light of the soul shall still remain; nor time, nor cloud, nor any power but its own perversity, shall ever quench its brightness. Again I would say, that whenever a human soul is born into the world, God stands over it, and pronounces the same sublime fiat, "Let there be light!" and may the time soon come, when all human governments shall coöperate with the divine government in carrying this benediction and baptism into fulfilment!

THE FORCE BILL. — *J. C. Calhoun.*

The bill violates the constitution, plainly and palpably, in many of its provisions, by authorizing the president, at his pleasure, to place the different ports of this Union on an unequal footing, contrary to that provision of the constitution which declares that no preference shall be given to one port over another. It also violates the constitution, by authorizing him, at his discretion, to impose cash duties on one port while credit is allowed in others; by enabling the president to regulate commerce, a power vested in Congress alone; and by drawing within the jurisdiction of the United States' courts powers never intended to be conferred on them. As great as these objections are, they become insignificant in the provisions of a bill, which, by a single blow, by treating the states as a mere lawless mass of individuals, prostrates all the barriers of the constitution. It proceeds on the ground that the entire sovereignty of this country belongs to the American people, as forming one great community, and regards the states as mere fractions or counties, and not as an integral part of the Union; having no more right to resist the encroachments of the government than a county has to resist the authority of a state; and treating such resistance as the lawless acts of so many individuals, without possessing sovereignty or political rights.

It has been said that the bill declares war against South Carolina. No! it decrees a massacre of her citizens! War has something ennobling about it, and, with all its horrors, brings into action the highest qualities, intellectual and moral. It was, perhaps, in the order of Providence that it should be permitted for that very purpose. But this bill declares no war, except, indeed, it be that which savages wage; a war, not against the community, but the citizens of whom that community is composed. But I regard it as worse than *savage* warfare, — as an attempt to take away life, under the color of law, without the trial by jury, or any other safeguard which the constitution has thrown around the life of the citizen! It authorizes the president, or even his deputies, when they may suppose the law to be violated, without the intervention of a court or jury, to kill without mercy or discrimination.

It has been said by the senator from Tennessee to be a measure of peace! Yes! such peace as the wolf gives to the lamb, — the kite to the dove! Such peace as Russia gives to Poland, or death

17

to its victim! A peace by extinguishing the political existence of the state, by awing her into an abandonment of the exercise of every power which constitutes her a sovereign community! It is to South Carolina a question of self-preservation; and I proclaim it, that, should this bill pass, and an attempt be made to enforce it, it will be resisted, at every hazard — even that of death itself! Death is not the greatest calamity; there are others still more terrible to the free and brave, and among them may be placed the loss of liberty and honor. There are thousands of her brave sons who, if need be, are prepared cheerfully to lay down their lives in defence of the state, and the great principles of constitutional liberty for which she is contending. God forbid that this should become necessary! It never can be, unless this government is resolved to bring the question to extremity; when her gallant sons will stand prepared to perform the last duty — to die nobly!

MASSACHUSETTS AND VIRGINIA. — *J. G. Palfrey.*

Three days ago I listened to another strain from the Ancient Dominion, with the delight which such graceful eloquence has the power to give, and certainly not without my share of the emotion which was stirred in every hearer. I trust that it was not a mere transient pleasure, but that I was warmed with something of the patriotic spirit which he has so powerfully exhorted us to cultivate. So far as that effect was produced, I shall be only the better qualified to sustain those views of the public well-being and honor of which I have occasionally come forward here as the very humble advocate. Admiring the elevated and generous tone of many of that gentleman's remarks, there were yet some things I could have wished otherwise, independent of his argument on the particular question now in hand, which, of course, did not satisfy me.

The gentleman thinks that Virginia laid Massachusetts under an obligation of gratitude and affection by her sympathy and aid in the disastrous time of the Boston port-bill. I think she did, and that the debt is mutual, at least. Does the gentleman suppose that the distresses incurred by Massachusetts, at the period of which he speaks, were solely for objects of her own; or that the exertions made by Virginia and others of her sister colonies,— whether regarded as made in her behalf, or for the common cause, for which she was standing the foremost champion,— were anything more than mitigations of her woe? When James Otis argued in the old state-house against the writs of assistance, and "then and there," according to John Adams, "the child Independence was born," for whom was that birth?—for Massachusetts, or for America? When, from her Faneuil Hall, and the meetings of her village democracies, the gauntlet was thrown down to the tremendous power of England, was Massachusetts alone in the prospect of advantage from that strife, or only most forward in its perils? When the vindictive "port bill," to which the gentleman referred, took effect, was it some Virginian city, or was it Boston, the chief mart of the continent, that saw its prosperity made desolation, and the grass springing in its streets? And if Massachusetts did incur a debt for the sympathy and succors which, as the gentleman correctly states, she then received, I think she paid some instalments of it when she bore the first furious brunt of the battle on her own soil, when she sent nearly one soldier in every three to the armies of the Revolution, and when the excess of her payments into the common treasury, for the prosecution of the war, over and above what she drew from it, was greater than that of the aggregate of her twelve sister states.

But when the gentleman, calling up affecting reminiscences of the past, appealed to us of Massachusetts to be faithful to the obligations of patriotism, I repeat that I trust his language fell profitably as well as pleasantly on my ear. He has reminded us of our stern but constant ancestry. I hope we shall be true to their great mission for freedom and right, and all the more true for having listened to his own impressive exhortation. The gentleman remembers the declaration of Hume, that "it was to the Puritans that the people of England owed its liberties." May their race never desert that work, as long as any of it is left to do! Sir, as I come of a morning to my duties here, I am apt to stop before the picture in your rotunda, of the departure from Delft Haven of that vessel, "freighted with the best hopes of the world," and refresh myself by looking in the faces of four ancestors of my own, depicted by the limner in the group on that dismal deck: the brave and prudent leader of the company, his head and knee bowed in prayer, — his faithful partner, blending in her mild but care-worn countenance the expression of the wife, the parent, the exile and the saint, — the young maiden and the youth, going out to the wide sea and the wide world, but already trained to masculine endurance and "perfect peace," by the precious faith of Christ. Not more steadfast than those forlorn wanderers were the men who, in the tapestried chambers of England's great sway, with stout sword on thigh, and a stouter faith in the heart, and the ragged flags of Cressy, and Agincourt, and the Armada, above their heads,

> "Sat, with Bibles open, around the council board,
> And answered a king's missive with a stern 'Thus saith the Lord.'"

Not hardier were they who, in the iron squadrons of Fairfax and Cromwell, had many a hard trot, on many a hot and dusty day, to get so much as a sight of the backs of those silk and velvet cavaliers of whom the eloquent gentleman discoursed with so much unction.

FRENCH AGGRESSIONS. — *R. T. Paine.*

The solemn oath of America has ascended to heaven. She has sworn to preserve her independence, her religion and her laws, or nobly perish in their defence, and be buried in the wrecks of her empire. To the fate of our government is united the fate of our country. The convulsions that destroy the one must desolate the other. Their destinies are interwoven, and they must triumph or fall together. Where, then, is the man so hardened in political iniquity as to advocate the victories of French arms, which would render his countrymen slaves, or to promote the diffusion of French principles, which would render them savages? Can it be doubted that the pike of a French soldier is less cruel and ferocious than the fraternity of a French philosopher? Where is the youth in this assembly who could, without agonized emotions, behold the Gallic invader hurling the brand of devastation into the dwelling of his father, or with sacrilegious cupidity plundering the communion-table of his God? Who could witness, without indignant desperation, the mother who bore him inhumanly murdered in the defence of her infants? Who could hear, without frantic horror, the shrieks of a sister flying from pollution, and leaping from the blazing roof to impale herself on the point of a halberd? "If any, speak, for him I have offended!" No, my fellow-citizens, these scenes are never to be witnessed by American eyes. The souls of your ancestors still live in the bosom of their descendants; and, rather than submit this fair land of their inheritance to ravage and dishonor, from hoary age to helpless infancy they will form one united bulwark, and oppose their breasts to the assailing foe.

RESISTANCE TO ENGLAND.—*P. Henry.*

MR. PRESIDENT, it is natural for man to indulge in the illusions of hope. We are apt to shut our eyes against a painful truth, and listen to the song of that siren till she transforms us into beasts. Is it the part of wise men, engaged in the great and arduous struggle for liberty? Are we disposed to be of the number of those who, having eyes see not, and having ears hear not, the things which so nearly concern their temporal salvation? For my part, whatever anguish of spirit it may cost, I am willing to know the whole truth, and to provide for it.

I have but one lamp by which my feet are guided, and that is the lamp of experience. I know of no way of judging of the future but by the past. And, judging by the past, I wish to know what there has been in the conduct of the British ministry, for the last ten years, to justify those hopes with which gentlemen have been pleased to solace themselves and the house? Is it that insidious smile with which our petition has been lately received? Trust it not, sir! it will prove a snare to your feet. Suffer not yourselves to be betrayed with a kiss. Ask yourselves how this gracious reception of our petition comports with those warlike preparations which cover our waters and darken our land.

Are fleets and armies necessary to a work of love and reconciliation? Have we shown ourselves so unwilling to be reconciled, that force must be called in to win back our love? Let us not deceive ourselves, sir. These are the implements of war and subjugation, the last arguments to which kings resort. I ask gentlemen, sir, what means this martial array, if its purpose be not to force us to submission? Can gentlemen assign any other motive for it?

Has Great Britain any other enemy in this quarter of the world, to call for all this accumulation of navies and armies? No, sir, she has none. They are meant for us; they can be meant for no other. They are sent over to bind and rivet upon us those chains which the British ministers have been so long forging.

And what have we to oppose them? Shall we try argument? Sir, we have been trying that for the last ten years. Have we anything new to offer on the subject? Nothing. We have held the subject up in every light of which it is capable; but it has been all in vain. Shall we resort to entreaty and humble supplication? What terms shall we find which have not been already exhausted? Let us not, I beseech you, sir, deceive ourselves longer. Sir, we have done everything that could be done, to avert the storm which is now coming on. We have petitioned, we have remonstrated, we have supplicated, we have prostrated ourselves before the throne, and have implored its interposition to arrest the tyrannical hands of the ministry and parliament. Our petitions have been slighted; our remonstrances have produced additional violence and insult; our supplications have been disregarded; and we have been spurned, with contempt, from the foot of the throne.

They tell us, sir, that we are weak — unable to cope with so formidable an adversary. But when shall we be stronger? Will it be the next week, or the next year? Will it be when we are totally disarmed, and when a British guard shall be stationed in every house? Shall we gather strength by irresolution and inaction? Shall we acquire the means of effectual resistance by lying supinely on our backs, and hugging the delusive phantom of hope, until our enemies shall have bound us hand and foot?

Sir, we are not weak, if we make a proper use of those means which the God of nature hath placed in our power. Three millions of people armed in the holy cause of liberty, and in such a country as that which we possess, are invincible by any force which our enemy can send against us. Besides, sir, we shall not fight alone. There is a just God who presides over the destinies of nations, and who will raise up friends to fight our battles for us.

The battle, sir, is not to the strong alone; it is to the active, the vigilant, the brave. Besides, sir, we have no election! If we were base enough to desire it, it is now too late to retire from the contest. There is no retreat — but in submission and slavery! Our chains are forged! Their clanking may be heard on the plains of Boston. The war is inevitable; — and let it come! I repeat, it sir; let it come!

It is in vain, sir, to extenuate the matter. Gentlemen may cry Peace! peace! — but there is no peace. The war is actually begun! The next gale that sweeps from the north will bring to our ears the clash of resounding arms! Our brethren are already in the field. Why stand we here idle? What is it that gentlemen wish? What would they have? Is life so dear, or peace so sweet, as to be purchased at the price of chains and slavery? Forbid it, Heaven! I know not what course others may take; but as for me, give me liberty, or give me death!

CHRISTIANITY THE BASIS OF LIBERTY. — *L. Beecher.*

Twice, in France, the physical power has gained the ascendency over law; and by the last victory the discovery has been made, that, to patriots, cities are fortresses, and pavements munitions. This is one of the most glorious and dreadful discoveries of modern days — glorious in its ultimate results, in the emancipation of the world, but dreadful in those intervening revolutions which power may achieve in the conquest of liberty, without corresponding intelligence and virtue for its permanent preservation.

The conquest of liberty is not difficult; — the question is, where to put it — with whom to intrust it. If to the multitude who achieved it it be committed, it will perish by anarchy. If national guards are employed in its defence, the bayonets which protect it are at any moment able to destroy it for a military despotism. If to a republican king it be intrusted, it will have to be regulated by state policy, and fed on bread and water, until the action of her heart, and the movement of her tongue, and the power of her arm, as under the deadly incubus, shall cease. There is not in this wide world a safe deposit for liberty, but the hearts of patriots, so enlightened as to be able to judge of correct legislation, and so patient and disinterested as to practise self-denial and self-government for the public good.

But can such a state of society be founded and maintained without the Bible and the institutions of Christianity? Did a condition of unperverted liberty, uninspired by Christianity, ever bless the world through any considerable period of duration? The power of a favoring clime, and the force of genius, did thrust up from the dead level of monotonous despotism the republics of Greece to a temporary liberty; but it was a patent model only, compared with such a nation as this; and it was partial, and capricious, and of short duration, and rendered illustrious rather by the darkness which preceded and followed, than by the benign influence of its own beams.

FEAR OF FOREIGN POWERS. — *G. Morris.*

Look at the conduct of America in her infant years. When there was no actual invasion of right, but only a claim to invade, she resisted the claim, she spurned the insult. Did we then hesitate? Did we then wait for foreign alliance? No! animated with the spirit, warmed with the soul of freedom, we threw our oaths of allegiance in the face of our sovereign, and committed our fortunes and our fate to the God of battles. We then were subjects. We had not then attained to the dignity of an independent republic. We then had no rank among the nations of the earth. But we had the spirit which deserved that elevated station. And, now that we have gained it, shall we fall from our honor?

Sir, I repeat to you that I wish for peace: real, lasting, honorable peace. To obtain and secure this blessing, let us, by a bold and decisive conduct, convince the powers of Europe that we are determined to defend our rights; that we will not submit to insult; that we will not bear degradation. This is the conduct which becomes a generous people. This conduct will command the respect of the world. Nay, it may rouse all Europe to a proper sense of their situation. They see that the balance of power, on which their liberties depend, is, if not destroyed, in extreme danger. They know that the dominion of France has been extended by the sword over millions who groan in the servitude of their new masters. These unwilling subjects are ripe for revolt. The empire of the Gauls is not, like that of Rome, secured by political institutions. It may yet be broken. But, whatever may be the conduct of others, let us act as becomes ourselves. I cannot believe, with my honorable colleague, that three-fourths of America are opposed to vigorous measures. I cannot believe that they will meanly refuse to pay the sums needful to vindicate their honor, and support their independence. This is a libel on the people of America. They will disdain submission to the proudest sovereign on earth. They have not lost the spirit of '76. But, if they are so base as to barter their rights for gold, — if they are so vile that they will not defend their honor, — they are unworthy of the rank they enjoy, and it is no matter how soon they are parcelled out among better masters.

Act as becomes America, and all America will be united in your support. What is our conduct? Do we endeavor to fetter and trammel the executive authority? Do we oppose obstacles? Do we raise difficulties? No! We are willing to commit into the hands of the chief magistrate the treasure, the power and the energies, of the country. We ask for ourselves nothing. We expect nothing. All we ask is for our country. And, although we do not believe in the success of treaty, yet the resolutions we move, and the language we hold are calculated to promote it.

I have now performed, to the best of my power, the great duty which I owed to my country. I have given that advice which in my soul I believe to be the best. But I have little hope that it will be adopted. I fear that, by feeble councils, we shall be exposed to a long and bloody war. This fear is perhaps ill-founded, and if so I shall thank God that I was mistaken. I know that, in the order of his providence, the wisest ends frequently result from the most foolish measures. It is our duty to submit ourselves to his high dispensations. I know that war, with all its misery, is not wholly without advantage. It calls forth the energies of character; it favors the manly virtues; it gives elevation to sentiment; it produces national union, generates patriotic love, and infuses a just sense of national honor. If, then, we are doomed to war, let us meet it as we ought; and, when the hour of trial comes, let it find us a band of brothers.

BRITISH INFLUENCE. — *J. Randolph.*

Against whom are these charges of British predilection brought? Against men who, in the war of the Revolution, were in the councils of the nation, or fighting the battles of your country.

Strange, that we should have no objection to any other people or government, civilized or savage, in the whole world! The great autocrat of all the Russias receives the homage of our high consideration. The dey of Algiers and his divan of pirates are a very civil, good sort of people, with whom we find no difficulty in maintaining the relations of peace and amity. "Turks, Jews, and infidels," or the barbarians and savages of every clime and color, are welcome to our arms. With chiefs of banditti, negro or mulatto, we can treat and can trade. Name, however, but England, and all our antipathies are up in arms against her. Against whom? Against those whose blood runs in our veins; in common with whom we claim Shakspeare, and Newton, and Chatham, for our countrymen; whose government is the freest on earth, our own only excepted; from whom every valuable principle of our own institutions has been borrowed — representation, trial by jury, voting the supplies, writ of habeas corpus — our whole civil and criminal jurisprudence. In what school did the worthies of our land, the Washingtons, Henrys, Hancocks, Franklins, Rutledges, of America, learn those principles of civil liberty which were so nobly asserted by their wisdom and valor? American resistance to British usurpation has not been more warmly cherished by these great men and their compatriots — not more by Washington, Hancock, and Henry — than by Chatham and his illustrious associates in the British Parliament.

It ought to be remembered, too, that the heart of the English people was with us. It was a selfish and corrupt ministry, and their servile tools, to whom we were not more opposed than they were. I trust that none such may ever exist among us; for tools will never be wanting to subserve the purposes, however ruinous or wicked, of kings and ministers of state. I acknowledge the influence of a Shakspeare and a Milton upon my imagination, of a Locke upon my understanding, of a Sidney upon my political principles, of a Chatham upon qualities which would to God I possessed in common with that illustrious man! This is a British influence which I can never shake off.

THE BRITISH TREATY. — *F. Ames.*

Wars, in all countries, and most of all in such as are free, arise from the impetuosity of the public feelings. The despotism of Turkey is often obliged by clamor to unsheath the sword. War might perhaps be delayed, but could not be prevented. The causes of it would remain, would be aggravated, would be multiplied, and soon become intolerable. More captures, more impressments, would swell the list of our wrongs, and the current of our rage. I make no calculation of the arts of those whose employment it has been, on former occasions, to fan the fire. I say nothing of the foreign money and emissaries that might foment the spirit of hostility, because the state of things will naturally run to violence. With less than their former exertion, they would be successful.

Will our government be able to temper and restrain the turbulence of such a crisis? The government, alas! will be in no capacity to govern. A divided people, and divided councils! Shall we cherish the spirit of peace, or show the energies of war? Shall we make our adversary afraid of our strength, or dispose him, by the measures of resentment and broken faith, to respect our rights? Do gentlemen rely on the state of peace because both nations will be worse disposed to keep it, — because injuries and insults still harder to endure will be mutually offered?

Such a state of things will exist, if we should long avoid war, as will be worse than war. Peace without security, accumulation of injury without redress or the hope of it, resentment against the aggressor, contempt for ourselves, intestine discord and anarchy. Worse than this need not be apprehended; for, if worse could happen, anarchy would bring it. Is this the peace gentlemen undertake with such fearless confidence to maintain? Is this the station of American dignity which the high-spirited champions of our national independence and honor could endure; nay, which they are anxious, and almost violent, to seize for the country? What is there in the treaty that could humble us so low? Are they the men to swallow their resentments who so lately were choking with them? If, in the case contemplated by them, it should be peace, I do not hesitate to declare it ought not to be peace.

Is there anything in the prospect of the interior state of the country to encourage us to aggravate the dangers of a war? Would not the shock of that evil produce another, and shake down the feeble and then unbraced structure of our government? Is this a chimera? Is it going off the ground of matter of fact to say the rejection of the appropriation proceeds upon the doctrine of a civil war of the departments? Two branches have ratified a treaty, and we are going to set it aside. How is this disorder in the machine to be rectified? While it exists, its movements must stop; and when we talk of a remedy, is that any other than the formidable one of a revolutionary interposition of the people? And is this, in the judgment even of my opposers, to execute, to preserve the constitution and the public order? Is this the state of hazard, if not of convulsion, which they can have the courage to contemplate and to brave, or beyond which their penetration can reach and see the issue? They seem to believe, and they act as if they believed, that our union, our peace, our liberty, are invulnerable and immortal, — as if our happy state was not to be disturbed by our dissensions, and that we are not capable of falling from it by our unworthiness. Some of them have no doubt better nerves and better discernment than mine. They can see the bright aspects and happy consequences of all this array of horrors. They can see intestine discords, our government disorganized, our wrongs aggravated, multiplied and unredressed, peace with dishonor, or war without justice, union or resources, in "the calm lights of mild philosophy."

After rejecting the treaty, what is to be the next step? They must have foreseen what ought to be done; they have doubtless resolved what to propose. Why, then, are they silent? Dare they not avow their plan of conduct, or do they wait till our progress towards confusion shall guide them in forming it?

Let me cheer the mind, weary, no doubt, and ready to despond on this prospect, by presenting another, which it is yet in our power to realize. Is it possible for a real American to look at the prosperity of this country without some desire for its continuance, without some respect for the measures which many will say produced, and all will confess have preserved it? Will he not feel some dread that a change of system will reverse the scene? The well-grounded fears of our citizens, in 1794, were removed by the treaty, but are not forgotten. Then they deemed war nearly inevitable; and would not this adjustment have been considered, at that day, as a happy escape from the calamity? The great interest and the general desire of our people was to enjoy the advantages of neutrality. This instrument, however misrepresented, affords America that inestimable security. The causes of our disputes are either cut up by the roots, or referred to a new negotiation after the end of the European war. This was gaining everything, because it confirmed our neutrality, by which our citizens are gaining everything. This alone would justify the engagements of the government. For, when the fiery vapors of the war lowered in the skirts of our horizon, all our wishes were concentred in this one, that we might escape the desolation of the storm. This treaty, like a rainbow on the edge of the cloud, marked to our eyes the space where it was raging, and afforded, at the same time, the sure prognostic of fair weather. If we reject it, the vivid colors will grow pale: it will be a baleful meteor, portending tempest and war.

THE SPIRIT OF LIBERTY.—*J. Otis.*

England may as well dam up the waters of the Nile with bulrushes, as to fetter the step of Freedom, more proud and firm in this youthful land than where she treads the sequestered glens of Scotland, or couches herself among the magnificent mountains of Switzerland. Arbitrary principles, like those against which we now contend, have cost one King of England his life,—another, his crown,—and they may yet cost a third his most flourishing colonies.

We are two millions—one-fifth fighting men. We are bold and vigorous, and we call no man master. To the nation from whom we are proud to derive our origin we were ever, and we ever will be, ready to yield unforced assistance; but it must not, and it never can, be extorted.

Some have sneeringly asked, "Are the Americans too poor to pay a few pounds on stamped paper?" No! America, thanks to God and herself, is rich. But the right to take ten pounds implies the right to take a thousand; and what must be the wealth that avarice, aided by power, cannot exhaust? True, the spectre is now small; but the shadow he casts before him is huge enough to darken all this fair land. Others, in sentimental style, talk of the immense debt of gratitude which we owe to England. And what is the amount of this debt? Why, truly, it is the same that the young lion owes to the dam, which has brought it forth on the solitude of the mountain, or left it amid the winds and storms of the desert.

We plunged into the wave, with the great charter of freedom in our teeth, because the fagot and torch were behind us. We have waked this new world from its savage lethargy; forests have been prostrated in our path; towns and cities have grown up suddenly as the flowers of the tropics; and the fires in our autumnal woods are scarcely more rapid than the increase of our wealth and population. And do we owe all this to the kind succor of the mother country? No! we owe it to the tyranny that drove us from her, — to the pelting storms which invigorated our helpless infancy.

But, perhaps others will say, "We ask no money from your gratitude, — we only demand that you should pay your own expenses." And who, I pray, is to judge of their necessity? Why, the king — and, with all due reverence to his sacred majesty, he understands the real wants of his distant subjects as little as he does the language of the Choctaws! Who is to judge concerning the frequency of these demands? The ministry. Who is to judge whether the money is properly expended? The cabinet behind the throne. In every instance, those who take are to judge for those who pay. If this system is suffered to go into operation, we shall have reason to esteem it a great privilege that rain and dew do not depend upon parliament; otherwise, they would soon be taxed and dried.

But, thanks to God, there is freedom enough left upon earth to resist such monstrous injustice. The flame of liberty is extinguished in Greece and Rome, but the light of its glowing embers is still bright and strong on the shores of America. Actuated by its sacred influence, we will resist unto death! But we will not countenance anarchy and misrule. The wrongs that a desperate community have heaped upon their enemies shall be amply and speedily repaired. Still, it may be well for some proud men to remember, that a fire is lighted in these colonies which one breath of their king may kindle into such fury that the blood of all England cannot extinguish it!

KNOWLEDGE IS POWER. — *E. H. Chapin.*

SUFFICIENT is it that men have felt and enunciated the sublime doctrine that "knowledge is power;" that, as mind is superior to matter, so are ideas more potent and enduring than prodigies of physical might. Archimedes' thought is stronger than his lever. The mind that planned the pyramids was more powerful than the hands that piled them. The inventors of the mariner's compass and the telescope have outdone the Macedonian, and won new worlds. And the influence of the Cæsars seems mean and narrow beside the imperial dominion of the printing-press. Physical force is sectional, and acts in defined methods. But knowledge defies gravitation, and is not thwarted by space. It is miraculous in the wonder of its achievements, and in its independence of precedent and routine. "Knowledge is power!" Man gains wider dominion by his intellect than by his right arm. The mustard-seed of thought is a pregnant treasury of vast results. Like the germ in Egyptian tombs, its vitality never perishes, and its fruit will spring up after it has been buried for long ages. To the superficial eye, the plain of modern history is merely an arena of battle and treaty, colonization and revolution. To the student, this modern history, so diversified and mutable, indicates more than this. Luther and Cromwell, Pilgrim Rock and the Declaration of Independence, are the results of an invisible but mighty power, — a levelling and exalting power, — a power which, with no mere Cyclopean effort, no fitful Ætna convulsion, but with silent throbbings, like some great tidal force in nature, is slowly undermining all falsehood, and heaving the mass of humanity upwards. But to dwell upon the power of knowledge, intellect, thought, is to run into trite declamation. The scholar who has wrung this power in toil and sacrifice knows it full well. He sees it, in secret places, distilling as the dew, and dropping as the gentle rain from heaven, and everywhere diffusing its potent spell. He experiences its superiority over nature and brute force. He knows its conquests in the past and in the future.

THE FALL OF SWITZERLAND. — *S. Smith.*

Amidst all the enormities of the French revolution, no one circumstance, perhaps, has excited such general sympathy and indignation as the fall of Switzerland. With the name of Switzerland have been connected, from our earliest years, all the worthy feelings of the heart, and all the exquisite beauties of nature, all that the eye of taste or the soul of benevolence could require. A race of brave, and happy, and good men animated her solemn rocks and glens; the climbing step of Freedom had scanned the summit of the mountains; the unwearied hand of labor had drawn from the barren rock sustenance for man; the peasant with his plough, and his sword, and his book, was at once a tiller of the earth, a soldier, and a Christian. Happiness never was more complete; imagination could not paint a more enviable lot upon earth, or could the earth afford it. For six hundred years they had remained firm as their native mountains, amidst all the convulsions of Europe; for two hundred years they had hardly drawn the sword, or never drawn it but to conquer.

Into these hallowed retreats, in the midst of a solemn truce, in spite of the strict neutrality observed by the Swiss, and the solemn and repeated promises of their own government, burst the common enemies of mankind, hot from the carnage and reeking with the blood of other nations. They came to no new work of horror; they had murdered other innocents, and pillaged other temples, and wasted other lands. They could dye the silvered hair of the aged man with his own blood; they could curse the tears of women, and dash down the tender child as it lifted its meek eyes for mercy.

In the midst of such horrid scenes as these, many actions of heroic valor characterized the last days of Switzerland; and she died with her face ever turned to the enemy, slowly yielding, and fiercely struggling to the last. At Oberland, an old peasant was observed in arms, fighting amidst his three children and his seven grandchildren; they sustained the combat with inconceivable bravery, calling upon each other by name, tenderly; the children thronging about the old man, and guarding with their manly limbs the hoary head of their parent. They were all murdered; and in a moment of time this valiant race was blotted from the book of living men!

The vengeance which the French took of the Swiss, for their determined opposition to the invasion of their country, was decisive and terrible. The history of Europe can afford no parallel of such cruelty. To dark ages, and the most barbarous nations of the East, we must turn in vain. The soldiers, dispersed over the country, carried fire and sword and robbery into the most tranquil and hidden valleys of Switzerland. From the depth of sweet retreats echoed the shrieks of murdered men, stabbed in their humble dwellings, under the shadow of the high mountains, in the midst of those scenes of nature which make solemn and pure the secret thought of man, and appal him with the majesty of God. The flying peasants saw, in the midst of the night, their cottages, their implements of husbandry, and the hopes of the future year, expiring in one cruel conflagration.

The Swiss was a simple peasant; the French are a mighty people, combined for the regeneration of Europe. O, Europe! what dost thou owe to this mighty people? — dead bodies, ruinous heaps, broken hearts, endless confusion, and unutterable woe! By this mighty people the Swiss have lost their country; that country which they loved so well, that, if they heard but the simple song of their childhood, tears fell down every manly face, and the hearts of intrepid soldiers sobbed with grief!

UNLAWFUL MILITARY COMBINATIONS. — *J. McLean.*

An obedience to the laws is the first duty of every citizen. It lies at the foundation of our noble political structure; and when this great principle shall be departed from, with the public sanction, the moral influence of our government must terminate.

If there be any one line of policy in which all political parties agree, it is that we should keep aloof from the agitations of other governments; that we shall not intermingle our national concerns with theirs; and much more, that our citizens shall abstain from acts which lead the subjects of other governments to violence and bloodshed.

A government is justly held responsible for the acts of its citizens. And if this government be unable or unwilling to restrain our citizens from acts of hostility against a friendly power, such power may hold this nation answerable — declare war against it. Every citizen is, therefore, bound by the regard he has for his country, by his reverence for its laws, and by the calamitous consequences of war, to exert his influence in suppressing the unlawful enterprises of our citizens against any foreign and friendly power.

History affords no example of a nation or people that uniformly took part in the internal commotions of other governments which did not bring ruin upon themselves. These pregnant examples should guard us against a similar policy, which must lead to a similar result. A war with a powerful nation, with whom we have the most extensive relations, commercial and social, would inflict upon our country the greatest calamity. It would dry up the sources of its prosperity, and deluge it in blood.

The great principles of our republican institutions cannot be propagated by the sword. This can be done by moral force, and not physical. If we desire the political regeneration of oppressed nations, we must show them the simplicity, the grandeur and the freedom, of our own government. We must recommend it to the intelligence and virtue of other nations by its elevated and enlightened action, its purity, its justice, and the protection it affords to all its citizens, and the liberty they enjoy. And if, in this respect, we shall be faithful to the high bequests of our fathers, to ourselves, and to posterity, we shall do more to liberalize other governments, and emancipate their subjects, than could be accomplished by millions of bayonets. This moral power is what tyrants have most cause to dread. It addresses itself to the thoughts and the judgment of men. No physical force can arrest its progress. Its approaches are unseen, but its consequences are deeply felt. It enters garrisons most strongly fortified, and operates in the palaces of kings and emperors. We should cherish this power, as essential to the preservation of our government, and as the most efficient means of ameliorating the political condition of our race. And this can only be done by a reverence for the laws, and by the exercise of an elevated patriotism.

I invoke, therefore, in behalf of the tribunals of justice, the moral power of society. I ask it to aid them in suppressing a combination of deluded or abandoned citizens, which imminently threatens the peace and prosperity of the country. And I have no fears that, when public attention shall be roused on this deeply important subject, when the laws are understood and the duties of the government, and when the danger is seen and properly appreciated, there will be an expression so potent, from an enlightened and patriotic people, as to suppress all combinations in violation of the laws, and which threaten the peace of the country.

AMBIGUITY OF SPEECH. — *R. Choate.*

Sir, I have been exceedingly struck, while listening to gentlemen, with the fact that while the ends and objects at which they aim are all so pacific, their speeches are strewn and sown thick, broad-cast, with so much of the food and nourishment of war. Their ends and objects are peace — a treaty of peace; but their means and their topics wear a certain incongruous grimness of aspect. The "bloom is on the rye;" but, as you go near, you see bayonet-points sparkling beneath, and are fired upon by a thousand men in ambush! The end they aim at is peace; but the means of attaining it are an offensive and absurd threat. Their ends and their objects are peace; yet how full have they stuffed the speeches we have been hearing with every single topic the best calculated to blow up the passions of kindred races to the fever-heat of battle!

I declare, sir, that while listening to senators whose sincerity and patriotism I cannot doubt, and to this conflict of topics and objects with which they half bewilder me, I was forcibly reminded of that consummate oration in the streets of Rome, by one who "came to bury Cæsar, not to praise him." He did not wish to stir up anybody to mutiny and rage! O, no! He would not have a finger lifted against the murderers of his and the people's friend — not he! He feared he wronged them; yet who has not admired the exquisite address and the irresistible effect with which he returns again and again to "sweet Cæsar's wounds, poor, poor dumb mouths," and put a tongue in each, — to the familiar mantle, first worn on the evening of the day his great friend overcame the Nervii, now pierced by the cursed steel of Cassius, of the envious Casca, of the well-beloved Brutus, — to his legacy of drachmas, arbors and orchards, to the people of Rome, whose friend, whose benefactor, he shows to them, all marred by traitors, — till the mob break away from his words of more than fire, with:

> "We will be revenged! —Revenge! About!
> Seek — burn — fire — kill — slay! —let not a traitor live!"

Antony was insincere. Senators are wholly sincere. Yet the contrast between their pacific professions and that revelry of belligerent topics and sentiments which rings and flashes in their speeches here half suggests a doubt to me, sometimes, whether they or I perfectly know what they mean or what they desire. They promise to show you a garden, and you look up to see nothing but a wall "with dreadful faces thronged, and fiery arms!" They propose to teach you how peace is to be preserved; and they do it so exquisitely that you go away half inclined to issue letters of marque and reprisal to-morrow morning.

The proposition is peace; but the audience rises and goes off with a sort of bewildered and unpleasing sensation, that if there were a thousand men in all America as well disposed as the orator, peace might be preserved; but that, as the case stands, it is just about hopeless! I ascribe it altogether to their anxious and tender concern for peace, that senators have not a word to say about the good she does, but only about the dangers she is in. They have the love of compassion, not the love of desire. Not a word about the countless blessings she scatters from her golden urn; but only "the pity of it, Iago! the pity of it!" to think how soon the dissonant clangor of a thousand brazen throats may chase that bloom from her cheek, —

"And Death's pale flag be quick advancéd there."

Sir, no one here can say one thing and mean another; yet much may be meant, and nothing directly said. "The dial spoke not, but pointed full upon the stroke of murder."

WARS OF KINDRED RACES. — *W. Gaston.*

THERE is something in the character of a war made upon the people of a country to force them to abandon a government which they cherish, and to become the subjects or associates of their invaders, which necessarily involves calamities beyond those incident to ordinary wars. Among us some remain who remember the horrors of the invasion of the Revolution; and "others of us have hung with reverence on the lips of narrative old age, as it related the interesting tale." Such a war is not a contest between those only who seek for renown in military achievements, or the more humble mercenaries "whose business 'tis to die." It breaks in upon all the charities of domestic life, and interrupts all the pursuits of industry. The peasant quits his plough, and the mechanic is hurried from his shop, to commence, without apprenticeship, the exercise of the trade of death. The irregularity of the resistance which is opposed to the invader, its occasional obstinacy and occasional intermission, provoking every bad passion of his soldiery, is the excuse for plunder, lust, and cruelty. These atrocities exasperate the sufferers to revenge; and every weapon which anger can supply, and every device which ingenious hatred can conceive, is used to inflict vengeance on the detested foe.

As there is no anger so deadly as the anger of a friend, there is no war so ferocious as that which is waged between men of the same blood, and formerly connected by the closest ties of affection. The pen of the historian confesses its inability to describe, the fervid fancy of the poet cannot realize, the horrors of a civil war. This invasion of Canada involves the miseries of both these species of war. It must be that such a war will rouse a spirit of sanguinary ferocity that will overleap every holy barrier of nature and venerable usage of civilization. Where will you find an authenticated instance of this ferocity, that more instantaneously compels the shuddering abhorrence of the heart, than the fact asserted by my eloquent friend from New Hampshire,—"the bayonet of the brother has been actually opposed to the breast of the brother"? Merciful Heaven! that those who have been rocked in the same cradle by the same maternal hand, who have imbibed the first genial nourishment of infant existence from the same blessed source, should be forced to contend in impious strife for the destruction of that being derived from their common parents! It should not be so! Every feeling of our nature cries aloud against it!

Before we enter upon this career of cold-blooded massacre, it behooves us, by every obligation which we owe to God, to our fellow-men, and to ourselves, to be certain that the right is with us, or that the duty is imperative. If, in a moment of excited feeling, we should heedlessly enact the fatal deed which consigns thousands of the gallant and the brave Americans and Britons to an ignominious death, and should afterwards discover that the deed was criminal,—that the blood of the innocent is upon us, and the cries of their fatherless infants have ascended against us to the throne of the Most High,—how shall we silence the reproaches of conscience, how atone for the wide-spread and irreparable mischief, or how efface from the American name the infamous stain that will be stamped upon it?

Think, for a moment, sir, on the consequences, and deem it not unworthy of you to regard them. True courage shuts not its eyes upon danger, or its result. It views steadily, and calmly resolves whether they ought to be encountered. Already has the Canadian war a character sufficiently cruel, as Newark, Buffalo and Niagara, can testify. But when the spirit of ferocity shall have been maddened by the vapor steaming from the innocent blood that shall stagnate around every depot of prisoners, then will it become a war, not of savage, but of demoniac character. Your part of it may, perhaps, be ably sustained. Your way through the Canadas may be traced afar off by the smoke of their burning villages. Your path may be marked by the blood of their furious peasantry. You may render your course audible by the frantic shrieks of their women and children. But your own sacred soil will also be the scene of this drama of fiends. Your exposed and defenceless seaboard, the seaboard of the south, will invite a terrible vengeance. That seaboard, which has been shamefully neglected, and is at this moment without protection, has been already invaded. But an invasion, after the war shall have assumed its unmitigated form of carnage, and woe, and wickedness, must be followed with horrors which imagination can but faintly conceive. I will say to the gentleman from Pennsylvania that when he alludes to the probability that an intestine foe may be roused to assassination and brutality, he touches a chord that vibrates to the very heart. I live in a state whose misfortune it is to contain the materials out of which may be made such a foe; — a foe that will be found everywhere — in our fields, our kitchens, and our chambers; a foe, ignorant, degraded by habits of servitude, uncurbed by moral restraints, whom no recollections of former kindness will soften, and whom the remembrance of severity will goad to frenzy; from whom nor age, nor infancy, nor beauty, will find reverence or pity; and whose subjugation will be but another word for extermination!

EULOGY UPON JOHN C. CALHOUN. — *D. Webster.*

THE eloquence of Mr. Calhoun, or the manner of his exhibition of his sentiments in public bodies, was part of his intellectual character. It grew out of the qualities of his mind. It was plain, strong, terse, condensed, concise; sometimes impassioned — still, always severe. Rejecting ornament, not often seeking far for illustration, his power consisted in the plainness of his propositions, in the closeness of his logic, and in the earnestness and energy of his manner. These are the qualities, as I think, which have enabled him through such a long course of years to speak often, and yet always command attention. His demeanor as a senator is known to us all, — is appreciated, venerated by us all. No man was more respectful to others; no man carried himself with greater decorum, no man with superior dignity. I think there is not one of us but felt, when he last addressed us from his seat in the senate, — his form still erect, with a voice by no means indicating such a degree of physical weakness as did, in fact, possess him, with clear tones, and an impressive, and, I may say, an imposing manner, — who did not feel that he might imagine that he saw before us a senator of Rome, when Rome survived.

He had the basis, the indispensable basis, of all high character; and that was, unspotted integrity — unimpeached honor and character. If he had aspirations, they were high, and honorable, and noble. There was nothing grovelling, or low, or mean, or meanly selfish, that came near the head or the heart of Mr. Calhoun. Firm in his purpose, perfectly patriotic and honest, as I am sure he was in the principles that he espoused, and in the measures that he defended, aside from that large regard for that species of distinction that conducted him to eminent stations for the benefit of the republic, I do not believe he had a selfish motive or selfish feeling.

However he may have differed from others of us in his political opinions or his political principles, those principles and those opinions will now descend to posterity under the sanction of a great name. He has lived long enough, he has done enough, and he has done it so well, so successfully, so honorably, as to connect himself for all time with the records of his country. He is now an historical character. Those of us who have known him here will find that he has left upon our minds and our hearts a strong and lasting impression of his person, his character, and his public performances, which while we live will never be obliterated. We shall hereafter, I am sure, indulge in it as a grateful recollection that we have been his contemporaries, — that we have seen him, and heard him, and known him. We shall delight to speak of him to those who are rising up to fill our places. And, when the time shall come when we ourselves shall go, one after another, in succession, to our graves, we shall carry with us a deep sense of his genius and character, his honor and integrity, his amiable deportment in private life, and the purity of his exalted patriotism.

THE ALIEN BILL. — *E. Livingston.*

Whenever our laws manifestly infringe the constitution under which they were made, the people ought not to hesitate which they should obey: if we exceed our powers, we become tyrants, and our acts have no effect. Thus, one of the first effects of measures such as this, if they be acquiesced in, will be disaffection among the states and opposition among the people to your government; tumults, violations, and a recurrence to first revolutionary principles: if they are submitted to, the consequences will be worse. After such manifest violation of the principles of our constitution, the form will not long be sacred, — presently every vestige of it will be lost and swallowed up in the gulf of despotism. But, should the evil proceed no further than the execution of the present law, what a fearful picture will our country present! The system of espionage thus established, the country will swarm with information-spies, delators, and all that odious tribe that breed in the sunshine of despotic power, that suck the blood of the unfortunate, and creep into the bosom of sleeping innocence only to awaken it with a burning wound. The hours of the most unsuspecting confidence, the intimacies of friendship, or the recesses of domestic retirement, afford no security; the companion in whom you must trust, the friend in whom you must confide, the domestic who waits in your chamber, are all tempted to betray your imprudence or guardless follies, to misrepresent your words, to convey them, distorted by calumny, to the secret tribunal where jealousy presides, where fear officiates as accuser, where suspicion is the only evidence that is heard.

Compared to the breach of our constitution, and the establishment of arbitrary power, every other topic is trifling; arguments of convenience sink into nothing; the preservation of wealth, the increase of commerce, however weighty on other occasions, here lose their importance, when the fundamental principles of freedom are in danger. I am tempted to borrow the impressive language of a foreign speaker, and exclaim, "Perish our commerce, let our constitution live;" perish our riches, let our freedom live. This would be the sentiment of every American, were the alternative between submission and wealth; but here it is proposed to destroy our wealth, in order to ruin our commerce; — not in order to preserve our constitution, but to break it; not to secure our freedom, but to abandon it.

Let me entreat gentlemen seriously to reflect, before they pronounce the decisive vote, that gives the first open stab to the principles of our government. Our mistaken zeal, like the patriarch of old, has bound one victim; it lies at the foot of the altar; a sacrifice of the first-born offspring of freedom is proposed by those who gave it birth. The hand is already raised to strike, and nothing, I fear, but the voice of Heaven, can arrest the impious blow.

Let not gentlemen flatter themselves that the fervor of the moment can make the people insensible to these aggressions. It is an honest, noble warmth, produced by an indignant sense of injury. It will never, I trust, be extinct, while there is a proper cause to excite it. But the people of America, though watchful against foreign aggressions, are not careless of domestic encroachment; they are as jealous of their liberties at home as of the power and prosperity of their country abroad; they will awake to a sense of their danger. Do not let us flatter ourselves, then, that these measures will be unobserved, or disregarded; do not let us be told that we excite a fervor against foreign aggressions only to establish tyranny at home; that, like the arch traitor, we cry "Hail, Columbia!" at the moment we are betraying her to destruction; that we sing out "Happy land!" when we are plunging it in ruin and disgrace; and that we are absurd enough to call ourselves "free and enlightened," while we advocate principles that would have disgraced the age of Gothic barbarity, and establish a code compared to which the ordeal is wise, and the trial by *battel* is merciful and just!

THE FUTURE AGE OF LITERATURE. — *H. Bushnell.*

I BELIEVE in a future age, yet to be revealed, which is to be distinguished from all others as the godlike age, — an age not of universal education simply, or universal philanthropy, or external freedom, or political well-being, but a day of reciprocity and free intimacy between all souls and God. Learning and religion, the scholar and the Christian, will not be divided as they have been. The universities will be filled with a profound spirit of religion, and the *bene orâsse* will be a fountain of inspiration to all the investigations of study and the creations of genius. And it will be found that Christianity has, at last, developed a new literary era — the era of religious love.

Hitherto, the love of passion has been the central fire of the world's literature. The dramas, epics, odes, novels, and even histories, have spoken to the world's heart chiefly through this passion, and through this have been able to get their answer. Hence there gathers round the lover a tragic interest, and we hang upon his destiny as if some natural charm or spell were in it. But this passion of love, which has hitherto been the staple of literature, is only a crude symbol in the life of nature, by which God designs to interpret, and also to foreshadow, the higher love of religion, — Nature's gentle Beatrice, who leaves her image in the youthful Dante, and is therefore to attend him afterwards in the spirit-flight of song, and be his guide upward through the wards of paradise to the shining mount of God. What, then, are we to think, but that he will some time bring us up out of the literature of the lower love, into that of the higher; that, as the age of passion yields, at last, to the age of reason, so the crude love of instinct shall give place to the pure intellectual love of God? And then, around that nobler love, or out of it, shall arise a new body of literature, as much more gifted as the inspiration is purer and more intellectual. Beauty, truth and worship, song, science and duty, will all be unfolded together in the common love of God.

Society must, of course, receive beauty into its character and feeling, such as can be satisfied no longer with the old barbaric themes of war and passion. To be a scholar and not to be a Christian, to produce the fruits of genius without a Christian inspiration, will no longer be thought of; and religion, heretofore looked upon as a ghostly constraint upon life, it will now be acknowledged is the only efficient fertilizer of genius, as it is the only real emancipator of man.

THE BATTLE OF BUNKER HILL.—*H. A. S. Dearborn.*

On Bunker's ever-memorable heights was first displayed the lofty spirit of invincible patriotism which impelled the adventurous soldier to brave the severest hardships of the tented field, and endure in northern climes the rugged toils of war, uncanopied from the boreal storm and rude inclemencies of Canadian winters. On that American Thermopylæ, where, wrapt in the dim smoke of wanton conflagration, fought the assembled sovereigns of their native soil, the everlasting bulwarks of freedom, and thrice rolled back the tremendous tide of war, was evinced that unconquerable intrepidity, that national ardor and meritorious zeal, which secured victory on the plains of Saratoga, stormed the ramparts of Yorktown, and bore the bannered eagle in triumph from the shores of the Atlantic to the furthest confines of the wilderness.

By that destructive battle were awakened the most exalted faculties of the mind. Reason, unrestrained, burst forth in the plenitude of its effulgence. Man, regenerated and disenthralled, beat down the walls of slavish incarceration, and trampled on the broken chains of regal bondage. The vast resources of an emancipated people were called into generous exertion. An enthusiastic spirit of independence glowed in every breast, and spread the uncontaminated sentiments of emulative freemen over the broad extent of an exasperated republic. The united energies of a virtuous people were strenuously directed to the effectual accomplishment of national independence. During those portentous times were achieved the most honorable deeds which are inscribed on the ever-during records of fame. Stimulated by accumulating wrongs, and elated by the purest feelings of anticipated success, no disastrous events could check the progress of their arms, — no fascinating allurements deflect them from that honorable path which they had sworn to pursue, or perish in the hazardous attempt. Inspired by the guardian genius of Liberty, no barriers could oppose their impetuous career. Like the "Pontic Sea, whose icy current and compulsive course ne'er feels retiring ebb," the irrefluent tide of freedom rolls unrestrained. By the courageous virtue of our illustrious heroes were secured those inestimable blessings which we have since enjoyed. To the warriors and statesmen of the Revolution are we indebted for all those distinguished privileges which place the citizens of the United States beyond the predatory vengeance of ruthless oppression. This invaluable inheritance is the prize of slaughter acquired by the lives of contending freemen, secured with the blood of battling patriots.

WAR PREFERABLE TO SUBMISSION. — *J. C. Calhoun.*

I ONLY know of one principle to make a nation great, — to produce in this country not the form, but real spirit, of union, — and that is, to protect every citizen in the lawful pursuit of his business. He will then feel that he is backed by the government, that its arm is his arms, and will rejoice in its increased strength and prosperity. Protection and patriotism are reciprocal. This is the road that all great nations have trod. I am not versed in this calculating policy, and will not, therefore, pretend to estimate in dollars and cents the value of national independence or national affection.

The gentleman from Virginia has not failed to touch on the calamity of war, that fruitful source of declamation, by which pity becomes the advocate of cowardice; but I know not what we have to do with that subject. If the gentleman desires to repress the gallant ardor of our countrymen by such topics, let me inform him that true courage regards only the cause, that it is just and necessary, and that it despises the pain and danger of war. If he really wishes to promote the cause of humanity, let his eloquence be addressed to Lord Wellesley or Mr. Percival, and not the American Congress. Tell them, if they persist in such daring insult and injury to a neutral nation, that, however inclined to peace, it will be bound in honor and interest to resist; that their patience and benevolence, however great, will be exhausted; that the calamity of war will ensue, and that they, in the opinion of wounded humanity, will be answerable for all its devastation and misery. Let melting pity, a regard to the interests of humanity, stay the hand of injustice, and, my life on it, the gentleman will not find it difficult to call off his country from the bloody scenes of war. We are next told of the dangers of war! I believe we are all ready to acknowledge its hazards and accidents; but I cannot think we have any extraordinary danger to contend with, — at least, so much as to warrant an acquiescence in the injuries we have received; on the contrary, I believe no war can be less dangerous to internal peace or national existence.

I think a regular force, raised for a period of actual hostilities, cannot be called a standing army. There is a just distinction between such a force and one raised as a peace establishment. Whatever may be the composition of the latter, I hope the former will consist of some of the best materials of the country. The ardent patriotism of our young men, and the reasonable bounty in land which is proposed to be given, will impel them to join their country's standard, and to fight her battles; they will not forget the citizen in the soldier, and, in obeying their officer, learn to contemn their constitution. In our officers and soldiers we will find patriotism no less pure and ardent than in the private citizen.

In speaking of Canada, the gentleman introduced the name of Montgomery with much feeling and interest. Sir, there is danger in that name to his argument. It is sacred to heroism! It is indignant of submission! This calls my memory back to the time of our Revolution — to the Congress of '74 and '75. Suppose a speaker of that day had risen and urged all the arguments which we have heard on this subject; had told that Congress, "Your contest is about the right of laying a tax; the attempt on Canada has nothing to do with it; the war will be expensive; danger and devastation will overspread our country, and the power of Great Britain is irresistible." With what sentiments, think you, would such doctrines have been then received? Happy for us, they had no force at that period of our country's glory. Had they been then acted on, this hall would never have witnessed a great nation convened to deliberate for the general good; a mighty empire, with prouder prospects than any nation the sun ever shone on, would not have risen in the west. No! we would have been vile, subjected colonies, governed by that imperious rod which Britain holds over her distant provinces.

ADAMS AND JEFFERSON.—*E. Everett.*

No, fellow-citizens, we dismiss not Adams and Jefferson to the chambers of forgetfulness and death. What we admired, and prized, and venerated in them, can never die, nor, dying, be forgotten. I had almost said that they are now beginning to live; to live that life of unimpaired influence, of unclouded fame, of unmingled happiness, for which their talents and services were destined. They were of the select few the least portion of whose life dwells in their physical existence; whose hearts have watched while their senses slept; whose souls have grown up into a higher being; whose pleasure is to be useful; whose wealth is an unblemished reputation; who respire the breath of honorable fame; who have deliberately and consciously put what is called life to hazard, that they may live in the hearts of those who come after. Such men do not, cannot die. To be cold, and motionless, and breathless,—to feel not and speak not,—this is not the end of existence to the men who have breathed their spirits into the institutions of their country, who have stamped their characters on the pillars of the age, who have poured their hearts' blood into the channels of the public prosperity. Tell me, ye who tread the sods of yon sacred height, is Warren dead? Can you not still see him, not pale and prostrate, the blood of his gallant heart pouring out of his ghastly wound, but moving resplendent over the field of honor, with the rose of heaven upon his cheek, and the fire of liberty in his eye? Tell me, ye who make your pious pilgrimage to the shades of Vernon, is Washington indeed shut up in that cold and narrow house? That which made these men, and men like these, cannot die. The hand that traced the charter of independence is indeed motionless, the eloquent lips that sustained it are hushed; but the lofty spirits that conceived, resolved, matured, maintained it, and which alone, to such men, "make it life to live,"—these cannot expire:

> "These shall resist the empire of decay,
> When time is o'er, and worlds have passed away;
> Cold in the dust the perished heart may lie,
> But that which warmed it once can never die."

RELIEF OF THE SURVIVORS OF THE REVOLUTION.—*T. Burgess.*

Permit me, then, to request each gentleman of this committee to look at this provision for the survivors of this army, and then to look at the kind, the amount, and the manner of their payment. In what country or age of the world, in modern times, was ever, before this, such an army kept in the field five years at a current expense of little more than two millions of dollars? Place over against this sum in the fiscal accounts of the nation the one hundred and twenty millions expended in the three years' war of 1812, and in the immense difference of these two sums you will be enabled, as if aided by a glass, to catch some faint outline of those times when a Revolutionary soldier fought your battles for sixty shillings per month, and while travelling home paid seventy-five dollars for a dinner. Examine the account. A fearful balance will be found standing against the nation in the forum of conscience. Wipe it off, I pray of you, by passing the provisions of this bill to our credit in that ever-during tribunal. Suffer not the impartial adjudication of history to be there recorded against us. You all must recollect the self-devotion of that young hero of Palestine, who, though fainting with thirst, yet refused to taste the waters of his native spring, presented to him by three of his youthful warriors, because they had put their lives in their hands, and cut their way through an enemy's camp, to obtain it. "As God liveth, it is your blood," exclaimed the generous chieftain; "I may not drink of it." This money in our treasury is, sir, the blood of these men. Give it back to them! It will not prosper in our hands.

If, notwithstanding these things, it should be said that this account has been compromised with these men, and ultimately settled, let it, if you please, be so considered; but do not forget the different results of this compromise. About the close of the war, the whole national debt, — all government had borrowed of foreigners, all they had borrowed of citizens, all the United States owed to the several states, all they owed to the army, — as by Madison, Hamilton and Ellsworth, is reported to Congress, in their address to the states, amounted to forty-two millions three hundred and seventy-five dollars. What would the amount have been, had you paid your armies in silver and gold? What, had you redeemed your two hundred millions of continental money, hundred for hundred, in Spanish milled dollars? The government saved some portion of the immense difference — how? By negotiations — with whom? Those men, who, in the cabinet, conducted our glorious Revolution, are worthy to be held in everlasting veneration. Let us, sir, from the savings made by the economical negotiations of those days, when the poverty and not the will of the government consented, draw some fair and honorable provision for this venerable remnant of the Revolutionary army; and, attentive to that voice of national magnanimity, calling to us from every region of our country, make one redeeming effort, now, in the times of maturity and abundance, to soften the rigor of those transactions, which grew up under a cold and unpropitious influence, in the years of oppressed and parsimonious minority.

Let us, however, give up this question to the cavils of debate, and allow that we owe these men nothing; that in settlement with them we saved nothing; that we have paid them, to the full, the amount of their wages, and in a manner, too, according to the literal terms of the contract. Between such an army and such a nation are there not some higher and holier feelings than those resulting from the gross working-day relations of mere debt and credit? Few men live now who lived in those days when first commenced those higher relations, now existing, between this army and this country, — few, I say, whose memory fully comprehends the stormy years of our Revolution, and the halcyon days of our prosperity. Indeed, since this provision was laid on the table, two men have left the world, whose illustrious lives did, like the bright bow of heaven, touch the two extremes of this varied horizon. They owed their glory to the darkness of its clouds, their lustre to the brightness of its sunshine. Enough, however, live, who do know that there never was before such an army, such a service, such a result.

Without this army our Revolution had never been achieved. Instead of "thus sitting, thus consulting," thus, in all the pride and power of self-government, we had to this hour been the mere appurtenances of foreign empire, dragging after us the weary chain of colonial dependence. The enterprising trade of your fathers was confined to the waters and the ports of Great Britain. This army conquered for you the freedom of the seas and the commerce of the world. They, too, conquered for you the lands from almost the waters of the Mexican Gulf to the head-springs of the Mississippi, and thus finally brought into your acquisition your whole present territory, extending over the broad breast of the continent, from ocean to ocean. What a wilderness of wealth! What a teeming parent of populous and powerful states! The old colonies were mere separate colonies. The Revolution united their hands, and formed them into a political brotherhood. This army sustained that union, placed us on the broad basis of independence, and we are, by their toils and jeopardies, now a nation, among the most efficient and prosperous. Does no spirit of gratitude call on this nation to remember and to relieve the survivors of that army, now, as they are "old, and weary with service"? I pray of you let their country give them this one look of kindness, pour this one beam of gladness on the desolate twilight of their days!

Does any one doubt whether the spirit of the nation will go

along with us, in making this provision? Why, when that venerable man, now standing in the canvas yonder on your wall, two years ago stood in his proper person on this floor, the whole nation seemed to spring forward to give him the hand of gratulation. Was this done because he was the noble descendant of a long line of illustrious ancestors, a warrior and a patriot in another country? Was it not rather because he was a soldier of our Revolutionary army? When he travelled from city to city, and the universal people went out to meet, to welcome, and to receive him to their abodes, was it not because he was a soldier of our Revolutionary army? When from state to state he moved under one continued shout of congratulation, it was not the great and illustrious nobleman, but the long-remembered and deeply-endeared soldier of our Revolutionary army, whom the people delighted to honor. At last, when he left our shores, carrying with him such testimonials as were appropriate for such a nation to give, and such a man to receive, no American imagined, though such was the fact, that we had been doing honors to the most meritorious man in Europe; all men believed that it was but the expression of national gratitude to the soldier, the Revolutionary soldier, who had devoted his youth, his fortune and his blood, in defence of our independence! Is there no such sentiment now in the bosom of our nation, embracing, warmly embracing, these, his venerable brothers in arms?

At the last great national festival of independence, the first jubilee of our country, why were these men, by a kind of simultaneous sentiment "beating in every pulse" through the nation, called out to assist at the solemnities, and to partake of the joys and festivities, of the day? Was this done, sir, merely to tantalize their hopes? or was it done to assure them that already the voice of the people had awarded to them this provision, and that they were only to wait until the forms of law had given efficiency to this award, until the recorded enactments of their representatives in Congress had embodied and promulgated this great voice of the people?

The character of your bestowment on Lafayette depends on the fate of this measure. Make this provision for the remainder of your Revolutionary army, and this and that will forever stand on the page of history as illustrious deeds of national gratitude. Send away these, his meritorious brothers in arms, to "beg their bread through realms their valor saved," and your gifts to that illustrious foreigner will, in the eyes of other nations and of posterity, serve only to purchase for you the character of a poor and a pitiful ostentation!

THE PATRIOT'S DUTY. — *J. Quincy.*

For my single self, did I support such projects as are avowed to be the objects of this bill, I should deem myself a traitor to my country. Were I even to aid them, by loan, or any other way, I should consider myself a partaker in the guilt of the purpose. But when these projects of invasion shall be abandoned; when men yield up schemes which not only openly contemplate the raising of a great military force, but also the concentrating them at one point, and placing them in one hand, — schemes obviously ruinous to the fates of a free republic, as they comprehend the means by which such have ever, heretofore, been destroyed; — when, I say, such schemes shall be abandoned, and the wishes of the cabinet limited to mere defence, and frontier and maritime protection, there will be no need of calls to union. For such objects there is not, there cannot be, but one heart and soul in this people.

I know that while I utter these things a thousand tongues and a thousand pens are preparing, without doors, to overwhelm me, if possible, by their pestiferous gall. Already I hear in the air the sound of "traitor," "British agent," "British gold," and all those changes of vulgar calumny by which the imaginations of the mass of men are affected, and by which they are prevented from listening to what is true and receiving what is reasonable.

It well becomes any man, standing in the presence of such a nation as this, to speak of himself seldom, — and such a man as I am, it becomes to speak of himself not at all, except, indeed, when the relations in which he stands to his country are little known, and when the assertion of those relations has some connection, and may have some influence on interests which it is peculiarly incumbent upon him to support. Under this sanction, I say, it is not for a man whose ancestors have been planted in this country, now, for almost two centuries, — it is not for a man who has a family, and friends, and character, and children, and a deep stake in the soil, — it is not for a man who is self-conscious of being rooted in that soil as deeply and exclusively as the oak which shoots among its rocks, — it is not for such a man to hesitate or swerve a hair's breadth from his country's purpose and true interests, because of the yelpings, the howlings and snarlings, of that hungry pack, which corrupt men keep, directly or indirectly, in pay, with the view of hunting down every man who dare develop their purposes; a pack composed, it is true, of some native curs, but for the most part of hounds and spaniels of very recent importation, whose backs are seared by the lash and whose necks are sore with the collars of their former masters. In fulfilling his duty, the lover of his country must often be obliged to breast the shock of calumny. If called to that service, he will meet the exigency with the same firmness as, should another occasion call, he would breast the shock of battle. No! I am not to be deterred by such apprehensions. May Heaven so deal with me and mine, as I am true or faithless to the best interests of this people! May it deal with me according to its just judgments, when I fail to bring men and measures to the bar of public opinion, and to expose projects and systems of policy which I realize to be ruinous to the peace, prosperity and liberties, of my country!

RESTLESS SPIRIT OF HUMANITY. — *W. Fisk.*

There is a spirit, an active, aspiring principle in man, which cannot be broken down by oppression, or satisfied by indulgence:

> "He has a soul of vast desires, —
> It burns within with restless fires;"

desires which no earthly good can satisfy; fires which no waters of affliction or discouragement can quench. And it is from this his nature that society derives all its interests, and here, also, lies all its danger. This spirit is at once the terror of tyrants and the destroyer of republics.

To form some idea of its strength, let us look at it in its different conditions, both when it is depressed and when it is exalted. See when it is bent down for a time by the iron grasp and leaden sceptre of tyranny, cramping, and curtailing, and hedging in the soul, and foiling it in all its attempts to break from its bonds and assert its native independence! In these cases the noble spirit, like a wild beast in the toils, sinks down at times into sullen inactivity, only that it may rise again, when exhausted nature is a little restored, to rush, as hope excites or madness impels, in stronger paroxysms, against the cords which bind it down.

This is seen in the mobs and rebellions of the most besotted and enslaved nations. Witness the repeated convulsions in Ireland, that degraded and oppressed country. Neither desolating armies, nor numerous garrisons, nor the most rigorous administration, enforced by thousands of public executions, can break the spirit of that restless people. Witness Greece. Generations have passed away since the warriors of Greece have had their feet put in fetters, and the race of heroes had apparently become extinct, and the Grecian lyre had long been unstrung, and her lights put out. Her haughty masters thought her spirit was dead; but it was not dead, it only slept. In a moment, as it were, we saw all Greece in arms; she shook off her slumbers, and rushed, with frenzy and hope, upon seeming impossibilities, to conquer or to die. And though the mother and the daughter, as well as the father and the son, have fought and fallen in the common cause, until her population grows thin, — though Missolonghi and many other strongholds have fallen, until her fortifications are few and feeble, — though Christian nations have looked on with a cruel inactivity, without lending their needed aid, — yet the spirit of Greece is no more subdued than at the commencement of the contest. It cannot be subdued.

We see, then, that man has a spirit which is not easily broken down by oppression. Let us inquire whether it can be more easily satisfied by indulgence. And in every step of this inquiry we shall find that no miser ever yet had gold enough, no office-seeker ever yet had honor enough, no conqueror ever yet subdued kingdoms enough. When the rich man had filled his store-houses, he must pull down and build larger. When Cæsar had conquered all his enemies, he must enslave his friends. When Bonaparte had become the Emperor of France, he aspired to the throne of all Europe. Facts, a thousand facts in every age and among all classes, prove that such is the ambitious nature of the soul, such the increasing compass of its vast desires, that the material universe, with all its vastness, richness and variety, cannot satisfy it. Nor is it in the power of the governments of this world, in their most perfect forms, so to interest the feelings, so to regulate the desires, so to restrain the passions, or so to divert, or charm, or chain the souls of a whole community, but that these latent and ungovernable fires will sooner or later burst out, and endanger the whole body politic.

The wise framers of our excellent political institutions, like the eclectic philosophers, have selected the best parts out of all the systems which preceded them, and to these have added others, according to the suggestions of their own wisdom, or the leadings of Providence, and have formed the whole into a constitution, the most perfect the world has ever witnessed. Here everything that is rational in political liberty is enjoyed; here the most salutary checks and restraints that have yet been discovered are laid upon men in office. Here the road to honor and wealth is open to all, and here is general intelligence. But here man is found to possess the same nature as elsewhere. And the stirrings of his restless spirit have already disturbed the peace of society, and portend future convulsions. Party spirit is begotten; ambitious views are engendered, and fed, and inflamed; many are running the race for office; rivals are envied, characters are aspersed, animosities are enkindled, and the whole community are disturbed by the electioneering contest.

No meanness is foregone, no calumny is too glaring, no venality is too base, when the mind is inflamed with strong desire, and elated with the hope of success in the pursuit of some favorite object. And when the doubtful question is decided, it avails nothing. Disappointment sours the mind, and often produces the most bitter enmity and the most settled and systematic opposition in the unsuccessful party, while success but imperfectly satisfies the mind of the more fortunate.

And if no other influence come in, to curb the turbulent spirits of men, besides that which is found in our general intelligence and constitutional checks, probably at no great distance of time such convulsions may be witnessed in our now happy country as shall make the ears of him that heareth it tingle, and the eyes of him that seeth it weep blood. State may be arrayed against state, section against section, and party against party, till all the horrors of civil war may desolate our land!

FREE DISCUSSION. — *D. Webster.*

Important as I deem it to discuss, on all proper occasions, the policy of the measures at present pursued, it is still more important to maintain the right of such discussion in its full and just extent. Sentiments lately sprung up, and now growing fashionable, make it necessary to be explicit on this point. The more I perceive a disposition to check the freedom of inquiry by extravagant and unconstitutional pretences, the firmer shall be the tone in which I shall assert, and the freer the manner in which I shall exercise it.

It is the ancient and undoubted prerogative of the people to canvass public measures, and the merits of public men. It is a "home-bred right," a fireside privilege. It hath ever been enjoyed in every house, cottage and cabin, in the nation. It is not to be drawn into controversy. It is as undoubted as the right of breathing the air or walking on the earth. Belonging to public life as a right, it belongs to public life as a duty; and it is the last duty which those whose representative I am shall find me to abandon. Aiming at all times to be temperate and courteous in its use, except when the right itself shall be questioned, I shall then carry it to its extent. I shall place myself on the extreme boundary of my right, and bid defiance to any arm that would move me from my ground.

This high constitutional privilege I shall defend and exercise within this house, and without this house, and in all places; in time of peace, and in all times. Living, I shall assert it; and, should I leave no other inheritance to my children, by the blessing of God I will leave them the inheritance of free principles, and the example of a manly, independent and constitutional defence of them.

CHARACTER OF GEN. JACKSON. — *G. Bancroft.*

The men of the American Revolution are no more! That age of creative power has passed away. The last surviving signer of the Declaration of Independence has long since left the earth! Washington lies near his own Potomac, surrounded by his family and his servants. Adams, the Colossus of independence, reposes in the modest grave-yard of his native region. Jefferson sleeps on the heights of his own Monticello, whence his eye overlooked his beloved Virginia. Madison, the last survivor of the men who made our constitution, lives only in our hearts. But who shall say that the heroes in whom the image of God shone most brightly do not live forever? They were filled with the vast conceptions which called America into being; they lived for those conceptions, and their deeds praise them.

We are met to commemorate the virtues of one who shed his blood for our independence, took part in winning the territory and forming the early institutions of the west, and was imbued with all the great ideas which constitute the moral force of our country.

South Carolina gave a birth-place to Andrew Jackson. On its remote frontier, far up on the forest-clad banks of the Catawba, in a region where the settlers were just beginning to cluster, his eye first saw the light. There his infancy sported in the ancient forests, and his mind was nursed to freedom by their influence. His boyhood grew up in the midst of the contest with Great Britain. The first great political truth that reached his heart was, that all men are free and equal; the first great fact that beamed on his understanding was, his country's independence.

The strife, as it increased, came near the shades of his upland residence. As a boy of thirteen he witnessed the scenes of horror that accompany civil war; and when but a year older, with an elder brother, he shouldered his musket, and went forth to strike a blow for his country. Joyous era for America and for humanity! But for him, the orphan boy, the events were full of agony and grief!

At the very time when Washington was pledging his own and future generations to the support of the popular institutions which were to be the light of the human race, — at the time when the institutions of the Old World were rocking to their centre, and the mighty fabric that had come down from the middle ages was falling in, — the adventurous Jackson, in the radiant glory and boundless hope and confident intrepidity of twenty-one, plunged into the wilderness, crossed the great mountain-barrier that divides the western waters from the Atlantic, followed the paths of the early hunters and fugitives, and, not content with the nearer neighborhood to his parent state, went still further and further to the west, till he found his home in the most beautiful region on the Cumberland.

On all great occasions, Jackson's influence was deferred to. When Jefferson had acquired for the country the whole of Louisiana, and there seemed some hesitancy on the part of Spain to acknowledge our possession, the services of Jackson were solicited by the national administration, and were not called into full exercise only from the peaceful termination of the incidents that occasioned the summons. In the long series of aggressions on the freedom of the seas and the rights of the American flag, Jackson was on the side of his country and the new maritime code of republicanism. In his inland home, where the roar of the breakers was never heard, and the mariner was never seen, he resented the continued aggression on our commerce and on our sailors.

A pupil of the wilderness, his heart was with the pioneers of American life towards the setting sun. No American statesman has ever embraced within his affections a scheme so liberal for the emigrants as that of Jackson. He longed to secure to them, not preëmption rights only, but more than preëmption rights. He longed to invite labor to take possession of the unoccupied fields without money and without price, with no obligation except the perpetual devotion of itself by allegiance to its country. Under the beneficent influence of his opinions, the sons of misfortune, the children of adventure, find their way to the uncultivated west. There, in some wilderness glade, or in the thick forest of the fertile plain, or where the prairies most sparkle with flowers, they, like the wild bee which sets them the example of industry, may choose their home, mark the extent of their possessions by driving stakes or blazing trees, shelter their log-cabins with the boughs and turf, and teach the virgin soil to yield itself to the ploughshare. Theirs shall be the soil, theirs the beautiful farms which they teach to be productive. Come, children of sorrow! you on whom the Old World frowns, crowd fearlessly to the forests; plant your homes in confidence, for the country watches over you; your children grow around you as hostages, and the wilderness, at your bidding, surrenders its grandeur of useless luxuriance to the beauty and loveliness of culture.

The portions of country that suffered most severely from a system of legislation which, in its extreme character, as it then existed, is now universally acknowledged to have been unequal and unjust, were less tranquil; and, rallying on the doctrines of freedom, which made our government a limited one, they saw in the oppressive acts an assumption of power which was nugatory, because it was exercised, as they held, without authority from the people. The contest that ensued was the most momentous in our annals. The greatest minds of America engaged in the discussion. Eloquence never achieved sublimer triumphs in the American senate than on those occasions. The country became deeply divided, and the antagonist elements were arrayed against each other under forms of clashing authority, menacing civil war; the freedom of the several states was invoked against the power of the United States; and, under the organization of a state in convention, the reserved rights of the people were summoned to display their energy, and balance the authority and neutralize the legislation of the central government. The states were agitated with prolonged excitement; the friends of freedom throughout the world looked on with divided sympathies, praying that the Union of the States might be perpetual, and also that the commerce of the world might be free.

Fortunately for the country, and fortunately for mankind, Andrew Jackson was at the helm of state, the representative of the principles that were to allay excitement, and to restore the hopes of peace and freedom. By nature, by impulse, by education, by conviction, a friend to personal freedom, — by education, political sympathies, and the fixed habit of his mind, a friend to the rights of the states, — unwilling that the liberty of the states should be trampled under foot, unwilling that the constitution should lose its vigor or be impaired, he rallied for the constitution, and in its name he published to the world, "THE UNION, IT MUST BE PRESERVED!" The words were a spell to hush evil passion and to remove oppression. Under his guiding influence the favored interests, which had struggled to perpetuate unjust legislation, yielded to the voice of moderation and reform, and every mind that had for a moment contemplated a rupture of the states discarded it forever. The whole influence of the past was invoked in favor of the constitution; from the council-chambers of the fathers who moulded our institutions, from the hall where American independence was declared, the clear, loud cry was uttered, "The Union, it must be preserved." From every battle-field of the Revolution, — from Lexington and Bunker Hill, from Saratoga and Yorktown, from the fields of Eutaw, from the cane-brakes that sheltered the men of Marion, — the repeated, long-prolonged echoes came up, "The Union, it must be preserved!" From every valley in our land, from every cabin on the pleasant mountain-sides, from the ships at our wharves, from the tents of the hunter in our westernmost prairies, from the living minds of the living millions of American freemen, from the thickly-coming glories of futurity, the shout went up like the sound of many waters, "The Union, it must be preserved!"

Behold the warrior and statesman, his work well done, retired to the Hermitage, to hold converse with his forests, to cultivate his farm, to gather around him hospitably his friends! Who was like HIM? He was still the loadstar of the American people. His fervid thoughts, frankly uttered, still spread the flame of patriotism through the American breast; his counsels were still listened to with reverence; and, almost alone among statesmen, he in his retirement was in harmony with every onward movement of his time. His prevailing influence assisted to sway a neighboring nation to desire to share our institutions; his ear heard the footsteps of the coming millions that are to gladden our western shores, and his eye discerned in the dim distance the whitening sails that are to enliven the waters of the Pacific with the social sounds of our successful commerce.

Age had whitened his locks, and dimmed his eye, and spread around him the infirmities and venerable emblems of many years of toilsome service; but his heart beat as warmly as in his youth, and his courage was as firm as it had ever been in the day of battle. But, while his affections were still for his friends and his country, his thoughts were already in a better world. That exalted mind, which in active life had always had unity of perception and will, which in action had never faltered from doubt, and which in counsel had always reverted to first principles and general laws, now gave itself up to communing with the Infinite. He was a believer, from feeling, from experience, from conviction. Not a shadow of scepticism ever dimmed the lustre of his mind. Proud philosopher, will you smile to know that Andrew Jackson perused reverently his Psalter and Prayer-Book and Bible? Know that Andrew Jackson had faith in the eternity of truth, in the imperishable power of popular freedom, in the destinies of humanity, in the virtues and capacity of the people, in his country's institutions, in the being and over-ruling providence of a merciful and ever-living God.

The last moment of his life on earth is at hand. It is the Sabbath of the Lord; the brightness and beauty of the summer clothe the fields around him; nature is in her glory; — but the sublimest spectacle on that day, on earth, was the victory of his unblenching spirit over death itself! In life, his career had been like the blaze of the sun in the fierceness of its noonday glory; his death was lovely as the mildest sunset of a summer's evening, when the sun goes down in tranquil beauty without a cloud!

SUFFERINGS AND DESTINY OF THE PILGRIMS. — *E. Everett.*

Methinks I see it now, that one solitary, adventurous vessel, the Mayflower of a forlorn hope, freighted with the prospects of a future state, and bound across the unknown sea. I behold it pursuing, with a thousand misgivings, the uncertain, the tedious voyage. Suns rise and set, and weeks and months pass, and winter surprises them on the deep, but brings them not the sight of the wished-for shore. I see them now, scantily supplied with provisions, crowded almost to suffocation in their ill-stored prison, delayed by calms, pursuing a circuitous route; and now driven in fury before the raging tempest, on the high and giddy wave. The awful voice of the storm howls through the rigging; the laboring masts seem straining from their base; the dismal sound of the pumps is heard; the ship leaps, as it were, madly from billow to billow; the ocean breaks, and settles with ingulfing floods over the floating deck, and beats, with deadening, shivering weight, against the staggered vessel. I see them, escaped from these perils, pursuing their all but desperate undertaking, and landed, at last, after a few months' passage, on the ice-clad rocks of Plymouth, weak and weary from the voyage, poorly armed, scantily provisioned, without shelter, without means, surrounded by hostile tribes.

Shut, now, the volume of history, and tell me, on any principle of human probability, what shall be the fate of this handful of adventurers? Tell me, man of military science, in how many months were they all swept off by the thirty savage tribes enumerated within the early limits of New England? Tell me, politician, how long did this shadow of a colony, on which your conventions and treaties had not smiled, languish on the distant coast? Student of history, compare for me the baffled projects, the deserted settlements, the abandoned adventures, of other times, and find the parallel of this! Was it the winter's storm, beating upon the houseless heads of women and children, was it hard labor and spare meals, was it disease, was it the tomahawk, — was it the deep malady of a blighted hope, a ruined enterprise, and a broken heart, aching, in its last moments, at the recollection of the loved and left, beyond the sea, — was it some, or all of these united, that hurried this forsaken company to their melancholy fate? And is it possible that neither of these causes, that not all combined, were able to blast this bud of hope? Is it possible that from a beginning so feeble, so frail, so worthy not so much of admiration as of pity, there has gone forth a progress so steady, a growth so wonderful, an expansion so ample, a reality so important, a promise, yet to be fulfilled, so glorious!

RELIGION AND POETRY. — *W. H. Hamersley.*

POETRY can adapt herself to all ages. She can weave a simple ballad for childhood, or a fervent song for the youth ripening into manhood; she has her pictures of fireside happiness and domestic comfort for the parent, and her voice has a tone for the ear of the aged. She can adapt herself to all conditions. She has her simple and affecting narrative for the poor and the humble; she has a trumpet voice for the soldier and the statesman, and a most refined speech for the scholar. She will be our companion at all times and in all seasons; she will give an additional zest to prosperity, and when the season of adversity shall arrive she will comfort the wounded spirit and bind up the broken heart.

The most groundless and anomalous objections urged against poetry are those which proceed from a certain class of religious men. The chief charge on the part of such men is the perversion of poetry to improper uses. As well might they tell the patriot not to draw the sword in behalf of his country because it is the weapon of the oppressor; as well might they cast away the book of life because its meaning is distorted by fools and fanatics. Poetry is most grand when connected with religious subjects; and in her purest and most sublime personification she does not, like Ajax, defy the lightning and the God who wields it, but, like the ethereal beings around the throne of heaven, she veils her burning eyes with her resplendent wings when in the solemn presence of the Almighty. He who has no love for poetry may lay to heart the precepts of the Bible; but there is a light upon the pages of that book which he sees not, there is a harmony in its language which he hears not, — for there is a vein of poetic fire, pure, simple and sublime, running through the whole sacred volume.

We not only find poetry in the abstract in the Scriptures, but it has been maintained that a portion of its contents are written in accordance with certain rules of composition, approximating in some degree to those which govern its construction in its most exclusive sense; as in the following, among many instances:

"My soul doth magnify the Lord,
And my spirit hath rejoiced in God my Saviour."

"He looketh on the earth,
And it trembleth;
He toucheth the hills,
And they smoke."

"I planted,
Apollos watered,
But God made to grow:
So that neither he who planteth is anything,
Nor he that watereth,
But God, who maketh to grow."

The life of Christ is a poem, and the argument comprehends the miraculous birth; the star, that God-appointed herald, leading the wise men to the cradle of the child Jesus; the youth disputing with the doctors; the celestial baptism; the man of sorrows expressing the perfect love of God; the little children gathered to his bosom as the exemplars of the simple and pure faith of the righteous; the blind seeing, and the lame walking, and the sick recovering, and the dead rising from their graves, at his command; the temptation, the fast, the transfiguration, the trial, the crucifixion, the prayer for the forgiveness of his persecutors, uttered amid the agony of the cross; the resurrection, and the mission of salvation fulfilled by an ascension welcomed by the harmonious hallelujahs of a heavenly chorus.

The doctrine of the immortality of the soul, which is "brought to light" in the Scriptures, infuses into the heart of the poet true life, and energy, and sublimity, and opens to his vision fields of eternal hope and beauty.

It is the chief glory of poetry that she bears us on spotless wings far above the sensuous sphere of earth, and, like the repentant tear which the Peri conveyed to the angel, removes the crystal bar that binds the gates of paradise.

I am well assured that poetry, although sometimes seen in connection with error, even as the sons of God held companionship with the daughters of men, is one of the choicest blessings bequeathed to this imperfect world. The Christian can trace her divine origin with the utmost certainty, and behold with an unclouded vision that she is born of God and baptized with inspiration. She diffuses a new light upon the face of nature, she weans us from the rule of our passions and the dominion of our lusts, and reveals the golden ladder that leads from earth to heaven.

IN BEHALF OF GREECE.—*H. Clay.*

It has been admitted by all that there is impending over this country a threatening storm, which is likely to call into action all our vigor, courage, and resources. Is it a wise way of preparing for this awful event, to talk to this nation of its incompetency to resist European aggression, to lower its spirit, to weaken its moral force, and do what we can to prepare it for base submission and easy conquest? If there be any reality in this menacing danger, I would rather adjure the nation to remember that it contains a million of freemen capable of bearing arms, and ready to exhaust their last drop of blood, and their last cent, in defending their country, its institutions, and its liberty. Are these to be conquered, by all Europe united? No; no united nation can be, that has the spirit to resolve not to be conquered, — such a nation is ever invincible. And has it come to this? Are we so humbled, so low, so despicable, that we dare not express our sympathy for suffering Greece, lest, peradventure, we might offend some one or more of their imperial and royal majesties? If gentlemen are afraid to act rashly on such a subject, suppose that we draw an humble petition addressed to their majesties, asking them that of their condescension they would allow us to express something on the subject. How shall it begin? "We, the representatives of the free people of the United States of America, humbly approach the thrones of your imperial and royal majesties, and supplicate that of your imperial and royal clemency" — I will not go through the disgusting recital; my lips have not yet learnt the sycophantic language of a degraded slave! Are we so low, so base, so despicable, that we may not express our horror, articulate our detestation, of the most brutal and atrocious war that ever stained earth or shocked high Heaven with the ferocious deeds of a brutal soldiery, set on by the clergy and followers of a fanatical and inimical religion, and rioting in excess of blood and butchery, at the mere details of which the heart sickens? If the great mass of Christendom can look coolly and calmly on while all this is perpetrated on a Christian people in their own vicinity, in their very presence, let us, at least, show that, in this distant extremity, there is still some sensibility and sympathy for Christian wrongs and sufferings, — that there are still feelings which can kindle into indignation at the oppression of a people endeared to us by every ancient recollection and every modern tie!

But it is not first and chiefly for Greece that I wish to see this measure adopted. It will give them but little aid — that aid purely of a moral kind. It is indeed soothing and solacing in distress to hear the accents of a friendly voice. We know this as a people. But it is principally and mainly for America herself, for the credit and character of our common country, that I hope to see this resolution pass; it is for our own unsullied name that I feel.

Go home, if you dare, — go home, if you can, — to your constituents, and tell them that you voted it down! Meet, if you dare, the appalling countenances of those who sent you here, and tell them that you shrank from the declaration of your own sentiments — that, you cannot tell how, but that some unknown dread, some indescribable apprehension, some indefinable danger, affrighted you, — that the spectres of scimetars, and crowns, and crescents, gleamed before you and alarmed you, and that you suppressed all the noble feelings prompted by religion, by liberty, by national independence, and by humanity!

THE MURDERER'S SECRET. — *D. Webster.*

The deed was executed with a degree of self-possession and steadiness equal to the wickedness with which it was planned. The circumstances, now clearly in evidence, spread out the whole scene before us. Deep sleep had fallen on the destined victim, and on all beneath his roof. A healthful old man, to whom sleep was sweet, the first sound slumbers of the night hold him in their soft but strong embrace. The assassin enters, through the window already prepared, into an unoccupied apartment. With noiseless foot he paces the lonely hall, half-lighted by the moon; he winds up the ascent of the stairs, and reaches the door of the chamber. Of this he moves the lock, by soft and continued pressure, till it turns on its hinges without noise; and he enters, and beholds his victim before him! The room was uncommonly open to the admission of light. The face of the innocent sleeper was turned from the murderer, and the beams of the moon, resting on the gray locks of his aged temple, showed him where to strike. The fatal blow is given! and the victim passes, without a struggle or a motion, from the repose of sleep to the repose of death! It is the assassin's purpose to make sure work; and he yet plies the dagger, though it was obvious that life had been destroyed by the blow of the bludgeon. He even raises the aged arm, that he may not fail in his aim at the heart, and replaces it again over the wounds of the poniard! To finish the picture, he explores the wrist for the pulse! He feels for it, and ascertains that it beats no longer. It is accomplished! The deed is done! He retreats, retraces his steps to the window, passes out through it as he came in, and escapes. He has done the murder; no eye has seen him, no ear has heard him. The secret is his own, and it is safe!

Ah! gentlemen, that was a dreadful mistake! Such a secret can be safe nowhere. The whole creation of God has neither nook nor corner where the guilty can bestow it, and say it is safe. Not to speak of that Eye which glances through all disguises, and beholds everything as in the splendor of noon, such secrets of guilt are never safe from detection, even by man.

True it is, generally speaking, that "murder will out." True it is, that Providence hath so ordained, and doth so govern things, that those who break the great law of Heaven by shedding man's blood seldom succeed in avoiding discovery: especially in a case exciting so much attention as this, discovery must and will come, sooner or later. A thousand eyes turn at once to explore every man, every thing, every circumstance, connected with the time and place; a thousand ears catch every whisper; a thousand excited minds intensely dwell on the scene, shedding all their light, and ready to kindle the slightest circumstance into a blaze of discovery. Meantime, the guilty soul cannot keep its own secret. It is false to itself; or, rather, it feels an irresistible impulse of conscience to be true to itself; it labors under its guilty possession, and knows not what to do with it. The human heart was not made for the residence of such an inhabitant; it finds itself preyed on by a torment, which it dares not acknowledge to God or man. A vulture is devouring it, and it asks no sympathy or assistance, either from heaven or earth. The secret which the murderer possesses soon comes to possess him; and, like the evil spirit of which we read, it overcomes him, and leads him whithersoever it will. He feels it beating at his heart, rising to his throat, and demanding disclosure. He thinks the whole world sees it in his face, reads it in his eyes, and almost hears its workings in the very silence of his thoughts. It has become his master. It betrays his discretion; it breaks down his courage; it conquers his prudence. When suspicions from without begin to embarrass him, and the net of circumstances to entangle him, the fatal secret struggles with still greater violence to burst forth. It must be confessed; it will be confessed; there is no refuge from confession but in suicide, — and suicide is confession!

ASPIRATIONS FOR AMERICA. — *C. M. Clay.*

WHILE the Union lasts, amid these fertile verdant fields, these ever-flowing rivers, these stately groves, this genial, healthful clime, this old Kentucky land, — hallowed by the blood of our sires, endeared by the beauty of her daughters, illustrious by the valor and eloquence of her sons, the centre of a most glorious empire, guarded by a cordon of states garrisoned by freemen, girt round by the rising and setting seas, — we are the most blessed of all people. Let the Union be dissolved, let that line be drawn where be drawn it must, and we are a border state: in time of peace with no outlet to the ocean, the highway of nations, a miserable dependency; in time of war the battle-ground of more than Indian warfare — of civil strife and indiscriminate slaughter! When, worse than Spanish provinces, we shall contend not for glory and renown, but, like the aborigines of old, for a contemptible life and miserable subsistence! Let me not see it! Among those proud courts and lordly coteries of Europe's pride, where fifty years ago we were regarded as petty provinces, unknown to ears polite, let me go forth great in the name of an American citizen. Let me point them to our statesmen and the laws and governments of their creation, the rapid advance of political science, the monuments of their fame, now the study of all Europe. Let them look at our rapidly increasing and happy population, see our canals, and turnpikes, and railroads, stretching over more space than combined Britain and Europe have reached by the same means. Let them send their philanthropists to learn of our penitentiary systems, our schools, and our civil institutions. Let them behold our skill in machinery, in steamboat and ship building, — hail the most gallant ship that breasts the mountain wave, and she shall wave from her flag-staff the stars and stripes. These are the images which I cherish; this the nation which I honor; and never will I throw one pebble in her track, to jostle the footsteps of her glorious march!

AMERICAN INDEPENDENCE. — *L. Woodbury.*

There seem to me some points of opinion common to us all in relation to the excellences and glories of the independence we celebrate. One of these points is the great importance of that event. On that account, inspired by one common gratitude, we all join heart and tongue in one chorus of thanksgiving to the statesmen and patriots and heroes who won our hallowed independence. They established among us its immortal principles, we hope, forever.

Lisping infancy, therefore, youth, manhood, and decrepit age, come together to-day; matron and maid, as well as the sunburnt millions from the plough and the vessel's decks, should come, — all professions and ranks, and forms of faith, political or religious, — from every hill, and valley, and prairie, of our beloved country, from Maine to California, — all gather in joyful throngs, and all bend in veneration before the glorious event, and its thrice-glorious doctrines.

This is not, that almost fourscore years ago some plain American farmers, planters, merchants and lawyers, assembled in a small room near Independence-square, in Philadelphia. It is not, that some among them, with iron heart and eagle eye, dared do all which had immortalized the Brutuses and Cromwells of other ages, and not only speak their wrongs, but redress and avenge them. It is not, that then and there was done a deed, to become a newspaper theme for a brief month only, or to be known not beyond the few cities and settlements then scattered over the eastern slope of the Alleghanies, containing a population but little larger than the State of New York now does alone; or to live in its influences only a generation, a half-century even, and then die out, as have perished from the page of history millions of other occurrences, at first far more dazzling to the inexperienced eye. But it was, that then occurred an event which has become incorporate with Liberty herself, — is a part of her substance no less than symbol, — and shall endure as long and spread as wide as the longest and widest portion of her magnificent empire. An event, which, if not destined to revolutionize all nations and people, has been already felt, in some degree, wherever civilization pervades mankind, and is likely, in coming ages, more and more, by "the war of opinion" it wages, to leaven the political views of the whole habitable globe. To dethrone a king by oppressed subjects has always been one of the most glowing themes in the annals of the human race. To change a dynasty of kings looms up still larger in the horizon of history and poetry. To alter the whole form of government in any country often has a bearing more important than either on its future destinies; and especially so if it be a change from slavery to freedom, for the people at large. But to do *all* these, — *more* than all, — to show consummate skill in the cabinet at the same time with heroic bravery in the field, and to accomplish a revolution in principles of government and legislation by the pen and the tongue, while another was carried on and gloriously sustained by the sword,— by the blood of freemen poured out in torrents wherever the invader polluted the soil, or a ruthless savage was let loose, with tomahawk and torch, on an exposed frontier, — this was an event that all the millions who have been signally blessed by it may well celebrate, for its grandeur, — may long and loudly celebrate, — and will, by God's permission, hold in holy remembrance, while they preserve any of the virtues of the patriots who accomplished it.

Myriads elsewhere, who have enjoyed only some of its *reflected* light, would shame us for any neglect of so great a revolution, by their heart-felt rejoicings over only so much of its influences as have reached and animated them in the cause of political reform;

because it has been the talisman and tocsin to freedom in all countries since. Whenever, for the last half-century, an oppressed people have broken their chains, — whether in France, or Hungary, or the classic soil of Italy, — the recollection of American independence has strengthened, if not guided, the blow; and, when tyrants since have trembled at popular indignation, and listened to remonstrances, and relented or reformed, the memory of American liberties and victories has struck terror to their hearts, and made them relent, oftener than arms or arguments, or a returning sense of justice towards the victims of their wrongs.

Not only have this western continent and some of its adjacent islands — both sides of the Andes — been thus made vocal with songs of gratitude for the example set this day, but Europe, from the Baltic to the Mediterranean, has felt the influence of some of its sacred principles, and been slowly but surely reforming, in order to save at all, a portion of its superannuated institutions. Even Asia has witnessed a grand vizier appealing through the press in favor of popular education and the welfare of the people at large; and ere another century closes, it would not be more extraordinary to see such principles prevailing in China, — in one kingdom alone of the populous east, — half of the whole human race. Misunderstood and misrepresented, I admit, often have been the character of our Revolution, and the designs and doctrines of the patriots who accomplished it; and many, it must be conceded, have been the outrages committed under a pretence of justification through its principles, as flagrant crimes have, in all ages, been committed under the sacred names of liberty and religion. But the establishment of American independence is no more answerable for such abuse, such perversions of her holy cause, than are religion and liberty for the profanations before, as well as since, committed under their consecrated banner; and proceeding, as we ought on occasions like this, to make some inquiry into the true civil consequences of that independence, no less than its military daring, in order to appreciate duly the greatness of the event, it will be found that their legitimate operation, their true essence, their full and perfect work, both here and elsewhere, is likely to prove most auspicious to the human race.

FAREWELL ADDRESS TO HIS TROOPS. — *A. Jackson.*

Possessing those dispositions which equally adorn the citizen and the soldier, the expectations of your country will be met in peace, as her wishes have been gratified in war. Go, then, my brave companions, to your homes, — to those tender connections and blissful scenes which render life so dear, — full of honor, and crowned with laurels which will never fade. When participating, in the bosoms of your families, the enjoyment of peaceful life, with what happiness will you not look back to the toils you have borne, to the dangers you have encountered! How will all your past exposures be converted into sources of inexpressible delight! Who that never experienced your sufferings will be able to appreciate your joys? The man who slumbered ingloriously at home during your painful marches, your nights of watchfulness and your days of toil, will envy you the happiness which these recollections will afford; still more will he envy the gratitude of that country which you have so eminently contributed to save. Continue, fellow-soldiers, on your passage to your several destinations, to preserve that subordination, that dignified and manly deportment, which have so ennobled your character.

While the commanding general is thus giving indulgence to his feelings towards those brave companions who accompanied him through difficulties and danger, he cannot permit the names of Blount, and Shelby, and Holmes, to pass unnoticed. With what generous ardor and patriotism have these distinguished governors contributed all their exertions to provide the means of victory! The recollections of their exertions, and of the success which has resulted, will be to them a reward more grateful than any which the pomp of title or the splendor of wealth can bestow.

What happiness it is to the commanding general, that, while danger was before him, he was, on no occasion, compelled to use towards his companions in arms either severity or rebuke! If, after the enemy had retired, improper passions began their empire in a few unworthy bosoms, and rendered a resort to energetic measures necessary for their suppression, he has not confounded the innocent with the guilty, the seduced with the seducers. Towards you, fellow-soldiers, the most cheering recollections exist, blended, alas! with regret that disease and war should have ravished from us so many worthy companions. But the memory of the cause in which they perished, and of the virtues which animated them while living, must occupy the place where sorrow would claim to dwell.

Farewell, fellow-soldiers! The expression of your general's is feeble, but the gratitude of a country of freemen is yours, — yours the applause of an admiring world.

MUSIC. — *H. Bushnell.*

It cannot be said that music is a human creation, and, as far as the substances of the world are concerned, a mere accident. As well can it be said that man creates the colors of the prism, and that they are not the properties of the light, because he shapes the prism by his own mechanical art. Or, if still we doubt, if it seems incredible that the soul of music is in the heart of all created being, then the laws of harmony themselves shall answer, one string vibrating to another, when it is not struck itself, and uttering its voice of concord simply because the concord is in it, and it feels the pulses on the air to which it cannot be silent. Nay, the solid mountains and their giant masses of rock shall answer, catching, as they will, the bray of horns or the stunning blast of cannon, rolling it across from one top to another in reverberating pulses, till it falls into bars of musical rhythm, and chimes and cadences of silver melody. I have heard some fine music, as men are wont to speak — the play of orchestras, the anthems of choirs, the voices of song that moved admiring nations. But in the lofty passes of the Alps I heard a music overhead from God's cloudy orchestra, the giant peaks of rock and ice, curtained in by the driving mist, and only dimly visible, athwart the sky, through its folds, such as mocks all sounds our lower worlds of art can ever hope to raise. I stood (excuse the simplicity) calling to them, in the loudest shouts

I could raise, even till my power was spent, and listening in compulsory trance to their reply. I heard them roll it up through their cloudy worlds of snow, sifting out the harsh qualities that were tearing in it as demon screams of sin, holding on upon it as if it were a hymn they were fining to the ear of the great Creator, and sending it round and round in long reduplications of sweetness, minute after minute, till, finally receding and rising, it trembled, as it were, among the quick gratulations of angels, and fell into the silence of the pure empyrean. I had never any conception before of what is meant by *quality* in sound. There was more power upon the soul, in one of those simple notes, than I ever expect to feel from anything called music below, or ever can feel till I hear them again in the choirs of the angelic world. I had never such a sense of purity, or of what a simple sound may tell of purity, by its own pure quality; and I could not but say, O, my God, teach me this! be this in me forever! And I can truly affirm that the experience of that hour has consciously made me better able to think of God ever since — better able to worship. All other sounds are gone, — the sounds of yesterday heard in the silence of enchanted multitudes are gone, — but that is with me still, and I hope will never cease to ring in my spirit, till I go down to the slumber of silence itself!

EARLY DAYS OF THE REVOLUTION. — *J. T. Austin.*

MASSACHUSETTS is the mother of the Revolution. Her efforts in its commencement are too honorable to be omitted in the heraldry of her fame. Earliest and alone, — without aid, without allies, connections or confederacy, — singly, by her own will, she dissolved the royal powers within her own territory and over her own people, and assumed to herself the prerogative of independence. When her congress of delegates assembled at Watertown, in defiance of the royal charter, and spurned the representatives of the crown, and assumed the powers of civil government, and took possession of the public treasury, and levied taxes, and established a navy, and commissioned that American vessel of war that first captured a British ship on the ocean, and erected maritime courts, and appointed judges, and administered justice to belligerent and neutral by the law of nations, and raised an army, and nominated officers, and gathered soldiers under the pine-tree banner of Massachusetts, and poured out a rich libation of blood on the battle-field of freedom, the colonial character was at an end. The Revolution had begun. The state was then free, sovereign, and independent.

Bring to the imagination that band of determined men, assembled at Watertown, unarmed and defenceless, within cannon-shot of a disciplined army; their fortunes in the camp of a military commander, whose dignity they had offended; their persons liable to be seized and sent to Europe, as traitors; their conduct impeached in a public proclamation, and two of them proscribed as rebels, whose offences were too heinous for the pardon of the king. Judge of their anxiety, in that time that tried men's souls; their immense responsibility to the country, whose destiny they directed; to their children, for the protection that was due to them; to posterity, for that political condition which would be a legacy of honor or of shame; to their God, before whom they were answerable, and felt themselves answerable, for all the blood of a war they might accelerate or prevent. How indistinct their vision of the future, even when a strong faith threw its light upon their souls! How difficult their task to keep up the courage of the timid, the hopes of the desponding, the strength of the feeble; to enlighten the ignorant, restrain the rash, supply the destitute, and impart to all the pure motives which consecrate success! Here was no mad ambition, no lust of power, no allurement of interest, no scheme of personal distinction. Few of them are remembered in history. Yet these are they whose light gave promise of a coming dawn. If they recede from the general gaze, it is in the noon-tide splendor of a brighter day.

"They set as sets the morning star, which goes
Not down behind the darkened west, nor hides
Obscured among the tempests of the sky,
But melts away into the light of heaven"

Had these men proved incompetent to the task, the battle for that generation would have been lost when it began. Independence might, indeed, have been obtained, for no foreign power could long hold a continent in its grasp; but the struggle must have been made in this age, and not that; and the desolation of civil war, which marks the times of our forefathers, would have been the melancholy history of our own.

THE MECHANICAL EPOCH. — *J. P. Kennedy.*

The world is now entering upon the mechanical epoch. There is nothing in the future more sure than the great triumphs which that epoch is to achieve. It has already advanced to some glorious conquests. What miracles of mechanical invention already crowd upon us! Look abroad, and contemplate the infinite achievements of the steam power. Reflect a moment on all that has been done by the railroad. Pause to estimate, if you can, with all the help of imagination, what is to result from the agency now manifested in the operations of the telegraph. Cast a thought over the whole field of scientific mechanical improvement and its application to human wants, in the last twenty years, — to go no further back, — and think what a world it has made; — how many comforts it has given to man, how many facilities; what it has done for his food and raiment, for his communication with his fellow-man in every clime, for his instruction in books, his amusements, his safety! — what new lands it has opened, what old ones made accessible! — how it has enlarged the sphere of his knowledge and conversancy with his species! It is all a great, astounding marvel, a miracle which it oppresses the mind to think of. It is the smallest boast which can be made for it to say that, in all desirable facilities in life, in the comfort that depends upon mechanism, and in all that is calculated to delight the senses or instruct the mind, the man of this day, who has secured himself a moderate competence, is placed far in advance of the most wealthy, powerful and princely, of ancient times, — might I not say, of the times less than a century gone by?

And yet we have only begun — we are but on the threshold of this epoch. A great celebration is now drawing to a close, — the celebration, by all nations, of the new era. A vast multitude of all peoples, nations and tongues, has been, but yesterday, gathered under a magnificent crystal palace, in the greatest city of the world, to illustrate and distinguish the achievements of art, — no less, also, to dignify and exalt the great mechanical fraternity who have filled that palace with wonders. Is not this fact, of itself, charged with a volume of comment? What is it but the setting of the great distinctive seal upon the nineteenth century? — an advertisement of the fact that society has risen to occupy a higher platform than ever before? — a proclamation from the high places, announcing honor, honor immortal, to the workmen who fill this world with beauty, comfort and power; honor to be forever embalmed in history, to be perpetuated in monuments, to be written in the hearts of this and succeeding generations!

JUSTICE TO ENGLAND. — *C. Sprague.*

If, in remembering the oppressed, you think the oppressors ought not to be forgotten, I might urge that the splendid result of the great struggle should fully reconcile us to the madness of those who rendered that struggle necessary. We may forgive the presumption which "declared" its right "to bind the American colonies," for it was wofully expiated by the humiliation which "acknowledged" those same "American colonies" to be "sovereign and independent states." The immediate workers, too, of that political iniquity, have passed away. The mildew of shame will forever feed upon their memories; — a brand has been set upon their deeds, that even Time's all-gnawing tooth can never destroy. But they *have* passed away; and of all the millions they misruled, the millions they *would* have misruled, how few remain! Another race is there to lament the folly, another here to magnify the wisdom, that cut the knot of empire. Shall these inherit and entail everlasting enmity? Like the Carthaginian Hamilcar, shall we come up hither with our children, and on this holy altar swear the pagan oath of undying hate? Even our goaded fathers disdained this. Let us fulfil their words, and prove to the people of England that "in peace" we know how to treat them "as friends." They have been twice told that "in war" we know how to meet them "as enemies;" and they will hardly ask another lesson, for, it may be that, when the *third* trumpet shall sound, a voice will echo along their sea-girt cliffs — "The glory has departed!"

Some few of their degenerate ones, tainting the bowers where they sit, decry the growing greatness of a land they will not love; and others, after eating from our basket, and drinking from our cup, go home to pour forth the senseless libel against a people at whose firesides they were warmed. But a few pens dipped in gall will not retard our progress; let not a few tongues festering in falsehood disturb our repose. We have those among us who are able both to pare the talons of the kite and pull out the fangs of the viper; who can lay bare, for the disgust of all good men, the gangrene of the insolent reviewer, and inflict such a cruel mark on the back of the mortified runaway, as will take long from him the blessed privilege of being forgotten.

These rude detractors speak not, we trust, the feelings of their nation. Time, the great corrector, is there fast enlightening both ruler and ruled. They are treading in our steps, even ours; and are gradually, though slowly, pulling up their ancient religious and political landmarks. Yielding to the liberal spirit of the age, — a spirit born and fostered here, — they are not only loosening their own long-riveted shackles, but are raising the voice of encouragement, and extending the hand of assistance, to the "rebels" of other climes.

In spite of all that has passed, we owe England much; and even on this occasion, standing in the midst of my generous-minded countrymen, I may fearlessly, willingly, acknowledge the debt. We owe England much; —nothing for her martyrdoms; nothing for her proscriptions; nothing for the innocent blood with which she has stained the white robes of religion and liberty; — these claims our fathers cancelled, and her monarch rendered them and theirs a full acquittance forever. But for the living treasures of her mind, garnered up and spread abroad for centuries by her great and gifted, who that has drank at the sparkling streams of her poetry, who that has drawn from the deep fountains of her wisdom, who that speaks and reads and thinks her language, will be slow to own his obligation? One of your purest ascended patriots, — Quincy, — he who compassed sea and land for liberty, whose early voice for her echoed round yonder consecrated hall, whose dying accents for her went up in solitude and suffering from the ocean, — when he sat down to bless, with the last token of a father's remembrance, the son who wears his mantle with his name, bequeathed him the recorded lessons of England's best and wisest, and sealed the legacy of love with a prayer, whose full accomplishment we live to witness, — "that the spirit of liberty might rest upon him."

EXAMPLE OF AMERICA. — *C. M. Clay.*

How many, like the great Emmet, have died, and left only a name to attract our admiration for their virtues, and our regret for their untimely fall, to excite to deeds which they would but could not effect! But what has Washington left behind, save the glory of a name? The independent mind, the conscious pride, the ennobling principle of the soul, — a nation of freemen. What did he leave? He left us to ourselves. This is the sum of our liberties, the first principle of government, the power of public opinion, — public opinion, the only permanent power on earth. When did a people flourish like Americans? Yet where, in a time of peace, has more use been made with the pen, or less with the sword of power? When did a religion flourish like the Christian, since they have done away with intolerance? Since men have come to believe and know that physical force cannot affect the immortal part, and that religion is between the conscience and the Creator only. He of 622, who with the sword propagated his doctrines throughout Arabia and the greater part of the barbarian world, against the power of whose tenets the physical force of all Christendom was opposed in vain, under the effective operations of freedom of opinion is fast passing the way of all error.

Napoleon, the contemporary of our Washington, is fast dying away from the lips of men. He who shook the whole civilized earth, — who, in an age of knowledge and concert among nations, held the world at bay, — at whose exploits the imagination becomes bewildered, — who, in the *eve* of his glory, was honored with the pathetic appellation of "the last lone captive of millions in war," — even *he* is now known only in history. The vast empire was fast tumbling to ruins whilst he yet held the sword. He passed away, and left "no successor" there! The unhallowed light which obscured *is gone;* but brightly beams *yet* the name of Washington!

This freedom of opinion, which has done so much for the political and religious liberty of America, has not been confined to this continent. People of other countries begin to inquire, to examine, and to reason for themselves. Error has fled before it, and the most inveterate prejudices are dissolved and gone. Such unlimited remedy has in some cases, indeed, apparently proved injurious, but the evil is to be attributed to the peculiarity of the attendant circumstances, or the ill-timed application. Let us not force our tenets upon foreigners. For, if we subject opinion to coercion, who shall be our inquisitors? No; let us do as we have done, as we are now doing, and then call upon the nations to examine, to scrutinize, and to condemn! No! they cannot look upon America, to-day, and pity; for the gladdened heart disclaims all woe. They cannot look upon her, and deride; for genius, and literature, and science, are soaring above the high places of birth and pageantry. They cannot look upon us, and defy; for the hearts of thirteen millions are warm in virtuous emulation — their arms steeled in the cause of their country. Her productions are wafted to every shore; her flag is seen waving in every sea. She has wrested the glorious motto from the once queen of the sea, and high on our banner, by the stars and stripes is seen:

E "Columbia needs no bulwark,
No towers along the steep,
Her march is o'er the mountain wave,
Her home is on the deep."

EULOGY UPON HENRY CLAY. — *J. J. Crittenden.*

I AM to address you in commemoration of the public services of Henry Clay, and in celebration of his obsequies. His death filled his whole country with mourning, and the loss of no citizen, save the Father of his Country, has ever produced such manifestations of the grief and homage of the public heart. His history has indeed been read "in a nation's eyes." A nation's tears proclaim, with their silent eloquence, its sense of the national loss. Kentucky has more than a common share in this national bereavement. To her it is a domestic grief, — to her belongs the sad privilege of being the chief mourner. He was her favorite son, her pride, and her glory. She mourns for him as a mother. But let her not mourn as those who have no hope nor consolation. She can find the richest and noblest solace in the memory of her son, and of his great and good actions; and his fame will come back, like a comforter, from his grave, to wipe away her tears. Even while she weeps for him, her tears shall be mingled with the proud feelings of triumph which his name will inspire; and Old Kentucky, from the depths of her affectionate and heroic heart, shall exclaim, like the Duke of Ormond, when informed that his brave son had fallen in battle, "I would not exchange my dead son for any living son in Christendom." From these same abundant sources we may hope that the widowed partner of his life, who now sits in sadness at Ashland, will derive some pleasing consolations. I presume not to offer any words of comfort of my own. Her grief is too sacred to permit me to use that privilege.

Henry Clay lived in a most eventful period, and the history of his life for forty years has been literally that of his country. He was so identified with the government for more than two-thirds of its existence, that, during that time, hardly any act which has redounded to its honor, its prosperity, its present rank among the nations of the earth, can be spoken of, without calling to mind involuntarily the lineaments of his noble person. It would be difficult to determine whether in peace or in war, in the field of legislation or of diplomacy, in the spring-tide of his life or in its golden ebb, he won the highest honor. It can be no disparagement to any one of his contemporaries to say, that, in all the points of practical statesmanship, he encountered no superior in any of the employments which his constituents or his country conferred upon him.

Henry Clay was indebted to no adventitious circumstances for the success and glory of his life. Sprung from an humble stock, "he was fashioned to much honor from his cradle;" and he achieved it by the noble use of the means which God and nature had given him. He was no scholar, and had none of the advantages of collegiate education. But there was a "divinity that stirred within him." He was a man of a genius mighty enough to supply all the defects of education. By its keen, penetrating observation, its quick apprehension, its comprehensive and clear conception, he gathered knowledge without the study of books; — he could draw it from the fountain head, — pure and undefiled; it was unborrowed; the acquisition of his own observation, reflection, and experience; and all his own. It entered into the composition of the man, forming part of his mind, and strengthening and preparing him for all those great scenes of intellectual exertion or controversy in which his life was spent. His armor was always on, and he was ever ready for the battle.

This mighty genius was accompanied, in him, by all the qualities necessary to sustain its action, and to make it most irresistible. His person was tall and commanding, and his demeanor —

> "Lofty and sour to them that loved him not;
> But to those men that sought him, sweet as summer."

He was direct and honest, ardent and fearless, prompt to form his opinions, always bold in their avowal, and sometimes impetuous, or even rash, in their vindication. In the performance of his duties he feared no responsibility. He scorned all evasion of untruth. No pale thoughts ever troubled his decisive mind.

"Be just and fear not" was the sentiment of his heart and the principle of his action. It regulated his conduct in private and public life; all the ends he aimed at were his country's, his God's, and truth's.

Such was Henry Clay, and such were his talents, qualities, and objects. Nothing but success and honor could attend such a character. For nearly half a century he was an informing spirit, brilliant and heroic figure in our political sphere, marshalling our country in the way she ought to go. The "bright track of his fiery car" may be traced through the whole space over which, in his day, his country and its government have passed in the way to greatness and renown. It will still point the way to further greatness and renown.

The great objects of his public life were to preserve and strengthen the Union; to maintain the constitution and laws of the United States; to cherish industry; to protect labor; and to facilitate, by all proper national improvements, the communication between all the parts of our widely-extended country. This was his American system of policy. With inflexible patriotism he pursued and advocated it to his end. He was every inch an American. His heart, and all that there was of him, were devoted to his country, to its liberty, and its free institutions. He inherited the spirit of the Revolution, in the midst of which he was born; and the love of liberty and the pride of freedom were in him principles of action.

A remarkable trait in the character of Mr. Clay was his inflexibility in defending the public interest against all schemes for its detriment. His exertions were, indeed, so steadily employed and so often successful in protecting the public against the injurious designs of visionary politicians or party demagogues, that he may be almost said to have been, during forty years, the guardian angel of the country He never would compromise the public interest for anybody, or for any personal advantage to himself.

He was the advocate of liberty throughout the world, and his voice of cheering was raised in behalf of every people who struggled for freedom. Greece, awakened from a long sleep of servitude, heard his voice, and was reminded of her own Demosthenes. South America, too, in her struggle for independence, heard his brave words of encouragement, and her fainting heart was animated, and her arm made strong.

Henry Clay is the fair representative of the age in which he lived; an age which forms the greatest and brightest era in the history of man; an age teeming with new discoveries and developments, extending in all directions the limits of human knowledge, — exploring the agencies and elements of the physical world, and turning and subjugating them to the uses of man, — unfolding and establishing, practically, the great principles of *popular rights* and free governments, and which, nothing doubting, nothing fearing, still advances in majesty, aspiring to and demanding further improvement and further amelioration of the condition of mankind.

With the chivalrous and benignant spirit of this great era Henry Clay was thoroughly imbued. He was, indeed, moulded by it, and made in its own image. That spirit, be it remembered, was not one of licentiousness, or turbulence, or blind innovation. It was a wise spirit, good and honest as it was resolute and brave; and truth and justice were its companions and guides.

These noble qualities of truth and justice were conspicuous in the whole public life of Henry Clay. On that solid foundation he stood erect and fearless; and when the storms of state beat around and threatened to overwhelm him, his exclamation was still heard, "Truth is mighty, and public justice certain." What a magnificent and heroic figure does Henry Clay here present to the world! We can but stand before and look upon it in silent reverence. His appeal was not in vain; — the passions of party subsided, truth and justice resumed their sway, and his generous countrymen repaid him for all the wrong they had done him with gratitude, affection and admiration, in his life, and tears for his death.

It has been objected to Henry Clay that he was ambitious. So he was. But in him ambition was virtue. It sought only the proper, fair objects of honorable ambition, and it sought these by honorable means only, — by so serving the country as to deserve its favors and its honors. If he sought office, it was for the purpose of enabling him, by the power it would give, to serve his country more effectually and preëminently; and, if he expected and desired thereby to advance his own fame, who will say that was a fault? Who will say that it was a fault to seek and desire office for any of the personal gratifications it may afford, so long as those gratifications are made subordinate to the public good?

That Henry Clay's object in desiring office was to serve his country, and that he would have made all other considerations subservient, I have no doubt. I knew him well, — I had full opportunity of observing him in his most unguarded moments and conversations, — and I can say that I have never known a more unselfish, a more faithful or intrepid representative of the *people*, of the people's rights, and the people's interests, than Henry Clay.

It was most fortunate for Kentucky to have such a representative, and most fortunate for him to have such a constituent as Kentucky; fortunate for him to have been thrown, in the early and susceptible period of his life, into the primitive society of her bold and free people. As one of her children, I am pleased to think that from that source he derived some of that magnanimity and energy which his after life so signally displayed. I am pleased to think, that, mingling with all his great qualities, there was a sort of *Kentuckyism* (I shall not undertake to define it), which, though it may not have polished or refined, gave to them additional point and power, and free scope of action.

You all knew Mr. Clay; your knowledge and recollection of him will present him more vividly to your minds than any picture I can draw of him. This I will add, — he was in the highest, truest sense of the term, a great man, and we ne'er shall look upon his like again. He has gone to join the mighty dead in another and better world. How little is there of such a man that can die! His fame, the memory of his benefactions, the lessons of his wisdom, all remain with us, — over these death has no power.

How few of the great of this world have been so fortunate as he! How few of them have lived to see their labors so rewarded! He lived to see the country that he loved and served advanced to great prosperity and renown, and still advancing. He lived till every prejudice which at any period of his life had existed against him was removed; and until he had become the object of the reverence, love and gratitude, of his whole country. His work seemed then to be completed, and fate could not have selected a happier moment to remove him from the troubles and vicissitudes of this life.

Glorious as his life was, there was nothing that became him like the leaving of it. I saw him frequently during the slow and lingering disease which terminated his life. He was conscious of his approaching end, and prepared to meet it with all the resignation and fortitude of a Christian hero. He was all patience, meekness, and gentleness; these shone round him like a mild, celestial light, breaking upon him from another world;

"And, to add greater honors to his age
Than man could give, he died fearing God."

COMPLETION OF THE WABASH AND ERIE CANAL. — *L. Cass.*

It is profitable in the career of life occasionally to pause to withdraw ourselves from the very busy scenes with which we mingle, and to look back upon the progress we have made, and forward, as far as it is given to us to look forward upon the prospect before us. These are high places in the journey of life, whence the region around is best contemplated and understood. In all time great events have been thus commemorated. The principle has its foundation in human nature, though perverted in its application by power or superstition. And many a monument, which has survived its own history and the objects of its founders, yet looks out upon the silence around it, the solitary evidence of some great but forgotten event in the fitful drama of life. And we have come up to-day to one of these high places to commune together. We have met from many a portion of our common country, and this great assemblage testifies, not less by its numbers than by the imposing circumstances which surround it, that there is here passing one of those scenes which mark the progress of society, and which form its character, and oftentimes its destiny. And so it is, and it is good for us to be here. We have not come to fight a battle, nor to commemorate one; we have not come to worship at the shrine of power, to celebrate the birth or the death of some unworthy ruler, the last step in political degradation. Nor have we come to commence, to complete, nor to commemorate, some useless but imposing structure, erected by pride, but paid for by poverty. I would not, however, be misunderstood. Far be it from us to censure or to check those feelings of love of country, or of religion, which seek their outpourings in the erection of memorials upon spots which have drank the blood of the patriot or of the martyr. It is a tribute of virtue, which honors the dead and the living. But let it be voluntary. Then it will neither be unjust in its object nor oppressive in its accomplishment. It will teach a lesson to after ages, which may stimulate virtue to action, and give fortitude to endure till the day of deliverance comes with its struggle and its reward. Look at the mighty pyramids which rise over the Arabian and the Libyan wastes, and which cast their shadow far in the desert, mocking the researches and the pride of man. They tell no tale but the old tale of oppression. They speak in their very massiveness of pride and power on the one side, and misery and poverty on the other. One of the little channels which the Fellah has diverted from the great river at their base, and which spreads verdure and fertility over the valley that owes so much to God and so little to man, is far dearer to the oppressed population than these useless and mighty structures.

Our eastern brethren, with the characteristic liberality and patriotism which make the descendants of the Pilgrims proud of the land of their ancestors, have just completed and dedicated a monument to mark the site of the battle which opened the greatest contest between a powerful empire and her young and distant provinces, and whose influence, if it did not give to the Revolution its fortunate issue, impressed its character upon the whole struggle. We have no such place to hallow; but we have the people to do the deeds by which places are sanctified, and where the pilgrims of liberty come, not to worship, but to reflect. We have not the wealth nor those "appliances" by which the long and imposing procession, and the gorgeous pageantry which a great city can arrange and display, affect, and almost subdue, the imagination. We have not the chief magistrate of the republic, with his official counsellors, to mark, as it were, with a national character, the occasion of our assemblage. Nor have we constructed an obelisk, simple and severe in its style, but lasting as the deeds it commemorates, whose foundation is laid in the graves of martyred patriots, but whose summit rises towards the heavens, telling the story of their fall, and proclaiming the gratitude of their countrymen. But there are here stout hearts and strong hands, — thousands who would devote themselves, as did the men of Bunker Hill, to the cause of freedom, and who would fight as they fought, and die as they died, should their country demand the sacrifice. On the face of the globe, liberty has no more zealous defenders, nor patriotism more ardent votaries, than is this great assembly, the convocation of a people who have made this region their own by all the ties that bind a man to his home, and who will defend it, and the institutions which belong to it, by all the means that energy and intelligence and devotedness have ever brought to the great day of trial, and by which they have made it a day of triumph.

We have come here to join in another commemoration. To witness the union of the lakes and the Mississippi. To survey one of the noblest works of man in the improvement of that great highway of nature, extending from New York to New Orleans, whose full moral and physical effects it were vain to seek even to conjecture. And fitly chosen is the day of this celebration. This work is another ligament which binds together this great confederated republic. Providence has given us union, and many motives to preserve it. The sun never shone upon a country abounding more than ours in all the elements of prosperity. It were needless to enumerate the advantages we enjoy, and which give us so distinguished a position among the nations of the world. They are seen and felt in all those evidences of prosperity and improvement which greet the traveller wherever he passes through our country. And still more striking are they when we contrast our situation with that of the older regions of the world. I shall not enter into the comparison. I could speak of it from personal knowledge; but the task would not be a pleasant one, for it would recall many a cause of discontent, and many a scene of misery, which meet the eye of the most careless observer who exchanges the new hemisphere for the old. An American, who does not return to his own country a wiser man and a better citizen, and prouder and more contented, for all he has seen abroad, may well doubt his own head or heart, and may well be doubted by his countrymen.

Still, it is not to be disguised that, from the very constitution of human nature, causes may occasionally exist, tending to weaken, though they cannot sever, the bonds which unite us; and happy is it that these causes may be counteracted, and ultimately, we may hope, rendered powerless, by measures now in progress, which will add the ties of interest to the dictates of patriotism. Our railroads and canals are penetrating every section of our territory. They are annihilating time and space. They are embracing in their folds the ocean and the lake frontiers, and the great region extending from the Alleghany to the Rocky Mountains, through which the mighty Mississippi and its countless tributaries find their way to the Gulf of Mexico. Once let this work be completed, and we are bound together by cords which no strength can sunder. The moral and political effect, therefore, of the great work before us, is even more important than the physical advantages it promises. It will bear upon its bosom the products of a thousand fertile valleys, and it will spread gladness and prosperity over regions which have just been rescued from the Indians, and from the animals, his co-tenants of the forest, which minister to his wants. But it will do more than this. It will make glad the heart of the patriot. As he sails along it, he will see, not merely the evidences and the cause of wealth and prosperity, but one of the ties which knit us together. By a process more fortunate than alchemist ever imagined, the feeblest element will be converted into the strongest bond. It will bear the boat and its freight to a market, where products may be interchanged and wealth acquired. But it will interchange interests and feelings which no wealth can purchase, and for which no price can pay. Well, then, may we rejoice, upon this day. The occasion and the time are in unison together. And, while we thank God for the services and sacrifices which he enabled our fathers to make in the acquisition of freedom and independence, let us thank him, also, that we are able to strengthen their work, and to transmit to our children, as they transmitted to theirs, the noblest inheritance that belongs to man. The ark of the constitution is yet untouched. Withered be the hand that would pollute it!

WISDOM OF THE ANCIENTS. — *C. Sumner.*

It is often said, "Let us not be wiser than our fathers." Rather, let us try to excel our fathers in wisdom. Let us imitate what in them was good, but not bind ourselves, as in the chains of fate, by their imperfect example. Principles are higher than human examples. Examples may be followed when they accord with the admonitions of duty. But he is unwise and wicked who attempts to lean upon these, rather than upon those truths which, like the Everlasting Arm, cannot fail!

In all modesty be it said, we have lived to little purpose, if we are not wiser than the generations that have gone before us. It is the grand distinction of man that he is a progressive being; that his reason at the present day is not merely the reason of a single human being, but that of the whole human race, in all ages from which knowledge has descended, in all lands from which knowledge has been borne away. We are heirs to an inheritance of truth, grandly accumulating from generation to generation. The child at his mother's knee is now taught the orbits of the heavenly bodies,

"Where worlds on worlds compose one universe,"

the nature of this globe, the character of the tribes of men by which it is covered, and the geography of nations, to an extent far beyond the ken of the most learned of other days. It is, therefore, true, as has been said, that antiquity is the real infancy of man; reason and the kindlier virtues of age, repudiating and abhorring force, now bear sway. We are the true ancients. The single lock on the battered forehead of Old Time is thinner now than when our fathers attempted to grasp it; the hour-glass has been turned often since; the scythe is heavier laden with the work of death. Let us cease, then, to look for a lamp to our feet in the feeble tapers that glimmer in the sepulchres of the past. Rather let us hail those ever-burning lights above, in whose beams is the brightness of noonday!

THE WEST AND THE SOUTH.—*T. H. Benton.*

Time and my ability would fail in any attempt to enumerate the names and acts of those generous friends in the South who then stood forth our defenders and protectors, and gave us men and money, and beat the domestic foe in the capitol, while we beat the foreign foe in the field. Time and my ability would fail to do them justice; but there is one state in the South, the name and praise of which the events of this debate would drag from the stones of the West, if they could rise up in this place and speak! It is the name of that state upon which the vials, filled with the accumulated wrath of years, have been suddenly and unexpectedly emptied before us, on a motion to postpone a land debate. That state whose microscopic offence in the obscure parish of Colleton is to be hung in equipoise with the organized treason and deep damnation of the Hartford Convention; that state whose present dislike to a tariff which is tearing out her vitals is to be made the means of exciting the West against the whole South; that state whose dislike to the tariff laws is to be made the pretext for setting up a despotic authority in the Supreme Court; that state which, in the old Congress in 1785, voted for the reduction of the price of public lands to about one-half the present minimum; which, in 1786, redeemed after it was lost, and carried by its single vote, the first measure that ever was adopted for the protection of Kentucky — that of the two companies sent to the Falls of Ohio; that state which in the period of the late war sent us a Lowndes, a Cheves, and a Calhoun, to fight the battles of the West in the capitol, and to slay the Goliaths in the North; that state which at this day has sent to this chamber the senator whose liberal and enlightened speech on the subject of the public lands has been seized upon and made the pretext for that premeditated aggression upon South Carolina and the whole South which we have seen met with a promptitude, energy, gallantry and effect, that has forced the assailant to cry out an hundred times that he was still alive, though we all could see that he was most cruelly pounded!

Memory is the lowest faculty of the human mind; — the irrational animals possess it in common with man — the poor beasts of the field have memory. They can recollect the hand that feeds and the foot that kicks them; and the instinct of self-preservation tells them to follow one and to avoid the other. Without any knowledge of Greek or Latin, these mute, irrational creatures "fear the Greek offering presents;" they shun the food offered by the hand that has been lifted to take their life. This is their instinct, — and shall man, the possessor of so many noble faculties, with all the benefits of learning and experience, have less memory, less gratitude, less sensibility to danger, than these poor beasts? And shall he stand less upon his guard, when the hand that smote is stretched out to entice? Shall man, bearing the image of his Creator, sink thus low? Shall the generous son of the West fall below his own dumb and reasonless cattle, in all the attributes of memory, gratitude, and sense of danger? Shall his "*Timeo Danaos*" have been taught him in vain? Shall he forget the things which he saw, and part of which he was, — the events of the late war, the memorable scenes of fifteen years ago? The events of former times, of forty years ago, may be unknown to those who are born since. The attempt to surrender the navigation of the Mississippi, — to prevent the settlement of the West, — the refusal to protect the early settlers of Kentucky and Tennessee, or to procure for them a cession of Indian lands, — all these trials, in which the South was the savior of the West, may be unknown to the young generation that has come forward since; and with respect to these events, being uninformed, they may be unmindful and ungrateful. They did not see them; and, like the second generation of the Israelites, in the land of promise, who knew not the wonders which God had done for their forefathers in Egypt, they may plead ignorance and go astray after strange gods, — after the Baals and the Astaroths of the heathen, — but not so of the events of the last war. These they saw! The aid of the South they felt! The deeds of a party in the north-east they felt, also! Memory will do its office for both; and base and recreant is the son of the West that can ever turn his back upon the friends that saved, to go into the arms of the enemy that mocked and scorned him, in the season of dire calamity!

THE LEXINGTON MARTYRS. — *E. Everett.*

And you, brave and patriotic men, whose ashes are gathered in this humble place of deposit, no time shall rob you of the well-deserved meed of praise! You, too, perceived not less clearly than the more illustrious patriots whose spirit you caught that the decisive hour had come. You felt with them that it could not, must not, be shunned. You had resolved it should not. Reasoning, remonstrance had been tried; from your own town-meetings, from the pulpit, from beneath the arches of Faneuil Hall, every note of argument, of appeal, of adjuration, had sounded to the foot of the throne, and in vain. The wheels of destiny rolled on; the great design of Providence must be fulfilled; the issue must be nobly met, or basely shunned. Strange it seemed, inscrutable it was, that your remote and quiet village should be the chosen altar of the first great sacrifice. But so it was; — the summons came and found you waiting; and here, in the centre of your dwelling-places, within sight of the homes you were to enter no more, between the village church where your fathers worshipped and the grave-yard where they lay at rest, bravely and meekly, like Christian heroes, you sealed the cause with your blood. Parker, Monroe, Hadley, the Harringtons, Muzzy, Brown, — alas! ye cannot hear my words, — no voice but that of the archangel shall penetrate your urns; but to the end of time your remembrance shall be preserved! To the end of time the soil whereon ye fell is holy, and shall be trod with reverence while America has a name among the nations!

And now ye are going to lie down beneath yon simple stone, which marks the place of your mortal agony. Fit spot for your last repose; —

"Where should the soldier rest, but where he fell?"

For ages to come the characters graven in the enduring marble shall tell the unadorned tale of your sacrifice; and ages after that stone itself has crumbled into dust as inexpressive as yours, history, undying history, shall transmit the record! Ay, while the language we speak retains its meaning in the ears of men, while a sod of what is now the soil of America shall be trod by the foot of a freeman, your names and your memory shall be cherished!

RESPECT FOR AMERICAN RIGHTS — *L. Woodbury.*

Among the coral reefs of the Pacific, or in sight of the halls of Montezuma, — wherever on land or ocean, in the western or eastern hemisphere or the south, by savage, semi-barbarian or civilized, by Pagan, Mahometan, Infidel, Turk or Christian, — wherever an American citizen is wronged, or American property plundered, or American rights invaded, there the stars and stripes should appear, and will protect and avenge. There, manfully, when all other reasons are exhausted, Americans will rush, like Warren at Bunker Hill, or Stark at Bennington, and hosts of others through the whole length and breadth of our Revolutionary campaigns; — in short, like Decaturs, McNeils and Jacksons, in the war of 1812, or Worths, Scotts and Taylors, since, they will prove themselves, on every fit occasion, ready to punish the enemies and redress the wrongs of their country. Such a spirit alone can save and perpetuate the glorious principles of this day.

It is not a thirst for conquest, but firm resolve to sustain national honor. We spare the vanquished; and if we scale the Alps, it is not to seize on new provinces, or ill-gotten gold, *auri sacra fames*, but we purchase and pay for empires, when needed, though we could have retained by the sword what we won by the sword; and thus, by the rights of war, have made our title as good to California, as it was, by treaty, to Louisiana. A different temper, shrinking from a vindication of national honor, would make us sheep to be devoured by the wolves around us; and allow Santa Annas to enforce their menaces to occupy our capital, rather than we to retaliate invasions, and hoist the stars and stripes over the walls of Mexico. A different temper, too, — not being magnanimous to the conquered, and forbearing to the fallen, — would tend to render our brave troops but marauders, or armed mobs, or fierce buccaneers. Our resistance even the matrons of the Revolution had the moral courage to inculcate; and deserve their full share in its glories, for inculcating it on their husbands and sons, and exhibiting so many virtues, and so much heroism, in the times which tried men's souls. Our pious mothers were not hostile to the common enemy wholly for the oppressive tax on their tea, but because they were educated by the Bible, and especially by Christianity, in the great doctrines of equal rights; and, like Spartan women, they taught their descendants — and deserve their gratitude for the patriotic lesson — that it was nobler to be brought home dead on their shields, than fly or submit to be slaves. A revolution originating and conducted like ours illustrates well the excellences of such a spirit, and embodies it. A revolution thus justified, guided, established, has become a model revolution for mankind; a great landmark, a colossal beacon-tower to all future times, and all future navigators on the rough sea of Liberty.

SOUTH CAROLINA UNDER FEDERAL LEGISLATION. — *G. McDuffie.*

A GREAT and solemn crisis is evidently approaching, and I admonish gentlemen that it is the part of wisdom, as well as of justice, to pause in this course of legislative tyranny and oppression, before they have driven a high-minded, loyal and patriotic people to something bordering on despair and desperation. If the ancestors of those who are now enduring — too patiently enduring — the oppressive burdens unjustly imposed upon them, could return from their graves and witness the change which the federal government, in one quarter of a century, has produced in the entire aspect of the country, they would hardly recognize it as the scene of their former activity and usefulness. Where all was cheerful, and prosperous, and flourishing, and happy, they would behold nothing but decay, and gloom, and desolation, without a spot of verdure to break the dismal continuity, or even

"A rose of the wilderness left on its stalk,
To tell where the garden had been."

Looking upon this sad reverse in the condition of their descendants, they would naturally inquire what moral or political pestilence had passed over the land, to blast and wither the fair inheritance they had left them. And, when they should be told that a despotic power of taxation infinitely more unjust and oppressive than that from which the country had been redeemed by their toils and sacrifices was now assumed and exercised over us by our own brethren, they would indignantly exclaim, like the ghost of the murdered Hamlet, when urging his afflicted son to avenge the tarnished honor of his house,

"If you have nature in you, bear it not"

I feel that I am called upon to vindicate the motives and the character of the people of South Carolina from imputations which have been unjustly cast upon them. There is no state in this Union distinguished by a more lofty and disinterested patriotism than that which I have the honor in part to represent. I can proudly and confidently appeal to history for proof of this assertion. No state has made greater sacrifices to vindicate the common rights of the Union, and preserve its integrity. No state is more willing to make those sacrifices now, whether of blood or treasure. But it does not belong to this lofty spirit of patriotism to submit to unjust and unconstitutional oppression; nor is South Carolina to be taunted with the charge of treason and rebellion, because she has the intelligence to understand her rights, and the spirit to maintain them. God has not planted in the breast of man a higher and a holier principle than that by which he is prompted to resist oppression. Absolute submission and passive obedience to every extreme of tyranny are the characteristics of slaves only.

The oppression of the people of South Carolina has been carried to an extremity which the most slavish population on earth would not endure without a struggle. Is it to be expected, then, that freemen will patiently bow down and kiss the rod of the oppressor? Freemen, did I say? Why, sir, any one who has the form and bears the name of a man, — nay, "a beast that wants discourse of reason," a dog, a sheep, a reptile, — the vilest reptile that crawls upon the earth, without the gift of reason to comprehend the injustice of its injuries, would bite, or bruise, or sting the hand by which they were inflicted. Is it, then, for a sovereign state to fold her arms and stand still in submissive apathy, when the loud clamors of the people whom Providence has committed to her charge are ascending to heaven for justice? Hug not this delusion to your breast, I pray you!

It is not for me to say, in this place, what course South Carolina may deem it her duty to pursue, in this great emergency. It is enough to say that she perfectly understands the ground which she occupies; and be assured, sir, that whatever attitude she may assume, in her highest sovereign capacity, she will firmly and fearlessly maintain it, be the consequences what they may. The responsibility will not rest upon her, but upon her oppressors.

I will say, in conclusion, that in all I have uttered there has not been mingled one feeling of personal unkindness to any human being, either in this house or out of it. I have used strong language, to be sure, but it has been uttered "more in sorrow than in anger." I have felt it to be a solemn duty which I owed to my constituents and to this nation, to make one more solemn appeal to the justice of their oppressors. Let me, then, beseech them, in the name of our common ancestors, whose blood was mingled together as a common offering at the shrine of our common liberty, — let me beseech them by all the endearing recollections of our common history, and by every consideration that gives value to liberty and the Union of these States, to retrace their steps as speedily as possible, and to relieve a high-minded and patriotic people from an unconstitutional and oppressive burden, which they cannot longer bear!

DEDICATION OF THE DAVIS MONUMENT, AT ACTON, MASS. — *G. S. Boutwell.*

THE events of the American Revolution can never fail to interest Americans. This assemblage, men of Middlesex, is an assurance that you cherish the Revolutionary character of your county, and will be true to the obligations and duties which it imposes. And may we not reverently believe that the Ruler of nations, in the partially shrouded natural beauties of the day, appropriate to funereal services and solemnities, crowns this occasion with his approval?

The event we commemorate is not of local interest only. It has, however, little value on account of the number of men who fought or who fell; but it lives as the opening scene of a great revolution, based on principle, and destined to change the character of human governments and the condition of the human race. The 19th of April, 1775, is not immortal because men fell in battle, but because they fell choosing death rather than servitude. The mere soldier, who fights without a cause, is unworthy our respect; but he who falls in defence of sound principles or valued rights deserves a nation's gratitude. Hence the battle-fields of the Revolution shall gain new lustre, while Austerlitz and Waterloo shall be dimmed by the lapse of ages. Each nation cherishes and recurs to the leading events in its history. Time increases the importance of some of them and diminishes the magnitude of others. Many of them are eras in the history of countries and the world. Such are the lives of great men — philosophers, poets, orators and statesmen. Such are battles and conquests, the foundation of new empires and the fall of old ones, changes in governments, and the administrations of renowned monarchs. Such were the conquests of Greece, the division of the Macedonian empire, the rise and fall of Rome, the discovery and settlement of this continent, the English commonwealth, the accession of William and Mary to the British throne, the American Revolution, and, finally, the wars, empire and overthrow, of Napoleon. A knowledge of these events is not only valuable in itself, but it enables us to penetrate the darkness which usually obscures the daily life and character of a people. A true view of the life of Socrates gives us an accurate idea of Athens and the Athenian people. The protectorate of Cromwell, the great event in all English history, presents a view of the British nation while passing from an absolute government to a limited monarchy, slowly but certainly tending to republicanism.

The American Revolution was a clear indication, in itself, of what the colonies had been, and what the republic was destined to be. Had the Revolution been delayed, no history, however minute, could have given to the world so accurate knowledge of the colonists from 1770 to 1780 as it now possesses. It was the full development of all their past history; it was the concise, vigorous, intelligible introduction to their future. It was a great illustration of preëxisting American character. Neither religious nor political fanaticism was an element of the American Revolution. It was altogether defensive; defensive in its assertion of principles, defensive in its warlike operations.

It is true that the Revolution was an important step towards freedom and equality; but the revolutionists did not primarily contemplate the destruction or abandonment of the principles of the British government, but rather their preservation and perpetuity; and this, in a great degree, they accomplished. The two governments are dissimilar in many respects; but the principles which lie at the foundation of the one led to the formation of the other.

On the 19th of April, 1775, the men of Acton left their homes upon these hills, and their families anxious and disconsolate, that they and their descendants might have homes undisturbed by the hand of the oppressor. On the 20th of April, 1775, these homes were deserted, that all might pay the last tribute of respect to Davis, Hayward and Hosmer. And now, after the lapse of seventy-six years, the descendants of that generation have met, not, as then, to mingle their tears at the grave of departed friends and heroes, but to utter with all of filial respect the names of worthy men, and to impress with new power upon their hearts the sentiment of gratitude for all who served and suffered in the cause of American freedom. And, as we contemplate the glorious death of those who fell, shall we not say,

"Since all must life resign,
Those sweet rewards which decorate the brave
'T is folly to decline,
And steal inglorious to the silent grave"?

As compared with the existence of the world, only a short space of time has intervened between the 19th of April, 1775, and this day; yet three generations of men have trodden these fields and aided in the great work of perfecting and preserving American institutions. With what confidence, fellow-citizens, did your ancestors look to independence, and the establishment of the form of government under which we have lived and prospered as a people? Beyond this form neither the patriot nor statesman can look with hope.

Who will propose to the now united American people either a return to the almost forgotten confederacy of 1778, or the establishment of separate governments? Nobody, nobody! When we contrast our institutions with those of any other country, how ought we to thank God for the measure of personal happiness and political security we have enjoyed! Not that our institutions are perfect, nor that there is nothing which the philanthropist may deplore or the statesman condemn. All the anticipations of our ancestors have not been realized. The past is not all perfect; the future will not always cheer us with sunshine and smiles: but he is a misanthrope who allows his opinions to be controlled by the exceptions to the general current of our national career.

Our years of independence have been years of almost uninterrupted prosperity, but they have borne to the grave those who took part in the later as well as earlier contests of the Revolution. Of Lexington and Concord only one remains; and from all the battle-fields of the war this occasion has brought together but two. But, fellow-citizens, the few survivors are not only venerable — they are sacred men. They are the last of a noble generation. They perilled their lives in behalf of liberty when

"'T was treason to love her and death to defend."

Fortunate all are you whose eyes rest to-day on these few surviving soldiers of the Revolution. Fortunate are the youth and children even who on this occasion and in this presence can pledge themselves to the cause of constitutional liberty. Of these men the next generation shall know only from history. Fortunate, then, that your lives begun before theirs ended.

The patriot should do homage to these men; the statesman may sit at their feet and learn lessons of fidelity to principle, and citizens all may see how nobly ends the life begun in the performance of duty.

To-day the commonwealth of Massachusetts and the town of Acton dedicate this monument to the memory of the early martyrs of the Revolution, and consecrate it to the principles of liberty and of patriotism. Here its base shall rest and its apex point to the heavens through the coming centuries. Though it bears the names of humble men, and commemorates services stern rather than brilliant, it shall be as immortal as American history. The ground on which it stands shall be made classical by the deeds which it commemorates. And may this monument exist only with the existence of the republic; and when God, in his wisdom, shall bring this government to naught, as all human governments must come to naught, may no stone remain to point the inquirer to fields of valor, or to remind him of deeds of glory! And, finally, may the republic resemble the sun in his daily circuit, so that none shall know whether its path were more glorious in the rising or in the setting!

THE PROBLEM FOR THE UNITED STATES.—*H. A. Boardman.*

This Union cannot expire as the snow melts from the rock, or a star disappears from the firmament. When it falls, the crash will be heard in all lands. Wherever the winds of heaven go, that will go, bearing sorrow and dismay to millions of stricken hearts; for the subversion of this government will render the cause of constitutional liberty hopeless throughout the world. What nation can govern itself, if this nation cannot? What encouragement will any people have to establish liberal institutions for themselves, if ours fail? Providence has laid upon us the responsibility and the honor of solving that problem in which all coming generations of men have a profound interest, — whether the true ends of government can be secured by a popular representative system. In the munificence of his goodness, he put us in possession of our heritage, by a series of interpositions scarcely less signal than those which conducted the Hebrews to Canaan; and he has, up to this period, withheld from us no immunities or resources which might facilitate an auspicious result. Never before was a people so advantageously situated for working out this great problem in favor of human liberty; and it is important for us to understand that the world so regards it.

If, in the frenzy of our base sectional jealousies, we dig the grave of the Union, and thus decide this question in the negative, no tongue may attempt to depict the disappointment and despair which will go along with the announcement, as it spreads through distant lands. It will be America, after fifty years' experience, giving in her adhesion to the doctrine that man was not made for self-government. It will be Freedom herself proclaiming that freedom is a chimera; Liberty ringing her own knell, all over the globe. And, when the citizens or *subjects* of the governments which are to succeed this Union shall visit Europe, and see, in some land now struggling to cast off its fetters, the lacerated and lifeless form of Liberty laid prostrate under the iron heel of despotism, let them remember that the blow which destroyed her was inflicted by their own country.

"So the struck eagle, stretched upon the plain,
No more through rolling clouds to soar again,
Viewed his own feather on the fatal dart,
And winged the shaft that quivered in his heart.
Keen were his pangs, but keener far to feel
He nursed the pinion which impelled the steel;
While the same plumage that had warmed his nest
Drank the last life-drop of his bleeding breast."

MORAL FORCE AGAINST PHYSICAL. — *D. Webster.*

The time has been, indeed, when fleets, and armies, and subsidies, were the principal reliances, even in the best cause. But, happily for mankind, there has come a great change in this respect. Moral causes come into consideration, in proportion as the progress of knowledge is advanced; and the public opinion of the civilized world is rapidly gaining an ascendency over mere brutal force. It is already able to oppose the most formidable obstruction to the progress of injustice and oppression; and, as it grows more intelligent, and more intense, it will be more and more formidable. It may be silenced by military power, but it cannot be conquered. It is elastic, irrepressible, and invulnerable to the weapons of ordinary warfare. It is that impassable, unextinguishable enemy of mere violence and arbitrary rule, which, like Milton's angels,

"Vital in every part,
Cannot, but by annihilating, die."

Until this be propitiated or satisfied, it is in vain for power to talk either of triumphs or of repose. No matter what fields are desolated, what fortresses surrendered, what armies subdued, or what provinces overrun. In the history of the year that has passed by us, and in the instance of unhappy Spain, we have seen the vanity of all triumphs, in a cause which violates the general sense of justice of the civilized world. It is nothing that the troops of France have passed from the Pyrenees to Cadiz; it is nothing that an unhappy and prostrate nation has fallen before them; it is nothing that arrests, and confiscation, and execution, sweep away the little remnant of national existence. There is an enemy that still exists, to check the glory of these triumphs. It follows the conqueror back to the very scene of his ovations; it calls upon him to take notice that Europe, though silent, is yet indignant; it shows him that the sceptre of his victory is a barren sceptre,— that it shall confer neither joy nor honor, but shall moulder to dry ashes in his grasp. In the midst of his exultation, it pierces his ear with the cry of injured justice; it denounces against him the indignation of an enlightened and civilized age; it turns to bitterness the cup of his rejoicing, and wounds him with the sting which belongs to the consciousness of having outraged the opinions of mankind.

PROGRESS OF THE CAUCASIAN RACE.—*T. H. Benton.*

It would seem that the white race alone received the divine command to subdue and replenish the earth; for it is the only race that has obeyed it—the only one that hunts out new and distant lands, and even a new world, to subdue and replenish. Starting from western Asia, taking Europe for their field and the sun for their guide, and leaving the Mongolians behind, they arrived, after many ages, on the shores of the Atlantic, which they lit up with the lights of science and religion, and adorned with the useful and the elegant arts. Three and a half centuries ago, this race, in obedience to the great command, arrived in the New World, and found new lands to subdue and replenish. For a long time it was confined to the border of the new field (I now mean the Celtic Anglo-Saxon division); and even fourscore years ago the philosophic Burke was considered a rash man because he said the English colonists would top the Alleghanies, and descend into the valley of the Mississippi, and occupy without parchment, if the crown refused to make grants of land. What was considered a rash declaration eighty years ago is old history, in our young country, at this day.

I cannot repine that this capitol has replaced the wigwam, this Christian people replaced the savages, white matrons the red squaws, and that such men as Washington, Franklin and Jefferson, have taken the place of Powhattan, Opechonecanough and other red men, however respectable they may have been as savages. Civilization or extinction has been the fate of all people who have found themselves in the track of the advancing whites, and civilization, always the preference of the whites, has been pressed as an object, while extinction has followed as a consequence of its resistance. The black and the red races have often felt their ameliorating influence. The yellow race, next to themselves in the scale of mental and moral excellence, and in the beauty of form, once their superiors in the useful and elegant arts and in learning, and still respectable, though stationary, — this race cannot fail to receive a new impulse from the approach of the whites, improved so much since so many ages ago they left the western borders of Asia. The apparition of the van of the Caucasian race, rising upon them in the east after having left them on the west, and after having completed the circumnavigation of the globe, must wake up and animate the torpid body of old Asia. Our position and policy will commend us to their hospitable reception; political considerations will aid the action of social and commercial influences. Pressed upon by the great powers of Europe, — the same that press upon us, — they must in our approach see the advent of friends, not of foes; of benefactors, not of invaders. The moral and intellectual superiority of the white race will do the rest; and thus the youngest people and the newest land will become the reviver and the regenerator of the oldest. It is in this point of view, and as acting upon the social, political and religious condition of Asia, and giving a new point of departure to her ancient civilization, that I look upon the settlement of the Columbia river by the van of the Caucasian race as the most momentous human event in the history of man since his dispersion over the face of the earth.

THE REIGN OF PEACE. — *C. Sumner.*

That future which filled the lofty visions of the sages and bards of Greece and Rome, which was foretold by the prophets and heralded by the evangelists, when man, in Happy Isles, or in a new paradise, shall confess the loveliness of peace, may be secured by your care, if not for yourselves, at least for your children. Believe that you can do it, and you can do it. The true golden age is before you, not behind you. If man has been driven once from paradise, while an angel, with a flaming sword, forbade his return, there is another paradise, even on earth, which he may form for himself, by the cultivation of knowledge, religion, and the kindly virtues of life; where the confusion of tongues shall be dissolved in the union of hearts, and joyous nature, borrowing prolific charms from the prevailing harmony, shall spread her lap with unimagined bounty, and there shall be a perpetual jocund spring, and sweet strains borne on "the odoriferous wing of gentle gales," through valleys of delight, more pleasant than the Vale of Tempe, richer than the garden of the Hesperides, with no dragon to guard its golden fruit.

Let it not be said that the age does not demand this work. The robber conquerors of the past, from their fiery sepulchres, demand it; the precious blood of millions unjustly shed in war, crying from the ground, demands it; the voices of all good men demand it; the conscience, even of the soldier, whispers "Peace." There are considerations, springing from our situation and condition, which fervently invite us to take the lead in this work. Here should bend the patriotic ardor of the land, the ambition of the statesman, the efforts of the scholar, the persuasive influence of the press, the mild persuasion of the sanctuary, the early teachings of the school. Here, in ampler ether and diviner air, are untried fields for exalted triumphs, more truly worthy the American name than any snatched from rivers of blood. War is known as the last reason of kings. Let it be no reason of our republic. Let us renounce, and throw off forever, the yoke of a tyranny more oppressive than any in the annals of the world. As those standing on the mountain-tops first discern the coming beams of morning, let us, from the vantage-ground of liberal institutions, first recognize the ascending sun of a new era! Lift high the gates, and let the King of glory in; the king of true glory — of peace!

It is a beautiful picture in Grecian story, that there was at least one spot, the small island of Delos, dedicated to the gods, and kept at all times sacred from war. No hostile foot ever sought to press this kindly soil; and the citizens of all countries here met, in common worship, beneath the ægis of inviolable peace. So let us dedicate our beloved country; and may the blessed consecration be felt, in all its parts, everywhere throughout its ample domain! The Temple of Honor shall be surrounded, here, at last, by the Temple of Concord, that it may never more be entered through any portal of war; the horn of abundance shall overflow at its gates; the angel of religion shall be the guide over its steps of flashing adamant; while within its enraptured courts, purged of violence and wrong, Justice, returned to the earth from her long exile in the skies, with mighty scales for nations as well as for men, shall rear her serene and majestic front; and by her side, greatest of all, Charity, sublime in meekness, hoping all and enduring all, shall divinely temper every righteous decree, and with words of infinite cheer shall inspire those good works that cannot vanish away. And the future chiefs of the republic, destined to uphold the glories of a new era, unspotted by human blood, shall be "the first in PEACE, and the first in the hearts of their countrymen."

But, while seeking these blissful glories for ourselves, let us strive to tender them to other lands. Let the bugles sound *the truce of God* to the whole world forever. Let the selfish boast of the Spartan women become the grand chorus of mankind, — that they have never seen the smoke of an enemy's camp. Let the iron belt of martial music which now encompasses the earth be exchanged for the golden cestus of peace, clothing all with celestial beauty. History dwells with fondness on the reverent homage that was bestowed, by massacring soldiers, upon the spot occupied by the sepulchre of the Lord. Vain man! to restrain his regard to a few feet of sacred mould! The whole earth is the sepulchre of the Lord; nor can any righteous man profane any part thereof. Let us recognize this truth, and now, on this Sabbath of our country, lay a new stone in the grand temple of universal peace, whose dome shall be as lofty as the firmament of heaven, as broad and comprehensive as the earth itself!

AGAINST FLOGGING IN THE NAVY. — *R. F. Stockton.*

There is one broad proposition upon which I stand. It is this: That an American sailor is an American citizen, and that no American citizen shall, with my consent, be subjected to the infamous punishment of the lash. If, when a citizen enters into the service of his country, he is to forego the protection of those laws for the preservation of which he is willing to risk his life, he is entitled, in all justice, humanity and gratitude, to all the protection that can be extended to him, in his peculiar circumstances. He ought, certainly, to be protected from the infliction of a punishment which stands condemned by the almost universal sentiment of his fellow-citizens; a punishment which is proscribed in the best prison-government, proscribed in the school-house, and proscribed in the best government on earth — that of parental domestic affection. Yes, sir, expelled from the social circle, from the school-house, the prison-house, and the army, it finds defenders and champions nowhere but in the navy!

Look to your history, — that part of it which the world knows by heart, — and you will find on its brightest page the glorious achievements of the American sailor. Whatever his country has done to disgrace him, and break his spirit, he has never disgraced *her;* he has always been ready to serve her; he always *has* served her faithfully and effectually. He has often been weighed in the balance, and never found wanting. The only fault ever found with him is, that he sometimes fights ahead of his orders. The world has no match for him, man for man; and he asks no odds, and he cares for no odds, when the cause of humanity, or the glory of his country, calls him to fight. Who, in the darkest days of our Revolution, carried your flag into the very chops of the British Channel, bearded the lion in his den, and woke the echoes of old Albion's hills by the thunders of his cannon, and the shouts of his triumph? It was the American sailor. And the names of John Paul Jones and the Bon Homme Richard will go down the annals of time forever. Who struck the first blow that humbled the Barbary flag, — which, for a hundred years, had been the terror of Christendom, — drove it from the Mediterranean, and put an end to the infamous tribute it had been accustomed to extort? It was the American sailor. And the name of Decatur and his gallant companions will be as lasting as monumental brass. In your war of 1812, when your arms on shore were covered by disasters, — when Winchester had been defeated, when the army of the north-west had surrendered, and when the gloom of despondency hung like a cloud over the land, — who first relit the fires of national glory, and made the welkin ring with the shouts of victory? It was the American sailor. And the names of Hull and the Constitution will be remembered, as long as we have left anything worth remembering. That was no small event. The wand of Mexican prowess was broken on the Rio Grandé. The wand of British invincibility was broken when the flag of the Guerrière came down. That one event was worth more to the republic than all the money which has ever been expended for the navy. Since that day, the navy has had no stain upon its escutcheon, but has been cherished as your pride and glory. And the American sailor has established a reputation throughout the world, — in peace and in war, in storm and in battle, — for heroism and prowess unsurpassed. He shrinks from no danger, he dreads no foe, and yields to no superior. No shoals are too dangerous, no seas too boisterous, no climate too rigorous, for him. The burning sun of the tropics cannot make him effeminate, nor can the eternal winter of the polar seas paralyze his energies. Foster, cherish, develop these characteristics, by a generous and paternal government. Excite his emulation, and stimulate his ambition, by rewards. But, above all, save him, save him from the brutalizing lash, and inspire him with love and confidence for your service! and then there is no achievement so arduous, no conflict so desperate, in which his actions will not shed glory upon his country. And, when the final struggle comes, as soon it will come, for the empire of the seas, you may rest with entire confidence in the persuasion that victory will be yours.

THE PURITAN. — *E. P. Whipple.*

There is a charm in that word which will never be lost on a New England ear. It is closely associated with all that is great in New England history. It is hallowed by a thousand memories of obstacles overthrown, of dangers nobly braved, of sufferings unshrinkingly borne, in the service of freedom and religion. It kindles at once the pride of ancestry, and inspires the deepest feelings of national veneration. It points to examples of valor in all its modes of manifestation, — in the hall of debate, on the field of battle, before the tribunal of power, at the martyr's stake. It is a name which will never die out of New England hearts. Wherever virtue resists temptation, wherever men meet death for religion's sake, wherever the gilded baseness of the world stands abashed before conscientious principle, there will be the spirit of the Puritans. They have left deep and broad marks of their influence on human society. Their children, in all times, will rise up and call them blessed. A thousand witnesses of their courage, their industry, their sagacity, their invincible perseverance in well-doing, their love of free institutions, their respect for justice, their hatred of wrong, are all around us, and bear grateful evidence daily to their memory. We cannot forget them, even if we had sufficient baseness to wish it. Every spot of New England earth has a story to tell of them; every cherished institution of New England society bears the print of their minds. The strongest element of New England character has been transmitted with their blood. So intense is our sense of affiliation with their nature, that we speak of them universally as our "fathers." And though their fame everywhere else were weighed down with calumny and hatred, — though the principles for which they contended, and the noble deeds they performed, should become the scoff of sycophants and oppressors, and be blackened by the smooth falsehoods of the selfish and the cold, — there never will be wanting hearts in New England to kindle at their virtues, nor tongues and pens to vindicate their name.

FOR PROSECUTING THE WAR, 1813. — *H. Clay.*

When the administration was striving, by the operation of peaceful measures, to bring Great Britain back to a sense of justice, the gentlemen of the opposition were for old-fashioned war. And, now they have got old-fashioned war, their sensibilities are cruelly shocked, and all their sympathies lavished upon the harmless inhabitants of the adjoining provinces. What does a state of war present? The united energies of one people arrayed against the combined energies of another; a conflict in which each party aims to inflict all the injury it can, by sea and land, upon the territories, property, and citizens of the other, — subject only to the rules of mitigated war, practised by civilized nations. The gentlemen would not touch the continental provinces of the enemy; nor, I presume, for the same reason, her possessions in the West Indies. The same humane spirit would spare the seamen and soldiers of the enemy. The sacred person of his majesty must not be attacked, for the learned gentlemen on the other side are quite familiar with the maxim that the king can do no wrong. Indeed, I know of no person on whom we may make war, upon the principles of the honorable gentlemen, but Mr. Stephen, the celebrated author of the orders in council, or the board of admiralty, who authorize and regulate the practice of impressment!

The disasters of the war admonish us, we are told, of the necessity of terminating the contest. If our achievements by land have been less splendid than those of our intrepid seamen by water, it is not because the American soldier is less brave. On the one element, organization, discipline, and a thorough knowledge of their duties, exist, on the part of the officers and their men. On the other, almost everything is yet to be acquired. We have, however, the consolation that our country abounds with the richest materials, and that in no instance, when engaged in action, have our arms been tarnished.

An honorable peace is attainable only by an efficient war. My plan would be, to call out the ample resources of the country, give them a judicious direction, prosecute the war with the utmost vigor, strike wherever we can reach the enemy, at sea or on land, and negotiate the terms of a peace at Quebec or at Halifax. We are told that England is a proud and lofty nation, which, disdaining to wait for danger, meets it half way. Haughty as she is, we once triumphed over her; and, if we do not listen to the counsels of timidity and despair, we shall again prevail. In such a cause, with the aid of Providence, we must come out crowned with success; but, if we fail, let us fail like men, — lash ourselves to our gallant tars, and expire together in one common struggle, fighting for FREE TRADE AND SEAMEN'S RIGHTS!

FOR INDEPENDENCE, 1776. — *R. H. Lee.*

THE time will certainly come when the fated separation between the mother country and these colonies must take place, whether you will or no; for so it is decreed by the very nature of things, — by the progressive increase of our population, the fertility of our soil, the extent of our territory, the industry of our countrymen, and the immensity of the ocean which separates the two countries. And, if this be true, — as it is most true, — who does not see that the sooner it takes place, the better; that it would be the height of folly, not to seize the present occasion, when British injustice has filled all hearts with indignation, inspired all minds with courage, united all opinions in one, and put arms in every hand? And how long must we traverse three thousand miles of a stormy sea, to solicit of arrogant and insolent men either counsels or commands to regulate our domestic affairs? From what we have already achieved, it is easy to presume what we shall hereafter accomplish. Experience is the source of sage counsels, and liberty is the mother of great men. Have you not seen the enemy driven from Lexington by citizens armed and assembled in one day? Already their most celebrated generals have yielded in Boston to the skill of ours. Already their seamen, repulsed from our coasts, wander over the ocean, the sport of tempests, and the prey of famine. Let us hail the favorable omen, and fight, not for the sake of knowing on what terms we are to be the slaves of England, but to secure to ourselves a free existence, to found a just and independent government.

Why do we longer delay, — why still deliberate? Let this most happy day give birth to the American republic. Let her arise, not to devastate and conquer, but to reëstablish the reign of peace and of the laws. The eyes of Europe are fixed upon us; she demands of us a living example of freedom, that may contrast, by the felicity of the citizens, with the ever-increasing tyranny which desolates her polluted shores. She invites us to prepare an asylum where the unhappy may find solace, and the persecuted repose. She entreats us to cultivate a propitious soil, where that generous plant which first sprang up and grew in England, but is now withered by the poisonous blasts of Scottish tyranny, may revive and flourish, sheltering under its salubrious and interminable shade all the unfortunate of the human race. This is the end presaged by so many omens: — by our first victories; by the present ardor and union; by the flight of Howe, and the pestilence which broke out among Dunmore's people; by the very winds which baffled the enemy's fleets and transports, and that terrible tempest which engulfed seven hundred vessels upon the coast of Newfoundland. If we are not this day wanting in our duty to our country, the names of the American legislators will be placed, by posterity, at the side of those of Theseus, of Lycurgus, of Romulus, of Numa, of the three Williams of Nassau, and of all those whose memory has been, and will be, forever dear to virtuous men and good citizens!

THE AMERICAN GOVERNMENT. — *M. Van Buren.*

In all the attributes of a great, happy and flourishing people, we stand without a parallel in the world. Abroad, we enjoy the respect, and, with scarcely an exception, the friendship of every nation; at home, while our government quietly, but efficiently, performs the sole legitimate end of political institutions, in doing the greatest good to the greatest number, we present an aggregate of human prosperity surely not elsewhere to be found.

How imperious, then, is the obligation imposed upon every citizen, in his own sphere of action, whether limited or extended, to exert himself in perpetuating a condition of things so singularly happy! All the lessons of history and experience must be lost upon us, if we are content to trust alone to the peculiar advantages we happen to possess. Position and climate, and the bounteous resources that nature has scattered with so liberal a hand, — even the diffused intelligence and elevated character of our people, — will avail us nothing, if we fail sacredly to uphold those political institutions that were wisely and deliberately formed with reference to every circumstance that could preserve, or might endanger, the blessings we enjoy. The thoughtful framers of our constitution legislated for our country as they found it. Looking upon it with the eyes of statesmen and of patriots, they saw all the sources of rapid and wonderful prosperity; but they saw, also, that various habits, opinions and institutions, peculiar to the various portions of so vast a region, were deeply fixed. Distinct sovereignties were in actual existence, whose cordial union was essential to the welfare and happiness of all. Between many of them there was, at least to some extent, a real diversity of interests, liable to be exaggerated through sinister designs; they differed in size, in population, in wealth, and in actual and prospective resources and power; they varied in the character of their industry and staple productions; and in some existed domestic institutions, which, unwisely disturbed, might endanger the harmony of the whole. Most carefully were all these circumstances weighed, and the foundations of the new government laid upon principles of reciprocal concession and equitable compromise. The jealousies which the smaller states might entertain of the power of the rest were allayed by a rule of representation confessedly unequal at the time, and designed forever to remain so. A natural fear that the broad scope of general legislation might bear upon and unwisely control particular interests, was counteracted by limits strictly drawn around the action of the federal authority; and to the people and the states was left unimpaired their sovereign power over the innumerable subjects embraced in the internal government of a just republic, excepting such only as necessarily appertain to the concerns of the whole confederacy, or its intercourse, as a united community, with the other nations of the world.

FROM AN ADDRESS AT BLOODY BROOK. — *E. Everett.*

Gathered in this temple not made with hands, to unroll the venerable record of our fathers' history, let our first thoughts ascend to Him whose heavens are spread out as a glorious canopy above our heads! As our eyes look up to the everlasting hills which rise before us, let us remember that in the dark and eventful days we commemorate the hand that lifted their eternal pillars to the clouds was the sole stay and support of our afflicted sires. While we contemplate the lovely scene around us, — once covered with the gloomy forest and the tangled swamps, through which the victims of this day pursued their unsuspecting path to the field of slaughter, — let us bow in gratitude to Him beneath whose paternal care a little one has become a thousand, and a small one a strong nation. Assembled under the shadow of this venerable tree, let us bear a thankful recollection that at the period when its sturdy limbs which now spread over us, hung with nature's rich and verdant tapestry, were all folded up within the narrow compass of their seminal germ, the thousand settlements of our beloved country, teeming with the life, energy and power of prosperous millions, were struggling with unimagined hardships for a doubtful existence, in a score of feeble plantations scattered through the hostile wilderness. Alas! it was not alone the genial showers, and the gentle dews, and the native richness of the soil, which nourished the growth of this stately tree. The sod from which it sprung was moistened with the blood of brave men who fell for their country, and the ashes of peaceful dwellings are mingled with the consecrated earth. In like manner, it is not alone the wisdom and the courage, the piety and the virtue, of our fathers, — not alone the prudence with which they laid the foundations of the state, to which we are indebted for its happy growth and all-pervading prosperity. No, we ought never to forget, — we ought this day especially to remember, — that it was in their sacrifices and trials, their heart-rending sorrows, their ever-renewed tribulations, their wanderings, their conflicts, their wants and their woes, that the corner-stone of our privileges and blessings was laid.

As I stand on this hallowed spot, my mind filled with the traditions of that disastrous day, surrounded by these enduring natural memorials, impressed with the touching ceremonies we have just witnessed, the affecting incidents of the bloody scene crowd upon my imagination. This compact and prosperous village disappears, and a few scattered log-cabins are seen, in the bosom of the primeval forest, clustering for protection around the rude blockhouse in the centre. A corn-field or two has been rescued from the all-surrounding wilderness, and here and there the yellow husks are heard to rustle in the breeze, that comes loaded with the mournful sighs of the melancholy pine-woods. Beyond, the interminable forest spreads in every direction, the covert of the wolf, of the rattle-snake, of the savage; and between its gloomy copses what is now a fertile and cultivated meadow stretches out a dreary expanse of unreclaimed morass. I look, — I listen. All is still, — solemnly, frightfully still. No voice of human activity or enjoyment breaks the dreary silence of nature, or mingles with the dirge of the woods and water-courses. All *seems* peaceful and still; — and yet there *is* a strange heaviness in the fall of the leaves in the wood that skirts the road; there is an unnatural flitting in those shadows; there is a plashing sound in the waters of that brook, which makes the flesh creep with horror. Hark! it is the click of a gun-lock from that thicket; — no, it is a pebble, that has dropped from the over-hanging cliff, upon the rock beneath. It is, it is the gleaming blade of a scalping-knife; — no, it is a sunbeam thrown off from that dancing ripple. It is, it is the red feather of a savage chief, peeping from behind that maple tree; — no, it is a leaf, which September has touched with her many-tinted pencil. And now a distant drum is heard; yes, that is a sound of life, — conscious, proud life. A single fife breaks upon the ear, — a stirring strain. It is one of the marches to which the stern warriors of Cromwell moved over the field at Naseby and Worcester. There are no loyal ears to take offence at a puritanical march in a trans-Atlantic forest; and hard by, at Hadley, there is a gray-haired fugitive, who followed the cheering strain at the head of his division in the army of the great usurper. The warlike note grows louder! I hear the tread of armed men! — but I run before my story.

EXTENT OF COUNTRY NO BAR TO UNION. — *E. Randolph.*

Extent of country, in my conception, ought to be no bar to the adoption of a good government. No extent on earth seems to me too great, provided the laws be wisely made and executed. The principles of representation and responsibility may pervade a large as well as a small territory; and tyranny is as easily introduced into a small as into a large district. Union is the rock of our salvation. Our safety, our political happiness, our existence, depend on the Union of these States. Without union, the people of this and the other states will undergo the unspeakable calamities which discord, faction, turbulence, war and bloodshed, have continually produced in other countries. Without union, we throw away all those blessings for which we have so earnestly fought. Without union, there is no peace in the land.

The American spirit ought to be mixed with American pride, — pride to see the Union magnificently triumph. Let that glorious pride which once defied the British thunder reänimate you again. Let it not be recorded of Americans, that, after having performed the most gallant exploits, after having overcome the most astonishing difficulties, and after having gained the admiration of the world by their incomparable valor and policy, they lost their acquired reputation, lost their national consequence and happiness, by their own indiscretion. Let no future historian inform posterity that Americans wanted wisdom and virtue to concur in any regular, efficient government. Catch the present moment. Seize it with avidity. It may be lost, never to be regained; and, if the Union be lost now, I fear it will remain so forever!

AMERICAN INNOVATIONS. — *J. Madison.*

Why is the experiment of an extended republic to be rejected, merely because it may comprise what is new? Is it not the glory of the people of America, that whilst they have paid a decent regard to the opinions of former times and other nations, they have not suffered a blind veneration for antiquity, for custom, or for names, to overrule the suggestions of their own good sense, the knowledge of their own situation, and the lesson of their own experience? To this manly spirit posterity will be indebted for the possession, and the world for the example, of the numerous innovations displayed on the American theatre, in favor of private rights and public happiness. Had no important step been taken by the leaders of the Revolution, for which a precedent could not be discovered, — no government established, of which an exact model did not present itself, — the people of the United States might, at this moment, have been numbered among the melancholy victims of misguided councils; must, at best, have been laboring under the weight of some of those forms which have crushed the liberties of the rest of mankind. Happily for America, — happily, we trust, for the whole human race, — they pursued a new and more noble course. They accomplished a revolution which has no parallel in the annals of human society. They reared the fabric of governments which have no model on the face of the globe. They formed the design of a great confederacy, which it is incumbent on their successors to improve and perpetuate. If their works betray imperfections, we wonder at the fewness of them. If they erred most in the structure of the Union, this was the most difficult to be executed; this is the work which has been new-modelled by the act of your convention, and it is that act on which you are now to deliberate and to decide.

DANGERS OF THE SPIRIT OF CONQUEST. — *T. Corwin.*

This uneasy desire to augment our territory has depraved the moral sense, and blighted the otherwise keen sagacity, of our people. What has been the fate of all nations who have acted upon the idea that they must advance? Our young orators cherish this notion with a fervid, but fatally mistaken zeal. They call it by the mysterious name of "destiny." "Our destiny," they say, "is onward;" and hence they argue, with ready sophistry, the propriety of seizing upon any territory and any people, that may lie in the way of our "fated" advance. Recently these progressives have grown classical; some assiduous student of antiquities has helped them to a patron saint. They have wandered back into the desolated Pantheon, and there, among the polytheistic relics of that "pale mother of dead empires," they have found a god, whom these Romans, centuries gone by, baptized "Terminus."

I have read much and heard somewhat of this gentleman, Terminus. Alexander was a devotee of this divinity. We have seen the end of him and his empire. It was said to be an attribute of this god, that he *must* always advance and never recede. So both republican and imperial Rome believed. It was, as they said, their destiny; and, for a while, it did seem to be even so. Roman Terminus did advance. Under the eagles of Rome, he was carried from his home on the Tiber to the furthest east on one hand, and to the far west, among the then barbarous tribes of Western Europe, on the other. But at length the time came when retributive justice had become a "destiny." The despised Gaul calls out to the contemned Goth, and Attila, with his Huns, answers back the battle-shout to both. The "blue-eyed nations of the north," in succession of united strength, pour forth their countless hosts of warriors upon Rome, and Rome's always advancing god, Terminus. And now the battle-axe of the barbarians strikes down the conquering eagle of Rome. Terminus at last recedes; slowly at first, but finally he is driven to Rome, and from Rome to Byzantium. Whoever would know the further fate of this Roman deity, may find ample gratification of his curiosity in the luminous pages of Gibbon's Decline and Fall. Such will find that Rome thought as you now think, that it was her destiny to conquer provinces and nations; and, no doubt, she sometimes said as you say, "I will conquer a peace." And where now is she, the mistress of the world? The spider weaves his web in her palaces; the owl sings his watch-song in her towers. Teutonic power now lords it over the servile remnant, the miserable memento of old and once omnipotent Rome. Sad, very sad are the lessons which time has written for us. Through and in them all I see nothing but the inflexible execution of that old law, which ordains as eternal the cardinal rule, "Thou shalt not covet thy neighbor's goods, nor *anything* which is his."

Since I have lately heard so much about the dismemberment of Mexico, I have looked back to see how, in the course of events which some call "Providence," it has fared with other nations who engaged in this work of dismemberment. I see that, in the latter half of the eighteenth century, three powerful nations, Russia, Austria and Prussia, united in the dismemberment of Poland. They said, too, as you say, "It is our destiny." They "wanted room." Doubtless each of these thought, with his share of Poland, his power was too strong ever to fear invasion, or even insult. One had his California, another his New Mexico, and a third his Vera Cruz. Did they remain untouched and incapable of harm? Alas! no; far, very far from it. Retributive justice must fulfil its destiny, too. A very few years pass off, and we hear of a new man, a Corsican lieutenant, the self-named "armed soldier of democracy," Napoleon. He ravages Austria, covers her land with blood, drives the northern Cæsar from his capital, and sleeps in his palace. Austria may now remember how her power trampled upon Poland. Did she not pay dear, very dear, for her California? But has Prussia no atonement to make? You see this same Napoleon, the blind instrument of Providence, at work there. The thunders of his cannon at Jena proclaim the work of retribution for Poland's wrongs; and the successors of the Great Frederick, the drill-sergeant of Europe, are seen flying across the sandy plains that surround their capital, right glad if they may escape captivity and death. But how fares it with the Autocrat of Russia? Is he secure in his share of the spoils of Poland? No; suddenly we see six hundred thousand armed men marching to Moscow. Does his Vera Cruz protect him now? Far from it. Blood, slaughter, desolation, spread abroad over the land, and, finally, the conflagration of the old commercial metropolis of Russia closes the retribution she must pay for her share in the dismemberment of her weak and impotent neighbor. A mind more prone to look for the judgments of Heaven in the doings of men than mine cannot fail in this to see the providence of God. When Moscow burned, it seemed as if the earth was lighted up, that the nations might behold the scene. As that mighty sea of fire gathered and heaved and rolled upward, and yet higher, till its flames licked the stars, and fired the whole heavens, it did seem as though the God of the nations was writing in characters of flame, on the front of his throne, that doom that shall fall upon the strong nation which tramples in scorn upon the weak. And what fortune awaits him, the appointed executor of this work, when it was all done? He, too, conceived the idea that his destiny pointed onward to universal dominion. France was too small; Europe, he thought, should bow down before him. But as soon as this idea took possession of his soul, he, too, became powerless. His Terminus must recede, too. Right there, while he witnessed the humiliation, and, doubtless, meditated the subjugation of Russia, He who holds the winds in his fist gathered the snows of the north, and blew them upon his six hundred thousand men; — they died, they froze, they perished. And now the mighty Napoleon, who had resolved on universal dominion, *he*, too, is summoned to answer for the violation of that ancient law, "Thou shalt not covet anything which is thy neighbor's." How are the mighty fallen! He, beneath whose proud footsteps Europe trembled, he is now an exile at Elba, and now finally a prisoner on the rock of St. Helena, — and there, on a barren island, in an unfrequented sea, in the crater of an extinguished volcano, *there* is the death-bed of the mighty conqueror. All his *annexations* have come to that! His last hour is now come; and he, the man of *destiny*, he who had rocked the world as with the throes of an earthquake, is now powerless, — still; even as the beggar, so he died. On the wings of a tempest that raged with unwonted fury, up to the throne of the only Power that controlled him while he lived, went the fiery soul of that wonderful warrior, another witness to that eternal decree, that they who do not rule in righteousness shall perish from the earth. He has found "room," at last. And France, — *she*, too, has found "room." Her eagles now no longer scream along the banks of the Danube, the Po, and the Borysthenes. They have returned home to their old eyrie, between the Alps, the Rhine and the Pyrenees. So shall it be with yours. You may carry them to the loftiest peaks of the Cordilleras, they may wave in insolent triumph in the halls of the Montezumas, the armed men of Mexico may quail before them, — but the weakest hand in Mexico, uplifted in prayer to the God of justice, may call down against you a Power, in the presence of which the iron hearts of your warriors shall be turned into ashes!

FOR THE BRITISH TREATY. — *F. Ames.*

ARE the posts of our frontier to remain forever in the possession of Great Britain? Let those who reject them, when the treaty offers them to our hands, say, if they choose, they are of no importance. Will the tendency to Indian hostilities be contested by any one? Experience gives the answer. Am I reduced to the necessity of proving this point? Certainly the very men who charged the Indian war on the detention of the posts will call for no other proof than the recital of their own speeches. "Until the posts are restored," they exclaimed, "the treasury and the frontiers must bleed." Can gentlemen now say that an Indian peace, without the posts, will prove firm? No! it will not be peace, but a sword; it will be no better than a lure to draw victims within the reach of the tomahawk.

On this theme my emotions are unutterable. If I could find words for them, if my powers bore any proportion to my zeal, I would swell my voice to such a note of remonstrance, it should reach every log-house beyond the mountains. I would say to the inhabitants, Wake from your false security! Your cruel dangers, your more cruel apprehensions, are soon to be renewed. The wounds, yet unhealed, are to be torn open again. In the day-time your path through the woods will be ambushed. The darkness of midnight will glitter with the blaze of your dwellings. You are a father, — the blood of your sons shall fatten your corn-fields! You are a mother, — the war-whoop shall wake the sleep of the cradle!

Who will say that I exaggerate the tendencies of our measures? Will any one answer, by a sneer, that all this is idle preaching? Will any one deny that we are bound, and, I would hope, to good purpose, by the most solemn sanctions of duty, for the vote we give? Are despots alone to be reproached for unfeeling indifference to the tears and blood of their subjects? Are republicans irresponsible? Can you put the dearest interest of society at risk, without guilt, and without remorse? It is vain to offer, as an excuse, that public men are not to be reproached for the evils that may happen to ensue from their measures. This is very true, where they are unforeseen or inevitable. Those I have depicted are not unforeseen; they are so far from inevitable, we are going to bring them into being by our vote. We choose the consequences, and become as justly answerable for them as for the measure that we know will produce them.

By rejecting the posts, we light the savage fires, we bind the victims. This day we undertake to render account to the widows and orphans whom our decision will make; — to the wretches that will be roasted at the stake; to our country, and, I do not deem it

26

too serious to say, to conscience and to God, we are answerable; and, if duty be anything more than a word of imposture, if conscience be not a bugbear, we are preparing to make ourselves as wretched as our country. There is no mistake in this case. There can be none. Experience has already been the prophet of events, and the cries of our future victims have already reached us. The western inhabitants are not a silent and uncomplaining sacrifice. The voice of humanity issues from the shade of the wilderness. It exclaims that, while one hand is held up to reject this treaty, the other grasps a tomahawk. It summons our imagination to the scenes that will open. It is no great effort to the imagination to conceive that events so near are already begun. I can fancy that I listen to the yells of savage vengeance, and the shrieks of torture! Already they seem to sigh in the western wind! Already they mingle with every echo from the mountains!

THE OLD WORLD AND THE NEW.—*L. Cass.*

WHAT American can survey the field of battle at Bunker Hill or at New Orleans, without recalling the deeds which will render these names imperishable? Who can pass the islands of Lake Erie, without thinking upon those who sleep in the waters below, and upon the victory which broke the power of the enemy, and led to the security of an extensive frontier? There no monument can be erected, for the waves roll and will roll over them. But he who met the enemy and made them ours, and his devoted companions, will live in the recollections of the American people, while there is virtue to admire, patriotism or gratitude to reward it. I have stood upon the plain of Marathon, the battle-field of liberty. It is silent and desolate. Neither Greek nor Persian is there, to give life and animation to the scene. It is bounded by sterile hills on one side, and lashed by the eternal waves of the Ægean Sea on the other. But Greek and Persian were once there, and that dreary spot was alive with hostile armies, who fought the great fight which rescued Greece from the yoke of Persia.

And I have stood also upon the hill of Zion, the city of Jerusalem, the scene of our Redeemer's sufferings and crucifixion, and ascension. But the sceptre has departed from Judah, and its glory from the capital of Solomon. The Assyrian, the Egyptian, the Greek, the Roman, the Arab, the Turk, and the crusader, have passed over this chief place of Israel, and have reft it of its power and beauty. Well has the denunciation of the prophet of misfortunes been fulfilled, when he declared that "the Lord had set his face against this city for evil, and not for good;" when he pronounced the words of the Most High, "I will cause to cease from the city of Judah and from the streets of Jerusalem the voice of mirth and the voice of gladness, the voice of the bridegroom and the voice of the bride; for the land shall be desolate."

In those regions of the East where society passed its infancy, it seems to have reached decrepitude. If the associations which the memory of the past glory excites are powerful, they are melancholy. They are without joy for the present, and without hope for the future. But here we are in the freshness of youth, and can look forward with national confidence to ages of progress in all that gives power and pride to man, and dignity to human nature. No deeds of glory hallow this region. But nature has been bountiful to it in its best gifts, and art and industry are at work to extend and improve them. You cannot pierce the barrier which shuts in the past, and separates you from the great highway of nations. You have opened a vista to the Atlantic and the Gulf of Mexico. From this elevated point two seas are before us, which your energy and perseverance have brought within reach. It is better to look forward to prosperity than back to glory. To the mental eye no prospect can be more magnificent than here meets the vision. I need not stop to describe it. It is before us in the long regions of fertile land which stretch off to the east and west, to the north and south, in all the advantages that Providence has liberally bestowed upon them, and in the changes and improvements which man is making. The forest is fading and falling, and towns and villages are rising and flourishing. And, better still, a moral, intelligent and industrious people are spreading themselves over the whole face of the country, and making it their own and their home. And what changes and chances await us? Shall we go on increasing and improving, and united? or shall we add another to the list of republics which have preceded us, and which have fallen the victims of their own follies and dissensions? My faith in the stability of our institutions is enduring, my hope is strong; for they rest upon public virtue and intelligence.

SUFFERINGS OF GREECE. — *R. Jarvis.*

In breathing our hopes of European emancipation, let not Greece — lovely, interesting Greece — be neglected or forgotten. O Greece! the cradle of the poet and the philosopher, the home of the hero and the statesman, — whose name awakens every sublime recollection, and whose ancient memory is bound to the American heart by every tie that literature, science, or love of liberty can weave, — when the American forgets thee, "may her right hand forget her cunning!" Where are thy glories now? The feet of barbarians have polluted thy soil, and the siroc of despotism has passed over thee. Thy Acropolis is crumbled in ruins; thy Parthenon lays low in dust; the Muses have fled thy Parnassus; thy Helicon murmurs in vain; the harp of thy Homer is broken; thy Sapphos are mute, and their lyres are unstrung! And could thy sufferings excite no sympathy in the bosoms of thy royal neighbors? Could not one faith, could not the worship of one Lord and one gospel, could not the voice of humanity, call forth the Holy Alliance to protect thee, or restrain them from monstrous combination with thy oppressors? O monarchs of Europe! members of the Holy Alliance! who claim to be Heaven's vicegerents, and to be set over mankind for dispensing that happiness which you profanely say they cannot procure for themselves, — how, in the days of your last account, will the genius of injured Greece stand before you, and point her accusing finger to your crimes! She will say, "My children sought refuge among you, and you shut your door against them! My daughters were carried into bondage, and your ships transported them! My sons implored your aid, and you gave it to their enemies! My cities were laid in ruins, and you furnished the firebrands! But for you, the barbarians had been long since subdued, and my land the abode of liberty, peace, and happiness! But for you, the fires of Scio had never been kindled, and the blood that now stains every blade of grass in my violated territory would still have warmed hearts more generous than your own!" But, however great the sufferings of this people, however formidable their enemies, or however efficiently aided by Christian kings, yet God will prosper their righteous cause, and scatter confusion among their enemies. The spirit of ancient Greece is waked from the slumber of ages! The tongue of Demosthenes is loosed; the sword of Miltiades is drawn; every strait is a Salamis, and every sailor a Themistocles; a Leonidas starts up in every peasant, and every mountain pass becomes a new Thermopylæ! And not only in Greece shall the Moloch of royalty be overturned, but in whatever corner of Europe the idol can find worshippers. The reign of kings is a violation of natural right. The cause of mankind is not their cause. The day of retribution approaches! The clouds are gathering! The tempest will soon burst! And when royalty shall be swept away in its avenging fury, the rainbow of republicanism shall span the heavens, giving promise of lasting peace and security!

GREAT BRITAIN NOT INVINCIBLE.—*J. C. Calhoun.*

THIS country is left alone to support the rights of neutrals. Perilous is the condition, and arduous the task. We are not intimidated. We stand opposed to British usurpation, and by our spirit and efforts have done all in our power to save the last vestiges of neutral rights. Yes, our embargoes, non-intercourse, non-importation, and, finally, war, are all manly exertions to preserve the rights of this and other nations from the deadly grasp of British maritime policy. But, say our opponents, these efforts are lost, and our condition hopeless. If so, it only remains for us to assume the garb of our condition. We must submit, humbly submit, crave pardon, and hug our chains. It is not wise to provoke where we cannot resist. But first let us be well assured of the hopelessness of our state before we sink into submission. On what do our opponents rest their despondent and slavish belief? On the recent events in Europe? I admit they are great, and well calculated to impose on the imagination. Our enemy never presented a more imposing exterior. His fortune is at the flood. But I am admonished by universal experience that such prosperity is the most precarious of human conditions. From the flood the tide dates its ebb. From the meridian the sun commences his decline. Depend upon it, there is more of sound philosophy than of fiction in the fickleness which poets attribute to fortune. Prosperity has its weakness, adversity its strength. In many respects our enemy has lost by those very changes which seem so very much in his favor. He can no more claim to be struggling for existence; no more to be fighting the battles of the world in defence of the liberties of mankind. The magic cry of "French influence" is lost. In this very hall we are not strangers to that sound. Here, even here, the cry of "French influence," that baseless fiction, that phantom of faction now banished, often resounded. I rejoice that the spell is broken by which it was attempted to bind the spirit of this youthful nation. The minority can no longer act under cover, but must come out and defend their opposition on its own intrinsic merits. Our example can scarcely fail to produce its effects on other nations interested in the maintenance of maritime rights. But if, unfortunately, we should be left alone to maintain the contest, and if — which may God forbid! — necessity should compel us to yield for the present, yet our generous efforts will not have been lost. A mode of thinking and a tone of sentiment have gone abroad which must stimulate to future and more successful struggles. What could not be done with eight millions of people will be done with twenty. The great cause will never be yielded; no, never, never! I hear the future audibly announced in the past, in the splendid victories over the Guerrière, Java and Macedonian. We, and all nations, by these victories are taught a lesson never to be forgotten. Opinion is power. The charm of British naval invincibility is gone.

THE FOURTH OF JULY. — *G. S. Hillard.*

It cannot be denied that we have been, for some time past, growing indifferent to the celebration of this day. It was once hailed — and some who hear me can remember the time — with emotions too deep for words. The full hearts of men overflowed in the copious, gushing tears of childhood, and silently went up to heaven on the wings of praise. With their own sweat and their own blood they had won their inheritance of peace, and they prized it accordingly. They were yet fresh from the great events which we read of as cold matters of history. The storm had passed by, but the swell of the troubled waters, rising in dark-heaving ridges, yet marked its duration and violence. All things then wore the beauty of novelty, and long possession had not dulled the sense of enjoyment. The golden light and glittering dews of the morning were above and around them. The wine of life sparkled and foamed in its freshly-poured cup. The lovely form of Liberty — to us so familiar — seemed like a bright vision, newly lighted upon this orb, from the starry courts of heaven; and men hung, with the rapture of lovers, upon her inspiring glances and her animating smiles. But a half-century has rolled by, and a new generation has sprung up, who seem to think that their social and political privileges belong to them as naturally as air and light, and reflect as little upon the way in which they came by them. The very magnitude of our blessings makes us insensible to their value, as the ancients supposed that the music of the spheres could not be heard, because it was so loud. The whole thing has become to us an old story. We have heard so much of the spirit of Seventy-six, and of the times that tried men's souls, that we are growing weary of the sound. The same feeling which made the Athenians tired of hearing Aristides called the just makes us tired of hearing this called a glorious anniversary. But that man is little to be envied who cannot disentangle this occasion from the secondary and debasing associations which cling to it, — from its noise, its dust, its confusion, its dull orations and vapid toasts, — and, ascending at once into a higher region of thought and feeling, recognize the full, unimpaired force of that grand manifestation of moral power which has consecrated the day. A cold indifference to this celebration would, in itself, be a sign of ominous import to the fortunes of the republic. He who greets the light of this morning with no throb of generous feeling is unworthy of a share in that heritage of glory which he claims by right of the blood which flows in his degenerate veins. That man, had he lived sixty years ago, would most surely have been found wanting to his country, in her hour of agony and struggle. Neither with tongue, nor purse, nor hand, would he have aided the most inspiring cause that ever appealed to a magnanimous breast. The same cast of character which makes one incapable of feeling an absorbing emotion, makes him incapable of heroic efforts and heroic sacrifices. He who cannot forget himself in admiring true greatness, can never be great; and the power of justly appreciating and heartily reverencing exalted merit is, in itself, an unequivocal sign of a noble nature.

FUTURE EMPIRE OF OUR LANGUAGE. — *G. W. Bethune.*

The products of the whole world are, or may soon be, found within our confederated limits. Already there had been a salutary mixture of blood, but not enough to impair the Anglo-Saxon ascendency. The nation grew morally strong from its original elements. The great work was delayed only by a just preparation. Now, God is bringing hither the most vigorous scions from all the European stocks, to make of them all one new man; — not the Saxon, not the German, not the Gaul, not the Helvetian, but the American. Here they will unite as one brotherhood, will have one law, will share one interest. Spread over the vast region from the frigid to the torrid, from the eastern to the western ocean, every variety of climate giving them choice of pursuit and modification of temperament, the ballot-box fusing together all rivalries, they shall have one national will. What is wanting in one race will be supplied by the characteristic energies of the others; and what is excesssive in either, checked by the counter action of the rest. Nay, though for a time the newly-come may retain their foreign vernacular, our tongue, so rich in ennobling literature, will be the tongue of the nation, the language of its laws, and the accent of its majesty. Eternal God, who seest the end with the beginning, Thou alone canst tell the ultimate grandeur of this people!

Such is the sphere, present and future, in which God calls us to work for him, for our country, and for mankind. The language in which we utter truth will be spoken on this continent, a century hence, by thirty times more millions than those dwelling on the island of its origin. The openings for trade on the Pacific coast, and the railroad across the isthmus, will bring the commerce of the world under the control of our race. The empire of our language will follow that of our commerce; the empire of our institutions, that of our language. The man who writes successfully for America will yet speak for all the world!

ADDRESS TO KOSSUTH.—*E. Hopkins.*

THE people of Massachusetts, sir, would have you accept this act of her constituted authorities as no unmeaning compliment. Never, in her history as an independent state, with one single and illustrious exception, has Massachusetts tendered such a mark of respect to any other than the chief magistrates of these United States. And even in the present instance, much as she admires your patriotism, your eloquence, your untiring devotedness and zeal,—deeply as she is moved by your plaintive appeals and supplications in behalf of your native and oppressed land,—greatly as she is amazed at the irrepressible elasticity with which you rise from under the heel of oppression, with fortitude increased under sufferings, and with assurance growing stronger as the darkness grows deeper,—still, it is not one or all of these qualities combined that can lead her to swerve from her dignity as an independent state to the mere worship of man. No. But it is because she views you as the advocate and providential representative of certain great principles which constitute her own vitality as a state, — because she views you as the representative of human rights and freedom in another and far distant land, — it is because she views you as the rightful but exiled governor of a people whose past history and whose recent deeds show them to be worthy of some better future than that of Russian tyranny and Austrian oppression, — that she seeks to welcome you to her borders; that she seeks to attest to a gazing world that to the cause of freedom she is not insensible, and that to the oppression of tyrants she is not indifferent.

It is well, sir, that your feet have not yet pressed the soil of Massachusetts. It is well that you landed elsewhere; that you have surveyed the most prosperous portions of the Atlantic coast; that you have surmounted the formidable Alleghanies, and planted your feet in the confines of this great valley. It is well that you should comprehend its vast extent; that you should float down these mighty streams, and survey these mighty valleys; that, when your soul has become expanded by these scenes, and gratified by the free institutions which adorn and bless them, then, and not till then, should you turn your footsteps on a holy pilgrimage to the spot where American liberty had its birth. Its embryo slumbered in the souls of those illustrious and highly accomplished Puritan exiles, when, with religion for their handmaid, they set foot on the rock of Plymouth, and encountered the stern rigors of a New England winter. Their first-born child was popular education. Their second was popular freedom. In what words can the history of any commonwealth be so gloriously emblazoned, as in those three words, and in the order in which I name them, — religion, education, freedom? Here, sir, is a tri-color for the world.

Such, preëminently such, is the record of Massachusetts. One word only need be added to bring her history to the present hour, and that is but a corollary of the former, — I mean, prosperity. As the man of piety surveys her borders, numbers her people, counts their wealth, he finds a new fact added to the proof of ages,

—"Never have I seen the righteous forsaken, nor his seed begging bread."

I have said, sir, that Massachusetts is the birth-place of American liberty. When, then, you have seen the full stature with which she fills these vast valleys and stretches herself over these mighty mountains, come to our little nursery, so retired from the turmoils and corruptions of the Old World, and we will show you the cradle where she was rocked to notes of eloquence, which, while they soothed her fears, awakened a mighty continent to her nurture and defence. Come, sir, and we will show you the holy spot where the first baptismal blood of the Revolution was sprinkled upon her consecrated head, the camp-ground where Washington first unsheathed his sword in her defence, and the fortifications which he first erected for her intrenchment. From the windows and balconies of the legislative halls whence this invitation to you has emanated, these spots can be seen.

Come, then, and stand amid these hallowed scenes; gaze upon them, listen to their silent eloquence, till it steals through every fibre, and breaks up every fountain of your soul. Drink with us of these first well-springs of American liberty, and you will find them still gushing and pure! Ah, sir, is it not fitting that your last pilgrimage on this continent should be to such a place, — that, as you embark for the Old World, your parting act should be to drink at the most hallowed fountains of the New? Sir, Massachusetts will welcome you. She is the descendant of illustrious exiles, who, fleeing from oppression in the Old World, sought freedom in the New. Her past history, her filial piety, bids you welcome as an exile. Herself the first in legal resistance to illegal acts, in constitutional resistance to unconstitutional oppression, how can she do otherwise than welcome those who follow in her footsteps? Prospered almost without a parallel as she has been under the smiles of a kind Providence, she can give but a poor account of her stewardship, unless her institutions of religion, of education, of philanthropy, of freedom, can afford most valuable information to all who seek to found new states, or, like yourself, to regenerate and revive those that are old.

I speak of her institutions of freedom. I mean her distinct municipalities. There is no centralization there. Distributed into three hundred and twenty-two cities and townships, it is in these, by her literally democratic assemblages, that her government is chiefly carried on. No central government established and patronizes our four thousand public schools. No central government levies our taxes to fill her coffers and feed her parasites. Each town provides for itself, levies its own taxes, sustains its own schools, establishes its own municipal regulations, and in each and all of these acts is independent of every other. The cause of education and of freedom is thus reposed in the hands and hearts of the people. Reposed, did I say? No, sir! it is because of those hands and hearts that freedom and education have no repose, but are pushed into the most active, vigorous and advancing life!

THE SOUTH DURING THE REVOLUTION — *R. Y. Hayne.*

If there be one state in the Union (and I say it not in a boastful spirit) that may challenge comparisons with any other, for an uniform, zealous, ardent and uncalculating devotion to the Union, that state is South Carolina. From the very commencement of the Revolution, up to this hour, there is no sacrifice, however great, she has not cheerfully made, — no service she has ever hesitated to perform. She has adhered to you in your prosperity; but in your adversity she has clung to you with more than filial affection. No matter what was the condition of her domestic affairs, — though deprived of her resources. divided by parties, or surrounded with difficulties, — the call of the country has been to her as the voice of God. Domestic discord ceased at the sound; every man became at once reconciled to his brethren, and the sons of Carolina were all seen crowding together to the temple, bringing their gifts to the altar of their common country.

What was the conduct of the South during the Revolution? I honor New England for her conduct in that glorious struggle. But, great as is the praise which belongs to her, I think at least equal honor is due to the South. They espoused the quarrel of their brethren, with a generous zeal, which did not suffer them to stop to calculate their interest in the dispute. Favorites of the mother country, possessed of neither ships nor seamen to create a commercial rivalship, they might have found in their situation a guarantee that their trade would be forever fostered and protected by Great Britain. But, trampling on all considerations either of interest or of safety, they rushed into the conflict, and, fighting for principle, perilled all, in the sacred cause of freedom. Never was there exhibited, in the history of the world, higher examples of noble daring, dreadful suffering and heroic endurance, than by the Whigs of Carolina, during the Revolution. The whole state, from the mountains to the sea, was overrun by an overwhelming force of enemy. The fruits of industry perished on the spot where they were produced, or were consumed by the foe. The "plains of Carolina" drank up the most precious blood of her citizens. Black and smoking ruins marked the places which had been the habitations of her children. Driven from their homes into the gloomy and almost impenetrable swamps, even there the spirit of liberty survived; and South Carolina, sustained by the example of her Sumpters and her Marions, proved, by her conduct, that, though her soil might be overrun, the spirit of her people was invincible.

LOUIS KOSSUTH. — *H. Mann.*

WITH what enthusiasm did we hail the birth of the South American republics! What hosannas did we shout forth for the emancipation of Greece! How deep the sigh of the nation's heart when Poland struggled in her death-agony and breathed her last! Even so late as 1848, this Congress sent resolutions congratulating France on her Magna Charta of "liberty, equality and fraternity." In one of the European revolutions of that year, on the banks of the Danube, a young man sprang, at a single bound, from comparative obscurity to universal fame. His heroism organized armies. His genius created resources. He abolished the factitious order of nobility; but his exalted soul poured the celestial ichor of the gods through ten millions of peasant hearts, and made them truly noble. Though weak in all but the energies of the soul, yet it took two mighty empires to break down his power. When he sought refuge in Turkey, the sympathies of the civilized world attended his exile. He was invited to our shores. He came, and spoke as man never before spake. It was Byron's wish that he could condense all the raging elements of his soul

> "into *one* word,
> And that one word were lightning."

Kossuth found what Byron in vain prayed for; for all *his* words were lightning; — not bolts, but a lambent flame, which he poured into men's hearts, not to kill, but to animate with a more exalted and a diviner life. In cities where the vast population went forth to hail him, in academic halls where the cultivation of eloquence and knowledge is made the business of life, in those great gathering places where the rivers of people have their confluence, he was addressed by the most eloquent men whom this nation of orators could select. More than five hundred of our selectest speakers spoke speeches before him which they had laboriously prepared from history and embellished from the poets, with severe toil, by the long-trimmed lamp. Save in two or three peculiar cases, his unprepared and improvised replies, in eloquence, in pathos, in dignity, in exalted sentiment, excelled them all. For their most profound philosophy, he gave them deeper generalizations; he outcircuited their widest ranges of thought, and in the whole sweep of the horizon revealed glories they had never seen; and, while they checked their ambitious flight beneath the sun, he soared into the empyrean, and brought down, for the guidance of men's hearts and deeds, the holy light that shines from the face of God. Though all their splendors were gathered to a focal point, they were outshone by his effulgence. His immortal theme was liberty — liberty for the nations, liberty for the people!

The person of this truly noble Hungarian has departed from our shores; but he has left a spirit behind him that will never die. He has scattered seeds of liberty and truth, whose flowers and fruit will become honors and glorious amaranthine. I trust he goes to mingle in sterner scenes; I trust he goes to battle for the right, not with the tongue and pen alone, but with all the weapons that freedom can forge and wield! Before the divine government I bow in reverence and adoration; but it tasks all my philosophy and all my religion to believe that the despots of Europe have not exercised their irresponsible and cruel tyrannies too long. It seems too long since Charles was brought to the axe, and Louis to the guillotine. Liberty, humanity, justice, demand more modern instances. The time has fully come when the despot, not the patriot, should feel the executioner's steel or lead. The time has fully come when, if the oppressed demand their inalienable and heaven-born rights of their oppressors, and this demand is denied, that they should say, not exactly in the language of Patrick Henry, "Give me liberty, or give me death;"—that was noble language in its day; but we have now reached an advanced stage in human development, and the time has fully come when the oppressed, if their rights are forcibly denied them, should say to the oppressor, "Give *me* liberty, or I will give *you* death!"

AMERICAN INSTITUTIONS.—*M. Van Buren.*

Half a century, teeming with extraordinary events, and elsewhere producing astonishing results, has passed along; but on our institutions it has left no injurious mark. From a small community we have risen to a people powerful in numbers and in strength; but with our increase has gone hand in hand the progress of just principles; the privileges, civil and religious, of the humblest individual, are still sacredly protected at home; while the valor and fortitude of our people have removed from us the slightest apprehension of foreign power, they have not yet induced us, in a single instance, to forget what is right. Our commerce has been extended to the remotest nations; the value and even nature of our productions have been greatly changed; a wide difference has arisen in the relative wealth and resources of every portion of our country; yet the spirit of mutual regard and of faithful adherence to existing compacts has continued to prevail in our councils, and never long been absent from our conduct. We have learned by experience a fruitful lesson, — that an implicit and undeviating adherence to the principles on which we set out can carry us prosperously onward through all the conflicts of circumstances, and the vicissitudes inseparable from the lapse of years.

The success that has attended our great experiment is, in itself, a sufficient cause for gratitude, on account of the happiness it has actually conferred, and the example it has unanswerably given. But to me, looking forward to the far-distant future with ardent prayers and confiding hopes, this retrospect presents a ground for still deeper delight. It impresses on my mind a firm belief that the perpetuity of our institutions depends upon ourselves; that, if we maintain the principles on which they were established, they are destined to confer their benefits on countless generations yet to come; and that America will present to every friend of mankind the cheering proof that a popular government, wisely formed, is wanting in no element of endurance or strength. Fifty years ago its rapid failure was boldly predicted. Latent and uncontrollable causes of dissolution were supposed to exist, even by the wise and the good; and not only unfriendly or speculative theorists anticipated for us the fate of past republics, but the fears of many an honest patriot overbalanced his sanguine hopes. Look back on these forebodings, not hastily but reluctantly made, and see how, in every instance, they have completely failed!

EARLY DEEDS OF OUR FATHERS. — *J. Q. Adams.*

Americans! let us pause for a moment to consider the situation of our country at that eventful day when our national existence commenced. In the full possession and enjoyment of all those prerogatives for which you then dared to adventure upon "all the varieties of untried being," the calm and settled moderation of the mind is scarcely competent to conceive the tone of heroism to which the souls of freemen were exalted in that hour of perilous magnanimity. Seventeen times has the sun, in the progress of his annual revolutions, diffused his prolific radiance over the plains of independent America. Millions of hearts, which then palpitated with the rapturous glow of patriotism, have already been translated to a brighter world, — to the abodes of more than mortal freedom! Other millions have arisen, to receive from their parents and benefactors the inestimable recompense of their achievements. A large proportion of the audience whose benevolence is at this moment listening to the speaker of the day, like him, were at that period too little advanced beyond the threshold of life to partake of the divine enthusiasm which inspired the American bosom, which prompted her voice to proclaim defiance to the thunders of Britain, which consecrated the banners of her armies, and, finally, erected the holy temple of American liberty over the tomb of departed tyranny. It is from those who have already passed the meridian of life, — it is from you, ye venerable assertors of the rights of mankind, — that we are to be informed what were the feelings which swayed within your breasts, and impelled you to action, when, like the stripling of Israel, with scarce a weapon to attack, and without a shield for your defence, you met, and, undismayed, engaged with the gigantic greatness of the British power. Untutored in the disgraceful science of human butchery, — destitute of the fatal materials which the ingenuity of man has combined to sharpen the scythe of death, — unsupported by the arm of any friendly alliance, and unfortified against the powerful assaults of an unrelenting enemy, — you did not hesitate at that moment, when your coasts were invaded by a numerous and veteran army, to pronounce the sentence of eternal separation from Britain, and to throw the gauntlet at a power the terror of whose recent triumphs was almost coëxtensive with the earth. The interested and selfish propensities, which in times of prosperous tranquillity have such powerful dominion over the heart, were all expelled; and, in their stead, the public virtues, the spirit of personal devotion to the common cause, a contempt of every danger in comparison with the subserviency of the country, had an unlimited control. The passion for the public had absorbed all the rest, as the glorious luminary of the heaven extinguishes, in a flood of refulgence, the twinkling splendor of every inferior planet. Those of you, my countrymen, who were actors in those interesting scenes, will best know how feeble and impotent is the language of this description to express the impassioned emotions of the soul with which you were then agitated; yet it were injustice to conclude from thence, or from the greater prevalence of private and personal motives in these days of calm serenity, that your sons have degenerated from the virtues of their fathers. Let it rather be a subject of pleasing reflection to you, that the generous and disinterested energies which you were summoned to display are permitted, by the bountiful indulgence of Heaven, to remain latent in the bosoms of your children. From the present prosperous appearance of our public affairs, we may admit a rational hope that our country will have no occasion to require of us those extraordinary and heroic exertions which it was your fortune to exhibit. But, from the common versatility of all human destiny, should the prospect hereafter darken, and the clouds of public misfortune thicken to a tempest, — should the voice of our country's calamity ever call us to her relief, — we swear, by the precious memory of the sages who toiled and of the heroes who bled in her defence, that we will prove ourselves not unworthy of the prize which they so dearly purchased, — that we will act as the faithful disciples of those who so magnanimously taught us the instructive lesson of republican virtue!

AMERICA. — *H. S. Legaré.*

What were the victories of Pompey to the united achievements of our Washingtons and Montgomerys and Greens, our Franklins and Jeffersons and Adams' and Laurens', — of the senate of sages whose wisdom conducted, of the band of warriors whose valor accomplished, of the "noble army of martyrs" whose blood sealed and consecrated, the Revolution of '76? What were the events of a few campaigns, however brilliant and successful, in the wars of Italy, or Spain, or Pontus, to by far the greatest era — excepting, perhaps, the Reformation — that has occurred in the political history of modern times, — to an era that has fixed forever the destinies of a whole quarter of the globe, with the numbers without number that are soon to inhabit it, and has already had, as it will probably continue to have, a visible influence upon the condition of society in all the rest? Nay, what is there, even in the most illustrious series of victories and conquests, that can justly be considered as affording, to a mind that dares to make a philosophic estimate of human affairs, a nobler and more interesting subject of contemplation and discoursé than the causes which led to the foundation of this mighty empire; than the wonderful and almost incredible history of what it has since done and is already grown to; than the scene of unmingled prosperity and happiness that is opening and spreading all around us; than the prospect, as dazzling as it is vast, that lies before us, the uncircumscribed career of aggrandizement and improvement which we are beginning to run under such happy auspices, and with the advantage of having *started* at a point where it were well for the species had it been the lot of many nations even to have *ended* theirs!

It is true, we shall not boast that the pomp of triumph has three hundred times ascended the steps of our capitol, or that the national temple upon its brow blazes in the spoils of a thousand cities. True, we do not send forth our prætors to plunder and devastate the most fertile and beautiful portions of the earth, in order that a haughty aristocracy may be enriched with booty, or a worthless populace be supplied with bread; nor, in every region under the sun, from the foot of the Grampian hills to the land of frankincense and myrrh, is the spirit of man broken and debased by us beneath the iron yoke of a military domination. No! *our* triumphs are the triumphs of *reason*, of happiness, of human nature. Our rejoicings are greeted with the most cordial sympathy of the cosmopolite and the philanthropist; and the good and the wise all round the globe give us back the echo of our acclamations. It is the singular fortune, or, I should rather say, it is the proud distinction of Americans, that, in the race of moral improvement which society has been everywhere running for some centuries past, we have outstripped every competitor, and have carried our institutions, in the sober certainty of waking bliss, to a higher pitch of perfection than ever warmed the dreams of enthusiasm or the speculations of the theorist. It is that a whole continent has been set apart, as if it were holy ground, for the cultivation of pure truth; for the pursuit of happiness upon rational principles, and in the way that is most agreeable to nature; for the development of all the sensibilities and capacities and powers of the human mind, without any artificial restraint or bias, in the broad daylight of modern science and political liberty. It is, that over the whole extent of this gigantic empire, — stretching, as it does, from the St. Croix to the Sabine, and from the waters of the Atlantic to those of the Pacific, — wherever man is found he is seen to walk abroad in all the dignity of his nature, with none to intimidate, or to insult, or to oppress him, with no superior upon this earth that does not deserve to be so, — and that, in the proud consciousness of his privileges, his soul is filled with the most noble apprehensions, and his aspirations lifted up to the most exalted objects, and his efforts animated and encouraged in the pursuit of whatever has a tendency to bless and adorn his existence!

EARLY ACHIEVEMENTS OF AMERICANS. — *J. L. Austin.*

What country, my friends, can produce so many events, in the course of a few years, as must ever distinguish the American page, — a young continent, contending with a nation whose establishment had been for ages, and whose armies had conquered the powers of the world? What spirit, short of a heavenly enthusiasm, could have animated these infant colonies, boldly to renounce the arbitrary mandates of a British parliament, and, instead of fawning like suppliants, to arm themselves for their common defence? You dared to appeal to that God who first planted the principles of natural freedom in the human breast, — principles repeatedly impressed on our infant minds by our great and glorious ancestors;

and may yonder sun be shorn of its beams, ere their descendants forget the heavenly admonitions!

When I behold so many worthy patriots, who, during the late glorious struggle, have shone conspicuous in the cabinet and in the field, — when I read in each smiling face and placid eye the happy occasion for joy and gratulation, — the transporting subject fires my bosom, and, with emotions of pleasure, I congratulate my country on the return of this anniversary. Hail, auspicious day! an era in the American annals to be ever remembered with joy, while, as a sovereign and independent nation, these United States can maintain with honor and applause the character they have so gloriously acquired! How shall we maintain, as a nation, our respectability, should be the grand subject of inquiry. This is the object to which we must attend; for the moment America sullies her name, by forfeiting her honor, the fame she has acquired from the heroism of her sons, and the virtues she has displayed in the midst of her distress, will only serve, like a train of mourners, to attend the funeral of her glory. But, by a due cultivation of manners, a firm adherence to the faith we have pledged, an union in council, a refinement in sentiment, a liberality and benevolence of conduct, we shall render ourselves happy at home and respectable abroad; our constellation will brighten in the political hemisphere, and the radiance of our stars sparkle with increasing lustre!

MASSACHUSETTS MEN IN THE REVOLUTION. — *R. C. Winthrop.*

Where should an American desire to be, on a Fourth of July, but in Faneuil Hall? Where else can he breathe the very natal air of independence? Where else can he quench his thirst at the very fountain-head of American liberty? Whatever part Massachusetts may have sustained in the great controversies which have agitated the country in later years, — and I am not ready to admit that it has been an unworthy or an inferior one, — no one will venture to suggest that she played anything less than the first part in that great drama whose opening scenes we are assembled to commemorate. Of how many of the great events of the Revolution was not Massachusetts the stage! How many of them were enacted almost within eye-shot and ear-shot of the spot on which we stand! The heights which overhang us on the right hand and on the left, the plains which lie behind them, the harbor at our feet, the hall in which we are assembled, State-street, the Old State-house, the Old South, — where else was engendered that noble spirit, that fearless purpose, that unconquerable resolve, of which the Declaration of Independence was, after all, only the mere formal and ceremonious proclamation? We sometimes talk playfully about the walls having ears. O, sir, if these walls could have had ears three-quarters of a century ago, and if they could find a tongue now, what a tale would they not unfold of the true rise and progress of American liberty!

Let me not seem to disparage the particular act which we meet to celebrate, or to be disposed to deck these hallowed columns with laurels stripped from other theatres. There are enough for all. The declaration itself was a bold and noble act. Honor to the pen which drafted it! Honor to the tongue which advocated it! Honor to the hands which signed it! Honor to the brave hearts and gallant arms which maintained and vindicated it! Honor to the five Massachusetts delegates in the Congress of that day, who were second to none in that illustrious body for ability, eloquence and patriotism, — Hancock, under whose sole signature it was originally published, the two Adamses, Elbridge Gerry, and Robert Treat Paine! Honor to them all!

Indeed, the more one reflects on the real character of that act, the more full of noble courage it appears. Remember, sir, that there was no divided responsibility in that Congress. There were no checks and balances in our confederated system. There was no concurrent vote of a second branch, there was no executive signature, or executive veto, to fall back upon. Fifty-six delegates, chosen long before there was any distinct contemplation of such a course, sitting in a single chamber, with closed doors, in the capital of a colony by no means the most ripe for such a movement, are found — doing what? Taking the tremendous responsibility of adopting a resolution, and promulgating an instrument, which may not only subject their own property to confiscation, and their own necks to the halter, but which must involve their constituents and their country in a war for existence, and of incalculable duration, with the most powerful nation on the face of the earth. There was no example for such a deed. There was no precedent on file for such a declaration. And who will say that, to put one's name to such an instrument, under such circumstances, in the clear, bold, unmistakable characters of John Hancock, was an exhibition of a courage less heroic than that which has rendered many a name immortal on the field of battle?

Still, sir, the way had been opened for such a proceeding; the popular heart had been prepared for it. As was well said by John Adams at the time, "the question was not whether by a declaration of independence we should make ourselves what we are not, but whether we should declare a fact which already exists." And how did that fact exist? How had it been brought about? By what events, but those which had occurred at Concord and Lexington, at Bunker Hill, and in Faneuil Hall? By what men, but by our own Otis, and Quincy, and Hancock, and Hawley, and Bowdoin, and Samuel Adams, and John Adams, and Paul Revere, and Prescott, and Warren, and all that glorious company of Massachusetts patriots, whose names will live forever?

I would associate with all the homage which we render to the memory of the Revolutionary patriots and heroes of our own state the Hamiltons and Jays, the Morrises and Franklins, the Laurenses and Marions, the Henrys and Jeffersons, and, above all, the unapproached and unapproachable WASHINGTON, of other states. I would think of our country, to-day and always, as one in the glories of the past, one in the grandeur of the present, and one, undivided and indivisible, in the destinies of the future. But, at a moment when there seems to be a willingness in some quarters to disparage our ancient commonwealth, and almost to rule her out from the catalogue of patriot states, I have not been unwilling to revive some recollections of our local history, and of the part which she has played in other days. I could hardly help feeling that, if we were to hold our peace, the very stones would cry out. In all that relates to liberty and union, Massachusetts, I am persuaded, is to-day just what she was seventy-five years ago. There is no variableness or shadow of turning in her devotion to the great principles of her Revolutionary fathers, nor will she ever, as I believe, be found wanting to any just obligation to her sister states.

It is for us to say whether we will be true to those great elements of free government, to those noble principles of liberty and law, and to that blessed compact of union, which our fathers have enshrined in the constitution of the United States. If we are but faithful to that great bond and bulwark of our Union, the constitution, critical periods may come and go, there may be grand climacterics and petty crises, stars may rise and set, the great and the good may fall on our right hand and our left, — but the country, the country, will survive them all, will survive us all, and will stand before the world as an imperishable monument of the patriotism of the sons, as well as of the wisdom and virtue of their sires!

PATRIOTISM. — *H. Giles.*

The patriotism which is worthy of this country, worthy of its advantages, worthy of its duties to the world, is a high and enlightened patriotism, — a patriotism of loyal devotion, but also of enlarged philanthropy. If man be only true, all here beside is full of inspiration and full of promise; if man will be but faithful to his opportunities, all around him here is strong in noble energies. Everything here tends to dilate the heart, — to send it upward in gratitude to a fatherly God, to send it outward in kindness to the brotherhood of man. The sky itself takes dimensions of grandeur fitted to the glorious scope of empire which it overhangs. It is high, deep, broad, lofty, and should upraise the freeman's soul whose step is on the freeman's earth. Nowhere is the calm more divinely fair; nowhere is the storm more awfully sublime; nowhere does the sun shine forth with a more peerless majesty; nowhere do the stars beam down with a more holy lustre. The atmosphere engenders no deadly plagues; health lives in the breeze, and plenty comes teeming from the soil. Broad dominions, to be measured in leagues only by a scale of hundreds, snatch imagination from every belittling influence, and carry it out from narrow thoughts to an ennobling excursiveness. Then there are ocean lakes, in which kingdoms might be buried, and leave on the surface no ripple of their grave; rivers, that sweep over half a world; cataracts, eternal and resistless, that hymn forever the omnipotence which they resemble; mountains, that stretch into the upper light, and mock, from their snow-crowned pinnacles, the clouds and the thunders that crash below them.

All these are your country's, — but your country is God's. It is God who has given you this country; it is God who has enriched it with these grand objects, and through these grand objects it is God who speaks. He speaks in the chorus of your woods; in the tempests of your valleys; in the ceaseless sobbings of your lakes and oceans; in the vague, low murmurs of forest and of prairie; in the mighty bass of waterfalls, in the silver melody of streams; — and the voice that he sends out from them is a voice for patriotism, but it is also a voice for equity and a voice for goodness. Who can look through the huge firmament; who can gaze upon the golden fires with which it is studded; who can float away on the wings of the spirit through the infinity of stars; who can watch the roll of the torrent, pouring out a sea in every gush — a sea of awful beauty; who can thus put his soul into communion with the universe, and not be enlarged by the communion? who can really put his soul into communion with the universe, and not be delivered from the slavery of prejudice into the glorious liberty of humanity and of God?

The measure of your duty is the greatness of your advantages, and the greatness of your advantages is the standard to which you will be subjected in the judgment of Heaven and the judgment of history. You are set for the hope or for the disappointment of the world. With such a mighty country, with such inestimable privileges, with such means of intelligence, virtue and happiness, with such means of increasing and dispensing them, so young and yet so strong, so late and yet so rich among the nations, there is room to look for good interminably to future generations, which the one departing shall leave more abundant for the one that comes. In order that such anticipations be not empty dreams, in order that they be not promises to change into mockery, vanity and grief, it should be the labor of a genuine and noble patriotism to raise the life of the nation to the level of its privileges, to harmonize its general practice with its abstract principles, to reduce to actual facts the ideals of its institutions, to elevate instruction into knowledge, to deepen knowledge into wisdom, to render knowledge and wisdom complete in righteousness, and to make the love of country perfect in the love of man.

GROWTH OF AMERICA.—*H. S. Legaré.*

ONE of the most fortunate and striking peculiarities of the Revolution is that it occurred in a New World. The importance that ought to be attached to this circumstance will be obvious to every one who will reflect for a moment upon the miracles which are exhibiting in the settlement of this country and the increase of its population. Behold how the pomœrium of the republic advances in the wilderness of the West! See how empires are starting up into being, in periods of time shorter even than the interval between infancy and manhood in the span allotted to the individuals that compose them! Contemplate the peaceful triumphs of industry, the rapid progress of cultivation, the diffusion of knowledge, the growth of populous cities, with all the arts that embellish life and soften while they exalt the character of man, and think of the countless multitudes that are springing up to inherit these blessings! The three millions by whom our independence was achieved, less than half a century ago, are already grown to *ten*, which, in the course of another half-century, will have swelled up to *fifty*, and so on, with a continually accelerated progress, until, at no distant day, the language of Milton shall be spoken from shore to shore, over the vastest portion of the earth's surface that was ever inhabited by a race worthy of speaking a language consecrated to liberty.

Now, to feel how deep an interest this circumstance is fitted to throw into the story of the Revolution, let us imagine a spectator, or let us rather suppose an *actor,* in that greatest and proudest of days, to have turned his thoughts upon the future which we see present and realized. Would he not, think ye, have trembled at the awful responsibility of his situation? Would he not have been overwhelmed with the unbounded anticipation? It depends upon *his* courage and conduct, and upon the strength of *his* right arm, whether, not his descendants only, not some small tract of country about his fireside, not Massachusetts alone, — no, nor all that shall inherit it in the ages that are to come, — shall be governed by satraps and viceroys, or as reason and nature dictate that they should be; but whether a republic, embracing upwards of twenty distinct and great empires, shall exist or not, — whether a host, worthy to combat and to conquer with Jackson, shall issue from the yet unviolated forests of Kentucky and Tennessee, to spurn from New Orleans the very foe whose vengeance he now dares, for the first time, to encounter in the field, when that foe shall be crowned with yet prouder laurels, and shall come in more terrible might, — whether the banks of the great lakes shall echo to the accents of liberty, and the Missouri and the Mississippi roll through the inheritance of freemen!

IMPORTANCE OF EDUCATION. — *R. C. Winthrop.*

We have been accustomed to regard a free-school system as the chief corner-stone of our republic, and popular education as the only safe and stable basis for popular liberty. So thought our fathers before us; and the principle may be found interwoven in a thousand forms into the very thread and texture of our political institutions. Education — religious and civil, the education of the sanctuary and the school-house — was, we all know, from the first establishment of these colonies, a matter in regard to which all property was held in common, and every man bound to contribute to the necessities of every other man; as much so as personal protection, public justice, or any other of the more obvious duties of government, or rights of the governed.

Children should be educated as those by whom the destinies of the nation are one day to be wielded, and free schools cherished as places in which those destinies are even now to be woven. It has been recorded as a saying of Mahomet that "the ink of the scholar and the blood of the martyr are equal." It would be difficult to bring an American of this generation, especially if he happened to be standing, as we now are, at the foot of Bunker Hill, to acknowledge that there could be anything equal — equal in its claim upon his regard and reverence, or equal in its influence upon our national welfare and freedom — to the blood of our Revolutionary martyrs. But in this we must all agree, that nothing but the ink of the scholar can preserve what the blood of the martyr has purchased. The experiment of free government is not one which can be tried once for all. Every generation must try it for itself. Our fathers tried it, and were gloriously successful. We are now engaged in the trial; and, thank God, we have not yet failed. But neither our success, nor that of our fathers, can afford anything but example and encouragement to those who are to try it next. As each new generation starts up to the reponsibilities of manhood, there is, as it were, a new launch of Liberty, and its voyage of experiment begins afresh. But the oracles have declared that its safety and success depend not so much upon the conduct of those engaged in it during the voyage, as upon their preparations before they embark. The winds and waves must be propitiated before the shore is left, or wreck and ruin will await them. But this propitiation consists, not in some cruel proceeding, like that prescribed by the heathen oracle to the Grecian fleet, in binding son or daughter upon the pile of sacrifice, and offering up their tortured bodies and agonized souls to appease an angry deity, but in a process which is not more certain to call down the best blessing of Heaven upon the enterprise, and to secure a peaceful and prosperous voyage, than it is to promote the truest happiness and welfare of those upon whom it is performed. Sons and daughters devoted to education are the only sacrifice which God has prescribed to render the progress of free government safe and certain.

SUCCESS OF AMERICAN INSTITUTIONS.—*M. Van Buren.*

The capacity of the people for self-government, and their willingness, from a high sense of duty, and without those exhibitions of coërcive power so generally employed in other countries, to submit to all needful restraints and exactions of the municipal law, have also been favorably exemplified in the history of the American states. Occasionally, it is true, the ardor of public sentiment, outrunning the regular process of the judicial tribunals, or seeking to reach cases not denounced as criminal by the existing law, has displayed itself in a manner calculated to give pain to the friends of free government, and to encourage the hopes of those who wish for its overthrow. These occurrences, however, have been far less frequent in our country than in any other of equal population on the globe; and, with the diffusion of intelligence, it may be hoped that they will constantly diminish in frequency and violence. The generous patriotism and sound common sense of the great mass of our fellow-citizens will assuredly, in time, produce this result; for, as every assumption of illegal power not only wounds the majesty of the law, but furnishes a pretext for abridging the liberties of the people, the latter has the most direct and permanent interest in preserving the great landmarks of social order, and maintaining on all occasions the inviolability of those constitutional and legal provisions which they themselves have made.

In a supposed unfitness of our institutions for those hostile emergencies which no country can always avoid, their friends found a fruitful source of apprehension, their enemies of hope. While they foresaw less promptness of action than in governments differently formed, they overlooked the far more important consideration, that with us war could never be the result of individual or irresponsible will, but must be a measure of redress for injuries sustained, voluntarily resorted to by those who were to bear the necessary sacrifice, and who would consequently feel an individual interest in the contest, and whose energy would be commensurate with the difficulties to be encountered. Actual events have proved their error; the last war, far from impairing, gave new confidence to our government; and, amid recent apprehensions of a similar conflict, we saw that the energies of our country would not be wanting in ample season to vindicate its rights. We may not possess, as we should not desire to possess, the extended and ever-ready military organization of other nations; we may occasionally suffer in the outset for the want of it; but among ourselves all doubt upon this great point has ceased, while a salutary experience will prevent a contrary opinion from inviting aggression from abroad.

Certain danger was foretold from the extension of our territory, the multiplication of states, and the increase of population. Our system was supposed to be adapted only to boundaries comparatively narrow. These have been widened beyond conjecture; the members of our confederacy are already doubled, and the numbers of our people are incredibly augmented. The alleged causes of danger have long surpassed anticipation, but none of the consequences have been followed. The power and influence of the republic have risen to a height obvious to all mankind; respect for its authority was not more apparent at its ancient than it is at its present limits; new and inexhaustible sources of general prosperity have been opened; the effects of distance have been averted by the inventive genius of our people, developed and fostered by the spirit of our institutions; and the enlarged variety and amount of interests, productions and pursuits, have strengthened the chain of mutual dependence, and formed a circle of mutual benefits too apparent ever to be overlooked.

In justly balancing the powers of the federal and state authorities, difficulties nearly insurmountable arose at the outset, and subsequent collisions were deemed inevitable. Amid these, it was scarcely believed possible that a scheme of government so complex in construction could remain uninjured. From time to time embarrassments have certainly occurred; but how just is the confidence of future safety imparted by the knowledge that each in succession has been happily removed! Overlooking partial and temporary evils as inseparable from the practical operations of all human institutions, and looking only to the general result, every patriot has reason to be satisfied. While the federal government has successfully performed its appropriate functions in relation to foreign affairs and concerns evidently national, that of every state has remarkably improved in protecting and developing local interests and individual welfare; and if the vibrations of authority have occasionally tended too much towards one or the other, it is unquestionably certain that the ultimate operation of the entire system has been to strengthen all the existing institutions, and to elevate our whole country in prosperity and renown!

ADAMS AND JEFFERSON. — *D. Webster.*

Adams and Jefferson are no more. On our fiftieth anniversary, the great day of national jubilee, in the very hour of public rejoicing, in the midst of echoing and reëchoing voices of thanksgiving, while their own names were on all tongues, they took their flight, together, to the world of spirits. Neither of these great men could have died at any time without leaving an immense void in our American society. They have been so intimately, and for so long a time, blended with the history of the country, and especially so united, in our thoughts and recollections, with the events of the Revolution, that the death of either would have touched the strings of public sympathy. We should have felt that one great link, connecting us with former times, was broken; that we had lost something more, as it were, of the presence of the Revolution itself, and of the act of independence; and were driven on, by another great remove, from the days of our country's early distinction, to meet posterity, and to mix with the future. Like the mariner, whom the ocean and the winds carry along, till he sees the stars which have directed his course and lighted his pathless way descend, one by one, beneath the rising horizon, we should have felt that the stream of time had borne us onward, till another great luminary, whose light had cheered us, and whose guidance we had followed, had sunk away from our sight.

Adams and Jefferson, I have said, are no more. As human beings, indeed, they are no more. They are no more, as in 1776, bold and fearless advocates of independence; no more, as on subsequent periods, the head of the government; no more, as we have recently seen them, aged and venerable objects of admiration and regard. They are no more. They are dead. But how little is there, of the great and good, which can die! To their country they yet live, and live forever. They live in all that perpetuates the remembrance of men on earth, — in the recorded proofs of their own great actions, in the offspring of their intellect, in the deep-engraved lines of public gratitude, and in the respect and homage of mankind. They live in their example, and they live emphatically, and will live, in the influence which their lives and efforts, their principles and opinions, now exercise, and will continue to exercise, on the affairs of men, not only in their own country, but throughout the civilized word. A superior and commanding human intellect, a truly great man, when Heaven vouchsafes so rare a gift, is not a temporary flame, burning bright for a while, and then expiring, giving place to returning darkness. It is rather a spark of fervent heat, as well as radiant light, with power to enkindle the common mass of human mind, so that when it glimmers in its own decay, and finally goes out in death, no night follows, but it leaves the world all light, all on fire, from the potent contact of its own spirit. Bacon died; but the human understanding, roused, by the touch of his miraculous wand, to a perception of the true philosophy, and the just mode of inquiring after truth, has kept on its course successfully and gloriously. Newton died; yet the courses of the spheres are still known, and they yet move on in the orbits which he saw and described for them, in the infinity of space.

We are not assembled, fellow-citizens, as men overwhelmed with calamity by the sudden disruption of the ties of friendship or affection, or as in despair for the republic, by the untimely blighting of its hopes. Death has not surprised us by an unseasonable blow. We have, indeed, seen the tomb close; but it has closed only over mature years, over long-protracted public service, over the weakness of age, and over life itself only when the ends of living had been fulfilled. These suns, as they rose slowly and steadily amidst clouds and storms in their ascendant, so they have not rushed from their meridian to sink suddenly in the west. Like the mildness, the serenity, the continuing benignity, of a summer's day, they have gone down with slow-descending, grateful, long-lingering light; and now that they are beyond the visible margin of the world, good omens cheer us from "the bright track of their fiery car."

No men ever served their country with more entire exemption from every imputation of selfish and mercenary motives than those to whose memory we are paying these proofs of respect. A suspicion of any disposition to enrich themselves, or to profit by their public employments, never rested on either. No sordid motive approached them. The inheritance which they have left to their children is of their character and their fame.

I will detain you no longer by this faint and feeble tribute to the memory of the illustrious dead. Even in other hands, adequate justice could not be performed within the limits of this occasion. Their highest, their best praise, is your deep conviction of their merits, your affectionate gratitude for their labors and services. It is not my voice, it is this cessation of ordinary pursuits, this arresting of all attention, these solemn ceremonies, and this crowded house, which speak their eulogy. Their fame, indeed, is safe. That is now treasured up, beyond the reach of accident. Although no sculptured marble should rise to their memory, nor engraved stone bear record of their deeds, yet will their remembrance be as lasting as the land they honored. Marble columns may, indeed, moulder into dust, time may erase all impress from the crumbling stone, but their fame remains; for with AMERICAN LIBERTY it rose, and with AMERICAN LIBERTY ONLY can it perish. It was the last swelling peal of yonder choir, "THEIR BODIES ARE BURIED IN PEACE, BUT THEIR NAME LIVETH EVERMORE." I catch that solemn song, I echo that lofty strain of funeral triumph, "THEIR NAME LIVETH EVERMORE."

Of the illustrious signers of the Declaration of Independence there now remains only CHARLES CARROLL. He seems an aged oak, standing alone on the plain, which time has spared a little longer, after all his contemporaries have been levelled with the dust. Venerable object! we delight to gather round its trunk, while yet it stands, and to dwell beneath its shadow. Sole survivor of an assembly of as great men as the world has witnessed, in a transaction one of the most important that history records, what thoughts, what interesting reflections, must fill his elevated and devout soul! If he dwell on the past, how touching its recollections; if he survey the present, how happy, how joyous, how full of the fruition of that hope which his ardent patriotism indulged; if he glance at the future, how does the prospect of his country's advancement almost bewilder his weakened conception! Fortunate, distinguished patriot! Interesting relic of the past! Let him know that, while we honor the dead, we do not forget the living, and that there is not a heart here which does not fervently pray that Heaven may keep him yet back from the society of his companions.

Let us not retire from this occasion without a deep and solemn conviction of the duties which have devolved upon us. This lovely land, this glorious liberty, these benign institutions, the dear purchase of our fathers, are ours; ours to enjoy, ours to preserve, ours to transmit. Generations past, and generations to come, hold us responsible for this sacred trust. Our fathers, from behind, admonish us, with their anxious paternal voices; posterity calls out to us from the bosom of the future; the world turns hither its solicitous eyes; — all, all conjure us to act wisely and faithfully in the relation which we sustain. We can never, indeed, pay the debt which is upon us; but by virtue, by morality, by religion, by the cultivation of every good principle and every good habit, we may hope to enjoy the blessing through our day, and to leave it unimpaired to our children. Let us feel deeply how much of what we are and of what we possess we owe to this liberty, and these institutions of government. Nature has, indeed, given us a soil which yields bounteously to the hands of industry; the mighty and fruitful ocean is before us, and the skies over our heads shed health and vigor. But what are lands, and seas, and skies, to civilized man, without society, without knowledge, without morals, without religious culture? and how can these be enjoyed, in all their extent and all their excellence, but under the protection of wise institutions and a free government? There is not one of us, there is not one of us here present, who does not, at this moment, and at every moment, experience, in his own condition, and in the condition of those most near and dear to him, the influence and the benefits of this liberty and these institutions. Let us, then, acknowledge the blessing; let us feel it deeply and powerfully, let us cherish a strong affection for it, and resolve to maintain and perpetuate it. The blood of our fathers, let it not have been shed in vain! the great hope of posterity, let it not be blasted!

It cannot be denied, but by those who would dispute against the sun, that with America and in America a new era commences in human affairs. This era is distinguished by free representative governments, by entire religious liberty, by improved systems of national intercourse, by a newly-awakened and an unconquerable spirit of free inquiry, and by a diffusion of knowledge through the community such as has been before altogether unknown and unheard of. America, America, our country, our own dear and native land, is inseparably connected, fast bound up, in fortune and by fate, with these great interests. If they fall, we fall with them; if they stand, it will be because we have upholden them. Let us contemplate, then, this connection, which binds the prosperity of others to our own, and let us manfully discharge all the duties which it imposes. If we cherish the virtues and the principles of our fathers, Heaven will assist us to carry on the work of human liberty and human happiness. Auspicious omens cheer us. Great examples are before us. Our own firmament now shines brightly upon our path. WASHINGTON is in the clear upper sky. These other stars have now joined the American constellation; they circle round their centre, and the heavens beam with new light.

Beneath this illumination let us walk the course of life, and at its close devoutly commend our beloved country, the common parent of us all, to the Divine Benignity.

BIRTH OF NATIONS.—*H. Bushnell.*

THE true increase of a nation is not that which is made by conquest and plunder, but that which is the simple development of its vital and prolific resources. Two centuries ago there came over to these western shores a few thousand men. These were the germ of a great nation, here to arise and come into the public history of the world, possibly as a leading member. Potentially speaking, these men had in themselves — that is, in their persons, their principles, their habits and other resources — all that now is, or is yet to be, of power and greatness in our republic. They went to work with a degree of spirit and energy never before exhibited. Habits of virtuous and frugal industry were unfolded by a wise and careful training. Simplicity of manners for the first time appeared, not as a barbaric virtue, but as the proper fruit of simplicity in religion. The mental vigor produced by the same causes was yet further sharpened by the necessities of a new state of existence. Population multiplied, wealth increased, the forest fell away at the sound of their axes, the natives retired before the potent and prolific energy of Saxon life, as before the Great Spirit himself. Cities rose upon the shores, the waters whitened to the sun under the sails of commerce, the civil order unfolded itself, as it were naturally, from the germ that blossomed in the Mayflower, — and, behold, a great, wealthy, powerful and free nation stalks into history with the tread of a giant, fastening the astonished gaze of the world, — all in the way of simple growth. We have made no conquests. We have only unfolded our original germ, the mustard-seed of our first colonization. There is no other kind of national advancement which is legitimate or safe. The civil order must grow as a creature of life, and unfold itself from within. If a nation will suddenly extend its boundaries and build up its splendor by conquest, as in the case of the Roman empire, or in the subjugation of Mexico by Spain, how different is the spectacle! The elements of the civil order, being piled together by mere accretion, are without coherency or unity. The public life does not fill the public mass; and, without the organic power of life, it is ready to fall to pieces at the earliest moment. Wealth itself is poverty; power is weakness; breadth is dissipation; numbers, discontent and anarchy. A nation built by growth is as different from a nation built by conquest, as the tree that stands erect, filled with vital sap, covered with joyful verdure, and, when the winter comes, tossing its bare arms victoriously to the storm, from a pile of driftwood which the floods have heaped upon the shore to rot and perish. Accordingly, the very word *nation* implies a nascent order and growth. It is no such pile of ruins as the external accidents of force and conquest may construct; but it is a birth, the unfolding of a vital germ through population, industry, art, literature, law, and religion.

SLOW GROWTH OF FREEDOM. — *R. C. Winthrop.*

The whole civilized world resounds with American opinions and American principles. Every vale is vocal with them. Every mountain has found a tongue for them. Everywhere the people are heard calling their rulers to account, and holding them to a just responsibility. Everywhere the cry is raised for the elective franchise, the trial by jury, the freedom of the press, written constitutions, representative systems, republican forms. In some cases, most fortunately, the rulers themselves have not escaped some seasonable symptoms of the pervading fervor for freedom, and have nobly anticipated the demands of their subjects. To the sovereign pontiff of the Roman states, in particular, belongs the honor of having led the way in the great movement of the day; and no American will withhold from him a cordial tribute of respect and admiration for whatever he has done or designed for the regeneration of Italy. Glorious, indeed, on the page of history, will be the name of Pius IX., if the rise of another Rome shall be traced to his wise and liberal policy. Yet not less truly glorious, if his own authority should date its decline to his noble refusal to lend his apostolical sanction to a war of conquest.

For Italy, however, and for France, and for the whole European world alike, a great work still remains. A rational, practical, enduring liberty cannot be acquired in a paroxysm, cannot be established by a proclamation. It is not, our own history proves that it is not,

"The hasty product of a day,
But the well-ripened fruit of wise delay."

The redress of a few crying grievances, the reform of a few glaring abuses, the banishment of a minister, the burning of a throne, the overthrow of a dynasty, — these are but scanty preparations for the mighty undertaking upon which they have entered. New systems are to be constructed; new forms to be established; new governments to be instituted, organized and administered, upon principles which shall reconcile the seeming conflict between liberty and law, and secure to every one the enjoyment of regulated constitutional freedom.

FOR THE IRISH PATRIOTS. — *J. Shields.*

The most friendly relations exist at this time between this country and Great Britain. There is a strong feeling of mutual regard and common interest, and, perhaps I may add, a sense of common danger, uniting the people of both countries at this moment in close and intimate connection. The English people, so far as I can observe, are beginning to appreciate the character, resources and institutions, of this country, and to look with something like admiration upon the growth of this continental republic. Not only England, but the world, begins to see and acknowledge that this nation is destined to future supremacy. America is the predestined mistress of the future. Such is not the condition of England herself. Great and powerful as England is at this day, — and the world admits that she is great and powerful, — her circumstances are such that she will be forced to compromise with the future. She has power, strength and energy; but her energies may be said to be fettered. She is like a giantess in chains. Her immense debt constitutes her chains and her fetters. The English people are strong and patient. They possess a great many sterling qualities, — industry, perseverance and fortitude; but, with all these qualities, such is the vast load which is now pressing upon them, they will be compelled, in my opinion, in the first general convulsion, the first political tempest, that shakes the continent of Europe, to fling off the load, or perish under its weight.

There is a volume of instruction in the present condition of England. Every American statesman should study it with attention. The debt which now weighs upon the heart of England — and which no other nation on this earth could support for a single day — was not contracted for any great English object or interest, but for what was plainly and emphatically a continental interest, — to crush Napoleon, to defend Austria, Russia and Prussia, to maintain the old royalties and aristocracies of Europe. Well; the object was accomplished, the old despotisms were sustained, England and Englishmen were mortgaged "to the last syllable of recorded time" to accomplish this desirable object. And what is the result? What is the state of the continent at this moment? Why, from the Frozen Ocean to the Mediterranean Sea the despotisms of Europe were never before as closely bound together in deep hostility to England as they are in 1852. This, too, after all her sacrifices in behalf of venerable despotism. This is her present position, and this is the present condition of Europe. At such a time, and after such experience, it is perfectly natural that the people of England should turn their hearts and thoughts to America. It is not only natural, but politic, that they should begin to cultivate the friendship of a great kindred people, who, from the rapid growth of their population and power, and the extraordinary advantages of their geographical position, will soon be able to influence the destinies of nations, by throwing their whole weight into the scale of liberty, justice and humanity. And permit me to say that, so far as I know the American heart, I feel to declare, that if the English people prove true to themselves and just to their fellow-subjects, if they assert and maintain the great principles of religious and political liberty, they will find a more generous sympathy, and a more effective, unbought and unpurchasable support, on this continent, in the hour of need, than they can ever hope to purchase or subsidize, with the duplicate of their national debt, upon the continent of Europe.

But I will confine myself on this occasion to a recent familiar instance, in relation to the Hungarians. England interfered directly in behalf of Kossuth and his companions, while we merely intercede for Smith O'Brien and his associates. She defended these Hungarians against Austria and Russia; we only appeal to her own clemency for the liberation of Irish patriots. She contributed to the liberation of Austrian subjects, although they are, in a certain sense, still dangerous to the Austrian government. We simply request the liberation of British subjects, whose freedom, in my opinion, at this time, will serve to strengthen the English government. We all recollect the universal delight with which the American people witnessed the first interference of England in behalf of the Hungarian exiles. When the British fleet appeared at the mouth of the Dardanelles, — when the red cross of England joined the crescent of Mahomet, and blazed in defence of the exile and the unfortunate, — all America, with one voice, shouted glory and honor to the flag of Old England. She acted gloriously on that occasion. Her conduct called forth the applause of the liberal world. But now we have to moderate this applause, when we think of Van Diemen's Land. We give her credit for her generosity abroad, but we are sorry to be compelled to refuse her equal credit for her clemency at home. Patriotism cannot be a virtue in Hungary and a crime in Ireland. England may be able to make some distinction between the two cases, but the world will refuse to recognize it. She will raise her national character in the estimation of the world, she will establish her disinterestedness before the tribunal of history and posterity, if she follow up her conduct towards the Hungarians with the liberation of the Irish exiles. As it is, her conduct is severely criticized on the continent of Europe. The Austrians and Russians, especially, accuse her of hypocrisy, of violating the great law of moral and political consistency, of traversing half the globe in defence and support of Hungarian patriots, while at the same time she proscribes, banishes and imprisons, Irish patriots. They say English philanthropy is like the philanthropy of the elder Mirabeau, who was styled "The Friend of Man" for his universal benevolence, while he practised, at the same time, within the bosom of his own family, the most cruel, heartless and unrelenting tyranny. This is the kind of indictment the continent prefers against England at this time. I am not prepared to endorse it. On the contrary, I am thoroughly convinced she will avail herself of the first favorable opportunity to clear her reputation from any such reproach. I am inclined to think she will feel thankful to this government for supplying her with a fair occasion, a graceful pretext, to perform a humane and politic act. The world will then see that she is not governed, either in her foreign or domestic policy, by jealousy of Russia or hatred of Austria, but by a great principle of philanthropy and humanity.

If we weigh the conduct of these Irish patriots, not in legal but in moral scales, we will find much to justify their attempt. They loved their native country. There is no moral guilt in this. On the contrary, the love of country is one of the noblest sentiments of our nature. When this sentiment fades from the soul, the soul has lost its original brightness. In Ireland, however, this sentiment is almost considered a political offence. There is something so unnatural in this state of things, that what the English law denounces as treason the Irish heart recognizes as patriotism. An Irish patriot hears himself pronounced guilty in what is called the sanctuary of justice, while he feels in the sanctuary of his heart that he stands guiltless before God and his country. This must be all perfectly understood, to appreciate the conduct of these men. In the eye of the law, they are convicted felons; but in every honest, manly Irish heart, they are received and recognized as Irish patriots. And why should it be otherwise? You must destroy the heart before you can destroy this sentiment. Ireland is their native country; they saw her lying around them in ruins. They made a desperate effort to collect the broken fragments, and bind them together into something like nationality. The effort failed; it was bound to fail. The spirit of Irish nationality is dead. But I will ask any generous American heart, I will put it even to any generous English heart, whether these men are to be blamed, in the present wretched condition of Ireland, for making the attempt. Who can blame Smith O'Brien, whose ancestors were kings in Ireland before Saxon, Dane or Norman, ever planted a foot on Irish soil, for making an attempt, however hopeless, to raise and resuscitate his fallen country? In fact, who can blame any Irishman for seeking to effect a radical change in the condition of his country, since no change consistent with social existence can make her condition worse than it is at this time? Poor Ireland! her history is a sad one. It is written in the tears and blood of her children. Her sons have been so long accustomed to injustice, that they regard themselves as aliens and outcasts in the very land that God gave them as a heritage. Yet they love their country with all the fervor of the Irish heart. The more she suffers, the more they love her. This love has become almost a part of their religion, and of their fervent devotion to their God. As her own sweet poet has so truly and beautifully said:

"Her chains as they rankle her blood as it runs,
But make her more painfully dear to her sons."

This is true; and in the midst of poverty and contempt her sons weep over her desolation, and pray for the hour of her deliverance. There is something incomprehensible to the human mind in the mysterious Providence that rules the destiny of nations. Israel gave a Saviour to the world; and the world, in return, has persecuted and denaturalized the children of Abraham. Greece instructed the world, taught it arts and sciences, lifted it out of a state of barbarism into a high state of civilization, — and look at the world's recompense! The Roman and Ottoman, in succession, trampled upon the susceptible heart and beautiful mind of Greece; and now that land of gods and godlike men is the footstool of the unsympathizing Goth. Poland and Hungary saved Christendom in the day of its weakness; they repulsed the crescent in the day of its power; and, in grateful return, three great Christian powers have dismembered Poland and distributed her bleeding members amongst them, and Christian Europe is now singing "Te Deums" and "Hosannas" over the prostrate and mangled body of Hungary!

ADDRESS TO THE SURVIVORS OF THE BATTLE OF LEXINGTON.

—*R. Rantoul, Jr.*

Living mementos of the glorious past! long may your valued presence remind us of our duty to the future, by showing what the past has done for us, by carrying back our thoughts to the times that tried men's souls. These are of the number that took their lives in their hand, and walked fearless among the death-shafts, counting all things earthly but as dross, that, surviving, they might point out to us, or, dying, might bequeath to us, a more excellent way, a career of pure, unshackled liberty.

Favorites of time, who has dealt so gently with you, what a contrast do your eyes behold when you compare the mighty empire which you helped to found with the feeble colony that gave you birth! The period of your life has been contemporaneous with the work of many ages: never before have a thousand years done for any nation under heaven what the last three-fourths of a century have done for us. A thousand years constructed and confirmed the majestic fabric of the Roman empire; sages and warriors, through a thousand years of fixed purpose, iron resolution and all-enduring fortitude, established the dominion of the eternal city, unshaken by the burthen of the world, and not to be destroyed, save in the wreck of the old heathen world passing away forever. But you, wonderful men, preceded by many years this empire; in the purple ripeness of maturely-developed youth, you stood by the cradle of this empire when the young Alcides strangled the monsters sent by his step-mother; when our home was a strip of land between the ocean and the Alleghanies, which scattered settlers, with no wealth but the labor of their hands, disputed with the savages. You have lived to be citizens of an empire broader than Rome, mightier than Rome, wealthier than Rome, wiser than Rome, holier than Rome. Machinery, the creation of the free mind, does more for us, ten-fold more, than all the arms of her many million subjects did for her. Look around you! all that you see, and all that your and our posterity shall see, is the fruit of liberty; and of that liberty it is for you to say truly, We and our comrades, on the nineteenth of April, planted the fructifying seed.

Look around you, and survey your work. It is not enough that we proclaim that a small one has become a great people; that day by day new nations rise up to call you blessed; that even now states, infant in years, but giants in vigor and proportions, press at your portals, asking admission as coördinate sovereignties, "demanding life, impatient for the skies." Look around you! measure the improvement of the condition of the individual denizens of all our towns and villages, and see if it tend not onward and upward in an accelerated ratio, equal, at least, to that of our political greatness. The hardy colonist extracted from the soil, with infinite labor, a frugal subsistence, uncertain how long he should hold even his earnings, — for the mother country claimed the right to bind the colonies in all cases whatsoever, — collecting few comforts, desiring no luxuries; without machinery, without capital, almost without intercourse, scarcely recovered from the exhaustion of ruinous French and Indian wars. The fair enchantress, Liberty, has waved her potent wand: prosperity and happiness crown all the hills and cover the plains; on every waterfall a city rises like an exhalation; the iron horse — the missionary which science despatches to lead the van of advancing refinement — snorts over the prairies scarcely abandoned by the disappearing buffalo; the electric nerve throbs with the impulse of intelligence from Halifax to New Orleans; internal commerce dips her silver oar in every lake; the birchen canoe of the native hunter is transformed to a water-borne palace, gorgeous with the adornments of high art, and steadying her upright keel against the wind with the miraculous energy of imprisoned fire. Of the rich exuberance of our plenty we may impart with a world-wide charity; and ocean smiles to transport upon her bosom the messengers freighted with salvation to the famine-stricken millions of slavery-blasted Ireland!

KOSSUTH IN MASSACHUSETTS. — *A. Burlingame.*

Our first invitation found him beyond the Alleghanies with the free sons of the West, — he had then visited the chief cities along the Atlantic slope. Since then, he has made the wide circuit of the republic, everywhere pouring out his life into the great bosom of the people, filling it with the loftiest sentiments. He kindled the bold spirit of our western land into a flame of enthusiasm. He laid his hand tenderly upon the fiery heart of the South, and soothed it into sympathy. This he did before he turned his feet toward New England; and many of his friends, in this home of his friends, feared — because of the long interval between his arrival in the country and his visit here — that the original interest awakened by the story of his heroic life might have somewhat declined; but the shouts of the people with which he is greeted — rising, as they do here to-night, like the voice of many waters — tell us that the interest in himself and country has rather deepened than diminished.

He does not feel the breeze from the distant prairies, or enjoy the fragrance of the magnolia's blossoms; but here, on these cold hills, and by this stormy sea, he has found hearts as God made them, open to the reception of truth, and responsive to the voice of humanity. And why is it that this people — taught from the cradle to the grave to conserve its own dignity — gives itself with child-like confidence to the voice of this one man, and he a stranger? Is it blind adoration of that form, not yet quite wasted by the dungeon or broken by the toils of a struggling life, — for that which may be cold in an hour? — No! no! It is because eternal truth dwells on those lips; it is because those eyes beam with the effulgence of principles which shall flourish in immortal vigor when all men are in the dust. But, gentlemen, I shall not give wing to speech, or do anything to break the delicious spell which now enthralls you. I leave you to the charms of the serene eloquence you have heard, feeling that its mournful melody will linger in your memories like the recollections of some grand old song, long after the voice which made it shall have died away!

THE PATRIOT'S HOPE. — *T. Ewing.*

Our republic has long been a theme of speculation among the savans of Europe. They profess to have cast its horoscope; and fifty years was fixed upon by many as the utmost limit of its duration. But those years passed by, and beheld us a united and happy people; our political atmosphere agitated by no storm, and scarce a cloud to obscure the serenity of our horizon; all of the present was prosperity, all of the future hope. True, upon the day of that anniversary two venerated fathers of our freedom and of our country fell; but they sunk calmly to rest, in the maturity of years and in the fulness of time, and their simultaneous departure, on that day of jubilee, for another and a better world, was hailed by our nation as a propitious sign, sent to us from heaven. Wandering, the other day, in the alcoves of the library, I accidentally opened a volume containing the orations delivered by many distinguished men on that solemn occasion, and I noted some expressions of a few who now sit in this hall, which are deep-fraught with the then prevailing, I may say universal feeling. It is inquired by one, "Is this the effect of accident or blind chance, or has that God who holds in his hand the destiny of nations and of men designed these things as an evidence of the permanence and perpetuity of our institutions?" Another says, "Is it not stamped with the seal of divinity?" And a third, descanting on the prospects, bright and glorious, which opened on our beloved country, says, "Auspicious omens cheer us!"

Yet it would have required but a tinge of superstitious gloom to have drawn from that event darker forebodings of that which was to come. In our primitive wilds, where the order of nature is unbroken by the hand of man, — there, where majestic trees arise, spread forth their branches, live out their age, and decline, — sometimes will a patriarchal plant, which has stood for centuries the winds and storms, fall when no breeze agitates a leaf of the trees that surround it. And when, in the calm stillness of a summer's noon, the solitary woodsman hears on either hand the heavy crash of huge, branchless trunks, falling by their own weight to the earth whence they sprung, prescient of the future, he foresees the whirlwind at hand, which shall sweep through the forest, break its strongest stems, upturn its deepest roots, and strew in the dust its tallest, proudest heads. But I am none of those who indulge in gloomy anticipation. I do not despair of the republic. My trust is strong, that the gallant ship, in which all our hopes are embarked, will yet outride the storm; saved alike from the breakers and billows of disunion, and the greedy whirlpool, the all-ingulfing maelstroom, of executive power; that, unbroken, if not unharmed, she may pursue her prosperous voyage far down the stream of time; and that the banner of our country, which now waves over us so proudly, will still float in triumph, borne on the wings of heaven, fanned by the breath of fame, every stripe bright and unsullied, every star fixed in its sphere, ages after each of us now here shall have ceased to gaze on its majestic folds forever!

DEATHS OF ADAMS AND JEFFERSON. — *E. Everett.*

The jubilee of America is turned into mourning. Its joy is mingled with sadness; its silver-trumpet breathes a mingled strain. Henceforward and forever, while America exists among the nations of the earth, the first emotion on the Fourth of July shall be of joy and triumph in the great event which immortalizes the day, — the second shall be one of chastised and tender recollection of the venerable men who departed on the morning of the jubilee. This mingled emotion of triumph and sadness has sealed the moral beauty and sublimity of our great anniversary. In the simple commemoration of a victorious political achievement, there seems not enough to occupy all our purest and best feelings. The Fourth of July was before a day of unshaded triumph, exultation, and national pride; but the angel of death has mingled in the all-glorious pageant, to teach us we are men. Had our venerated fathers left us on any other day, the day of the united departure of two such men would henceforward have been remembered but as a day of mourning. But now, while their decease has gently chastened the exultations of the triumphant festival, the banner of independence will wave cheerfully over the spot where they repose. The whole nation feels, as with one heart, that since it must sooner or later have been bereaved of its revered fathers, it could not have wished that any other had been the day of their decease. Our anniversary festival was before triumphant; it is now triumphant and sacred. It before called out the young and ardent to join in the public rejoicings; it now also speaks, in a touching voice, to the retired, to the gray-headed, to the mild and peaceful spirits, to the whole family of sober freemen. With some appeal of joy, of admiration, of tenderness, it henceforth addresses every American heart. It is henceforward what the dying Adams pronounced it,— a great and a good day. It is full of greatness, and full of goodness. It is absolute and complete. The death of the men who declared our independence — their death on the day of the jubilee — was all that was wanting to the Fourth of July. To die on that day, and to die together, was all that was wanting to Jefferson and Adams.

Think not, fellow-citizens, that, in the mere formal discharge of my duty this day, I would overrate the melancholy interest of the great occasion. Heaven knows I do anything but intentionally overrate it. I labor only for words to do justice to your feelings and to mine. I can say nothing which does not sound as cold, as tame, and as inadequate, to myself as to you. The theme is too great and too surprising, the men are too great and good, to be spoken of in this cursory manner. There is too much in the contemplation of their united characters, their services, the day and coïncidence of their death, to be properly described, or to be fully felt at once. I dare not come here and dismiss, in a few summary paragraphs, the characters of men who have filled such a space in the history of their age. It would be a disrespectful familiarity with men of their lofty spirits, their rich endowments, their deep counsels and wise measures, their long and honorable lives, to endeavor thus to weigh and estimate them. I feel the mournful contrast in the fortunes of the first and best of men, that after a life in the highest walks of usefulness; after conferring benefits, not merely on a neighborhood, a city, or even a state, but on a whole continent, and a posterity of kindred men; after having stood in the first estimation for talents, services and influence, among millions of fellow-citizens, — a day should come which closes all up, pronounces a brief blessing on their memory; gives an hour to the actions of a crowded life; describes in a sentence what it took years to bring to pass, and what is destined for years and ages to continue and operate on posterity; forces into a few words the riches of busy days of action and weary nights of meditation; passes forgetfully over many traits of character, many counsels and measures, which it cost, perhaps, years of discipline and effort to mature; utters a funeral prayer, chants a mournful anthem, and then dismisses all into the dark chambers of death and forgetfulness.

GENIUS. — *H. Giles.*

Genius, to enjoy and to communicate happy and exalting life, must have union with the moral and the spiritual, — with the truth which they inspire, with the beauty which they sanctify. These belong to the soul's moral and progressive being; and these, good and fair forever, no genius can exhaust, and no genius can transcend. Genius, therefore, to ask in freedom, and in a right direction, must be of faith, and love, and hope: of the faith which can reverence and can trust; of the love which can receive and give; of the hope which faith and love sustain, which gleams cheeringly over the path of humanity, and which, by large sympathy, has large wisdom. These are the principles which connect us with the universe of highest thought and of most enduring beauty. It is by faith that poetry, as well as devotion, soars above this dull earth; that imagination breaks through its clouds, breathes a purer air, and lives in a softer light. It is love that gives the poet the whole heart of man; and it is by love that he speaks to the whole heart of man forever. Hope, which is but our ideal future, lives even in our most prosaic experience, and is a needful solace to our daily toils. We can then but ill spare it from our poetic dreams. We can but ill endure, among so many sad realities, to rob anticipation of its pleasant visions.

In speaking thus, I would not imply that life can be always sunshine. By no means. Its afflictions are many; they are universal, they are inevitable. Because they are so, life can afford to lose none of its alleviations. Much that belongs merely to the present it must of necessity lose. Wretched it is, indeed, if it must likewise resign the future. Much will be carried from us, as our years decline, which years that come never can restore. Hours there are, brief, happy hours, in experience, which may not be forgotten, but are no more to be renewed. They can be but once, and the effort to repeat is to destroy them. They go to the past as a dream; they are no more, except that now and then their shadows mock us through the mist of days. Pure enjoyments and bright expectances the most meagre souls have known some time in their existence; and the most meagre souls, in feeling that they shall never know them again, are capable of deep regret. They are as a melody when the lute is broken; they are as a tale the minstrel tells — and dies. The inanimate universe itself seems to undergo the changes of our own spirits, and to sympathize with the transitions of our own experience. The stars, it is true, rise as brightly in the heavens, the flowers spring as lovely from the earth, the woodlands bloom as freshly as before; but, O, the glory and the joy within, the fancy and the hope which made the stars more beautiful, and the flowers more graceful, and the woods more elysian, and the birds more musical, will not last with passing suns, nor come back again with returning seasons! I do not decry this characteristic of our nature. I do not decry the genius which has affinity with it, and appeals to it. A high and solemn melancholy is the sighing of our immortality; it is the struggle of a divine aspiration with our earthly imperfections. The capacity of sorrow belongs to our grandeur; and the loftiest of our race are those who have had the profoundest grief, because they have had the profoundest sympathies. There is a sadness which is an attribute of our spiritual humanity; and it is only when this spiritual humanity is dormant that misery approaches the limitation of simple physical suffering or physical want. To be happy as moral and intellectual beings, we must feel the joy which has its centre in the soul; from that centre springs also the anguish which testifies our exaltation. This very sorrow of ours is one of the strongest reasons why nothing should dissociate the soul from principles which are not dependent on externals, but which, when suns grow dim, will come out into brighter revelation!

AGAINST ALLIANCE WITH ENGLAND.—*J. Clemens.*

It was an inflexible rule of the Roman senate never to make peace with a victorious enemy, lest amid the sufferings and humiliations of defeat they might be tempted to sacrifice the interests of the republic. No wonder that a people governed by such rules became the masters of the world. Over them the passions had no sway; reason ruled supreme. Cold as the marble columns about them, no wild fancies led them into profitless adventures, no vain dreams of universal philanthropy taught them to forget the higher duties they owed to Rome.

The present project of intervention does not come recommended to me by the company in which it proposes to place us. We are asked to act in conjunction with England, who may well find it for her own interest and her own safety, but who will offer us nothing in exchange for our share in the common danger and the common expense. The policy of England is known to the world; and all history is false, if she ever formed an alliance without a selfish end in view. Whatever nation subserves her purposes is her ally for the time being, but not a moment longer. A league with England out of which any good could arise to America is an Utopian dream, of which a schoolboy should be ashamed.

In her case, also, even feeling prompts us to reject the proffered fellowship. There are many wounds inflicted in the past whose "poor dumb mouths" plead eloquently against such an alliance. The fierce Tarlton and the merciless Rawdon are not yet forgotten. The house-burnings of Cockburn and the savage massacres of Proctor still blacken the page of history. Time has not abated the deep indignation excited by the brutal war-cry which rang over the plains of New Orleans; and none of us remember, without a feeling of resentment, the Vandal inroad to which this capital was subjected. That large class of our population who are of Irish birth or Irish extraction have darker memories to cherish, and deeper wrongs to avenge. Many of them have had their infant slumbers broken by the rattle of musketry and the fierce yell of an infuriated soldiery; and none of them have forgotten that there was a time when the frightened peasant who fled to the mountain or the morass for safety was lighted on his way by the flames bursting from the roof of his cottage; when the dungeon was filled with the noblest in the land, and the scaffold groaned with the weight of its victims; when terror walked side by side with the paid informer, and desolation made its home in Ireland.

These are the souvenirs connected with the name of England; and I will not so libel a gallant people as to suppose for a moment that they have any great anxiety to clasp in friendship hands red with the best blood of their native land. Let me not be misunderstood. I seek no quarrel with England; but I do not forget what she has done, and I want no alliance with her. So long as she attends to her own business, and does not presume to meddle with ours, I am willing that our present relations should continue. But let her beware how she arouses the animosities now slumbering in the American bosom. The bones and sinews of the young giant of the west are fast hardening into mature manhood, and the next time we meet in hostile conflict, the proud boast that the roll of the English drum may be heard from the rising to the setting sun will be nothing but a tale of the past. Then, too, may the Irish heart leap with a proud joy, for the time will have come when the epitaph of Emmett may at last be written.

We have all read recently, and none of us, I trust, without deep feeling, the opinions of the venerable statesman whose bodily infirmity now keeps him from among us. Who is there with a higher wisdom than his? Who is there with a wider experience? Who is there with so few motives to deceive himself or others as to the true interests of his country? His voice comes to us clothed with all the sanctity the grave can give, with the added knowledge of existing things which the grave must take away. Standing upon the verge of two worlds, and looking back upon that which he is about to leave, his heart swelling with a patriotism little less than holy, his vision clear and unclouded by the passions and prejudices which dim our sight, he tells us that ours is a mission of peace, not a mission of blood; that to avoid all interference in the affairs of other nations, to preserve our own independence, to live for America, to labor for America, and, if need be, to die for America, is a sacred duty, the performance of which will best serve the cause of human liberty in every land beneath the sun. I shall follow his advice. If my own judgment differed from his, I should distrust it, and feel inclined rather to be governed by the suggestions of him whom all men of every party have agreed to name patriot, statesman, sage!

THE LAST HOURS OF DANIEL WEBSTER. — *E. Everett.*

Among the many memorable words which fell from the lips of our friend just before they were closed forever, the most remarkable are those, — "I STILL LIVE." They attest the serene composure of his mind, the Christian heroism with which he was able to turn his consciousness in upon itself, and explore, step by step, the dark passage (dark to us, but to him, we trust, already lighted from above) which connects this world with the world to come.

But I know not what words could have been better chosen to express his relation to the world he was leaving. "I still live. This poor dust is just returning to the dust from which it was taken; but I feel that I live in the affections of the people to whose services I have consecrated my days. I still live. The icy hand of death is already laid on my heart, but I shall still live in those words of counsel which I have uttered to my fellow-citizens, and which I now leave them as the last bequest of a dying friend."

In the long and honored career of our lamented friend there are efforts and triumphs which will hereafter fill one of the brightest pages in our history. But I greatly err if the closing scene — the height of the religious sublime — does not, in the judgment of other days, far transcend in interest the brightest exploits of public life. Within that darkened chamber at Marshfield was witnessed a scene of which we shall not readily find the parallel. The serenity with which he stood in the presence of the king of terrors, without trepidation or flutter, for hours and days of expectation; the thoughtfulness for the public business, when the sands were so nearly run out; the hospitable care for the reception of the friends who came to Marshfield; that affectionate and solemn leave separately taken, name by name, of wife, and children, and kindred, and friends, and family, down to the humblest members of the household; the designation of the coming day, then near at hand, when "all that was mortal of Daniel Webster would cease to exist;" the dimly-recollected strains of the funeral poetry of Gray, — last faint flash of the soaring intellect; the feebly-murmured words of Holy Writ repeated from the lips of the good physician, who, when all the resources of human art had been exhausted, had a drop of spiritual balm for the parting soul; the clasped hands; the dying prayers; — O! my fellow-citizens, this is a consummation over which tears of pious sympathy will be shed, ages after the glories of the forum and the senate are forgotten.

"His sufferings ended with the day, yet lived he at its close,
And breathed the long, long night away in statue-like repose;
But ere the sun, in all his state, illumed the eastern skies,
He passed through glory's morning gate, and walked in Paradise."

THE SACRED TRUST OF LIBERTY. — *W. F. Otis.*

Do we suppose that we can shed our liberty upon other countries without exertion, and let it fall upon them like the dew which stirs not the leaf? No; liberty must be long held suspended over them in the atmosphere, by our unseen and unwearied power. The more intense the heat which oppresses them, the more must it saturate and surcharge the air, till, at last, when the ground is parched dry, when vegetation is crisped up, and the gasping people are ready to plunge into destruction for relief, then will it call forth its hosts from every quarter of the horizon; then will the sky be overcast, the landscape darkened, and liberty, at one peal, with one flash, will pour down her million streams; then will she lift up the voice which echoed, in days of yore, from the peaks of Otter to the Grand Monadnock; then will

> "Jura answer through her misty cloud,
> Back to the joyous Alps, who call to her aloud."

We are asked upon what is our reliance in times of excitement; what checks have we upon popular violence; what compensation for human infirmities; what substitutes for bayonets, dragoons, and an aristocracy? I answer, the religion and morality of the people. Not the religion of the state; not the morality of the fashionable. Thank Heaven, our house is of no Philistine architecture! Our trust — our only trust — is where it ought to be, — the religion and morality of the whole people. Upon that depends, and ought to depend, all that we enjoy or hope. Our strength is in length, in breadth, and in depth. It is in us, and must be felt and exercised by each one and all of us, or our downfall is doomed. For we are the people; we are our governors; we are the Lord's anointed; we are the powers that be, and we bear not the sword in vain. And upon us is the responsibility; humble and obscure, domestic and retiring, secluded and solitary, we may be, — but ours is still the great national trust, go where we will; and to God are we, one and all, accountable. Our responsibility is with us; it weighs upon us; it overhangs us, like the dome of this house; its universal pressure is the great principle of our protection. If the just rules of religion and morality pervade through all its parts, the prodigious weight is gracefully sustained; but if vice and corruption creep in its divided circles, the enfeebled fabric will yawn in dread chasms, and, crumbling, will overwhelm us with unutterable ruin!

CHARITY SHOULD COMMENCE AT HOME. — *J. C. Jones.*

If this Union is to endure with all its brilliancy, we are the agents and the instrumentalities by which it is to be accomplished; and I submit to every senator here, who loves this Union, — and I would to God that all of them did love it! — if they are ready to take a step which, by possibility, may endanger this Union. What are your sympathies, broad, boundless as they are, compared to the interest, to the honor, to the duty, we owe to our own country? We go throughout the whole world in quest of objects of sympathy, forgetting that we have a country to be saved, and a country that is to be honored, and made prosperous and happy. Sir, I love this Union in all its length, in all its breadth, in all its height, in all its depth. Yes, sir, from the Aroostook to the Rio Grandé, from the Pacific to the Atlantic, throughout all our borders, I love this Union. For it I am ready to live, and, by the grace of God, if necessary, for it I am ready to die. I love it, and, because I love it, I want to act so as to preserve it. Why should we endanger this Union by faction, either north or south? I have no affinities for the one or the other. Wherever there is a man, or a community, or principles which endanger the Union, if I had the power, I would borrow some thunderbolt from the armory of heaven, and dash the accursed wretch into utter annihilation!

I love this Union, — love of the Union is idolatry with me; and it is because I love and cherish it with the fondness of devoted affection, that I am against any of those Utopian schemes, any of those modern doctrines of progress, or manifest destiny, or higher or lower law, come from what sources they may. Why should we go abroad? Have we not enough to do at home? Have we not a field broad enough for the sympathies of senators? Are all our sympathies to be exhausted on Hungary? Weep over her wrongs to your heart's content; I will join you in the holy office; but I ask you to come back in the hours of quietude and look to your own country. Have you not enough here to engage your time, to enlist your talents, to enlist the talents of the loftiest intellect of the age? See your country, with twenty-five millions of population, extending from ocean to ocean, — a territory of empires in extent, and yet not enough for the enlarged capacity of some gentlemen. The world itself seems scarcely large enough to contain their boundless sympathies. It is enough for me to know that there are interests here that command and demand my attention. Look at the interests of this country! You have a territory almost boundless; unnumbered millions and hundreds of millions of public domain, that might be made the basis upon which the hopes, the prosperity, the happiness, the grandeur and the glory, of the mightiest nation upon earth might be established. And yet, sir, that is a small matter, that concerns nobody. We must go and weep over Hungary. If your sympathies are so large, go into the valley of the Mississippi, that I have the honor in part to represent. I see the honored representative of my district here now. Go there, and see the unnumbered and numberless lives that are constantly sacrificed to the imbecility and weakness of this government of ours. There is a hecatomb of living spirits carried down into the deep and angry waters of the Mississippi and its tributaries. There is no sympathy for them. We must go abroad, and shed tears of blood and compassion for the sufferings of Hungary. Better come home, and weep over widows and orphans, left husbandless and fatherless by the neglect of the government to give protection, and to improve her inland and her external commerce. That is enough to engage the time and the talents of the whole Senate — of the loftiest genius that ever lived. Yet these are very small matters — we may forget them all! We have a sea-coast almost boundless, with harbors to improve, interests to protect, thousands and tens of thousands of American citizens languishing for the want of that paternal regard which the government ought to extend them, in giving protection to the honest labor of the country. All that moves no sympathetic chord in those hearts that sympathize with the oppressed of all nations. Come home, gentlemen, come home, and let us see if we cannot do something here. When we shall have made our own people happy and prosperous, when the treasury shall be overflown, when the navy shall find nothing to do, when the army shall be a burden upon our hands, then you may go out and fight the battles of other people. But first let us establish ourselves upon a basis not only honorable, but safe and perpetual.

I hope to see this government go on in the course in which our fathers guided it. I hope to see her growing stronger and stronger every day. My sympathies for the oppressed of other nations are as acute as those of other gentlemen; but I remember that I have a country myself, and that, while I sympathize with the oppressed of other nations, my first duty is to my own country. When I go back, and inquire what have been the achievements, what have been the results that have flown from the policy of our fathers, I confess that I am astounded that gentlemen should choose to change. Why, from feeble colonies, thirteen in number, and three millions in population, we have grown to be a people of about twenty-five millions, with thirty-one states, instead of thirteen. With such results as these, so stupendous and overwhelming, I ask, is it possible that any American can desire to change the policy which has produced such results? As for myself, I desire to see this country go onward. I would invoke the spirit of Him who seems to preside over the deliberations of the Senate, to watch, and guard, and protect, and defend the institutions of our country. I hope that the column which has been laid by Washington may go on rising higher and higher, and higher still, until its proud head shall have pierced the clouds of heaven, and be bathed in eternal light! From its proud summit may the light and the truth of freedom and liberty go out into the whole world, until all its dark recesses shall be enlightened by the revivifying rays that flow from it, and all the world be filled with glory, and be wrapped in one eternal flame of liberty and freedom, now and forever!

DEATH OF DANIEL WEBSTER.—*J. C. Park.*

Daniel Webster, the patriot, the jurist, the statesman, is no more. I rise to pronounce no panegyric, no eulogy! This is neither the time nor occasion; nor am I the man. When the avalanche has fallen from the mountain top, when the thunderbolt has cleft the forest-oak, deep silence succeeds the shock; and now the public pulse has ceased its throbbings, and holy, silent awe is the loudest oratory. Time will be when we shall awake to a full realization of the event; and then eloquent lips will pour forth a nation's feelings.

How many thousands sympathize in the emotions of this hour! The news, lightning-winged, has already pervaded the continent. The fisherman on the banks pauses in his toil to echo back the wail which reaches him from the shore. The trapper in the valleys of the Rocky Mountains catches it, as it rolls across the prairies. The industry of the nation feels that it has lost its best friend; and even on the thrones of Europe the monarchs of the Old World tremble as they learn that that master-spirit, which has wielded a moral power over the destinies of nations more potent than their armed legions or their diplomatic machinery, now stands with the prophets of old and apostles of truth in humble adoration before the throne of Omnipotence!

Around us, in our very midst, how everything speaks to us of him! Yonder monument to Liberty, baptized in the blood of his eloquence; yonder Pilgrim Rock, consecrated by his lips, in the spirit of Puritan truth; the very landmarks and boundaries of our land, from the bleak north-east to the sultry south-west, are established under his wise, far-seeing guidance. Not a waterfall or a cataract in all New England, rendered useful to mankind by those discreet measures which always met his cordial support, that did not seem, on yesterday's holy morn, to have rolled its course seaward with a more subdued and plaintive murmur.

The Indian, when his chief goes on his long pilgrimage to the spirit-land, buries with him his implements, his tomahawk and arrows. We, of a Christian faith, bury *far away from* our chief the barbed arrows of political strife and party rancor, and gaze with mournful gratitude on the countless benefits which he has conferred upon us. Three-score years and ten he has been spared to us. Thirty, at least, of the number, he has been leaving the impress of his gigantic intellect upon every prominent measure which has conduced to our country's advancement and prosperity.

But I forbear. The glorious sun has set. Unclouded to the last, its latest beams were of meridian splendor, and the twilight of good influences which it leaves will endure forever.

ENGLAND'S DISLIKE OF AMERICA. — *J. Bell.*

The next great war which is to fill the world with its desolations will be a war between the old continent and the new; between the Old World and the New World; between the ideas, the principles, and the interests, and the passions, of European or eastern civilization, and the ideas, the principles, the interests and the passions, belonging to the new and more vigorous civilization of the continent of America. This is the natural order of progress in the civilization of the world. The jealousy of all Europe has been effectually roused and excited by the late and vast accession to our territory, foreshadowing in its results the profits and resources of the trade of the gorgeous East. As long as this republic shall continue united and prosperous, it must continue to be a standing rebuke to despotic power. It will haunt the dreams of the enthroned masters of Europe like the ghosts of murdered princes, and they can never be at heart's ease until they shall have made one great and united effort to crush this disturber of their repose. Principles of government so diverse, adverse interests so deep and imperishable, cannot exist on continents between which the barrier of an ocean is removed by modern inventions, without bringing jealousies, rivalries, hatreds and collisions, which, sooner or later, must result in war, — fierce, protracted war, — which can only be terminated by the mutual exhaustion of the parties, or the final triumph of one over the other.

A voice whispers me, Where will England be in a contest between the despotic powers of the continent and this republic? What guarantee have we that she would be disposed to interpose her broad shield between America and her assailants? Will kindred race and language be a guarantee of the friendship of England? Never, sir, as long as the story of the Revolution shall be handed down; never, while the brightest pages of our history shall still be those which record our triumphs over British valor and British domination. The dire and lasting hate engendered by family feuds is proverbial; and the lasting enmity of England is decreed by an inexorable law.

But may not kindred institutions be a guarantee of her alliance and protection? No! The throne, the altar, the aristocracy, the whole governing race, including the wealthy middle classes of England, have as great a horror of republicanism, and of the levelling theories of the fierce democracy of the continent, as the Czar of Russia himself. Nothing can be more unmeaning, hollow and deceitful, than what we hear so often announced through some of our own journals, of the desire of Great Britain to draw more closely the bonds of amity between the two countries. Neither the cause of liberty, nor any interest in the diffusion of constitutional monarchies, has been the basis of British policy in this age, or in any other, in her relations with the continent, or with America. These were not the causes of her involvement in the last general war of Europe. They were purely and simply the protection of her own interests and her own safety.

Will her trade, will her rich commercial connections with the United States, bind her to our cause against the powers of the continent? I still answer, unhesitatingly, No! If there is one great fact in the future history of the world that can be foretold with greater certainty than any other, it is the great conflict, not now, but soon to be, between Great Britain and the United States, for the empire of the seas, and the command of the trade of the world. Instead of becoming our ally in a war with the despotic powers of the continent, Great Britain would have cause to exult; and let me say that she has at this moment cause to exult, and her far-seeing statesmen doubtless do exult, in the dawning of a state of things which may place all the powers of the continent, even Russia, — heretofore in her policy friendly to the United States, — in an attitude of lasting hostility and resentment to this republic. Great Britain may see, in recent events on the continent and in this country, causes equally new and unexpected, which may prolong her power and her ocean dominion to a date in the future far beyond all former hope or calculation. She would rejoice to see our commerce cut up, and our youthful energies paralyzed and crushed, under the weight of a European combination. She may stand off, to be sure; but, if the powers on the continent will only pursue a pacific policy towards her,— if they will keep their ports and commercial marts open, on liberal terms, to her trade and manufactures, — they will have her free consent to model their governments upon principles of the purest absolutism; they may extinguish every spark of liberty among their own subjects, and crumble into dust every republic on the globe.

NEW ENGLAND AND VIRGINIA. — *R. C. Winthrop.*

New England does not require to have other parts of the country cast into shade, in order that the brightness of her own early days may be seen and admired. Least of all would any son of New England be found uttering a word in wanton disparagement of "our noble, patriotic sister colony, Virginia," as she was once justly termed by the patriots of Faneuil Hall. There are circumstances of peculiar and beautiful correspondence in the careers of Virginia and New England, which must ever constitute a bond of sympathy, affection and pride, between their children. Not only did they form respectively the great northern and southern rallying-points of civilization on this continent, — not only was the most friendly competition, or the most cordial coöperation, as circumstances allowed, kept up between them during their early colonial existence, — but who forgets the generous emulation, the noble rivalry, with which they continually challenged and seconded each other in resisting the first beginnings of British aggression, in the persons of their James Otises and Patrick Henrys? Who forgets that, while that resistance was first brought to a practical test in New England, at Lexington, and Concord, and Bunker Hill, fortune, as if resolved to restore the balance of renown between the two, reserved for the Yorktown of Virginia the last crowning victory of independence? Who forgets that, while the hand by which the original declaration of that independence was drafted was furnished by Virginia, the tongue by which the adoption of that instrument was defended and secured was supplied by New England, — a bond of common glory, upon which not death alone seemed to set his seal, but Deity, I had almost said, to affix an immortal sanction, when the spirits by which that hand and that tongue were moved were caught up together to the clouds on the same great day of the nation's jubilee!

CHARACTER OF DANIEL WEBSTER. — *R. Choate.*

WITH the peace of 1815, his more cherished public labors began; and thenceforward has he devoted himself — the ardor of his civil youth, the energies of his maturest manhood, the autumnal wisdom of the ripened years — to the offices of legislation and diplomacy; of preserving the peace, keeping the honor, establishing the boundaries, and vindicating the neutral rights, of his country; restoring a sound currency, and laying its foundation sure and deep; in upholding public credit; in promoting foreign commerce and domestic industry; in developing our uncounted material resources; giving the lake and river to trade, and vindicating and interpreting the constitution and the law. On all these subjects, on all measures practically in any degree affecting them, he has inscribed his opinions, and left the traces of his hand. Everywhere the philosophical and patient statesman and thinker will find that he has been before him, lighting the way, sounding the abyss. His weighty language, his sagacious warnings, his great maxims of empire, will be raised to view, and live to be read when the final catastrophe shall lift the granite foundation in fragments from its bed.

Mr. Webster, by his acts, words, thoughts, or the events of his life, associated himself forever in the memory of all of us with every historical incident,— or, at least, with every historical epoch, — with every policy, with every glory, with every great name, and fundamental institution, and grand or beautiful image, which are peculiarly and properly American. Look back to the planting of Plymouth and Jamestown; to the various scenes of colonial life in peace and war; to the opening and march and close of the Revolutionary drama; to the age of the constitution; to Washington, and Franklin, and Adams, and Jefferson; to the whole train of causes, from the Reformation downward, which prepared us to be republicans; to that other train of causes which led us to be unionists; — look round on field, workshop and deck, and hear the music of labor rewarded, fed and protected; look on the bright sisterhood of the states, each singing as a seraph in her motion, yet blending in a common beam and swelling a common harmony, and there is nothing which does not bring him by some tie to the memory of America.

We seem to see his form, and hear his deep, grave speech, everywhere. By some felicity of his personal life; by some wise, deep, or beautiful word, spoken or written; by some service of his own, or some commemoration of the services of others, — it has come to pass that "our granite hills, our inland seas, and prairies, and fresh, unbounded, magnificent wilderness;" our encircling ocean, the rock of the Pilgrims; our new-born sister of the Pacific; our popular assemblies; our free schools, all our cherished doctrines of education, and of the influence of religion, and material policy and law and the constitution, give us back his name. What American landscape will you look on, what subject of American interest will you study, what source of hope or of anxiety as an American will you acknowledge, that it does not recall him?

I shall not venture, in this rapid and general recollection of Mr. Webster, to attempt to analyze that intellectual power which all admit to have been so extraordinary, or to compare or contrast it with the mental greatness of others, in variety or degree, of the living or the dead; or even to attempt to appreciate exactly, and in reference to canons of art, his single attribute of eloquence. Consider, however, the remarkable phenomenon of excellence in three unkindred, one might have thought incompatible, forms of public speech; that of the forum, with its double audience of bench and jury, of the halls of legislation, and of the most thronged and tumultuous assemblies of the people.

Consider, further, that this multiform eloquence, exactly as his words fell, became at once so much accession to permanent literature, in the strictest sense solid, attractive and rich, and ask how often in the history of public life such a thing has been exemplified. Recall what pervaded all these forms of display, and every effort in every form; — that union of naked intellect in its largest measure, which penetrates to the exact truth of the matter in hand by intuition or by inference, and discerns everything which may make it intelligible, probable and credible, to another, with an emotional and moral nature profound, passionate, and ready to kindle, and with imagination enough to supply a hundred-fold more of illustration and aggrandizement than his taste suffered him to accept; that union of greatness of soul with depth of heart, which made his speaking almost more an exhibition of character than of mere genius; the style not merely pure, clear Saxon, but so constructed, so numerous as far as becomes prose, so forcible, so abounding in unlabored felicities, the words so choice, the epithet so pictured, the matter absolute truth, or the most exact and spacious resemblance the human wit can devise; the treatment of the subject, if you have regard to the kind of truth he had to handle, — political, ethical, legal, — as deep, as complete, as Paley's, or Locke's, or Butler's, or Alexander Hamilton's, of their subjects, yet that depth and that completeness of sense, made transparent as though crystal waters, all embodied in harmonious or well-composed periods, — raised on winged language, vivified, fused, and poured along in a tide of emotion fervid, and incapable to be withstood.

I should indicate it as an influence of his life, acts and opinions, that it was in an extraordinary degree uniformly and liberally conservative. He saw with vision as of a prophet that if our system of united government can be maintained till a nationality shall be generated of due intensity and due comprehension, a glory indeed millennial, a progress without end, a triumph of humanity hitherto unseen, were ours.

Standing on the rock of Plymouth, he bid distant generations hail; and saw them rising, "demanding life, impatient from the skies," from what then were "fresh, unbounded, magnificent wildernesses," from the shore of the great, tranquil sea, not yet become ours. But observe to what he welcomes them, by what he would bless them. It is to "good government." It is to "treasures of science and delights of learning." It is to the "sweets of domestic life, the immeasurable good of a rational existence, the immortal hopes of Christianity, the light of everlasting truth."

It will be happy if the wisdom and temper of his administration of our foreign affairs shall preside in the time which is at hand. Sobered, instructed by the examples and warnings of all the past, he yet gathered from the study and comparison of all the eras that there is a silent progress of the race, without pause, without haste, without return, to which the counsellings of history are to be accommodated by a wise philosophy. More than, or as much as, that of any of our public characters, his statesmanship was one which recognized a Europe, an Old World, but yet grasped the capital idea of the American position, and deduced from it the whole fashion and color of its policy; which discerned that we are to play a high part in human affairs, but discerned, also, what part it is, — peculiar, distant, distinct and grand, as our hemisphere; an influence, not a contact, — the stage, the drama, the catastrophe, all but the audience, all our own; and if ever he felt himself at a loss, he consulted reverently the genius of Washington.

Among the eulogists who have just uttered the eloquent sorrow of England at the death of the Great Duke, one has employed an image and an idea which I venture to modify and appropriate.

"The Northmen's image of death is finer than that of other climes; no skeleton, but a gigantic figure, that envelops men within the massive folds of its dark garment. Webster seems so enshrouded from us, as the last of the mighty three, themselves following a mighty series, the greatest closing the procession. The robe draws round him, and the era is past."

Yet how much there is which that all-ample fold shall not hide! The recorded wisdom, the great example, the assured immortality. They speak of monuments:

> "Nothing can cover his high fame but Heaven.
> No pyramid sets off his memories,
> But the eternal substance of his greatness;
> To which I leave him."

THE BACKWOODSMEN. — *A. Burlingame.*

The great spirit of the backwoods has been felt in our country's destiny. We have heard its manly eloquence in Congress, where it has sometimes seized with rude hand the sceptre of power. Give it a more cultivated intelligence, impress it with a higher morality, and it will breathe its thoughts round the world in language worthy of Milton, Chatham and Shakspeare.

I have spoken warmly of the backwoodsmen, for I could do no otherwise. Their strong arms shielded my boyhood, and my memory is full of their wild border tales. The bold lines of their character are fast fading out. They themselves are falling like autumn leaves. In a few more years "the places which now know them shall know them no more forever." Already the sound of the settler's axe and the hunter's rifle grows fainter in the forest. The "voyageur's" songs have died away from our western waters. Gone, too, are the "rangers of the woods," with their bright eyes and irrepressible spirits; and the poor Indians, those down-trodden children of nature, are pressing with their flying feet the leaves of a still more distant wilderness. The railroad track has obliterated the Indian trail, and the iron horse awakens new echoes in the forest. Upon the broad foundations laid by the hardy woodsmen in the midst of unutterable sorrows, and along the huge paths beaten by buffaloes' hoofs before the courage of man struggled with the wilderness, there has sprung up a civilization, which, for energy and magnificence, is without a parallel in the world's history. It outruns the imagination of the poet, who tells us —

"A thousand years scarce serve to form a state."

In our time, states are born of the wild wood in a day, with rights the Romans never knew, and clothed with more than the thunders of Olympian Jove. O! little thought Boone and a few straggling hunters, as they passed through the gap of the Alleghanies, long ago, and hid themselves in the reeds fringing the great rivers of the west, that they were the van of a mighty empire. Little thought Dr. Cutler, when he went forth from Beverly, in Massachusetts, and first settled in Ohio, that the first spot where his feet should find rest would become the home of commerce, and the birth-place of ships swifter and grander than those which went forth annually from his early home to the land of the orient. Little thought the brave men who filled the valleys of the Muskingum, the Maumee, the Wabash, and the Kaskaskias, that ere the grass would grow green upon their graves, mighty cities would spring up where the wolf howled; that the Christian's shining cross would stand where the Indian told his love and breathed his prayer to the offended Manito; that the lakes, so calm, so still, more beautiful than the blue sea beyond the pillars of Hercules, would whiten with sails, and literally murmur with the rush of keels; that the rivers upon which they gazed in silent wonder, whose sources were away in hills beyond the regions of their imaginations, would bear on their bosoms the rich argosies of ten millions of people; and that steamboats, not then born in the brain of their inventor, would go roaring down their waters with a thousand men on their decks. These things they have seen, — we have seen. They are more like magic, or the dream of some fairy tale, than like reality. Yet still the mighty stream of emigration pours westward. "At first a little rivulet winding its way through some beautiful valley, now fed by a thousand springs welling up the wayside, anon increased by other rills mingling with its smiling waters, it has flowed on, and rolled onward, widening and deepening its channel, until now it laves with its rising flood the base of the stony mountains," Ay, it has overleaped them, and this day pours its wild torrent of living, breathing humanity upon the far-off shores of the peaceful Pacific. The star of empire has passed the Atlantic slope, and now stands glittering above the summit of the Alleghanies. In a few more years it will have sped its way to the regions of the setting sun; for true is it now, as in the days of Bishop Berkeley, that

"Westward the course of empire takes its way."

THE EXPERIMENT OF SELF-GOVERNMENT. — *J. P. Hale.*

We live in a remarkable age of the world. And it would seem, casting our eyes back, by the aid of history, over the long vista of ages that are past, as if the Divine Ruler had said that he would not forever be wearied with the importunities of man for liberty; but that here he would make the best experiment. And, as if to render everything favorable for the fullest and fairest experiment to exhibit the capacity of man for self-government, in the fulness of time the eye of science disclosed a new continent, to which the lovers of liberty could resort, to lay deep the foundations of the temple of liberty that they were about to erect.

It is a great mistake to say that the experiment has succeeded. It has not yet succeeded. We are now making it. We are now trying it. Why, the old men of the Revolution, thank God! have not all gone down to their graves in peace. And shall we presumptuously boast, and say that we have succeeded in the great experiment which has baffled the ingenuity and the piety of men in all the ages that have gone before us? No, my friends! It has devolved upon us, with all the lights of a new era shining upon us, — with the friends of civil and religious liberty, the world over, watching with painful interest every step of our progress, — to decide for ourselves and the world whether man is capable of self-government. And if we fail, we fail not alone for ourselves, but for those that shall come after us.

When, in the progress of ages, the traveller from distant climes and shores shall visit the places we now occupy, shall that traveller of some future century, like him that now wanders over the plains of Greece, find his interest only kept alive because he is wandering amidst the monuments of a liberty that is dead, a patriotism that is departed, and a virtue that is gone? Or shall it be that he is doubly interested because he finds living here, fresh and perennial, the streams of liberty and of truth? These are questions that we may ask to-day. The answer is with the future.

If we were to undertake to compare ourselves with our fathers, — we are fond of saying it is a progressive age, and that we are a progressive people, but if we were to undertake to compare ourselves with the old men of the Revolution, after the most liberal allowances that self-love could suggest, how would the account stand? Have we improved upon their ideas of liberty of thought, and of independence of private judgment, which could stand unawed before the face of power, and announce deliberately the possession of a proscribed opinion against which the penalty of death was denounced, and then declare that such conduct as that opinion demanded and that faith required should be pursued at any hazard and at every peril? It is true, my friends, that we have no dread sovereign king interposing his royal prerogative as a terror against the expression of our free thoughts. But let us not flatter ourselves that kings are the only foes that stand in the way of free principles.

It is not to be denied, and it is not to be winked out of sight, that there are adverse influences at work in our midst to-day. We have not realized the full idea of our fathers. We have not fully come up to the idea that the great rights for which they nobly contended were maintained by them because they were conferred by God; not because they were the gift of any government, of any prince, of any potentate, but were inalienable in man. We have failed to come up to that. I do not propose to call away your thoughts and reflections from the joy which the return of such an anniversary should occasion in every breast; and, therefore, will leave this subject, expressing a confident hope and a firm faith that the mist which may for a time envelop, and the clouds which may temporarily hover around the beams of liberty, shall burst away. The eye of faith can already see a dawning of a more glorious sun that is about rising to illuminate the whole heavens. The ear of faith can already hear the shouts of the thousands that shall go up to heaven when the principles of the Declaration of American Independence shall have exerted their influences broadcast as the glorious light of heaven in which we to-day rejoice!

RESISTANCE TO OPPRESSION IN ITS RUDIMENTS.—*D. Webster.*

EVERY encroachment, great or small, is important enough to awaken the attention of those who are intrusted with the preservation of a constitutional government. We are not to wait till great public mischiefs come, till the government is overthrown, or liberty itself put in extreme jeopardy. We should not be worthy sons of our fathers, were we so to regard great questions affecting the general freedom. Those fathers accomplished the Revolution on a strict question of principle. The Parliament of Great Britain asserted a right to tax the colonies in all cases whatsoever; and it was precisely on this question that they made the Revolution turn. The amount of taxation was trifling, but the claim itself was inconsistent with liberty; and that was, in their eyes, enough. It was against the recital of an act of Parliament, rather than against any suffering under its enactments, that they took up arms. They went to war against a preamble. They fought seven years against a declaration. They poured out their treasures and their blood like water, in a contest, in opposition to an assertion, which those less sagacious and not so well schooled in the principles of civil liberty would have regarded as barren phraseology, or mere parade of words. They saw in the claim of the British Parliament a seminal principle of mischief, the germ of unjust power; they detected it, dragged it forth from underneath its plausible disguises, struck at it, nor did it elude either their steady eye, or their well-directed blow, till they had extirpated and destroyed it, to the smallest fibre. On this question of principle, while actual suffering was yet afar off, they raised their flag against a power to which, for purposes of foreign conquest and subjugation, Rome, in the height of her glory, is not to be compared; a power which has dotted over the surface of the whole globe with her possessions and military posts; whose morning drum-beat, following the sun, and keeping company with the hours, circles the earth daily with one continuous and unbroken strain of the martial airs of England!

WASHINGTON'S FAREWELL ADDRESS. — *E. Everett.*

THAT address was the most carefully prepared product of a mind from which nothing crude or ill-considered ever went forth, — the maturest result of his life-long experience. At the close, as he believed, of his political and military career, having fought through two great wars, one of which ended in establishing the independence of his country, having in posts of high responsibility assisted in bringing about two organic changes of government, — having been twice unanimously called to the chief magistracy, and about to withdraw from office for the last time, and, as he thought, forever, into that beloved retirement, as he called it, which he so earnestly coveted, he gave to the people of the United States the last counsels, as he calls them, in language I can never repeat without emotion, "of an old and affectionate friend." You have read it a thousand times. You place it in the hands of your children. You appreciate as you ought those last words of wisdom and love which gushed from that noble heart but a few years before it ceased to beat forever.

And what is the leading advice of this ever-memorable address? Is it not ADHERENCE TO THE UNION? I believe, if its pages were counted, a full fourth part of it would be found devoted to this theme. He tells us to watch over its preservation with the most jealous anxiety. As to love of liberty, which you might suppose would be the principal topic in an address from one who had devoted his life to promote it, there is but a single sentence, a couple of lines, — he just alludes to it as an indwelling sentiment of the American heart which needs no recommendation from him. As for the preservation of state rights, which forms so leading a topic in modern systems of policy, I believe that Washington does not so much as allude to them. I think he does not name them

— not that he undervalued state rights, but he knew there were centrifugal tendencies enough in so large a body of states for their preservation. No, gentlemen, it is union, union, union — the first, the last, the constant strain of this immortal address.

What could my poor voice add, if I were presumptuous enough to attempt to do it, to the parting counsels of Washington? If their influence ceases to be felt, it is not because Washington is dead, but because we are dead and cold, buried in the grave of criminal indifference and apathy, absorbed in the gilded cares of that prosperity which we enjoy under the constitution which he did so much to procure for us, — or, what is worse, misled by prejudice, by false theories of government, by imaginary sectional interests, or, still worse, blinded by party and maddened by faction. It is time for every man to utter his voice in accordance with the parting voice of Washington. I know it is said, and by many excellent and patriotic, but, as I think, greatly-mistaken citizens, that the Union is not seriously threatened, that the alarm is factitious, that the danger is wholly imaginary, or greatly overrated. I wish I could think so; but I must say that, in the result of all the anxious inquiry I have been able to make, I have come to the conclusion that the Union is in great danger. I am not so much moved by the acts of organized bodies, of legislatures, of conventions, or by acts of riot, disorder and lawlessness, in any part of the country. These things carry with them their own corrective, to a certain extent, in the North and South. I know how much has been done by excellent and patriotic citizens of the South to stay the disaffection to the Union in that quarter. I am not so much led to the opinion I have expressed by public acts and demonstrations, as I am most deeply grieved by symptoms I have seen, in both extremes of the country, of a deep feeling of bitterness and ill-will, a spirit of denunciation of the motives, character and policy, of the opposite sections of the Union, and of all at home who are suspected of having any charity or sympathy with their fellow-citizens at a distance. This, sir, is what grieves and alarms me. Why, if the several portions of the country belonged to different nations, — if they were alien in language, in religion and in race, — if they were sworn, like Hannibal at the altar, to wage a war of destruction against each other, they could not use stronger or more bitter language than I have read within a few weeks, by men, both at the North and the South, who entertain extreme opinions on the agitating subjects of the day. I say it is this which gives me the greatest alarm for the continuance of the Union. The outward facts are but the manifestation of the spirit of disaffection and bitterness which, if not checked, sooner or later, or, rather, very soon, will cause the Union to crumble.

I am not an alarmist; I never have been. If I may allude to a matter so unimportant, I would say that, in all my humble addresses to the public, I have ever looked on the bright side in reference to the future of America. But if there is to be no relaxation of those unkind feelings between the different sections of the country, — if men will not make up their minds to live in good feeling and good faith under the constitution and the laws — that constitution which was framed by our fathers, as good, as wise, as patriotic as ourselves, and under which the country has enjoyed a degree of prosperity unexampled in the world, — if they will go on indulging this fierce spirit of mutual hostility, it will, at no distant day, result in a separation of the states, to be followed by a war, or, rather, a series of wars, which will change the aspect of this country, and injuriously affect the cause of constitutional liberty forever. I do regard it as demonstrable that, in the event of a separation of this Union, as certain as the sun in heaven in mid-day, that the sun of the republic will go down from the meridian and set in blood. I know that some persons of sanguine temperament, dallying, as I think, unwarrantably with these dreadful futurities, have persuaded themselves that it would only be a change of two confederacies instead of one, and that in other respects all would go on much as it did before. Sir, I am very loth to enter into any speculations of this kind, on one side or the other; but, in my humble judgment, there will not be two confederacies, nor any confederacies, but as many despotic governments as, in the chances of conquest and re-conquest, military chieftains may be able and willing to establish. Gentlemen, let Germany teach us.

How did she come out of the chaos of the dark ages, after a thousand years of internecine war? Did she come out with two or three confederacies? Gentlemen, she counted more than three hundred independent principalities, as they called themselves, but all lying at the mercy of the nearest despot and the strongest army.

I presume not to look into that dark abyss. I turn from it with the same horror, a thousand-fold increased, that I felt when in my youth I was surprised on the black and calcined edge of the crater of Vesuvius, when the sides of the mountain were already quivering with the convulsive throes of an approaching eruption. To attempt to give form and outline, to measure the force, to calculate the direction of the molten elements, boiling and bellowing in the fiery gulf below, and just ready to be let loose by the hand of God on this pathway of destruction, would be as unavailing and presumptuous in the political as it is in the natural world. One thing, however, I think, is certain. We talk of the separation of these states, assuming that they would still remain the states which they now are, — but I think it is certain as demonstration, that their ancient sacred boundaries, founded, in many cases, not at all on features of physical geography, running, as they do, in open defiance of the mountains and rivers, drawn without the slightest regard to military defence, as if it were the design of Providence that we should be bound together, not by material barriers, but by the cords of love, — boundaries resting on charters, on prescription and agreement, and rendered at last sacred by the constitution and union of the United States, — I think it is certain that some of those boundaries would fall the first sacrifice to a separation of the Union. Do you suppose, sir, that thirty-one states, when the constitutional ties which now bind them are broken, and when this new scramble for separate power shall begin, are going to pay strict regard to those unseen and mystical intrenchments within which stout little Rhode Island — which, in comparison with some other states, is rather a cornfield or a flower-garden than a state — lies as safely fortified as your own imperial New York, which holds the Hudson in the hollow of her hand, and extends her colossal limbs from the lakes to the ocean? When the Union is dissolved, do you think that holy constitutional spell will remain unbroken which prevents your powerful neighbor, Pennsylvania, enthroned upon the Alleghanies, with the broad Susquehanna for her sparkling cincture, and the twin tributaries of the Ohio for the silver fillets of her temples, from raising so much as a finger against gallant little Delaware, which nestles securely within the fringes of the gorgeous robe of her queenly sister?

THE JUDICIARY. — *W. E. Channing.*

There is one branch of government which we hold in high veneration, which we account an unspeakable blessing. We refer to the judiciary. From this tribunal, as from a sacred oracle, go forth the responses of justice.

To us there is nothing in the whole fabric of civil institutions so interesting and imposing as this impartial and authoritative exposition of the principles of moral legislation. The administration of justice in this country, where the judge, without a guard, without a soldier, without pomp, decides upon the dearest interests of the citizen, trusting chiefly to the moral sentiment of the community for the execution of his decrees, is the most beautiful and encouraging aspect under which our government can be viewed. We repeat it, there is nothing in public affairs so venerable as the voice of justice speaking through her delegated ministers, reaching and subduing the high as well as the low, setting a defence around the splendid mansion of wealth and the lowly hut of poverty, repressing wrong, vindicating innocence, humbling the oppressor, and publishing the rights of human nature to every human being.

We confess that we often turn with pain and humiliation from the hall of Congress, where we see the legislator forgetting the majesty of his function, forgetting his relation to a vast and growing community, and sacrificing to his party or to himself the public weal; and it comforts us to turn to the court of justice, where the dispenser of the laws, shutting his ear against all solicitations of friendship or interest, dissolving, for a time, every private tie, forgetting public opinion, and withstanding public feeling, asks only what is RIGHT. To our courts, the resorts and refuge of weakness and innocence, we look with hope and joy. We boast, with a virtuous pride, that no breath of corruption has as yet tainted their pure air. To this department we cannot ascribe too much importance. Over this we cannot watch too jealously. Every encroachment on its independence we should resent and repel, as the chief wrong our country can sustain. Woe, woe to the impious hand which would shake this most sacred and precious column of the social edifice!

AN APPEAL FOR UNION. — *J. McDowell.*

GIVE us but a part of that devotion which glowed in the heart of the younger Pitt, and of our own elder Adams, who, in the midst of their agonies, forgot not the countries they had lived for, but mingled with the spasms of their dying hour a last and imploring appeal to the Parent of all mercies, that he would remember, in eternal blessings, the land of their birth, — give us their devotion, — give us that of the young enthusiast of Paris, who, listening to Mirabeau in one of his surpassing vindications of human rights, and seeing him fall from his stand, dying, as a physician proclaimed, for the want of blood, rushed to the spot, and, as he bent over the expiring man, bared his arm for the lancet, and cried again and again, with impassioned voice, "Here, take it, — O, take it from me! let me die, so that Mirabeau and the liberties of my country may not perish!" Give us something only of such a love of country, and we are safe, forever safe; the troubles which shadow over and oppress us now will pass away like a summer cloud; the fatal element of all our discord will be removed from among us.

It is said, sir, that at some dark hour of our Revolutionary contest, when army after army had been lost, when, dispirited, beaten, wretched, the heart of the boldest and faithfullest died within them, and all, for an instant, seemed conquered, except the unconquerable soul of our father-chief, — it is said that at that moment, rising above all the auguries around him, and buoyed up by the inspiration of his immortal work for all the trials it could bring, he aroused anew the sunken spirit of his associates by this confident and daring declaration: "Strip me (said he) of the dejected and suffering remnant of my army, take from me all that I have left, leave me but a banner, give me but the means to plant it upon the mountains of West Augusta, and I will yet draw around me the men who shall lift up their bleeding country from the dust, and set her free!" Give to me, who am a son and representative of the same West Augusta, — give to me as a banner the propitious measure I have endeavored to support, help me to plant it upon this mountain-top of our national power, and the land of Washington, undivided and unbroken, will be our land, and the land of our children's children forever! So help me to do this at this hour, and, generations hence, some future son of the South, standing where I stand, in the midst of our legitimate successors, will bless, and praise, and thank God that he, too, can say of them, as I of you, and of all around me, These, these are *my* brethren, and, O, THIS, THIS TOO, IS MY COUNTRY!

ADDRESS TO THE CITIZENS OF LEXINGTON. — *E. H. Kellogg.*

BORNE away by emotions not to be repressed, we can scarcely do more than felicitate you on your good fortune. Happy men! you have in your veins the blood, and in your keeping the graves, of the first martyrs to the great cause. Their glorious slumbers bless this quiet vale. But that cause poured its tide of blessings over a wider field than Concord,— on other heads than those of their children. In the full and abounding fruition of those blessings, we appear here, to-day, to join you in paying homage to the spot and the memory of those whose deaths hallow it. The same filial piety that leads you to observe the day brings us here to join you. Indeed, sir, you can hardly appropriate the glorious lineage exclusively to yourselves. Opportunity did not serve our ancestors all alike. But your fathers did not raise the battle-shout on that morning in firmer or fiercer tones than it was echoed back from the hearts of our fathers, resident in other and more distant parts of the state. All hearts leaped alike to the field, though all hands did not close with the foe in the fight. Sir, these fields of Concord and Lexington expand, as I am contemplating them, to the full dimensions of Massachusetts. The hearts of all her sons, seventy-five years ago, beat responsive to those in Concord. And so, I must be allowed to believe, does the chord that you strike here to-day vibrate throughout the same wide limits. Whether we live on that cape that stretches her mighty arm so far into the sea, or within the charmed circle of Faneuil Hall's influence, or whether we live in the great central county, or in the velvet vale of the queen of New England waters, or breathe the air of my own dear mountain land, — however distant our abodes, we would this day bow with you around this early altar of our country's freedom, with equal gratitude to those who consecrated it, and to God who so abundantly blessed their cause.

The great volume of history does not present an instance of more noble services in behalf of other states than that of Massachusetts affords. The fight we celebrate was not begun for Concord, but the country. It was but a few short months after the event before the last foot of the invaders left our state forever. But did Massachusetts halt on her borders, when she found her own soil free? No! For seven long years, wherever the front of battle lowered darkest, there was she found in numbers and in spirit in the foremost ranks of the Revolutionary army. Around the Green Mountain lakes, on the banks of the Hudson, the Delaware or the Susquehanna, on the plains of Virginia or the savannas of the South, — on whatever part of our country the power of England descended, there she bared her breast to the shock. When the country found itself incapable of exertion, almost incapable of defence, under the old confederation of independent states, she waived her state pride, and contributed the wisdom of her Kings, her Gerrys, her Gorhams, and Strongs, to the establishment of the present political fabric — the wonder of the world. Under that Union she has exhibited the same patriotism with which she led the states through the weary way of the Revolution.

THE SHIP OF STATE.— *W. P. Lunt.*

Break up the Union of these States, because there are acknowledged evils in our system! Suppose the fatal blow were struck, would the evils and mischiefs that would be experienced by those who are actually members of this vast republican community be all that would ensue? Certainly not. We are connected with the several nations and races of the world as no other people has ever been connected. We have opened our doors, and invited emigration to our soil from all lands. Our invitation has been accepted. We are in this way teaching the world a great lesson. It may safely be asserted that this Union could not be dissolved without disarranging and convulsing every part of the globe. Not in the indulgence of a vain confidence did our fathers build the ship of state, and launch it upon the waters. We will exclaim, in the noble words of one of our poets:

"Thou, too, sail on, O ship of state!
Sail on, O Union, strong and great!
Humanity with all its fears,
With all the hopes of future years,
Is hanging breathless on thy fate!
We know what master laid thy keel,
What workmen wrought thy ribs of steel,
Who made each mast, and sail, and rope,
What anvils rang, what hammers beat,
In what a forge and what a heat
Were shaped the anchors of thy hope!
Fear not each sudden sound and shock,—
'T is of the wave and not the rock;
'T is but the flapping of the sail,
And not a rent made by the gale!
In spite of rock and tempest roar,
In spite of false lights on the shore,
Sail on, nor fear to breast the sea!
Our hearts, our hopes, are all with thee.
Our hearts, our hopes, our prayers, our tears,
Our faith triumphant o'er our fears,
Are all with thee,—are all with thee!"

APPENDIX.

DECLARATION OF INDEPENDENCE.

When, in the course of human events, it becomes necessary for one people to dissolve the political bands which have connected them with another, and to assume among the powers of the earth the separate and equal station to which the laws of nature and of nature's God entitle them, a decent respect to the opinions of mankind requires that they should declare the causes which impel them to the separation.

We hold these truths to be self-evident, that all men are created equal; that they are endowed by their Creator with certain unalienable rights; that among these are life, liberty, and the pursuit of happiness. That, to secure these rights, governments are instituted among men, deriving their just powers from the consent of the governed; that, whenever any form of government becomes destructive of these ends, it is the right of the people to alter or to abolish it, and to institute a new government, laying its foundation on such principles, and organizing its powers in such form, as to them shall seem most likely to effect their safety and happiness. Prudence, indeed, will dictate that governments long established should not be changed for light and transient causes; and, accordingly, all experience hath shown that mankind are more disposed to suffer, while evils are sufferable, than to right themselves by abolishing the forms to which they are accustomed. But, when a long train of abuses and usurpations, pursuing invariably the same object, evinces a design to reduce them under absolute despotism, it is their right, it is their duty, to throw off such government, and to provide new guards for their future security. Such has been the patient sufferance of these colonies, and such is now the necessity which constrains them to alter their former systems of government. The history of the present King of Great Britain is a history of repeated injuries and usurpations, all having in direct object the establishment of an absolute tyranny over these states. To prove this, let facts be submitted to a candid world :

He has refused his assent to laws the most wholesome and necessary for the public good.

He has forbidden his governors to pass laws of immediate and pressing importance, unless suspended in their operation till his assent should be obtained; and, when so suspended, he has utterly neglected to attend to them.

He has refused to pass other laws for the accommodation of large districts of people, unless those people would relinquish the right of representation in the legislature; a right inestimable to them, and formidable to tyrants only.

He has called together legislative bodies at places unusual, uncomfortable, and distant from the depository of their public records, for the sole purpose of fatiguing them into compliance with his measures.

He has dissolved representative houses repeatedly, for opposing, with manly firmness, his invasions on the rights of the people.

He has refused, for a long time after such dissolutions, to cause others to be elected; whereby the legislative powers, incapable of annihilation, have returned to the people at large for their exercise; the state remaining, in the mean time, exposed to all the danger of invasion from without and convulsions within.

He has endeavored to prevent the population of these states; for that purpose, obstructing the laws for naturalization of foreigners; refusing to pass others to encourage their migration hither, and raising the conditions of new appropriations of lands.

He has obstructed the administration of justice, by refusing his assent to laws for establishing judiciary powers.

He has made judges dependent on his will alone, for the tenure of their offices and the amount and payment of their salaries.

He has erected a multitude of new offices, and sent hither swarms of officers to harass our people and eat out their substance.

He has kept among us, in times of peace, standing armies, without the consent of our legislature.

He has affected to render the military independent of and superior to the civil power.

He has combined with others to subject us to a jurisdiction foreign to our constitution, and unacknowledged by our laws; giving his assent to their acts of pretended legislation :

For quartering large bodies of armed troops among us :

For protecting them, by a mock trial, from punishment, for any murders which they should commit on the inhabitants of these states :

For cutting off our trade with all parts of the world :

For imposing taxes on us without our consent :

For depriving us, in many cases, of the benefits of trial by jury:

For transporting us beyond seas to be tried for pretended offences :

For abolishing the free system of English laws in a neighboring province, establishing therein an arbitrary government, and enlarging its boundaries, so as to render it at once an example and fit instrument for introducing the same absolute rule into these colonies :

For taking away our charters, abolishing our most valuable laws, and altering fundamentally the powers of our governments :

For suspending our own legislatures, and declaring themselves invested with power to legislate for us in all cases whatsoever.

He has abdicated government here, by declaring us out of his protection, and waging war against us.

He has plundered our seas, ravaged our coasts, burnt our towns, and destroyed the lives of our people.

He is, at this time, transporting large armies of foreign mercenaries to complete the works of death, desolation and tyranny, already begun, with circumstances of cruelty and perfidy scarcely paralleled in the most barbarous ages, and totally unworthy the head of a civilized nation.

He has constrained our fellow-citizens, taken captive on the high seas, to bear arms against their country, to become the executioners of their friends and brethren, or to fall themselves by their hands.

He has excited domestic insurrections amongst us and has endeavored to bring on the inhabitants of our frontiers the merciless Indian savages, whose known rule of warfare is an undistinguished destruction of all ages, sexes, and conditions.

In every stage of these oppressions we have petitioned for redress in the most humble terms. Our repeated petitions have been answered only by repeated injury. A prince whose character is thus marked by every act which may define a tyrant is unfit to be the ruler of a free people.

Nor have we been wanting in attention to our British brethren. We have warned them, from time to time, of attempts made by their legislature to extend an unwarrantable jurisdiction over us. We have reminded them of the circumstances of our emigration and settlement here. We have appealed to their native justice and magnanimity, and we have conjured them, by the ties of our common kindred, to disavow these usurpations, which would inevitably interrupt our connections and correspondence. They, too, have been deaf to the voice of justice and consanguinity. We must, therefore, acquiesce in the necessity which denounces our separation, and hold them, as we hold the rest of mankind, enemies in war, in peace friends.

We, therefore, the representatives of the UNITED STATES OF AMERICA, in GENERAL CONGRESS assembled, appealing to the Supreme Judge of the world for the rectitude of our intentions, do, in the name and by the authority of the good people of these colonies, solemnly publish and declare, That these United Colonies are, and of right ought to be, FREE AND INDEPENDENT STATES; that they are absolved from all allegiance to the British crown, and that all political connection between them and the state of Great Britain is and ought to be totally dissolved; and that, as FREE AND INDEPENDENT STATES, they have full power to levy war, conclude peace, contract alliances, establish commerce, and to do all other acts and things which INDEPENDENT STATES may of right do. And, for the support of this declaration, with a firm reliance on the protection of DIVINE PROVIDENCE, we mutually pledge to each other our lives, our fortunes, and our sacred honor.

John Hancock

MASSACHUSETTS.

Saml Adams

John Adams

Robt Treat Paine

Elbridge Gerry

NEW HAMPSHIRE.

Josiah Bartlett

Wm Whipple

Matthew Thornton

RHODE ISLAND.

Step. Hopkins

William Ellery

DELAWARE.

Cæsar Rodney

CONNECTICUT.

Roger Sherman

Saml Huntington

Wm Williams

Oliver Wolcott

MARYLAND.

Samuel Chase

Wm. Paca

Thos. Stone

Charles Carroll of Carrollton

NEW YORK.

Wm. Floyd

Phil. Livingston

Fran.s Lewis

Lewis Morris

VIRGINIA.

George Wythe

Richard Henry Lee

Th Jefferson

Benja Harrison

Thos Nelson jr

Francis Lightfoot Lee

Carter Braxton

NEW JERSEY.

Richd Stockton

Jno Witherspoon

Fras Hopkinson

John Hart

Abra Clark

NORTH CAROLINA.

Wm Hooper

Joseph Hewes

John Penn

PENNSYLVANIA.

Robt Morris

Benjamin Rush

Benj.ⁿ Franklin

John Morton

Geo Clymer

Ja.ˢ Smith

Geo. Taylor

James Wilson

Geo Ross

SOUTH CAROLINA.

Edward Rutledge

Thos. Heyward Junr.

Thomas Lynch Junr.

Arthur Middleton

GEORGIA.

Button Gwinnett

Lyman Hall

Geo Walton

CONSTITUTION OF THE UNITED STATES.

WE the people of the United States, in order to form a more perfect union, establish justice, insure domestic tranquillity, provide for the common defence, promote the general welfare, and secure the blessings of liberty to ourselves and our posterity, do ordain and establish this CONSTITUTION for the United States of America.

ARTICLE I.

SEC. 1. All legislative powers herein granted shall be vested in a Congress of the United States, which shall consist of a Senate and House of Representatives.

SEC. 2. The House of Representatives shall be composed of members chosen every second year by the people of the several states, and the electors in each state shall have the qualifications requisite for electors of the most numerous branch of the State Legislature. No person shall be a representative who shall not have attained to the age of twenty-five years, and been seven years a citizen of the United States, and who shall not, when elected, be an inhabitant of that state in which he shall be chosen. Representatives and direct taxes shall be apportioned among the several states which may be included within this Union, according to their respective numbers, which shall be determined by adding to the whole number of free persons, including those bound to service for a term of years, and excluding Indians not taxed, three-fifths of all other persons. The actual enumeration shall be made within three years after the first meeting of the Congress of the United States, and within every subsequent term of ten years, in such manner as they shall by law direct. The number of representatives shall not exceed one for every thirty thousand, but each state shall have at least one representative; and, until such enumeration shall be made, the State of New Hampshire shall be entitled to choose three, Massachusetts eight, Rhode Island and Providence Plantations one, Connecticut five, New York six, New Jersey four, Pennsylvania eight, Delaware one, Maryland six, Virginia ten, North Carolina five, South Carolina five, and Georgia three. When vacancies happen in the representation from any state, the executive authority thereof shall issue writs of election to fill such vacancies. The House of Representatives shall choose their speaker and other officers; and shall have the sole power of impeachment.

SEC. 3. The Senate of the United States shall be composed of two senators from each state, chosen by the legislature thereof, for six years; and each senator shall have one vote. Immediately after they shall be assembled in consequence of the first election, they shall be divided as equally as may be into three classes. The seats of the senators of the first class shall be vacated at the expiration of the second year, of the second class at the expiration of the fourth year, and of the third class at the expiration of the sixth year, so that one-third may be chosen every second year; and if vacancies happen by resignation, or otherwise, during the recess of the legislature of any state, the executive thereof may make temporary appointments until the next meeting of the legislature, which shall then fill such vacancies. No person shall be a senator who shall not have attained the age of thirty years, and been nine years a citizen of the United States, and who shall not, when elected, be an inhabitant of that state for which he shall be chosen. The Vice-president of the United

States shall be President of the Senate, but shall have no vote, unless they be equally divided. The Senate shall choose their other officers, and also a president pro tempore, in the absence of the vice-president, or when he shall exercise the office of President of the United States. The Senate shall have the sole power to try all impeachments. When sitting for that purpose, they shall be on oath or affirmation. When the President of the United States is tried, the chief-justice shall preside : And no person shall be convicted without the concurrence of two-thirds of the members present. Judgment in cases of impeachment shall not extend further than to removal from office, and disqualification to hold and enjoy any office of honor, trust or profit, under the United States; but the party convicted shall nevertheless be liable and subject to indictment, trial, judgment and punishment, according to law.

SEC. 4. The times, places and manner of holding elections for senators and representatives, shall be prescribed in each state by the legislature thereof; but the Congress may at any time by law make or alter such regulations, except as to the places of choosing senators. The Congress shall assemble at least once in every year, and such meeting shall be on the first Monday in December, unless they shall by law appoint a different day.

SEC. 5. Each house shall be the judge of the elections, returns and qualifications of its own members, and a majority of each shall constitute a quorum to do business ; but a smaller number may adjourn from day to day, and may be authorized to compel the attendance of absent members, in such manner and under such penalties as each house may provide. Each house may determine the rules of its proceedings, punish its members for disorderly behavior, and, with the concurrence of two-thirds, expel a member. Each house shall keep a journal of its proceedings, and from time to time publish the same, excepting such parts as may in their judgment require secrecy ; and the yeas and nays of the members of either house on any question shall, at the desire of one-fifth of those present, be entered on the journal. Neither house, during the session of Congress, shall, without the consent of the other, adjourn for more than three days, nor to any other place than that in which the two houses shall be sitting.

SEC. 6. The senators and representatives shall receive a compensation for their services, to be ascertained by law, and paid out of the treasury of the United States. They shall in all cases, except treason, felony, and breach of the peace, be privileged from arrest during their attendance at the session of their respective houses, and in going to and returning from the same ; and for any speech or debate in either house they shall not be questioned in any other place. No senator or representative shal', during the time for which he was elected, be appointed to any civil office under the authority of the United States, which shall have been created, or the emoluments whereof shall have been increased, during such time; and no person holding any office under the United States shall be a member of either house during his continuance in office.

SEC. 7. All bills for raising revenue shall originate in the House of Representatives ; but the Senate may propose or concur with amendments, as on other bills. Every bill which shall have passed the House of Representatives and the Senate shall, before it become a law, be presented to the President of the United States. If he approve, he shall sign it; but, if not, he shall return it, with his objections, to that house in which it shall have originated, who shall enter the objections at large on their journal, and proceed to reconsider it. If, after such reconsideration, two-thirds of that house shall agree to pass the bill, it shall be sent, together with the objections, to the other house, by which it shall likewise be reconsidered, and if approved by two-thirds of that house, it shall become a law. But in all such cases the votes of both houses shall be determined by yeas and nays, and the names of the persons voting for and against the bill shall be entered on the journal of each house respectively. If any bill shall not be returned by the president within ten days (Sundays excepted) after it shall have been presented to him, the same shall be a law, in like manner as if he had signed it, unless the Congress by their adjournment prevent its return, in which case it shall not be a law. Every order, resolution or vote, to which the concurrence of the Senate and House of Representatives may be necessary (except on a question of adjournment), shall be presented to the President of the United States ; and before the same shall take effect, shall be approved by him, or, being disapproved by him, shall be repassed by two-thirds of the Senate and House of Representatives, according to the rules and limitations prescribed in the case of a bill.

SEC. 8. The Congress shall have power : To lay and collect taxes, duties, imposts and excises, to pay the debts and provide for the common defence and general welfare of the United States, but all duties, imposts and excises, shall be uniform throughout the United States ; to borrow money on the credit of the United States ; to regulate commerce with foreign nations, and among the states, and with the Indian tribes; to establish an uniform rule of naturalization, and uniform laws on the subject of bankruptcies, throughout the United States ; to coin money, regulate the value thereof, and of foreign coin, and fix the standard of weights and measures ; to provide for the punishment of counterfeiting the securities and current coin of the United States; to establish post offices and post roads ; to promote the progress of science and useful arts, by securing for limited times to authors and inventors the exclusive right to their respective writings and discoveries ; to constitute tribunals inferior to the Supreme Court ; to define and punish piracies and felonies committed on the high seas, and offences against the law of nations ; to declare war, grant letters of marque and reprisal, and make rules concerning captures on land and water ; to raise and support armies, but no appropriation of money to that use shall be for a longer term than two years ; to provide and maintain a navy ; to make rules for the government and regulation of the land and naval forces ; to provide for calling forth the militia to execute the laws of the Union, suppress insurrections, and repel invasions ; to provide for organizing, arming and disciplining the militia, and for governing such part of them as may be employed in the service of the United States, reserving to the states respectively the appointment of the officers and the authority of training the militia according to the discipline prescribed by Congress ; to exercise exclusive legislation, in all cases whatsoever, over such district (not exceeding ten miles square) as may, by cession of particular states, and the acceptance of Congress, become the seat of the government of the United States, and to exercise like authority over all places purchased by the consent of the legislature of the state in which the same shall be, for the erection of forts, magazines, arsenals, dock-yards, and other needful buildings ; and to make all laws which shall be necessary and proper for carrying into execution the foregoing powers, and all other powers vested by this constitution in the government of the United States, or in any department or officer thereof.

SEC. 9. The migration or importation of such persons as any of the states now existing shall think proper to admit shall not be prohibited by the Congress prior to the year one thousand eight hundred and eight, but a tax or duty may be imposed on such importation, not exceeding ten dollars for each person. The privilege of the writ of habeas corpus shall not be suspended, unless when in cases of rebellion or invasion the public safety may require it. No bill of attainder or *ex post facto* law shall be passed. No capitation or other direct tax shall be laid, unless in proportion to the census or enumeration hereinbefore directed to be taken. No tax or duty shall be laid on articles exported from any state. No preference shall be given by any regulation of commerce or revenue to the ports of one state over those of another ; nor shall vessels bound to or from one state be obliged to enter, clear or pay duties, in another. No money shall be drawn from the treasury but in consequence of appropriations made by law ; and a regular statement and account of the receipts and expenditures of all public money shall be published from time to time. No title of nobility shall be granted by the United States ; and no person holding any office of profit or trust under them shall, without the consent of the Congress, accept of any present, emolument, office or title, of any kind whatever, from any king, prince, or foreign state.

SEC. 10. No state shall enter into any treaty, alliance or confederation; grant letters of marque and reprisal; coin money; emit bills of credit; make anything but gold and silver coin a tender in payment of debts; pass any bill of attainder, *ex post facto* law, or law impairing the obligation of contracts, or grant any title of nobility. No state shall, without the consent of the Congress, lay any imposts or duties on imports or exports, except what may be absolutely necessary for executing its inspection laws; and the net produce of all duties and imposts laid by any state on imports or exports shall be for the use of the treasury of the United States; and all such laws shall be subject to the revision and control of the Congress. No state shall, without the consent of Congress, lay any duty of tonnage, keep troops or ships of war in time of peace, enter into any agreement or compact with another state, or with a foreign power, or engage in war, unless actually invaded, or in such imminent danger as will not admit of delay.

ARTICLE II.

SEC. 1. The executive power shall be vested in a President of the United States of America. He shall hold his office during the term of four years, and, together with the vice-president, chosen for the same term, be elected as follows: Each state shall appoint, in such manner as the legislature thereof may direct, a number of electors equal to the whole number of senators and representatives to which the state may be entitled in the Congress; but no senator or representative, or person holding an office of trust or profit under the United States, shall be appointed an elector. [* The electors shall meet in their respective states, and vote by ballot for two persons, of whom one at least shall not be an inhabitant of the same state with themselves. And they shall make a list of all the persons voted for, and of the number of votes for each; which list they shall sign and certify, and transmit sealed to the seat of the government of the United States, directed to the President of the Senate. The President of the Senate shall, in the presence of the Senate and House of Representatives, open all the certificates, and the votes shall then be counted. The person having the greatest number of votes shall be the president, if such number be a majority of the whole number of electors appointed; and if there be more than one who have such majority, and have an equal number of votes, then the House of Representatives shall immediately choose by ballot one of them for president; and if no person have a majority, then from the five highest on the list the said house shall in like manner choose the president. But, in choosing the president, the votes shall be taken by states, the representation from each state having one vote; a quorum for this purpose shall consist of a member or members from two-thirds of the states, and a majority of all the states shall be necessary to a choice. In every case, after the choice of the president, the person having the greatest number of votes of the electors shall be the vice-president. But, if there should remain two or more who have equal votes, the Senate shall choose from them by ballot the vice-president.] The Congress may determine the time of choosing the electors, and the day on which they shall give their votes; which day shall be the same throughout the United States. No person except a natural-born citizen, or a citizen of the United States at the time of the adoption of this constitution, shall be eligible to the office of president; neither shall any person be eligible to that office who shall not have attained to the age of thirty-five years, and been fourteen years a resident within the United States. In case of the removal of the president from office, or of his death, resignation, or inability to discharge the powers and duties of the said office, the same shall devolve on the vice-presi-

* This clause within brackets has been superseded and annulled by the 12th amendment.

dent, and the Congress may by law provide for the case of removal, death, resignation or inability, both of the president and vice-president, declaring what officer shall then act as president, and such officer shall act accordingly, until the disability be removed, or a president shall be elected. The president shall, at stated times, receive for his services a compensation, which shall neither be increased nor diminished during the period for which he shall have been elected, and he shall not receive within that period any other emolument from the United States or any of them. Before he enter on the execution of his office, he shall take the following oath or affirmation: "I do solemnly swear (or affirm) that I will faithfully execute the office of President of the United States, and will to the best of my ability preserve, protect and defend, the constitution of the United States."

SEC. 2. The president shall be commander-in-chief of the army and navy of the United States, and of the militia of the several states when called into the actual service of the United States; he may require the opinion, in writing, of the principal officer in each of the executive departments, upon any subject relating to the duties of their respective offices; and he shall have power to grant reprieves and pardons for offences against the United States, except in cases of impeachment. He shall have power, by and with the advice and consent of the Senate, to make treaties, provided two-thirds of the senators present concur; and he shall nominate, and by and with the advice and consent of the Senate shall appoint ambassadors, other public ministers and consuls, judges of the Supreme Court, and all other officers of the United States whose appointments are not herein otherwise provided for, and which shall be established by law: but the Congress may by law vest the appointment of such inferior officers as they think proper in the president alone, in the courts of law, or in the heads of departments. The president shall have power to fill up all vacancies that may happen during the recess of the Senate, by granting commissions which shall expire at the end of their next session.

SEC. 3. He shall from time to time give to the Congress information of the state of the Union, and recommend to their consideration such measures as he shall judge necessary and expedient; he may, on extraordinary occasions, convene both houses, or either of them, and in case of disagreement between them with respect to the time of adjournment, he may adjourn them to such time as he shall think proper; he shall receive ambassadors and other public ministers; he shall take care that the laws be faithfully executed, and shall commission all the officers of the United States.

SEC. 4. The president, vice-president, and all civil officers of the United States, shall be removed from office, on impeachment for, and conviction of, treason, bribery, or other high crimes and misdemeanors.

ARTICLE III.

SEC. 1. The judicial power of the United States shall be vested in one Supreme Court, and in such inferior courts as the Congress may from time to time ordain and establish. The judges both of the supreme and inferior courts shall hold their offices during good behavior, and shall at stated times receive for their services a compensation, which shall not be diminished during their continuance in office.

SEC. 2. The judicial power shall extend to all cases in law and equity arising under this constitution, the laws of the United States, and treaties made or which shall be made under their authority; to all cases affecting ambassadors, other public ministers, and consuls; to all cases of admiralty and maritime jurisdiction; to controversies to which the United States shall be a party; to controversies between two or more states; between a state and citizens of another state; between citizens of different states; between citizens of the same state claiming lands under grants of different states; and between a state, or the citizens thereof, and foreign states, citizens or subjects. In all cases affecting ambassadors, other public ministers and consuls, and those in which a state shall be party, the Supreme Court shall have original jurisdiction. In all the other cases before mentioned, the Supreme Court shall have appellate jurisdiction, both as to law and fact, with such exceptions and under such regulations as the Congress shall make. The trial of all crimes, except in cases of impeachment, shall be by jury; and such trial shall be held in the state where the said crimes shall have been committed; but when not committed within any state, the trial shall be at such place or places as the Congress may by law have directed.

SEC. 3. Treason against the United States shall consist only in levying war against them, or in adhering to their enemies, giving them aid and comfort. No person shall be convicted of treason unless on the testimony of two witnesses to the same overt act, or on confession in open court. The Congress shall have power to declare the punishment of treason, but no attainder of treason shall work corruption of blood, or forfeiture, except during the life of the person attainted.

ARTICLE IV.

SEC. 1. Full faith and credit shall be given in each state to the public acts, records, and judicial proceedings, of every other state. And the Congress may by general laws prescribe the manner in which such acts, records and proceedings, shall be proved, and the effect thereof.

SEC. 2. The citizens of each state shall be entitled to all privileges and immunities of citizens in the several states. A person charged in any state with treason, felony, or other crime, who shall flee from justice, and be found in another state, shall, on demand of the executive authority of the state from which he fled, be delivered up, to be removed to the state having jurisdiction of the crime. No person held to service or labor in one state, under the laws thereof, escaping into another, shall, in consequence of any law or regulation therein, be discharged from such service or labor, but shall be delivered up on claim of the party to whom such service or labor may be due.

SEC. 3. New states may be admitted by the Congress into this Union; but no new state shall be formed or erected within the jurisdiction of any other state; nor any state be formed by the junction of two or more states, or parts of states, without the consent of the legislatures of the states concerned, as well as of the Congress. The Congress shall have power to dispose of and make all needful rules and regulations respecting the territory or other property belonging to the United States; and nothing in this constitution shall be so construed as to prejudice any claims of the United States, or of any particular state.

SEC. 4. The United States shall guarantee to every state in this Union a republican form of government, and shall protect each of them against invasion, and on application of the legislature, or of the executive (when the legislature cannot be convened), against domestic violence.

ARTICLE V.

The Congress, whenever two-thirds of both houses shall deem it necessary, shall propose amendments to this constitution, or, on the application of the legislatures of two-thirds of the several states, shall call a convention for proposing amendments, which, in either case, shall be valid to all intents and purposes, as part of this constitution, when ratified by the legislatures of three-fourths of the several states, or by conventions in three-fourths thereof, as the one or the other mode of ratification may be proposed by the Congress; provided that no amendment which may be made prior to the year one thousand eight hundred and eight shall in any manner affect the first and fourth clauses in the ninth section of the first article; and that no state, without its consent, shall be deprived of its equal suffrage in the Senate.

ARTICLE VI.

All debts contracted and engagements entered into, before the adoption of this constitution, shall be as valid against the United States under this constitution as under the confederation. This constitution, and the laws of the United States which shall be made in pursuance thereof, and all treaties made, or which shall be made, under the authority of the United States, shall be the supreme law of the land; and the judges in every state shall be bound thereby, anything in the constitution or laws of any state to the contrary notwithstanding. The senators and representatives before mentioned, and the members of the several state legislatures, and all executive and judicial officers, both of the United States and of the several states, shall be bound by oath or affirmation to support this constitution; but no religious test shall ever be required as a qualification to any office or public trust under the United States.

ARTICLE VII.

The ratification of the conventions of nine states shall be sufficient for the establishment of this constitution between the states so ratifying the same.

Done in convention, by the unanimous consent of the states present, the seventeenth day of September, in the year of our Lord one thousand seven hundred and eighty-seven, and of the independence of the United States of America the twelfth. In witness whereof, we have hereunto subscribed our names.

GEORGE WASHINGTON, *President,*
and Deputy from Virginia.

NEW HAMPSHIRE.
John Langdon,
Nicholas Gilman.

MASSACHUSETTS.
Nathaniel Gorham,
Rufus King.

CONNECTICUT.
Wm. Samuel Johnson,
Roger Sherman.

NEW YORK.
Alexander Hamilton.

NEW JERSEY.
William Livingston,
David Brearley,
William Paterson,
Jonathan Dayton.

PENNSYLVANIA.
Benjamin Franklin,
Thomas Mifflin,
Robert Morris,
George Clymer,
Thomas Fitzsimons,
Jared Ingersoll,
James Wilson,
Gouverneur Morris.

DELAWARE.
George Read,
Gunning Bedford, jun.,
John Dickinson,
Richard Bassett,
Jacob Broom.

MARYLAND.
James M'Henry,
Daniel of St. Thomas Jenifer,
Daniel Carroll.

VIRGINIA.
John Blair,
James Madison, jun.

NORTH CAROLINA.
William Blount,
Richard Dobbs Spaight,
Hugh Williamson.

SOUTH CAROLINA.
John Rutledge,
Charles Cotesworth Pinckney,
Charles Pinckney,
Pierce Butler.

GEORGIA.
William Few,
Abraham Baldwin.

Attest, WILLIAM JACKSON, *Secretary.*

The constitution was adopted on the 17th September, 1787, by the convention appointed in pursuance of the resolution of the Congress of the Confederation of the 21st February, 1787, and was ratified by the conventions of the several states, as follows, namely: Delaware, Dec. 7, 1787; Pennsylvania, Dec. 12, 1787; New Jersey, Dec. 18, 1787; Georgia, Jan. 2, 1788; Connecticut, Jan. 9, 1788; Massachusetts, Feb. 6, 1788; Maryland, April 28, 1788; South Carolina, May 23, 1788; New Hampshire, June 21, 1788; Virginia, June 26, 1788; New York, July 26, 1788; North Carolina, Nov. 21, 1789; Rhode Island, May 29, 1790.

AMENDMENTS TO THE CONSTITUTION.

At the first session of the first Congress, twelve amendments to the constitution were recommended to the states, ten of which were adopted; the others have since been adopted.

ARTICLE I.

Congress shall make no law respecting an establishment of religion, or prohibiting the free exercise thereof; or abridging the freedom of speech, or of the press; or the right of the people peaceably to assemble, and to petition the government for a redress of grievances.

ARTICLE II.

A well-regulated militia being necessary to the security of a free state, the right of the people to keep and bear arms shall not be infringed.

ARTICLE III.

No soldier shall, in time of peace, be quartered in any house, without the consent of the owner; nor in time of war, but in a manner to be prescribed by law.

ARTICLE IV.

The right of the people to be secure in their persons, houses, papers and effects, against unreasonable searches and seizures, shall not be violated; and no warrants shall issue but upon probable cause, supported by oath or affirmation, and particularly describing the place to be searched, and the persons or things to be seized.

ARTICLE V.

No person shall be held to answer for a capital or otherwise infamous crime, unless on a presentment or indictment of a grand jury, except in cases arising in the land or naval forces, or in the militia, when in actual service, in time of war or public danger; nor shall any person be subject for the same offence to be twice put in jeopardy of life or limb; nor shall be compelled, in any criminal case, to be a witness against himself; nor be deprived of life, liberty or property, without due process of law; nor shall private property be taken for public use without just compensation.

ARTICLE VI.

In all criminal prosecutions the accused shall enjoy the right to a speedy and public trial, by an impartial jury of the state and district wherein the crime shall have been committed, which district shall have been previously ascertained by law, and to be informed of the nature and cause of the accusation; to be confronted with the witnesses against him; to have compulsory process for obtaining witnesses in his favor; and to have the assistance of counsel for his defence.

ARTICLE VII.

In suits at common law, where the value in controversy shall exceed twenty dollars, the right of trial by jury shall be preserved; and no fact tried by a jury shall be otherwise reëxamined, in any court of the United States, than according to the rules of the common law.

ARTICLE VIII.

Excessive bail shall not be required, nor excessive fines imposed, nor cruel and unusual punishments inflicted.

ARTICLE IX.

The enumeration in the constitution of certain rights shall not be construed to deny or disparage others retained by the people.

ARTICLE X.

The powers not delegated to the United States by the constitution, nor prohibited by it to the states, are reserved to the states respectively, or to the people.

ARTICLE XI.

The judicial power of the United States shall not be construed to extend to any suit in law or equity, commenced or prosecuted against one of the United States by citizens of another state, or by citizens or subjects of any foreign state.

ARTICLE XII.

The electors shall meet in their respective states, and vote by ballot for president and vice-president, one of whom, at least, shall not be an inhabitant of the same state with themselves ; they shall name in their ballots the person voted for as president, and in distinct ballots the person voted for as vice-president ; and they shall make distinct lists of all persons voted for as president, and of all persons voted for as vice-president, and of the number of votes for each, which lists they shall sign and certify, and transmit sealed to the seat of the government of the United States, directed to the President of the Senate ; the President of the Senate shall, in presence of the Senate and House of Representatives, open all the certificates, and the votes shall then be counted ; the person having the greatest number of votes for president shall be the president, if such number be a majority of the whole number of electors appointed : and if no person have such majority, then from the persons having the highest numbers, not exceeding three, on the list of those voted for as president, the House of Representatives shall choose immediately, by ballot, the president. But, in choosing the president, the votes shall be taken by states, the representation from each state having one vote ; a quorum for this purpose shall consist of a member or members from two-thirds of the states, and a majority of all the states shall be necessary to a choice. And if the House of Representatives shall not choose a president, whenever the right of choice shall devolve upon them, before the fourth day of March next following, then the vice-president shall act as president, as in the case of the death or other constitutional disability of the president. The person having the greatest number of votes as vice-president shall be the vice-president, if such number be a majority of the whole number of electors appointed ; and if no person have a majority, then from the two highest numbers on the list the Senate shall choose the vice-president ; a quorum for the purpose shall consist of two-thirds of the whole number of senators, and a majority of the whole number shall be necessary to a choice. But no person constitutionally ineligible to the office of president shall be eligible to that of vice-president of the United States.

WASHINGTON'S FAREWELL ADDRESS TO THE PEOPLE OF THE UNITED STATES.

Friends and Fellow-citizens : — The period for a new election of a citizen to administer the executive government of the United States being not far distant, and the time actually arrived when your thoughts must be employed in designating the person who is to be clothed with that important trust, it appears to me proper, especially as it may conduce to a more distinct expression of the public voice, that I should now apprize you of the resolution I have formed, to decline being considered among the number of those out of whom a choice is to be made.

I beg you, at the same time, to do me the justice to be assured that this resolution has not been taken without a strict regard to all the considerations appertaining to the relation which binds a dutiful citizen to his country ; and that, in withdrawing the tender of service which silence, in my situation, might imply, I am influenced by no diminution of zeal for your future interest, no deficiency of grateful respect for your past kindness, but am supported by a full conviction that the step is compatible with both.

The acceptance of, and continuance hitherto in, the office to which your suffrages have twice called me, have been a uniform sacrifice of inclination to the opinion of duty, and to a deference for what appeared to be your desire. I constantly hoped that it would have been much earlier in my power, consistently with motives which I was not at liberty to disregard, to return to that retirement from which I had been reluctantly drawn. The strength of my inclination to do this, previous to the last election, had even led to the preparation of an address to declare it to you ; but mature reflection on the then perplexed and critical posture of our affairs with foreign nations, and the unanimous advice of persons entitled to my confidence, impelled me to abandon the idea.

I rejoice that the state of your concerns, external as well as internal, no longer renders the pursuit of inclination incompatible with the sentiment of duty or propriety; and am persuaded, whatever partiality may be retained for my services, that, in the present circumstances of our country, you will not disapprove my determination to retire.

The impressions with which I first undertook the arduous trust were explained on the proper occasion. In the discharge of this trust, I will only say, that I have with good intentions contributed towards the organization and administration of the government the best exertions of which a very fallible judgment was capable. Not unconscious in the outset of the inferiority of my qualifications, experience, in my own eyes, — perhaps still more in the eyes of others, — has strengthened the motives to diffidence of myself ; and every day the increasing weight of years admonishes me, more and more, that the shade of retirement is as necessary to me as it will be welcome. Satisfied that, if any circumstances have given peculiar value to my services, they were temporary, I have the consolation to believe that, while choice and prudence invite me to quit the political scene, patriotism does not forbid it.

In looking forward to the moment which is intended to terminate the career of my public life, my feelings do not permit me to suspend the deep acknowledgment of that debt of gratitude which I owe to my beloved country for the many honors it has conferred upon me ; still more for the steadfast confidence with which it has supported me, and for the opportunities I have thence enjoyed of manifesting my inviolable attachment, by services faithful and persevering, though in usefulness unequal to my zeal. If benefits have resulted to our country from these services, let it always be remembered to your praise, and as an instructive example in our annals, that, under circumstances in which the passions, agitated in every direction, were liable to mislead; amidst appearances sometimes dubious, vicissitudes of fortune often discouraging; in situations in which, not unfrequently, want of success has countenanced the spirit of criticism, — the constancy of your support was the essential prop of the efforts, and a guarantee of the plans by which they were effected. Profoundly penetrated with this idea, I shall carry it with me to my grave, as a strong incitement to unceasing vows that Heaven may continue to you the choicest tokens of its beneficence; that your union and brotherly affection may be perpetual; that the free constitution, which is the work of your hands, may be sacredly maintained; that its administration, in every department, may be stamped with wisdom and virtue; that, in fine, the happiness of the people of these states, under the auspices of liberty, may be made complete, by so careful a preservation and so prudent a use of this blessing as will acquire to them the glory of recommending it to the applause, the affection and the adoption, of every nation which is yet a stranger to it.

Here, perhaps, I ought to stop; but a solicitude for your welfare, which cannot end but with my life, and the apprehension of danger natural to that solicitude, urge me, on an occasion like the present, to offer to your solemn contemplation, and to recommend to your frequent review, some sentiments, which are the result of much reflection, of no inconsiderable observation, and which appear to me all-important to the permanency of your felicity as a people. These will be afforded to you with the more freedom, as you can only see in them the disinterested warnings of a parting friend, who can possibly have no personal motive to bias his counsel; nor can I forget, as an encouragement to it, your indulgent reception of my sentiments on a former and not dissimilar occasion.

Interwoven as is the love of liberty with every ligament of your hearts, no recommendation of mine is necessary to fortify or confirm the attachment.

The unity of government, which constitutes you one people, is also now dear to you. It is justly so; for it is a main pillar in the edifice of your real independence, the support of your tranquillity at home, your peace abroad, of your safety, of your prosperity, of that very liberty which you so highly prize. But, as it is easy to foresee that from different causes and from different quarters much pains will be taken, many artifices employed, to weaken in your minds the conviction of this truth, — as this is the point in your political fortress against which the batteries of internal and external enemies will be most constantly and actively (though often covertly and insidiously) directed, — it is of infinite moment that you should properly estimate the immense value of your national union to your collective and individual happiness; that you should cherish a cordial, habitual and immovable attachment to it, accustoming yourselves to think and speak of it as of the palladium of your political safety and prosperity; watching for its preservation with jealous anxiety; discountenancing whatever may suggest even a suspicion that it can, in any event, be abandoned; and indignantly frowning upon the first dawning of every attempt to alienate any portion of our country from the rest, or to enfeeble the sacred ties which now link together the various parts.

For this you have every inducement of sympathy and interest. Citizens, by birth or choice, of a common country, that country has a right to concentrate your affections. The name of *American*, which belongs to you in your national capacity, must always exalt the just pride of patriotism, more than any appellation derived from local discriminations. With slight shades of difference, you have the same religion, manners, habits, and political principles. You have, in a common cause, fought and triumphed together; the independence and liberty you possess are the work of joint counsels and joint efforts, of common dangers, sufferings and successes.

But these considerations, however powerfully they address themselves to your sensibility, are greatly outweighed by those which apply more immediately to your interest ; here every portion of our country finds the most commanding motives for carefully guarding and preserving the union of the whole.

The North, in an unrestrained intercourse with the South, protected by the equal laws of a common government, finds, in the productions of the latter, great additional resources of maritime and commercial enterprise, and precious materials of manufacturing industry. The South, in the same intercourse, benefiting by the agency of the North, sees its agriculture grow, and its commerce expand. Turning partly into its own channels the seamen of the North, it finds its particular navigation invigorated ; and while it contributes, in different ways, to nourish and increase the general mass of the national navigation, it looks forward to the protection of a maritime strength to which itself is unequally adapted. The East, in like intercourse with the West, already finds, and, in the progressive improvement of interior communication, by land and water, will more and more find, a valuable vent for the commodities which it brings from abroad, or manufactures at home. The West derives from the East supplies requisite to its growth and comfort, and, what is perhaps of still greater consequence, it must, of necessity, owe the secure enjoyment of indispensable outlets for its own productions to the weight, influence, and the future maritime strength, of the Atlantic side of the Union, directed by an indissoluble community of interest as one nation. Any other tenure by which the West can hold this essential advantage, whether derived from its own separate strength, or from an apostate and unnatural connection with any foreign power, must be intrinsically precarious.

While, then, every part of our country thus feels an immediate and particular interest in union, all the parts combined cannot fail to find, in the united mass of means and efforts, greater strength, greater resource, proportionably greater security from external danger, a less frequent interruption of their peace by foreign nations, and, what is of inestimable value, they must derive from union an exemption from those broils and wars between themselves, which so frequently afflict neighboring countries, not tied together by the same government, which their own rivalships alone would be sufficient to produce, but which opposite foreign alliances, attachments and intrigues, would stimulate and embitter Hence, likewise, they will avoid the necessity of those overgrown military establishments, which, under any form of government, are inauspicious to liberty, and which are to be regarded as particularly hostile to republican liberty ; in this sense it is that your union ought to be considered as the main prop of your liberty, and that the love of the one ought to endear to you the preservation of the other.

These considerations speak a persuasive language to every reflecting and virtuous mind, and exhibit the continuance of the Union as a primary object of patriotic desire. Is there a doubt whether a common government can embrace so large a sphere ? Let experience solve it. To listen to mere speculation, in such a case, were criminal. We are authorized to hope that a proper organization of the whole, with the auxiliary agency of governments for the respective subdivisions, will afford a happy issue to the experiment. It is well worth a fair and full experiment. With such powerful and obvious motives to union, affecting all parts of our country, while experience shall not have demonstrated its impracticability, there will always be reason to distrust the patriotism of those who, in any quarter, may endeavor to weaken its bands.

In contemplating the causes which may disturb our Union, it occurs, as a matter of serious concern, that any ground should have been furnished for characterizing parties by geographical discriminations, — northern and southern, Atlantic and western, — whence designing men may endeavor to excite a belief that there is a real difference of local interests and views. One of the expedients of party to acquire influence within particular districts is to misrepresent the opinions and aims of other districts. You cannot shield yourselves too much against the jealousies and heart-burnings which spring from these misrepresentations; they tend to render alien to each other those who ought to be bound together by fraternal affection. The inhabitants of our western country have lately had a useful lesson on this head; they have seen in the negotiation by the executive, and in the unanimous ratification by the Senate, of the treaty with Spain, and in the universal satisfaction at that event throughout the United States, a decisive proof how unfounded were the suspicions propagated among them, of a policy in the general government, and in the Atlantic states, unfriendly to their interests in regard to the Mississippi; they have been witnesses to the formation of two treaties — that with Great Britain and that with Spain — which secure to them everything they could desire in respect to our foreign relations, towards confirming their prosperity. Will it not be their wisdom to rely for the preservation of these advantages on the Union by which they were procured? Will they not henceforth be deaf to those advisers, if such there are, who would sever them from their brethren and connect them with aliens?

To the efficacy and permanency of your Union, a government for the whole is indispensable. No alliance, however strict, between the parts, can be an adequate substitute; they must inevitably experience the infractions and interruptions which all alliances, in all time, have experienced. Sensible of this momentous truth, you have improved upon your first essay, by the adoption of a constitution of government better calculated than your former for an intimate Union, and for the efficacious management of your common concerns. This government, the offspring of our own choice, uninfluenced and unawed, adopted upon full investigation and mature deliberation, completely free in its principles, in the distribution of its powers, uniting security with energy, and containing within itself a provision for its own amendment, has a just claim to your confidence and your support. Respect for its authority, compliance with its laws, acquiescence in its measures, are duties enjoined by the fundamental maxims of true liberty. The basis of our political systems is the right of the people to make and to alter their constitutions of government; but the constitution which at any time exists, till changed by an explicit and authentic act of the whole people, is sacredly obligatory upon all. The very idea of the power and the right of the people to establish government, pre-supposes the duty of every individual to obey the established government.

All obstructions to the execution of the laws, all combinations and associations, under whatever plausible character, with the real design to direct, control, counteract or awe, the regular deliberation and action of the constituted authorities, are destructive to this fundamental principle, and of fatal tendency. They serve to organize faction, to give it an artificial and extraordinary force, to put in the place of the delegated will of the nation the will of a party, — often a small but artful and enterprising minority of the community, — and, according to the alternate triumphs of different parties, to make the public administration the mirror of the ill-concerted and incongruous projects of faction, rather than the organ of consistent and wholesome plans, digested by common counsels, and modified by mutual interests.

However combinations or associations of the above description may now and then answer popular ends, they are likely, in the course of time and things, to become potent engines, by which cunning, ambitious and unprincipled men will be enabled to subvert the power of the people, and to usurp for themselves the reins of government; destroying, afterwards, the very engines which had lifted them to unjust dominion.

Towards the preservation of your government, and the permanency of your present happy state, it is requisite, not only that you steadily discountenance irregular oppositions to its acknowledged authority, but also that you resist with care the spirit of innovation upon its principles, however specious the pretexts. One method of assault may be to effect, in the forms of the constitution, alterations which will impair the energy of the system, and thus to undermine what cannot be directly overthrown. In all the changes to which you may be invited, remember that time and habit are at least as necessary to fix the true character of governments as of other human institutions ; that experience is the surest standard by which to test the real tendency of the existing constitution of a country ; that facility in changes, upon the credit of mere hypothesis and opinion, exposes to perpetual change, from the endless variety of hypothesis and opinion ; and remember, especially, that for the efficient management of your common interests, in a country so extensive as ours, a government of as much vigor as is consistent with the perfect security of liberty is indispensable. Liberty itself will find in such a government, with powers properly distributed and adjusted, its surest guardian. It is, indeed, little else than a name, where the government is too feeble to withstand the enterprises of faction, to confine each member of the society within the limits prescribed by the laws, and to maintain all in the secure and tranquil enjoyment of the rights of person and property.

I have already intimated to you the danger of parties in the state, with particular reference to the founding of them on geographical discriminations. Let me now take a more comprehensive view, and warn you, in the most solemn manner, against the baneful effects of the spirit of party generally.

This spirit, unfortunately, is inseparable from our nature, having its root in the strongest passions of the human mind. It exists, under different shapes, in all governments, more or less stifled, controlled or repressed ; but in those of the popular form it is seen in its greatest rankness, and is truly their worst enemy.

The alternate domination of one faction over another, sharpened by the spirit of revenge, natural to party dissension, which, in different ages and countries, has perpetrated the most horrid enormities, is itself a frightful despotism. But this leads, at length, to a more formal and permanent despotism. The disorders and miseries which result gradually incline the minds of men to seek security and repose in the absolute power of an individual ; and, sooner or later, the chief of some prevailing faction, more able or more fortunate than his competitors, turns this disposition to the purposes of his own elevation on the ruins of public liberty.

Without looking forward to an extremity of this kind (which, nevertheless, ought not to be entirely out of sight), the common and continual mischiefs of the spirit of party are sufficient to make it the interest and duty of a wise people to discourage and restrain it.

It serves always to distract the public councils, and enfeeble the public administration. It agitates the community with ill-founded jealousies and false alarms ; kindles the animosity of one part against another ; foments, occasionally, riot and insurrection. It opens the door to foreign influence and corruption, which find a facilitated access to the government itself through the channels of party passions. Thus the policy and the will of one country are subjected to the policy and will of another.

There is an opinion that parties, in free countries, are useful checks upon the administration of the government, and serve to keep alive the spirit of liberty. This, within certain limits, is probably true ; and in governments of a monarchical cast, patriotism may look with indulgence, if not with favor, upon the spirit of party. But in those of the popular character, in governments purely elective, it is a spirit not to be encouraged. From their natural tendency, it is certain there will always be enough of that spirit for every salutary purpose. And there being constant danger of excess, the effort ought to be, by force of public opinion to mitigate and assuage it. A fire not to be quenched, it demands a uniform vigilance to prevent its bursting into a flame, lest, instead of warming, it should consume.

It is important, likewise, that the habits of thinking, in a free country, should inspire caution in those intrusted with its administration, to confine themselves within their respective constitutional spheres, avoiding, in the exercise of the powers of one department, to encroach upon another. The spirit of encroachment tends to consolidate the powers of all the departments in one, and thus to create, whatever the form of government, a real despotism. A just estimate of that love of power and proneness to abuse it which predominates in the human heart is sufficient to satisfy us of the truth of this position. The necessity of reciprocal checks in the exercise of political power, by dividing and distributing it into different depositories, and constituting each the guardian of the public weal, against invasions by the others, has been evinced by experiments, ancient and modern, — some of them in our own country, and under our own eyes. To preserve them must be as necessary as to institute them. If, in the opinion of the people, the distribution or modification of the constitutional powers be, in any particular, wrong, let it be corrected by an amendment in the way which the constitution designates. But let there be no change by usurpation; for though this, in one instance, may be the instrument of good, it is the customary weapon by which free governments are destroyed. The precedent must always greatly overbalance, in permanent evil, any partial or transient benefit which the use can, at any time, yield.

Of all the dispositions and habits which lead to political prosperity, religion and morality are indispensable supports. In vain would that man claim the tribute of patriotism, who should labor to subvert these great pillars of human happiness, these firmest props of the duties of men and citizens. The mere politician, equally with the pious man, ought to respect and to cherish them. A volume could not trace all their connections with private and public felicity. Let it simply be asked, Where is the security for property, for reputation, for life, if the sense of religious obligation *desert* the oaths which are the instruments of investigation in courts of justice? And let us with caution indulge the supposition that morality can be maintai ıed without religion. Whatever may be conceded to the influence of refined education on minds of peculiar structure, reason and experience both forbid us to expect that national morality can prevail in exclusion of religious principles.

It is substantially true, that virtue or morality is a necessary spring of popular government. The rule, indeed, extends with more or less force to every species of free government. Who that is a sincere friend to it can look with indifference upon attempts to shake the foundation of the fabric?

Promote, then, as an object of primary importance, institutions for the general diffusion of knowledge. In proportion as the structure of a government gives force to public opinion, it is essential that public opinion should be enlightened.

As a very important source of strength and security, cherish public credit. One method of preserving it is to use it as sparingly as possible; avoiding occasions of expense by cultivating peace, but remembering, also, that timely disbursements to prepare for danger frequently prevent much greater disbursements to repel it; avoiding, likewise, the accumulation of debt, not only by shunning occasions of expense, but by vigorous exertions in time of peace to discharge the debts which unavoidable wars may have occasioned; not ungenerously throwing upon posterity the burden which we ourselves ought to bear. The execution of these maxims belongs to your representatives, but it is necessary that public opinion should coöperate. To facilitate to them the performance of their duty, it is essential that you should practically bear in mind that towards the payment of debts there must be revenue; that to have revenue there must be taxes; that no taxes can be devised which are not more or less inconvenient and unpleasant; that the intrinsic embarrassment inseparable from the selection of the proper objects (which is always a choice of difficulties), ought to be a decisive motive for a candid construction of the conduct of the government in making it, and for a spirit of acquiescence in the measures for obtaining revenue which the public exigencies may at any time dictate

Observe good faith and justice towards all nations; cultivate peace and harmony with all; — religion and morality enjoin this conduct, and can it be that good policy does not equally enjoin it? It will be worthy of a free, enlightened, and, at no distant period, a great nation, to give to mankind the magnanimous and too novel example of a people always guided by an exalted justice and benevolence. Who can doubt that, in the course of time and things, the fruits of such a plan would richly repay any temporary advantages which might be lost by a steady adherence to it? Can it be that Providence has not connected the permanent felicity of a nation with its virtue? The experiment, at least, is recommended by every sentiment which ennobles human nature. Alas! is it rendered impossible by its vices?

In the execution of such a plan, nothing is more essential than that permanent inveterate antipathies against particular nations, and passionate attachments for others, should be excluded, and that, in place of them, just and amicable feelings towards all should be cultivated. The nation which indulges towards another an habitual hatred, or an habitual fondness, is, in some degree, a slave. It is a slave to its animosity or to its affection, either of which is sufficient to lead it astray from its duty and its interest. Antipathy in one nation against another disposes each more readily to offer insult and injury, to lay hold of slight causes of umbrage, and to be haughty and intractable when accidental or trifling occasions of dispute occur. Hence, frequent collisions, obstinate, envenomed and bloody contests. The nation, prompted by ill-will and resentment, sometimes impels to war the government, contrary to the best calculations of policy. The government sometimes participates in the national propensity, and adopts, through passion, what reason would reject; at other times it makes the animosity of the nation subservient to projects of hostility, instigated by pride, ambition, and other sinister and pernicious motives. The peace often, sometimes perhaps the liberty of nations, has been the victim.

So, likewise, a passionate attachment of one nation to another produces a variety of evils. Sympathy for the favorite nation, facilitating the illusion of an imaginary common interest, in cases where no real common interest exists, and infusing into one the enmities of the other, betrays the former into a participation in the quarrels and wars of the latter, without adequate inducement or justification. It leads also to concessions to the favorite nation of privileges denied to others, which is apt doubly to injure the nation making the concessions, by unnecessarily parting with what ought to have been retained, and by exciting jealousy, ill-will, and a disposition to retaliate, in the parties from whom equal privileges are withheld; and it gives to ambitious, corrupted, or deluded citizens (who devote themselves to the favorite nation), facility to betray or sacrifice the interest of their own country, without odium, sometimes even with popularity; gilding with the appearance of a virtuous sense of obligation, a commendable deference for public opinion, or a laudable zeal for public good, the base or foolish compliances of ambition, corruption, or infatuation.

As avenues to foreign influence in innumerable ways, such attachments are particularly alarming to the truly enlightened and independent patriot. How many opportunities do they afford to tamper with domestic factions, to practise the art of seduction, to mislead public opinion, to influence or awe the public councils! Such an attachment of a small or weak towards a great and powerful nation dooms the former to be the satellite of the latter.

Against the insidious wiles of foreign influence (I conjure you to believe me, fellow-citizens) the jealousy of a free people ought to be *constantly* awake, since history and experience prove that foreign influence is one of the most baneful foes of republican government. But that jealousy, to be useful, must be impartial, else it becomes the instrument of the very influence to be avoided, instead of a defence against it. Excessive partiality for one foreign nation, and excessive dislike for another, cause those whom they actuate to see danger only on one side, and serve to veil, and even second, the arts of influence on the other. Real patriots, who may resist the intrigues of the favorite, are liable to become suspected and odious, while its tools and dupes usurp the applause and confidence of the people, to surrender their interests.

The great rule of conduct for us, in regard to foreign nations, is, in extending our commercial relations, to have with them as little political connection as possible. So far as we have already formed engagements, let them be fulfilled with perfect good faith. Here let us stop.

Europe has a set of primary interests, which to us have none or a very remote relation. Hence she must be engaged in frequent controversies, the causes of which are essentially foreign to our concerns. Hence, therefore, it must be unwise in us to implicate ourselves, by artificial ties, in the ordinary vicissitudes of her politics, or the ordinary combinations and collisions of her friendships or enmities.

Our detached and distant situation invites and enables us to pursue a different course. If we remain one people, under an efficient government, the period is not far off when we may defy material injury from external annoyance, when we may take such an attitude as will cause the neutrality we may at any time resolve upon to be scrupulously respected, — when belligerent nations, under the impossibility of making acquisitions upon us, will not lightly hazard the giving us provocation, — when we may choose peace or war, as our interest, guided by justice, shall counsel.

Why forego the advantages of so peculiar a situation? Why quit our own to stand upon foreign ground? Why, by interweaving our destiny with that of any part of Europe, entangle our peace and prosperity in the toils of European ambition, rivalship, interest, humor, or caprice?

It is our true policy to steer clear of permanent alliances with any portion of the foreign world; so far, I mean, as we are now at liberty to do it; for let me not be understood as capable of patronizing infidelity to existing engagements. I hold the maxim no less applicable to public than to private affairs, that honesty is always the best policy. I repeat it, therefore, let those engagements be observed in their genuine sense. But, in my opinion, it is unnecessary, and would be unwise, to extend them.

Taking care always to keep ourselves, by suitable establishments, on a respectable defensive posture, we may safely trust to temporary alliances for extraordinary emergencies.

Harmony, and a liberal intercourse with all nations, are recommended by policy, humanity and interest. But even our commercial policy should hold an equal and impartial hand; neither seeking nor granting exclusive favors or preferences; consulting the natural course of things; diffusing and diversifying, by gentle means, the streams of commerce, but forcing nothing; establishing, with powers so disposed, in order to give trade a stable course, to define the rights of our merchants, and to enable the government to support them, conventional rules of intercourse, the best that present circumstances and mutual opinions will permit, but temporary, and liable to be, from time to time, abandoned or varied, as experience and circumstances shall dictate; constantly keeping in view that it is folly in one nation to look for disinterested favors from another; that it must pay, with a portion of its independence, for whatever it may accept under that character; that by such acceptance it may place itself in the condition of having given equivalents for nominal favors, and yet of being reproached with ingratitude for not giving more. There can be no greater error than to expect, or calculate upon, real favors from nation to nation. It is an illusion which experience must cure, which a just pride ought to discard.

In offering to you, my countrymen, these counsels of an old and affectionate friend, I dare not hope they will make the strong and lasting impression I could wish, — that they will control the usual current of the passions, or prevent our nation from running the course which has hitherto marked the destiny of nations; but if I may even flatter myself that they may be productive of some partial benefit, some occasional good, that they may now and then recur to moderate the fury of party spirit, to warn against the mischiefs of foreign intrigues, to guard against the impostures of pretended patriotism, — this hope will be a full recompense for the solicitude for your welfare by which they have been dictated.

How far, in the discharge of my official duties, I have been guided by the principles which have been delineated, the public records, and other evidences of my conduct, must witness to you and the world. To myself, the assurance of my own conscience is, that I have at least believed myself to be guided by them.

In relation to the still subsisting war in Europe, my proclamation of the 22d of April, 1793, is the index to my plan. Sanctioned by your approving voice, and by that of your representatives in both houses of Congress, the spirit of that measure has continually governed me, uninfluenced by any attempts to deter or divert me from it.

After deliberate examination, with the aid of the best lights I could obtain, I was well satisfied that our country, under all the circumstances of the case, had a right to take, and was bound in duty and interest to take, a neutral position. Having taken it, I determined, as far as should depend upon me, to maintain it with moderation, perseverance and firmness.

The considerations which respect the right to hold this conduct, it is not necessary on this occasion to detail. I will only observe that, according to my understanding of the matter, that right, so far from being denied by any of the belligerent powers, has been virtually admitted by all.

The duty of holding a neutral conduct may be inferred, without anything more, from the obligation which justice and humanity impose on every nation, in cases in which it is free to act, to maintain inviolate the relations of peace and amity towards other nations.

The inducements of interest, for observing that conduct, will best be referred to your own reflections and experience. With me, a predominant motive has been to endeavor to gain time to our country to settle and mature its yet recent institutions, and to progress, without interruption, to that degree of strength and consistency which is necessary to give it, humanly speaking, the command of its own fortunes.

Though, in reviewing the incidents of my administration, I am unconscious of intentional error, I am, nevertheless, too sensible of my defects not to think it probable that I may have committed many errors. Whatever they may be, I fervently beseech the Almighty to avert or mitigate the evils to which they may tend. I shall also carry with me the hope that my country will never cease to view them with indulgence, and that, after forty-five years of my life dedicated to its service with an upright zeal, the faults of incompetent abilities will be consigned to oblivion, as myself must soon be to the mansions of rest.

Relying on its kindness in this, as in other things, and actuated by that fervent love towards it which is so natural to a man who views in it the native soil of himself and his progenitors for several generations, I anticipate, with pleasing expectation, that retreat in which I promise myself to realize, without alloy, the sweet enjoyment of partaking, in the midst of my fellow-citizens, the benign influence of good laws under a free government — the ever favorite object of my heart — and the happy reward, as I trust, of our mutual cares, labors, and dangers.

GEORGE WASHINGTON.

UNITED STATES, 17*th September*, 1796.

AUTOGRAPHS.

W H Harrison

Fitz-Greene Halleck

O Ellsworth W. Wirt

David Wilmot

Emma C Embury

C. Hoffman Whitefield

J. C. Bates

Theophilus Parsons John G. Saxe

Saml L Knapp

J Trumbull

Gilbert Stuart

Trumbull E. P. Whipple

James Abercromby

Rich. H. Dana

Thos. Ritchie J Davis

Thomas H. Benton

Livingston Nath'l Bowditch

J: Burgoyne

J. C. Calhoun

I Toucey Roger William

M Van Buren

H Clay Erastus Hopkins

Wm Penn

Cullen Sawtelle R. B. Taney

John Randolph

W C Rives Edgar A Poe

Lindley Murray

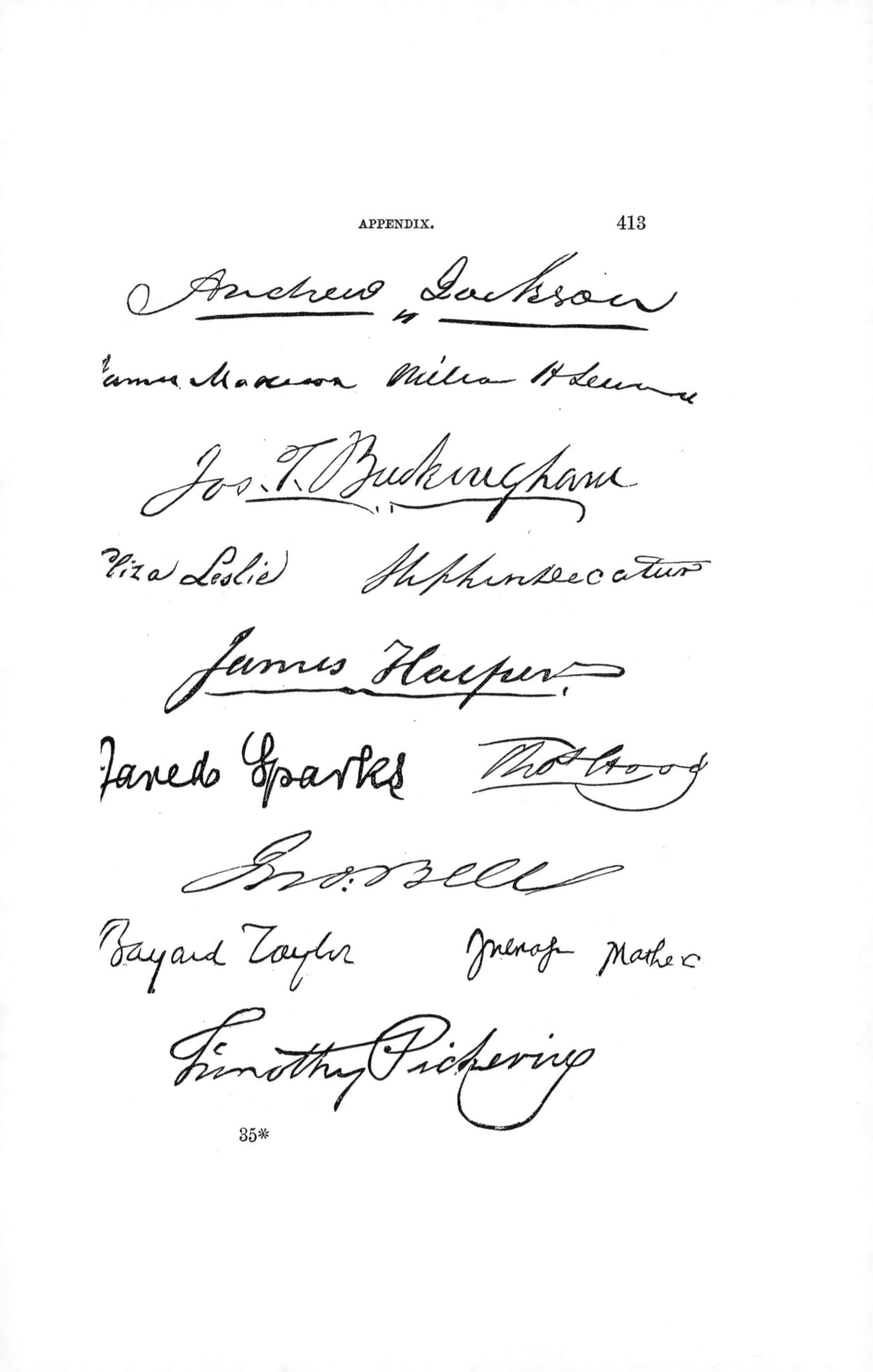

Rvdy Johnson

Isaac Hull G. M. Dallas

James G. Percival

W. Pitt Geo. P. Morris

Charles Sumner

Edmund Pendleton Gaines

Saml F. B. Morse Thos Starr King

C. M. Sedgwick

W. Gilmore Simms

W. W. Seaton T. Carlyle

F. Wayland

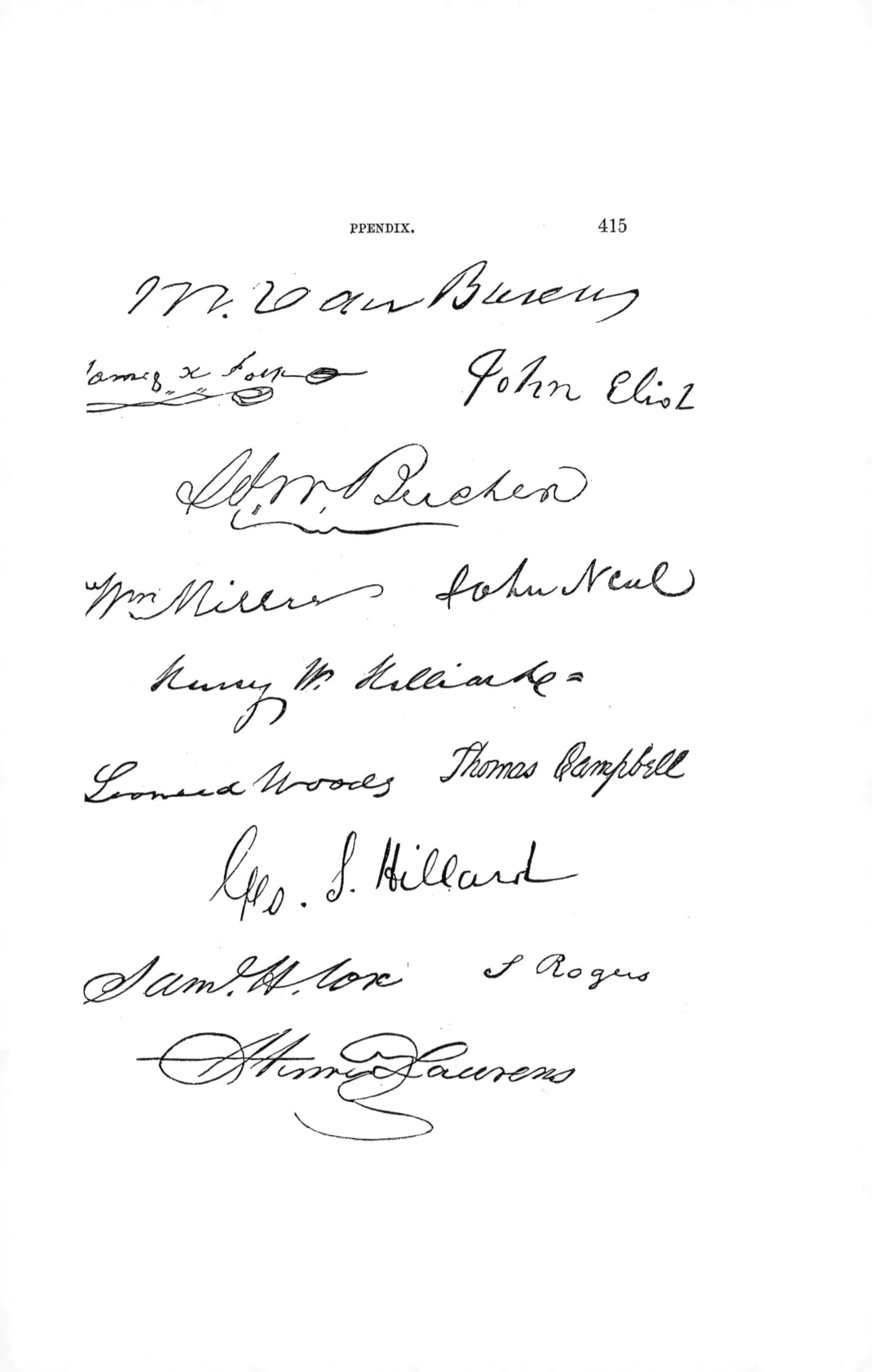

Solomon Foot

Joseph Mazzini   Silas Wright Jr

Martha Washington

Cornwallis   Frances S Osgood

B. F. Butler.

Seba Smith   J Hawes—

Wm Bainbridge

O. A. Brownson   Humboldt.

Alexr Campbell

Nath Greene

Robert Southey

J. K. Paulding

Geo. S. Boutwell

H. Dearborn

John M. Niles

Susan Fenimore Cooper

C. Lyell

Chas. Thos. Russell

J. J. Crittenden

J. Burgoyne

J. Vanderlyn

Robt. Y. Hayne

Albert Barnes   Nathl Bowditch

N. P. Banks Jr

S. C. Phillips   Paul Revere

John J. Audubon

Wm. Upham   Theo. S. Fay

Rufus Dawes

P. S. Gilmore

Leslie Combs

Winfield Scott

Anna Maria Hall — J. P. Kennedy

W. L. Marcy.

Wm H Prescott W Ware

Wm Jas Hammersley

James Buchanan Geo. Combe

W. C. Bryant

S. A. Douglas O. W. Holmes.

Amos Lawrence

Daniel Webster

Geo. Grenville Geo. Canning

Edwin Croswell.

Maria Edgeworth A. P. Peabody.

E. H. Chapin

John Forsyth Eliza Cook

John Allen

W C Bond. R Hildreth

Martin F. Tupper

Levi Woodbury

Freeman Hunt

Richard Frothingham Jr

Robt Rantoul Jr

Sam Houston

C. Johnson

Lafayette

George Bancroft

Geo. N Briggs

…A Wickliffe Noah Webster

Abbott Lawrence

…Palmerston H. G. Otis

Chas. G Greene

…ackeray Fredrika Bremer

Henry Grattan

…ashington Irving A. H. Everett

T Dwight

William R. King

Jo. Gales.

William Foster Otis

Richard Rus

J. Pierpont

Israel Putnam

Jenny Lind

C. Tollen

Wm E Channing

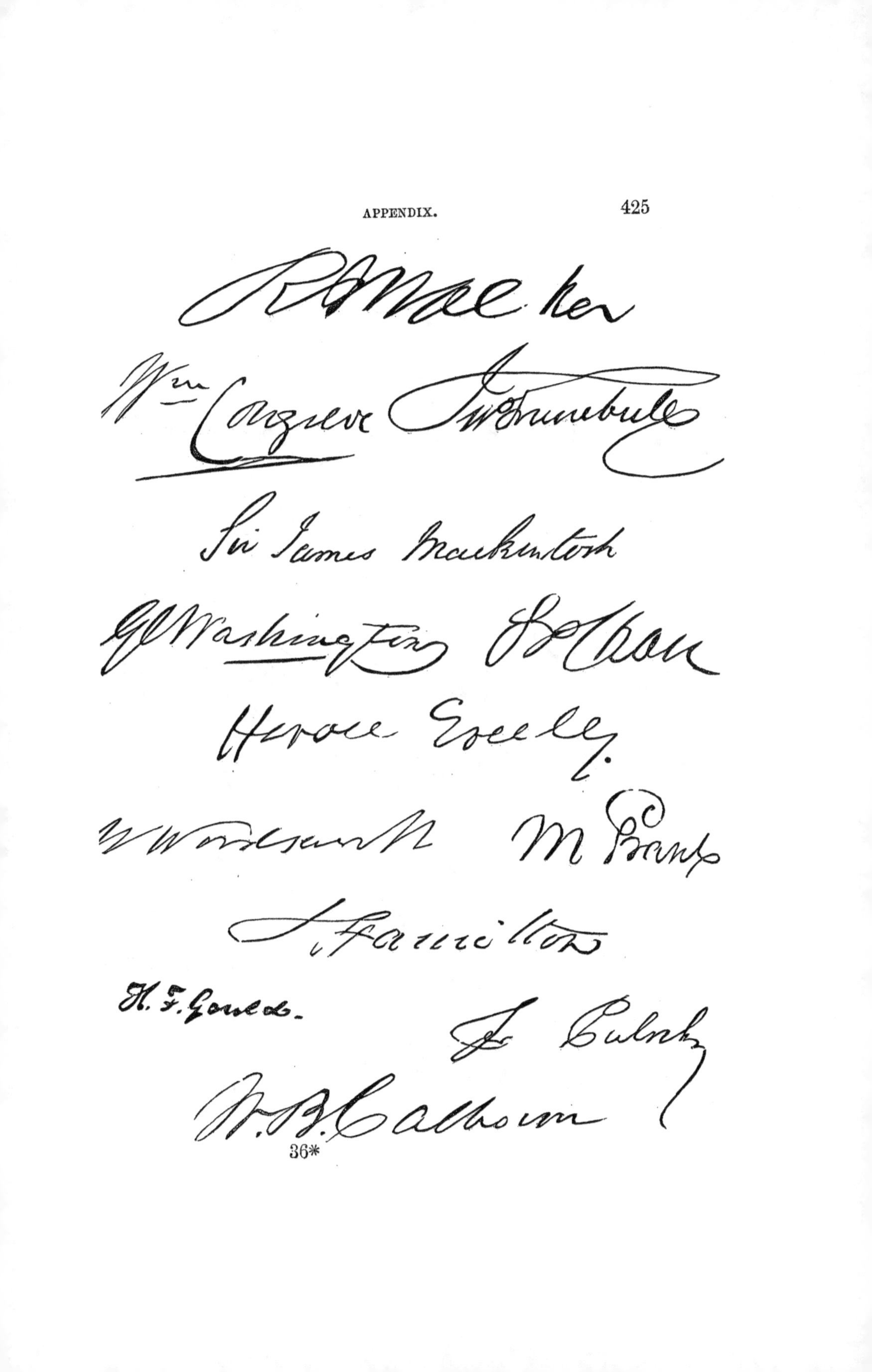

John Quincy Adams.

Dan'l Morgan Geo Poindexter

John A. Dix

Hosea Ballou. Jacob Abbott

A. P. Upshur

Theobald Mathew Thomas Moore

Th. S. Jesup

Fenimore Cooper, J. N. Maffitt.

Therese Pulszky

Will. A. Graham

W. Eustis. John Frost

Epes Sargent

Elihu Burritt   Caroline M. Kirkland

Emily C. Judson.

H. S. Legaré.   James T. Fields

Park Benjamin.

Jonathan Edwards   John Wesley

R. W. Emerson

Edward Everett.

Henry Knox

Theo. Frelinghuysen.

T. C. Brownell Samuel C. Edgerton

Edward Hitchcock

J. Taylor J. R. Ingersoll

Orville Dewey

David Henshaw Wm Cobbett.

J. T. Morehead

Millard Fillmore

[illegible] Rich. H. Dana Jr

John C. Park

Pierre Soulé L. H. Sigourney

Wm H Crawford

Ethan Allen Amos Kendall

Joseph Warren

Philip Hone George Ripley

Marcus Morton

James Monroe

Henry Giles Daniel O'Connell

Washington Allston.

Charles Sprague Mary Howitt

William Biggs

J. G. Whittier Robert Peel

Jas. Watson Webb.

Robt Fulton R. Womb

H More Dixon H Lewis

DeWitt Clinton

John Sergeant

H Brougham John Hubbard

Edward Beecher

W Wilberforce Gerrit Smith

Mahlon Dickerson.

Charles Allen. Andw Combe

Geo. W. Julian

C. E. Beecher Samuel Sewall

Alvan Stewart

Wilson Lumpkin

Josiah Quincy. D D Tompkins

Henry B Anthony

John Cotton Smith John Farmer

Chs Stewart

Geo Evans James E De Kay

Anson Burlingame

Horatio Gates J. Knipfell

Joshua Leavitt

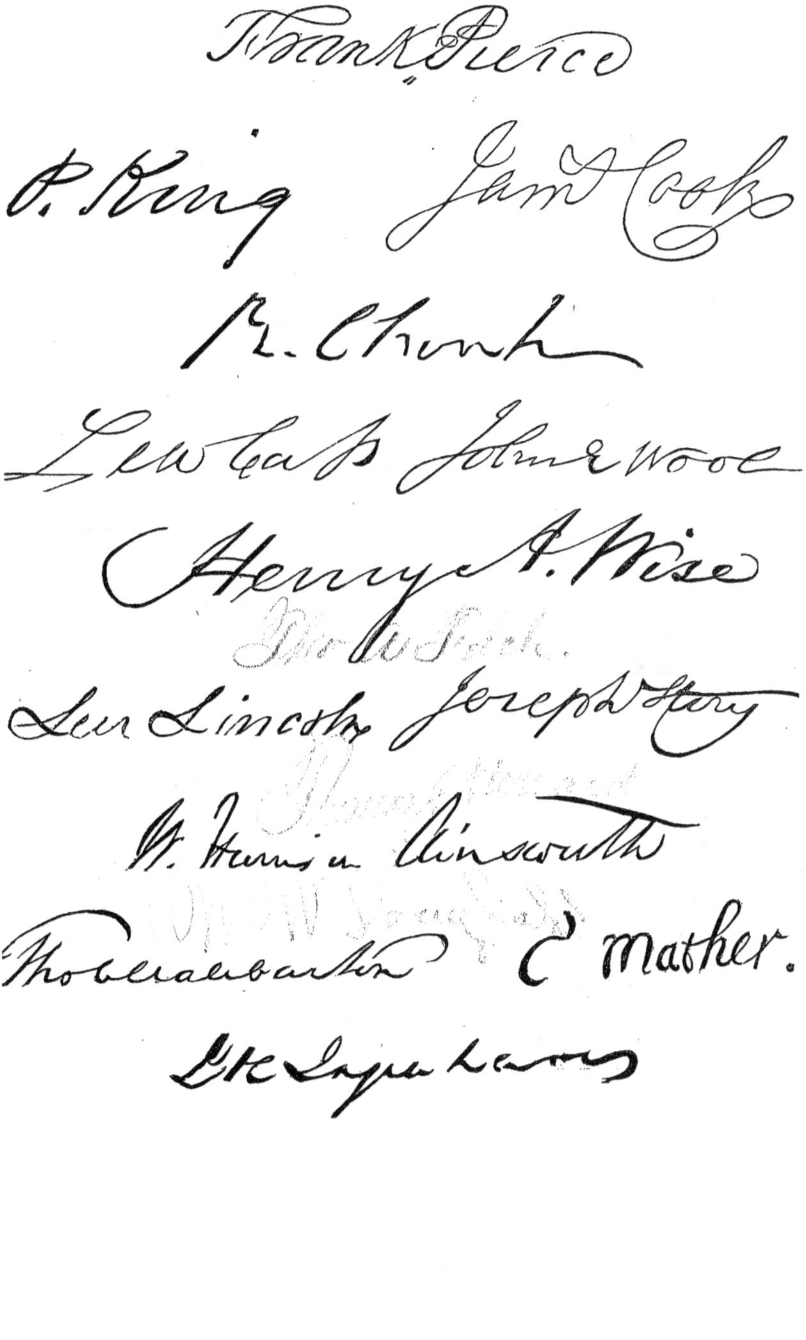

Charles Gordon Atherton.

Daniel Boone

Alpheus Felch

T H Perkins

J C Warren

Ensign H. Kellogg

Samuel Hutter §

Henry R Schoolcraft

C D Humphrys

Alex Wilson

Lemuel Shaw

Christ^r Gadsden

Isaac Davis

John Catron Abr Baldwin

David Daggett Benjn West

Wm L. Dayton.

John J. Wells John Barry

Richard Fletcher

Richd Cobden B Frazier

[illegible]

Edwd D. Ingraham

Robt: G: Harper

John Alden Charles Dickens

James Biddle

Geo. B. Cheever Wm A Alcott

T. H. Chivers

Mark Hopkins Daniel Gookin

Bernard Barton

Benjamin Church W Shirley

Saml G Drake

J. W. Bradbury

Wil: Livingston Horace Holley.

Justin Edwards

Jared Ingersoll William Bradford

Joshua Barney

Wm. C. Dawson J. M. Porter

Roger S. Baldwin

Rufus W. Griswold. Andrews Norton

James E. Murdoch

Pliny Merrick

Green Kendrick

B. F. Hallett

Henry Wilson.

Wm Parmenter

J. A. Hillhouse

David Crockett

Jas Sullivan

GOVERNORS OF PLYMOUTH COLONY, CHOSEN ANNUALLY BY THE PEOPLE.

[John Carver's autograph not found.]

GOVERNORS OF MASS. UNDER THE FIRST CHARTER, CHOSEN ANNUALLY.

GOVERNORS OF MASSACHUSETTS UNDER THE SECOND CHARTER, APPOINTED BY THE KING.

William Phips

J Dudley

J Belcher

W Shirley

T Hutchinson

Thos Gage

Bellomont

Saml Shute

W Burnet

T Pownall

Fra Bernard

Wm C. Bouck

R. Coffey   Samuel Hoar.

Simon Greenleaf

Jn W. Steele   John E. Howard

John B. Gough

Louisa Catherine Adams   James Barron

Thos. Addis Emmet

Chs W. Cathcart

George Hull   Leigh Hunt

Thomas Francis Meagher

Napoleon

Chas Chapman

C. Gore

Thomas De Quincey

Thos W Dorr.

Byron

J. L. Petigru

W M Thackeray

J Watts.

Louis McLane

R Pakenham

J Russell

Felix Grundy

H Hallam

A. L. de Sta Anna

Wellington

John Murray

E. Braddock

Horace Mann

Grace Greenwood

G. W. Bethune

Anty Wayne

Nath Hawthorne

J. C. Fremont

L. Saltonstall

J. E. Holmes

www.ingramcontent.com/pod-product-compliance
Lightning Source LLC
LaVergne TN
LVHW021131110826
845150LV00005B/999

* 9 7 8 1 4 2 5 5 4 9 6 5 7 *